Praise for *Hidden Heroes*

Pamela Cohen wrote a very important memoir, *Hidden Heroes*. Being the former head of the Union of Councils for Soviet Jews, the biggest grassroots activist organization in the world of the struggle for Soviet Jewry, Pamela portrays many Jewish leaders of this organization from different communities all over the United States, as well as Jewish refuseniks from different places all over the Soviet Union.

It is this personal, intimate connection between these two groups that gave inspiration, encouragement, and strength to the people on both sides of the Iron Curtain and made our struggle in general so powerful.

Natan Sharansky, former Prisoner of Zion

Pam Cohen's *Hidden Heroes* tells an important part of the unique story of brave and courageous individuals who effected immense change for human rights worldwide. As president of the grassroots activist organization Union of Councils for Soviet Jews, Pamela was there from the outset. This inspiring read gives us hope that we can continue to make this world a better place.

Alan Dershowitz, Professor Emeritus,
Harvard University; lawyer for many Soviet
refuseniks and dissidents

Pamela Cohen wrote a book. It is not only hers. It is OURS. We wrote the book together, the page in the history of Am Israel.

In June 1970, I was arrested with my friends in an airport in Leningrad for an attempt to voice our struggle for the freedom of Soviet Jewry. We never considered whether there would be somebody from the other side of the Iron Curtain to join us in our struggle. As naturally as we stood up for the fight for Jewish freedom, for me it was obvious that there should be people like us in the free world. The striving for freedom, for human rights, is basic for every Jew.

Only later, being in prison already for eight years, I met a fresh prisoner, Anatoly Sharansky, who told me the story of the public effort of the Jews in the US and elsewhere. The first public organization was the Union of Councils for Soviet Jews (and, naturally, the SSSJ). This is how we met with Pam, not in person but in the spirit of the struggle.

I still regret that I never met that lady of beautiful spirit. But we were soldiers. A soldier cannot know the name of his compatriots fighting on the front lines, but he knows that he can rely on them.

It is what I expect from every Jew – to be a fighter for our nation. And that is why Pam's book is so important. It is not about the past – it is a textbook for a Jewish fighter. Learn it and join our ranks. Am Israel CHAI!

Yosef Mendelevich, former Prisoner of Zion

In 1969, at the height of the Cold War, when I was twenty-one years old, the Israeli government sent me into the Soviet Union to smuggle in Jewish items and smuggle out the names of Jews who wanted to emigrate. I was sent because I was a committed Jew and because I spoke Russian and Hebrew. Those languages enabled me to talk to Soviet Jews whenever talking was possible (always outdoors, always while walking).

As the spokesman for the Student Struggle for Soviet Jewry, I knew of Pam Cohen's and the UCSJ's work on behalf of Soviet Jewry. Few people are as qualified to write about the Soviet Jewry movement as she is. This is one of those books that can with no exaggeration be called important. It is also riveting.

Soviet Jews proved a lesson we should never forget: big things happen only when a few brave souls — "hidden heroes," as Pam Cohen calls them — take on the majority. *Hidden Heroes* is filled with such relevant lessons. Here's another: America is at its best when it fights for liberty. America (and Israel) led the worldwide fight for Soviet Jews. Ironically, the fight for liberty is, for the first time since the Civil War, now an intra-American battle. Americans who read this inspiring book may well resolve to adopt the distinguishing trait of the Soviet Jewish heroes of this book, and the only trait that can keep any people free: courage.

Dennis Prager, *New York Times* bestselling author of ten books, including *The Rational Bible*

Just as memory of the historic struggle of Soviet Jewry is fading, Pamela Cohen has written an irreplaceable history of the movement. This is a very personal tale told through a thousand names and stories, but the sum total is a panoramic picture: the refuseniks, the American Jews who fought for them (and the American Jews who did not), the State Department and the White House, and of course the Kremlin. Natan Sharansky called Pamela Cohen the "five-star general of the army of students and housewives," and this is her account of how students and housewives defeated the Soviet Union – and pushed aside plenty of American and even Israeli bigshots who did not share their uncompromising commitment to free the Jews of Russia. One woman's story here illuminates a vast historic movement that changed Jewish and Israeli history.

> **Elliott Abrams,** former Deputy National
> Security Advisor and
> Assistant Secretary of State for Human Rights

The Soviet Jewry movement, perhaps the most successful human rights campaign in history, succeeded thanks to its determined army of "students and housewives." Here the unassuming commander of that army, Pamela B. Cohen, recounts the story of her leadership of the Union of Councils for Soviet Jews. She details how she inspired others, transformed herself, and most importantly "changed the world" – sometimes over the objections of men much more famous than herself. An essential historical memoir and a great read.

> **Jonathan D. Sarna,** University Professor and
> Joseph H. and Belle R. Braun Professor of
> American Jewish History, Brandeis University

Pamela Cohen's book *Hidden Heroes* is a moving account of how she went from a stay-at-home mom to lead a remarkable grassroots group, the Union of Councils for Soviet Jews (UCSJ), which sprouted up almost spontaneously in response to the arrest and trial of Soviet Jews desperately seeking to leave the anti-Semitic prison of the Soviet Union. She grippingly describes how the 1967 Six-Day War was a catalyst for Soviet Jews to redis-cover their Jewish identity brutally suppressed by the USSR, and how the UCSJ tirelessly worked, sometimes in opposition to more establishment Jewish groups and the Israeli foreign ministry, to prod US government and

Western action that produced the most successful mass rescue of Jews in history. As their outside legal adviser, I was privileged to witness firsthand and to be inspired by Pamela's tireless work and that of her colleagues, including Micah Naftalin, the head of the UCSJ's Washington office. *Hidden Heroes* demonstrates how dedication at the grassroots level for a just cause can profoundly change history.

> **Ambassador (ret.) Stuart E. Eizenstat,**
> former chief domestic policy adviser to
> President Carter (1977–1981);
> former US Ambassador to the European Union

Hidden Heroes unlocks and humanizes, for the first time, the power of the global Soviet Jewry movement and the tenacious housewives and students who successfully took on not only the Kremlin, but also, when needed, the Jewish establishment and even the State of Israel. The secret formula for creating a modern exodus unfolds with each engaging chapter, from suburban dining rooms to cramped Moscow apartments; from the halls of Congress to superpower summits. *Hidden Heroes* celebrates the refuseniks in the Soviet Union and the voice of the refuseniks in the West, whose bond was stronger than the KGB. Any opponent of totalitarianism will find hope in this historic human and Jewish drama. It is not an accident that the Soviet Union fell on the watch of the leadership of Pam Cohen, Micah Naftalin, and a whole generation of mostly volunteers. It was, in retrospect and prophetically, inevitable. Now their story is finally told.

> **Josef I. Abramowitz,** President and CEO,
> Gigawatt Global Coöperatief U.A.

HIDDEN HEROES

PAMELA BRAUN COHEN

gefen גפן
publishing house בית הוצאה לאור
Est. 1981
JERUSALEM ♦ NEW YORK

Grateful acknowledgment is made to Remember and Save, the digital refusenik archives, for the use of multiple photos for the cover and interior of this book.

Bottom left cover photo by Robert P. Turtil, courtesy of the archives of the Student Struggle for Soviet Jewry (SSSJ).

Cover Design: Leah Ben Avraham/Noonim Graphics
Typesetting: Optume Technologies
ISBN: 978-965-7023-36-5

1 3 5 7 9 8 6 4 2

Gefen Publishing House Ltd.
6 Hatzvi Street
Jerusalem 9438614
Israel
972-2-538-0247
orders@gefenpublishing.com

Gefen Books
c/o Baker & Taylor Publisher Services
30 Amberwood Parkway
Ashland, Ohio 44805
516-593-1234
orders@gefenpublishing.com

www.gefenpublishing.com

Printed in Israel
Library of Congress Control Number: 2021902814

Contents

PART FOUR: RIDING THE STORMS

PART FIVE: ENDINGS AND BEGINNINGS

Foreword

In 1987, while I served as Assistant Secretary of State for Human Rights and Humanitarian Affairs, I became fully engaged in the effort to effect basic changes in the human rights policy of the Soviet Union in light of the changed outlook brought about by Gorbachev's perestroika. One item on my agenda was Soviet emigration policy, which had prevented thousands of Soviet citizens from leaving the Soviet Union. The overwhelming majority of applicants for exit visas were Jews. In August 1987, while in Moscow, I was able, following conversations with Soviet officials, to help bring about a basic change in Soviet policy that was reflected in the 1988 emigration figures and the ever-increasing numbers in the years immediately following.

Let me make it clear that when I use the phrase "help bring about," I am well aware of who else played a role in bringing about that change. To start with, the person whose outlook was of real interest to the Soviets and whom they wanted to accommodate was Secretary of State George Shultz, who had made it very clear to Foreign Minister Eduard Shevardnadze that Jewish emigration from the Soviet Union was an issue that was important to the United States. Similarly, President Reagan had emphasized his concern about Jewish emigration to Soviet leader Gorbachev.

That takes us to the next question. There had been decades in which the Soviet Union had engaged the United States in the Cold War. There were now numerous issues on the US agenda in dealing with the Soviet Union, including a number in the field of human rights. What had placed the issue so high on the agenda of President Reagan and Secretary Shultz?

I have long believed that it was the Union of Councils for Soviet Jews (UCSJ) that had, in the first instance, in the 1970s, placed the Soviet Jewish emigration issue on the agenda of the US general public, with the media increasingly engaged. The message had reached members of Congress and caused many members to express their concern. That brought about a brief improvement in the Soviet exit visa issuance in the 1970s. It came to an end following a decline in bilateral relations with the Soviets after the invasion of Afghanistan.

But UCSJ never stopped. Once the Reagan administration had taken over, the new administration, too, was concerned that many thousands of Soviet Jews, who wanted to escape the antisemitic discrimination they suffered in the Soviet Union, were prevented from doing so by the Soviet exit visa policy. The term *refusenik*, used to describe a person whose exit visa application had been turned down, began to be commonly used. The refusenik problem was so often an issue of public discussion that all those concerned with US foreign policy were highly conscious of the fact that this was an issue of great public interest.

That takes us to the question of how UCSJ was able to get the Soviet Jewry issue so high on the US public agenda. What this book describes is how a group of dedicated volunteers, a group that included Pamela Cohen in its leadership, was so extraordinarily effective in following developments in the Soviet Union affecting its Jewish population and was then able to get the message out to the US general public. The message that the Reagan administration conveyed to the Soviet leadership was very much in keeping with what the US public considered to be the right message. So, as we look back and ask ourselves who it was that opened the Soviet door to allow emigration, it was Pamela Cohen and those associated with her in UCSJ.

Ambassador Richard Schifter, 1923–2020

Assistant Secretary of State for Human Rights and
Humanitarian Affairs, 1985–92

Preface

Throughout the Soviet Jewry movement, countless volunteers traveled to the Soviet Union as tourists to meet with refuseniks, Jews who were refused permission to emigrate. An astounding number of those people have told me that the week they spent in Moscow and Leningrad was the most meaningful experience of their lives. They were changed by their encounter with refuseniks – by their moral courage and tenacity, their resistance in the face of persecution, their personalities and drive.

In more than twenty years as a full-time volunteer activist committed to Jewish emigration from the Soviet Union, I too experienced the galvanizing impact of the refuseniks' struggle, and I witnessed the movement's impact on American Jewry.

I have often wondered what made these refuseniks such indefatigable moral protagonists. Were they born with an innate predisposition to resist the state's intimidating demands for political and social conformity? They were for the most part highly educated and assimilated Jews, ordinary in many ways, who made themselves extraordinary when they asserted the most precious of all personal freedoms, the freedom to choose. In the face of persecution, they chose Jewish identity and the struggle for the right to go to their Jewish national home.

In the West, too, a similar transformation took place: otherwise quite ordinary people, mostly women and students, inspired by refuseniks, made choices that made them extraordinary.

And extraordinary they were. Voluntarily committing hours, days, years, even decades of their lives, my colleagues – a small group of American Jews obsessed with the failures of the past – dedicated themselves to rescuing their beleaguered people and became changed in the process.

This is the story, then, of extraordinary people in America and in the USSR, on two sides of the ocean, who saw themselves as one people, refusing to be separated by an Iron Curtain. This is the story of hidden heroes who might have otherwise been lost to history.

Forged together by will and purpose, these activists built a grassroots movement that helped drive the rescue of two million Jews from the Soviet Union – the largest rescue mission of Jews in history – ultimately contributing to the collapse of the structure that made them captives in the first place.

In my involvement with the Union of Councils for Soviet Jews (UCSJ), I was privileged to work with countless refuseniks and UCSJ activists. Each of them could write a book detailing their struggles; their acts of courage, kindness, and selflessness; their victories and defeats. I have written about many of their stories, but I am painfully aware that I am just scratching the surface, and that I simply could not include all the stories of those who impacted the movement and my life.

Looking back at my own story, I'm aware that nothing was coincidental, nothing happened by chance. Every step of the way, I was given precisely the help I needed to move forward. The right people appeared at the right time, people who would become partners and friends, mentors and protégés. Each of them contributed to the movement and to my own personal growth, and we all changed history in the process. For them, and for all of my experiences along the way, I am so grateful.

One anecdote from the very beginning of my life seems to point to the path I would follow. When I was born, my mother asked my great-grandmother's opinion about whether my English name should be Penelope or Pamela. Without hesitation, my *bubbe* answered in Yiddish: "*Penelope iz nisht kein nommen*" (Penelope is not a name). "But Pom-ella, Pom-ella… this is a name!" I grew up as Pam, but to refuseniks, I was Pamela, which they pronounced as my *bubbe* did: *Pom-ella*. Some thirty years later, long after she left this world, the name on my *bubbe*'s lips was echoed by Jews in the Soviet Union who ultimately transformed my life.

An editorial note: The word I use for the Sabbath varies between *Shabbat* and *Shabbos*, depending on context. In writing about the early years of our family, I use the term *Shabbat*, because that's how we pronounced it at the time. In writing about refuseniks who identified as religious Zionists, I use *Shabbat*, in keeping with the Sephardic pronunciation used in Israel. As I grew religiously, I decided not to abandon the traditional Yiddish pronunciation of my great-grandparents from Lithuania.

Therefore, when I write about events later in my life, after I became observant, I use the term *Shabbos*.

A final caveat: This book is based solely on information from my personal and UCSJ archives, my research, and my reflections of events as they happened. I take full responsibility for any omissions or errors.

Acknowledgments

I wrote *Hidden Heroes* with an imagined cast of Russian and American former colleagues – many of whom are no longer living – at my side, coaching, reminding, whispering memories.

The book's production has been a team effort, with so many people urging me to bring memory to life, to record history as I saw it, to show the enormous potential of the individual to change the world.

Enid Wurtman in Jerusalem has been focused for over thirty years on the trajectory of refuseniks – documenting and advocating their struggle to live in Israel and providing material and moral support once they arrived. Her confidence in my ability to write the story of the rescue of Soviet Jews encouraged me throughout the years it has taken. Enid was the book's first reader and fact-checker. In addition to being a longtime friend, she was invaluable due to her phenomenal memory, extensive personal archives, and complete dedication to the players of the movement and its history. I am ever grateful to her.

Profound thanks goes to my Israel-based editing support system. Rabbi Jonathan Rosenblum, internationally known author, columnist, and lecturer in Jerusalem, has consistently acted as a guardian angel, sure of my ability to tell this story from my firsthand perspective. His confidence and guidance encouraged me to overcome what I thought were insurmountable challenges. Jonathan also led me to Avigail Sharer, who refined the book's chronology. I'm especially appreciative to her for arranging the publication of "Fighting Apathy with Fire," an excerpt from the book that appeared in the September 20, 2018, edition of *Mishpacha*'s *Family First* magazine. Thanks also to Gila Greene for her guidance. I'm very grateful to award-winning writer Benjamin Balint for his insights. Benji released me from my reluctance to write in the first person singular by helping me to see that "I" could be collective, representing those activists on whose shoulders I was standing.

I was spurred on and encouraged by a few people who probably had no idea the influence they had on me. Though he might have forgotten, historian and Brandeis professor Jonathan Sarna, who had traveled to visit refuseniks and had been briefed by Sandy Spinner at UCSJ's Cincinnati Council for Soviet Jews, was the first to urge me to write this book, decades before I decided to do so. Elliott Abrams, former deputy national security advisor and assistant secretary of state for human rights, wrote in the *Jewish Review of Books* about the need to learn from the success of the Soviet Jewry movement. His article has stayed on my desk for the last two years, challenging me to provide some of those lessons.

When I was looking for an editor, our son Scott asked his friend, writer and editor Mark Swartz, to whom I am ever indebted for leading me to Judy Galens. Judy is a demanding perfectionist, a researcher, a consummate wordsmith and grammarian. I have come to learn she is all of the above but also an endlessly patient, focused listener and an unrelenting psychiatrist who aids the reader's understanding with an uncanny ability to push out unexpressed or repressed realities from the writer. Judy has been a true partner in the birth of this book. I am deeply indebted to you, Judy, not least for a job much larger than you expected. It couldn't have been done without you.

Gefen Publishing House's CEO Ilan Greenfield has inherited his father's vision to publish books of importance to the State of Israel and the Jewish people, to reveal what is hidden, to open the doors to the historic record. From our first meeting in 2011, when Lenny, Judy Balint, and I approached him to publish Yosef Mendelevich's book *Unbroken Spirit*, we have found him to be a vigorous champion of the important lessons of the Soviet Jewry movement. I am eternally grateful to him for believing in this book from our very first conversation. Everyone at Gefen has been helpful in moving this project from manuscript to final product. Thanks to Kezia Raffel Pride for her editorial rigor; Daphne Abrahams, who pulled the many elements of this book together; and Leah Ben Abraham for her outstanding cover design.

I am grateful for the patience and support of friends and colleagues who have borne with me throughout the progress of this work. I am ever indebted to Leonid and Natasha Stonov for their encouragement, their help, and their friendship. I am deeply appreciative to Morey Schapira and Glenn Richter and to Aba Taratuta and Edward Markov of Remember and

Save, the digital refusenik archives, for their help with research and for providing photos for the cover. And I am so grateful for the patience and moral support of June and Ron Daniels, Jackie and Michael Abels, Luba Bar Menachem, Judy Balint, Robert Kleinman, Earl and Faye Newman, Craig and Fredi Weiss, Rabbi Ezra Belsky, Marcia Zuckerman, Jerry and Judy Fishman. My sister-in-law, Lessa Roskin, herself an activist, has stood solidly behind my efforts at every stage. There are so many people I'm grateful for that I have not mentioned by name. Please know that your friendship and support have not been forgotten.

I am so very thankful that Ambassador Richard Schifter graciously agreed to write the foreword for this book. As I was in the final stages of writing and editing, I was eager for him to read the book, and especially my tribute to him as a quiet giant, but, to my great sadness, he passed away before he had the chance. I hope this book brings him out of the shadows that hide our Jewish heroes. May his memory be a blessing for all of Israel.

My boundless love and appreciation go to our children, Brooke, Scott, and Joshua, and their spouses, whom I call "children of choice" – David Warso, Kathy Fromm Cohen, and Lizzy Isaacson Cohen. It's not enough that our children had to live through their mother's compulsion for Jewish rescue, they then had to endure years of reports of the book's laborious development. But through it all, they have been unremittingly supportive and are truthfully among the hidden heroes of this story. You are all blessings.

I am and have always been profoundly grateful for Lenny, my *bashert* (soul mate) and best friend. We were both raised with a focus on family, Jewish tradition, and good deeds. He shared my concerns and supported my activity, morally and financially, from the beginning, helping sustain Chicago Action after we moved the office to Highland Park. Throughout the struggle, he had unremitting confidence in my activity. To him, this work was a natural consequence of our shared values, and he felt we were shouldering it together and passing those values on to our children. He was ever confident and reassuring. More times than not, when driving me to the airport, he reminded me I was leaving the children with their capable father, reassuring me that I wasn't abandoning them and that "everything will be fine." We were a team: I was operating within the movement, and his capable hands were on the rudder, keeping us steady and secure. This book is a result of his insistence that I tell my story and share my perspective on a monumental period of history. Not least, I am always impressed by his ability to be inspired, to change, to grow, to take new paths. Our partnership has given us a richly textured life. My gratitude knows no bounds.

To our most loved, treasured grandchildren, our *kinderlach* of all ages: You have waited expectantly for this book. Aaron, as a great reader of non-fiction, you tracked my progress unrelentingly, week by week, encouraging me every step of the way. Every word of this book was written with you all in mind. *Hidden Heroes* is dedicated to all of you and to those who are destined to come from you; much of the Jewish future rests in your hands. It is our prayerful hope that you will follow in your people's footsteps along the path of history: Aaron and Nechama Schwartz Warso, Simmy and Talya Rosenwasser Warso, Hannah Warso, Ezra Warso, Ephraim Warso, Gavi Warso, Shai Warso, Naftali Warso, Betzalel Warso, Sophie Cohen, Zev Cohen, Mayta Cohen, Maya Cohen, Hayle Cohen, Leah Cohen, and our first great-grandchild, Jack Warso.

December 2020 (Kislev 5781)

PART ONE

Awakenings –
The Soviet Jewish
Emigration Movement

CHAPTER 1

The Birth of a Movement, 1970s

The Leningrad Trials

It all started on a warm June evening in 1970. Our kids were already asleep. Lenny and I were in our family room when we heard the news broadcast that would change our lives forever. John Chancellor was on national news reporting that a group of Soviet Jews had been arrested for trying to hijack a plane from Leningrad to the West. We were both astounded. It was inconceivable. We couldn't wrap our heads around it. Jewish hijackers?

Then the news seemed to dry up. Over the next few days, I heard no further reports from the press, our synagogue, or Jewish organizations. I went looking for more information, a difficult task in those pre-internet years. I soon found that a Philadelphia Jewish weekly, the *Jewish Exponent*, published a regular column on Soviet Jewry. It revealed that the hijackers, unable to get permission to leave the Soviet Union, had planned to seize a plane in a desperate attempt to attract the attention of the West to their plight. They were struggling to leave a police state where the twin policies of state anti-Semitism and assimilation made it impossible to live as Jews, and they had defied both, risking everything by trying to emigrate from the USSR to Israel.

Encompassing eleven time zones, the Union of Soviet Socialist Republics (USSR) was in fact a vast prison that held about 240 million people in fifteen republics within a guarded, thirty-six-thousand-mile border. More than a million KGB agents and informants, over fifteen hundred in Moscow alone, spied on the population, "creating a spy state pitting all against all, in which phones were tapped and letters opened, and everyone was encouraged to inform on everyone else, everywhere, all the time."[1]

---

1.   Ben MacIntyre, *The Spy and the Traitor: The Greatest Espionage Story of the Cold War* (New York: Broadway Books, 2018), 86.

Interned in this vast prison were at least four million Jews – about one-third of world Jewry – cut off from their people and from Israel, deprived of Jewish books, institutions, and Hebrew language. With Stalin's accession to power in the 1920s, and with his goal of creating a new genus of homo sapiens – "Homo Sovieticus" – he wiped away all individual identity and consequently eradicated Jewish life. There were no synagogues except for those controlled by the government and thus avoided by most activists out of contempt. There were no Jewish schools, no Jewish organizations, and no Jewish printing houses; in fact, there was no unofficial printing allowed at all. Intermarriage was rampant. The evisceration of Judaism and Jewish culture produced a generation of millions of Jews who would have assimilated and disappeared entirely were it not for the unrelenting state anti-Semitism. For many, it was actually the poisonous anti-Semitic press, teachers and professors who promulgated and encouraged anti-Semitic bullying in classrooms, and the universities' and scientific institutes' restrictive admission of Jews that shaped their last tenuous link to Jewish identity. That link was made conspicuous by the requirement to list their national identity as Jewish on line five of their internal passports, regardless of which republic they came from.

But then something unforeseen happened. In 1967, the Six-Day War broke out in the Middle East. The Soviet propagandists, on state-controlled television, repeatedly broadcast the onslaught of Arab armies, thus signaling the imminent defeat of the fledgling Jewish state. On their television screens, Soviet Jews watched their brethren, proud uniformed Israeli soldiers, ready to die for a Jewish state – a national homeland where Jews weren't pariahs, where they could live with pride. Like a lightning bolt piercing the propaganda smokescreen, the cognitive recognition of a Jewish home gave Soviet Jews a new sense of peoplehood, dignity, and national purpose. Leon Uris's book *Exodus*, published in 1958 and later translated into Russian, made its way into the USSR, where it was copied by hand or photographed and smuggled as far away as the Siberian prison camps. The Six-Day War and books like *Exodus* stimulated a process of renewed Jewish self-identity, blossoming national pride, and a longing to go home. *Exodus* and others like it were the very same books that were affecting me, thousands of miles away.

By 1970, with no hope of emigrating, one small group conspired to take an empty plane from Leningrad to Sweden in a desperate attempt to marshal international attention. From the start, they knew the plan was doomed, but they had to make a stand. They were Jews and they wanted to go home. Predictably, they were arrested on the tarmac before they even boarded the plane.

In a flash of recognition, I knew that Yosef Mendelevich, Hillel Butman, Sylva Zalmanson, her husband Edward Kuznetsov, and the rest of this group were Jewish moral giants who had pitted themselves against the Kremlin. But I wanted to know more. Who were they? How had they come to make a decision that would result in years of imprisonment and hard labor in Siberia?

The Trials and the Aftermath

In the Soviet Union, news of the ensuing Leningrad trials raced through the underground whisper system that flourishes in police states, spread largely through foreign radio reports. Free thinkers learned early to read between the lines in Soviet anti-Semitic propaganda. The trials concluded with two of the defendants sentenced to death (sentences that were later commuted) and the others condemned to long sentences in prison camps.

Instead of suppressing the embryonic drive for Jewish emigration, the arrests and trials of the "hijackers" had an unintended consequence, launching what would be a decades-long, hard-fought exodus of Jews from the Soviet Union. Jews across the breadth of the USSR applied for exit visas. What started as scores multiplied quickly, turning into hundreds and then thousands of Jews requesting permission to leave the country. The Kremlin's reaction was to plug the flow, refusing most applications and creating a "head tax" on those given permission to leave. The Kremlin turned those who were refused – known as refuseniks – into vocational and social pariahs by identifying them on television news, firing them from their jobs, removing them from scientific institutes, stripping them of academic degrees, and allowing them only menial work. Some, unable to find work of any kind, were then arrested for not working, on the grounds of parasitism. Some refuseniks were sent to prison and work camps to serve as examples for others who were considering emigrating. No longer casting themselves in the mold of "Homo Sovieticus," many Jews began treading the path toward their Jewish identity, studying Hebrew and Judaism in underground seminars – taught by refuseniks who knew a little more than they did.

From the beginning, refuseniks believed their future depended on whether we in the West would struggle with them – together, with one voice and as one people. They knew that alone, without support from the free world, their resistance would be brutally quelled.

The question loomed before me. Would we? Would I? I thought of the Jews of Europe during World War II, believing their brothers and sisters in America wouldn't let the unthinkable happen. But now, for American Jews who were far removed from events in the Soviet Union, the Leningrad hijackers had broadcast an unmistakable call for action.

Their call was based on a two-thousand-year-old Talmudic dictum: "*Kol Yisrael areivin zeh la'zeh*" (all Jews are responsible for one another).[2] I had to do something. I, too, was responsible.

So, I started writing. The *Jewish Exponent* columnist posted addresses of both refuseniks and Soviet officials, assuring readers that publicity and mail beamed a spotlight of protection on the struggle inside the Soviet Union. It put the Soviets on notice that Americans were watching. Armed with those addresses, I wrote letters to Soviet officials in protest of the Leningrad defendants and requests for intervention to my representatives and senators.

Ultimately the Leningrad defendants achieved their goal. The media coverage raced across the globe. Spontaneously in Paris, Rome, London, and across the United States, Jews took to the streets in protest. It was an explosion of outrage, demonstrating our refusal to tolerate the suppression of Jews' right to reunite with their people, in their homeland. We, the pro-testers, spanned generations and held diverse political and religious views, but we shared one goal: freedom for the Leningrad trial defendants and for the countless numbers they represented.

I waited impatiently each week for reports in the *Jewish Exponent* of the imprisoned Leningrad trial defendants and the resulting crackdown on all Jews learning Hebrew or publishing *tarbut*, clandestine self-pub-lished pamphlets on Jewish culture. Authorities were using the attempted hijacking to justify shutting down all underground Jewish activities. Throughout the Soviet Union, there was a surge of house searches, inter-rogations, detainments, and arrests by KGB.

---

2.   Talmud, *Shevuot* 39a.

Soon enough, my dining room table, spotted with coffee stains, was covered with newspaper clippings. I was part of a group of activist-oriented mothers who met regularly to discuss affairs of the nation and write to our congressional representatives on various upcoming legislative issues. With babies on our laps and toddlers at our feet, we discussed compelling civil rights setbacks and the Vietnam War. Referencing the *Jewish Exponent*, I urged our group to protest the Kremlin's denial of the right of Jews to emigrate and rail against the head tax imposed on would-be Jewish emigrants.

In those early years, my days consisted of looking for more information on Jewish refuseniks, writing protest letters, and reading *The Wind in the Willows* to our kids, Brooke, Scott, and Joshua. Sundays, Lenny and I took them apple-picking in the country or to the Brookfield Zoo. In winter, we pulled them through the snow on our sled, with our dog happily trotting alongside. With an eye on our Jewish past, I became increasingly grateful that our family and friends were the exceptions, a privileged generation living within secure borders, not forced to live behind ghetto walls, living blessed if insulated lives.

I was also increasingly aware that on the other side of the Iron Curtain, thousands of Jews were refused permission to emigrate. Five thousand miles from our home, another Jewish woman, in her mid-thirties like me, was imprisoned for her Jewish activity. Raisa Palatnik, a librarian in Odessa, was charged with disseminating materials that slandered the USSR. She was accused of being a renegade, under the influence of Zionist propaganda. Some of her books that were seized by KGB were the same books as those on my nightstand.

In the Soviet Union, the incipient Jewish movement was percolating. Jews were on a road to self-awareness, awakening to their historical and cultural roots with newfound pride. On the other side of the world, I was traveling without threat or intimidation on a converging road of Jewish self-discovery, and it wouldn't be long before those two roads intersected.

Chicago Action for Soviet Jewry

One afternoon in the mid-1970s, a telephone call put me on a trajectory I didn't know existed. In a lightly accented voice, the caller identified herself as Hetty Deleeuwe. She had recently moved to Chicago from Baltimore, where she had been active in the Soviet Jewry movement. She was now selling commemorative cards for Chicago Action for Soviet Jewry (CASJ) and had heard about my interest. I nearly dropped the receiver. What? There were other people working for Soviet Jewry in Chicago?

I soon learned that CASJ, under the guidance of Lorel Pollack, had emerged out of another group of young women who were advocating for Soviet Jewish emigration. At one of their letter-writing sessions, Lorel arranged a telephone call to Moscow refusenik Lydia Kornfeld and invited the press to listen in on the call. With local CBS-TV cameras rolling in Lorel's Oak Park apartment, Lydia reported that KGB had raided the Moscow apartment of prominent refusenik Dr. Alexander Lerner. Preposterously, KGB had apprehended a congressman, James Scheuer of New York, who was part of a congressional delegation visiting the USSR. Lorel reported the incident to the *New York Times*, and as the news spread, KGB released Scheuer. The incident set a remarkable precedent: from then on, every US legislator who traveled to the Soviet Union met with refuseniks.

With newly won visibility and credibility from the Scheuer affair, Lorel incorporated CASJ as a 501(c)(3) nonprofit and, with some donated seed money, rented an office at Spertus College of Judaica in the heart of the city. She affiliated the new organization with a string of other independent grassroots groups that had sprung up across the nation after the Leningrad trials, the Union of Councils for Soviet Jews (UCSJ).

A vice president of the Union of Councils, Lorel had a vibrant personality. She was sometimes acerbic, always articulate, and she had an exhaustive understanding of the political intricacies and complexities of the Soviet Jewry movement, Soviet policy, and Soviet-Israel relations. Operating out of her tiny office on Michigan Avenue, Lorel was a one-woman grassroots powerhouse who achieved a sympathetic political response from the Illinois congressional delegation in Washington, DC.

In no time, I found myself spending hours in late-night phone briefings with Lorel. With the kids sleeping soundly, she briefed me on CASJ's political role. Under her chairmanship, CASJ was among the UCSJ councils to press for the Jackson-Vanik Amendment. This amendment to the Trade Act of 1974 was a strategic lever that denied most-favored-nation trade status to non-market-economies that prevented freedom of emigration. Thanks in part to a big thrust by UCSJ and another grassroots organization, the Student Struggle for Soviet Jewry (SSSJ), the Jackson-Vanik amendment managed to overcome the opposition of Secretary of State Henry Kissinger and the Nixon White House, big business, and some

Jewish Establishment leaders. Lorel played a key role: the entire Illinois congressional delegation, Democrats and Republicans alike, voted in favor of the Jackson-Vanik Amendment.

Methodically, Lorel moved me through the complexities of the emigration and Jewish renewal movements inside the USSR, bringing to life the personalities and positions of the refusenik leaders. She peeled back the veils to reveal how Soviet Jews were affected by the complex relationships between Moscow and Washington, Moscow and Jerusalem, and Jerusalem and Washington. Lorel began supplying me with refusenik cases for our informal group of activist letter-writers on the North Shore.

Meanwhile, like the refuseniks, I was experiencing a growing Jewish identity. I jumped at the opportunity to take a weekly Jewish history class that was taught by the brilliant and indomitable Marillyn Tallman. Like me, the other women in the class were secular and part of one of the most illiterate Jewish generations in history. But we were mesmerized by Marillyn as she sizzled through centuries of Jewish life.

Marillyn was about twenty years older than me, with curly hair she liked to complain about when the humidity was high. She wore big glasses and sparkled with intelligence. She was quick-witted, energetic, funny, and brilliant. A widely recognized national speaker for Jewish United Fund, Marillyn had a sterling reputation, an enviable collection of Jewish history books, and experience in the Jewish communal world.

Becoming more and more concerned with the persecution of Soviet Jews, I nervously took my campaign to Marillyn's class. Although I hated speaking publicly, even in a small group, I managed to take the floor to urge my fellow students to bombard the Soviet embassy with letters and telephone calls protesting the persecution and arrests of refuseniks. Marillyn's inherent understanding of the rescue process made her an enthusiastic co-conspirator, my ideal partner. After the Holocaust, Marillyn had worked with Abe Sachar at the University of Illinois to bring in Jewish refugees from Europe on student visas. (One of those students, Tom Lantos, would later be elected to Congress from California and would serve as cochairman of the Congressional Human Rights Caucus.) In the 1970s and 1980s, her classes were inspiring hundreds of young women and men. At first, she was my teacher, mentor, and inspiration. She became my partner, sister, and treasured friend. Once she said we were attached at the hip, and when her hip broke, mine hurt too.

At the same time that I was studying Jewish history with Marillyn, Lorel was intensifying my Soviet studies education on late-night talks, delivering a masterfully eloquent history of Soviet anti-Jewish policy and an exegesis on political and public advocacy. She also conveyed a vitriolic opprobrium against a secret office of the Israel Foreign Ministry, the Lishkat Hakesher, also known as the Lishka, which was charged with administering to the needs of Soviet Jewry. I listened with some skepticism; I was not accustomed to hearing any criticism of Israel. I scraped together all the filaments of her narrative to assess how much of her perspective was reality-based, and how much might be the result of a deep persecution complex. Ultimately I would come to see that she was right, that the Lishka had its own objectives and methodology that put us at odds.

With Lorel's encouragement, I decided to go to the UCSJ Annual Meeting outside Washington, DC, representing our letter-writing Soviet Jewry advocates. Leaving the children with Lenny, the freezer loaded with food, and the refrigerator decorated with my obsessive lists of reminders and schedules, I departed for the airport.

Union of Councils for Soviet Jews

After checking into the hotel in Arlington, Virginia, I made my way to the first session of the meeting, expecting a large gathering of national Jewish leaders and organizational professionals. I was shocked to discover that the task of saving millions of Soviet Jews was limited to a group of about thirty activists, grassroots volunteers who operated their local independent council in the United States, London, or Paris. But these unsalaried activists projected an image of strength that vastly magnified the reality of their numbers and the limitations imposed by their self-supporting local activities. These women and men clearly had harnessed their distinctly individual personalities and skills in a united struggle to mobilize a grassroots movement.

I was a teenager when Lou Rosenblum, the director of NASA's Solar and Electrochemistry division at Cleveland's Glenn Research Center, built the historic grassroots groundswell on behalf of the Jews held hostage in the Soviet Union.

In 1963, he and Herb Caron founded the Cleveland Council on Soviet Anti-Semitism, at a time when American Jews were far more focused on Vietnam, the student movement, and the women's movement than on

Soviet Jewry. When the Kremlin banned matzah production before Pesach in 1963, Lou tried to unite Jewish leaders in an effort to tie American grain sales to a lifting of the Soviet matzah ban. But moving the US organizational bureaucracy was like turning around a battleship with a towboat. Lou came to realize that, in order to light a fire under the mainstream US Jewish organizations, it would be necessary to mobilize a sustained call to action by independent, grassroots players.

In 1970, Lou united the Cleveland Council with five other independent grassroots councils, creating the national Union of Councils for Soviet Jews and becoming its first president. By 1986, the year I became national president, the UCSJ represented thirty-two member councils across the United States and was the largest independent Soviet Jewry grassroots organization in the world.

In those early years, a handful of charismatic, street-smart women and a few men were at the forefront of UCSJ. During the course of that Washington meeting, they referenced the opinions of specific refusenik leaders with such frequency that it was as if they were in the room together with us, contributing to the discussion on strategy and tactics. The focus of UCSJ's activists on the refuseniks was unremitting and all-consuming. It seemed from the beginning that they exhibited a uniquely authentic form of leadership.

Irene Manekovsky was the prototype of the kind of leader I admire. With razor-sharp intelligence, she was UCSJ's national president and also headed the Washington, DC, Committee on Soviet Jewry. A commanding presence, she was consumed, like everyone else in the room, with the case of Anatoly Sharansky. That commitment ultimately made the Sharansky case an international cause célèbre.

A refusenik since 1973, Sharansky had been arrested in March 1977 in Moscow on a fabricated charge after months of KGB surveillance. Charismatic, quick-witted, and fluent in English, he had been the spokesman for dissidents and refuseniks alike who were collecting evidence of Soviet human rights abuses. He was now in pretrial isolation, accused of espionage and treason. Because of his cooperation with the dissident movement, as opposed to the exclusively Zionist movement, the Lishka wasn't promoting his case. Further, it encouraged his wife Avital, formerly Natasha Stiglitz, who had been given permission and left for Israel the day after their wedding, to "sit quietly and not make noise." But that wasn't what Anatoly (later known as Natan) wanted. Before his arrest, Sharansky had asked prominent activists June and Ron Daniels, who were in Moscow from the Des Moines Jewish Federation, to take a message to his wife in Jerusalem. He wanted them to tell Avital to speak out and take action, not to rely on the Lishka's policy of quiet diplomacy. Then he directed Avital and June and Ron to work with the UCSJ and Irene Manekovsky.

It was Irene who was putting Sharansky's name in front of the public. In fact, Avital was with Irene in Washington when she saw the news reporting her husband's sentence: thirteen years of prison and hard labor. It was around that time that I met her, a young beauty with soft, dark eyes, raven hair, and a slow, shy smile. She was slated to speak at a luncheon hosted by UCSJ's Congressional Wives Committee. The smartly dressed women filled the room with a social buzz that abruptly broke when Avital was introduced. Avital faced the wives of the congressmen and addressed them in her quiet, halting English: "My husband, Natan…" The words choked in her throat and she turned aside, eyes filling with tears. "You have to help my husband. Please." Avital was irresistible.

Avital met the challenges of her husband's incarceration with an uncanny capacity to change. She grew in stature and became a compelling speaker and a consummate leader of the movement to free her husband; in doing so, she became a symbol of all Soviet Jewish refuseniks. Anatoly likes to tell the story of when he was imprisoned and his jailer showed him the video of demonstrations in the United States, telling him, "You think people care about you in the West? Just look who is supporting you. Nobody. Only a group of housewives and students." And there, at the head of the demonstration, was Avital, whom he hadn't seen since she left Moscow. He asked the jailer to play the video again. And again.

Intended by Sharansky's interrogator to be demeaning, the characterization *housewives and students* represented the achievements of dedicated activist volunteers who operated as professionals working overtime. Sharansky's inscription to me in his book reads, "To Pam Cohen, Five-Star General of the army of students and housewives."

The other activists I met at the Washington meeting were equally obsessed with the Sharansky case and the climate of fear pervading the refusenik communities. Lynn Singer headed the Long Island Committee for Soviet Jewry and would become UCSJ's president in the early 1980s. Lynn was a gutsy, street-smart New Yorker with a determined gait and an authoritative presence. She was also a soft touch for the refuseniks and prisoners of conscience,[3] who knew her as their "Yiddishe Momma." She forged connections with the New York congressional representatives and the US State Department. She manned the phone lines to refuseniks, bringing out vital information. When necessary, she interfaced with the New York Jewish bureaucracy and the Lishka, with whom she was able to maintain dignified and civil dialogue even as she held tough against their positions.

Under her presidency, she convened a biennial UCSJ conference in Israel, where we could debrief newly arrived refuseniks or meet with the families of those still in refusal. At one of them, she met artist Evgeny Abezgauz, Leningrad refusenik and founder of the Alef Group for Jewish underground artists in the USSR. She had spoken with him on the phone regularly when he was in the USSR; now, finally together face to face, she found he was suddenly struggling for words. She led him to the hotel lobby, installed him in a phone booth, and handed him the phone; she went into the adjacent booth, from where she loudly called out to him, "Evgeny. Hello! Now talk. How are you?"

Often, over the years, people I spoke to about our work on behalf of Soviet Jewry challenged me. "You are trying to do *what*? Who do you think you are? You think you can take on the Kremlin, the second greatest military power in the world? You think you can pit yourself against KGB's apparatus?"

But the people I met at that first UCSJ Annual Meeting – self-educated Sovietologists, politically savvy activists, volunteers – were doing just that, taking on the Kremlin and KGB to rescue Jews. Selma Light, Shirley Goldstein, Lil Hoffman, and Rae Sharfman: all were strong, gutsy women, half a generation older than me, capable of facing down any KGB goon, each running her own council. Harvard-educated Morey Schapira in San Francisco's Bay Area Council; Bob Gordon, a successful Boston businessman; and Joel Sandberg, a Miami doctor, were leading the campaign locally at home, driving the grassroots forces to pressure their congressional representatives on Capitol Hill. Enid and Stuart Wurtman, from the Philadelphia Council, would later make aliyah themselves, inspired by

---

3.   UCSJ used the term *prisoners of conscience* to refer to those refuseniks who were sent to prison or labor camps; the Israeli government and Jewish Establishment referred to them as prisoners of Zion.

the activists. All were consumed with the right of Jews to emigrate in the face of anti-Jewish persecution. The Washington meeting was dedicated to exploring the methodology of making that happen.

From early morning on, an intense agenda addressed a host of challenges confronting individual refuseniks and the emigration movement as well as what we needed to supply the refuseniks to aid their physical, emotional, and spiritual survival while they struggled for their right to leave. White House officials and State Department representatives were brought in for us to question. Late that night, on the phone to Lenny, I realized that the attendees reminded me of the characters in Steven Spielberg's film *Close Encounters of the Third Kind*. They, too, were driven by a compulsion to implement a shared vision and willing to go to extremes to fulfill it. To them, the defense of Soviet Jewry wasn't a job, it was their life. They lived and breathed it night and day.

I was the newest and among the youngest of them, but I knew I was home.

With Lenny on our first trip to the USSR, Moscow, 1978

Yuli Kosharovsky, Moscow, 1978

Professor Alexander Lerner, Moscow, 1978

Lev Blitshtein, Moscow, 1978

Ari Volvovsky, Moscow, 1980

Marillyn Tallman, me, Jean Freed, Hetty Deleeuwe,
Chicago Action for Soviet Jewry (CASJ)

With Prime Minister Menachem Begin,
UCSJ meeting, Jerusalem, 1981

Misha Edelman at our home in Deerfield, Illinois, 1984

Open letter to Secretary of State George Shultz, UCSJ's *Wall Street Journal* ad, January 2, 1985

"Hang Tough, Mr. President," UCSJ's *New York Times* ad, November 10, 1985

Mikhail Shirman in Reykjavik, speaking to his sister in Moscow: "I've come to meet my killer," Reagan-Gorbachev summit, Iceland, 1986

Yosef Mendelevich arrives in Reykjavik, Iceland, with a *sefer Torah*, Reagan-Gorbachev summit, Iceland, 1986

Morris Abram (*fifth from left*) and I flank Secretary of State George Shultz, White House, 1986

With Natan Sharansky at the UCSJ Annual Meeting, Washington, DC, 1986

Speaking at Freedom Sunday, Washington, DC, December 6, 1987

First meeting with Vladimir Slepak, Freedom Sunday, US Capitol Building, December 6, 1987

UCSJ rally, Capitol Building, Washington, DC, 1987

Zachar Zunshine, recently released from prison, and his wife Tatiana thank
Chicago's Mayor, Harold Washington, for his support, September 29, 1987

White House meeting with President Reagan, 1987. I'm fourth from the left, next to Secretary Shultz. Vladimir Slepak is seated first on the right.

Student Struggle for Soviet Jewry's demonstration in Helsinki, 1988;
left to right: Jacob Ner-David (in cage), me, Rabbi Avi Weiss, Glenn Richter

Pamela B. Cohen explains UCSJ policy and procedures to a wide representation of Jewish Refuseniks and activists in Refusenik Vladimir Kislik's Moscow apartment.

THE MOSCOW SUMMIT:
UCSJ KEEPS HUMAN RIGHTS ON THE AGENDA

President Reagan's fourth and possibly final Summit meeting with General Secretary Mikhail Gorbachev presented an important opportunity for the Union of Councils for Soviet Jews to ensure that human rights — and specifically Jewish emigration — were kept high on the official agenda.

Prior to the Summit, UCSJ National President Pamela B. Cohen and National Director Micah H. Naftalin were invited, by the White House, to prepare a written statement of their human rights goals for Summit IV. In a report entitled "Verification of Soviet Agreements in Human Rights," the two UCSJ leaders outlined the critical elements of a human rights verification policy negotiation. Additionally, they urged the President and Secretary of State to reaffirm their unwavering support of the Helsinki Final Act and Jackson-Vanik Amendment, and to seek areas of linkage, especially in the fields of trade and finance, to offer opportunities for increased leverage in the area of human rights and Jewish emigration.

"Helsinki Action to Free Soviet Jews"

To coincide with President Reagan's stopover in Helsinki, Finland — the site of the 1975 human rights accords — a delegation from UCSJ and the New York-based Student Struggle for Soviet Jewry (SSSJ) travelled to Helsinki to highlight the human rights component of the President's mission.

(continued on page two)

With a last-minute visa issued in Helsinki, I meet with refuseniks in Moscow during the Reagan-Gorbachev Summit, 1988

Speaking at UCSJ's "Annual" Meeting in Moscow: the first open meeting in Soviet history between Soviet Jews and Jews from the West, 1989

White House meeting with President George H. W. Bush, 1990;
first from left: Malcolm Hoenlein; *third from left:* me

Left to right: Micah Naftalin, me, and Leonid Stonov, circa 1989

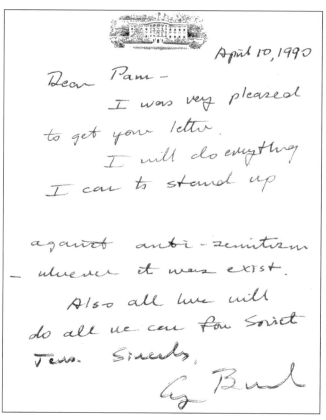

April 10, 1990

Dear Pam —
 I was very pleased
to get your letter.
 I will do everything
I can to stand up

against anti-semitism
— whenever it may exist.
 Also all we will
do all we can for Soviet
Jews. Sincerely,

G Bush

Personal assurance from President George H. W. Bush, 1990

Briefing Congressional Helsinki Commission co-chairman Senator Dennis
DeConcini and Representative Steny Hoyer, Vilnius Alternative Human Rights
meeting, Lithuania 1991

UCSJ, Moscow Bureau, Jewish Russian and Ukrainian activists meeting with Lithuania's new president, Vilnius, Lithuania, 1991; *from left:* Leonid Stonov, Micah Naftalin, Emmanuel Zingeris, Steven Cohen, President Vytauta Lansbergis, David Waksberg, me, Roman Gefter, Alla Gerber, former prisoner Josef Zissels, UCSJ Moscow bureau director Dima Kalmanson

Bureau head and former prisoner of conscience Semyon Gluzman (*center*) and Leonid Stonov (*right*) at the opening of UCSJ's Kiev Bureau on Human Rights, 1992

Lenny and I meet President Bush at the White House state dinner for Russian president Boris Yeltsin, June 16, 1992

With Ambassador Richard Schifter (*center*) and former prisoner of conscience Yuli Edelstein (*right*), who later became Speaker of Knesset, at the Knesset committee on aliyah honoring former refuseniks, Jerusalem, 2010

With Leonid Stonov and writer Evgeny Yevtushenko, whose groundbreaking poem "Babi Yar" in 1961 was the first and for decades the only monument to Jews slaughtered on Soviet soil in the Holocaust, Skokie, Illinois, 1992

UCSJ leadership in Jerusalem; *from left, with former UCSJ presidents indicated by asterisk:* Joel Sandberg, me*, Bob Gordon*, Enid Wurtman (obscured), Natasha Stonov, Leonid Stonov, Larry Lerner*, Yossi Abramowitz*, Judy Balint, Morey Schapira*

Marillyn welcoming Chicago-born long-term refusenik Abe Stolar to freedom,
Chicago, 1989

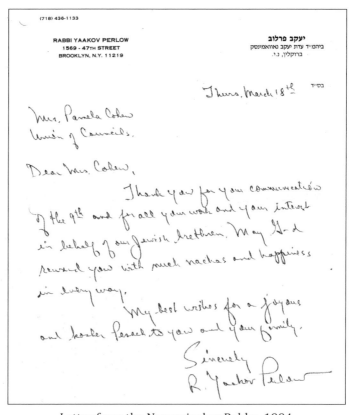

Letter from the Novominsker Rebbe, 1994

CHAPTER 2

Into the Storm, 1978

Russia and Ukraine

I went home, called a travel agency, and booked a trip to Russia.

And so it was, in the autumn of 1978, that Lenny and I found ourselves anxiously waiting in the long customs line at Moscow's Sheremetyevo Airport. Our suitcases were crammed with contraband – goods that were permissible under international agreement but were prohibited in the Soviet Union: Jewish and Hebrew books, prayer books, Hebrew-Russian dictionaries, tallitot, tefillin, kosher mezuzah *klafim*. We also had cameras, tape recorders, jeans, and other goods for refuseniks to sell on the black market to financially sustain themselves and the movement. Lorel had briefed us on the rights of tourists to convey critical goods and information for refuseniks, an effective method used by UCSJ.

The long lines were moving imperceptibly. With mounting anxiety, we watched KGB customs officials force tourists to open their suitcases so the officials could rummage through them and examine their contents. They confiscated *Time* and *Newsweek* magazines, books and newspapers, anything published in the West, all piled in growing heaps on the floor.

I silently prayed: "Please God, let us pass through without our suitcases opened. These are not for us; everything is for Your children. Please let us go through safely and unimpeded. Please." Miraculously, we might have been the only travelers who passed through without incident. Our luggage went uninspected.

As the bus drove through the streets of Moscow, I peered out the windows to see the grim faces of heavy-footed men and women trudging along the sidewalks, many waiting in long lines in front of gray, grimy shops. It was a world without color, filled with people beaten into submission. They avoided eye contact, especially with foreigners.

Ari Volvovsky

Marillyn had arranged for us to meet with several refuseniks and had briefed us about how to make contact without being detected by KGB. She instructed us to use the kopeks she had given us to call the refuseniks from a payphone far from the hotel. Hotel rooms were bugged. We had also been told that on every hotel floor sat a "key lady" who methodically collected the room keys of tourists as they headed out. Ostensibly hotel employees, these Russian women were part of KGB's arsenal, responsible for reporting the movement of "suspicious" tourists and inspecting their rooms for evidence that could link them to "undesirables," like our Jewish activists. Upon arriving, Lenny and I removed from our luggage all of the Jewish books, the tefillin, every obviously Jewish item we were to distribute in five cities over the next two weeks, and crammed it all into our backpacks. We then set out to find a public phone booth to arrange our meeting with a Jew whom officials considered undesirable.

It would be a fateful meeting, one that set off a chain reaction that has lasted more than forty years. The man we were to meet – Leonid "Ari" Volvovsky – was the archetypal Moscow Jewish scientist, with years of research in cybernetics under his belt. Accomplished in his field, he, like us, had no Jewish education. In 1974, one hour after Ari had asked his boss for the character reference required to apply to emigrate, he was fired. Now he was cleaning streets.

An hour after making initial contact by phone, clutching a Cyrillic-language map of Moscow, Lenny and I were hurtling down the impossibly deep escalator of Moscow's metro into the bowels of the earth. As planned, at the end of the Red Line we were met by a short woman with light brown curls. In a nervous staccato of broken English, she confirmed she was Mila Volvovsky, Ari's wife. We silently trailed after her until we arrived in their small, warm, book-filled apartment on Automobilskaya. We waited. Ari was due back in a few minutes. The phone rang, and Mila picked it up immediately, answered, and after a few seconds, handed it to me. "I am on my way," a man told me in heavily accented English. When I handed her back the phone, I saw that her face had drained white. She shook her curly head. "No, it wasn't Ari you spoke to." Someone must have followed us. We waited anxiously. Who would come to the door? By now, Mila's face was not white but flushed red.

Finally, the door opened. Ari Volvovsky burst into the room. Mila gasped. We looked at her, then at him, waiting to hear what had happened. It was simple enough: Mila did not recognize her husband's voice speaking English. It was a tiny misunderstanding, but it gave us a glimpse of the fear that pervaded the Volvovskys' world – and that of all those who dared want a life outside of Mother Russia.

Ari Volvovsky had a full beard and broad shoulders. His effervescent style left an impression of a big man, though he wasn't particularly tall. He took off his jacket, sat down with us at the small table in front of his bookshelf-lined walls, and started talking. He bubbled, boiled, erupted, and intermittently broke out in laughter. He spoke English, but his understanding of the language seemed clouded. His outgoing personality suffocated our stammering attempts to identify ourselves and establish our credibility. He was a man with an agenda maximized for each of his contacts with the West. Somehow, who we were seemed irrelevant. He trusted us.

In the rush of his buoyancy, the gravity of his situation could be missed. No one in Moscow could forget the unpredictability of the escalated crackdown, which some traced to October 1976, when KGB reacted with violence to a standard sit-in of refuseniks in the visa office. The authorities rounded up a group of protesters, bused them to a forest, and beat them. Twenty-two people were jailed for fifteen days, and Boris Chernobilsky and Yosef Ahss were charged and held until massive pressure from the West forced their release.

After he was fired from his work, Ari started learning Hebrew. Five years later he joined the newest generation of unofficial Hebrew teachers who were prevented from registering officially and resorted to teaching underground, thereby subverting the Kremlin's war against the Hebrew language. A Zionist, Ari recognized that knowledge of Hebrew could play a decisive role in determining whether Jews would pick Israel as their destination rather than America.

Ari's personal aims aside, for the refusenik, the pariah who was fired and socially ostracized, the underground Hebrew classes were the beginnings of community. The classes were a supportive way for Jews to explore their Jewish identities and to celebrate newly discovered Jewish holidays with other families. They served as the platform upon which life in the "transit camp" of Soviet refusal was built.

Sitting with us in his apartment, Volvovsky began explaining to us, as if we were novices, that Jewish books had to be brought into the Soviet Union by tourists. However, he emphasized, we should also be pressuring Soviet authorities to allow Jewish books to be delivered by international mail. We didn't interrupt as he enthusiastically explained our own methodology. Correspondence and books, he told us, must be mailed in strict accordance with the Helsinki Final Act,[1] which guaranteed citizens of the signatory countries (including the Soviet Union) the right to their cultural identity.

"Look at this," he instructed. With his back to the book-laden shelves, his eyes focused directly on us, he blindly reached behind and slipped out one of the scores of books from his crowded shelf. Thumbing through its pages, he arrived at his objective, the blue label pasted on the inside cover. This label "officially verifies that the book's contents are admissible under the provisions of Helsinki Final Act's 'Right to Identity.'" At the bottom are the names of the book's donors. The label acknowledged that this particular book was sent by registered mail to Dr. Leonid Volvovsky. It was sent by none other than Leonard and Pamela Cohen. Incredulous, we pointed at ourselves. "Ari, that's *us*!"

Instantly there was a lightning bolt of recognition and connection. Marillyn, who sent us to him, was in the room with us. Time and space ceased to exist.

For years, Volvovsky's activities had brought down the wrath of the authorities. Two years before our meeting, he was interrogated, his apartment was searched by KGB, and he was held under house arrest along with other refuseniks for participating in the Jewish Cultural Symposium. The symposium was organized to attract Jews who had lost all connections to their Jewish religious and cultural roots. Ultimately, authorities closed it down. During the winter of 1977, Volvovsky had been arrested and taken to KGB's notorious Lefortovo Prison in connection with the investigation of Anatoly Sharansky, who was arrested in March of that year. Volvovsky was brought from his cell for interrogation. Instead of appearing intimidated,

---

1. The Helsinki Final Act was an agreement signed by thirty-five nations, including the Soviet Union; it concluded the Conference on Security and Cooperation (CSCE) in Europe, held in Helsinki, Finland, in 1975. The multifaceted act addressed a range of prominent global issues and gave human rights obligations equal stature with disarmament and economic issues.

he went on the offensive and authoritatively placed a book on his interrogator's table. It was written by Vladimir Albrecht, a well-known dissident lawyer. The subject addressed citizens' rights during interrogations.

"What's that book?" questioned his interrogator.

"What do you mean, 'what's this book?'" answered Volvovsky sardonically. "It's a book of our laws. You and I are here to make sure that we protect our laws and we do it together. Now, what am I doing here?"

Volvovsky was subjected to a ten-hour interrogation without food or water. Throughout, he consulted the book on each question and answered only if the question was admissible under Soviet law. Ari wasn't alone. Jewish activists operated openly and within the legal parameters. The Soviets had to be pressured to adhere to their own legal system. In the end, in this instance, KGB released him.

Nevertheless, Ari was hounded by the authorities. They intercepted his mail. Intermittently, they disconnected his phone. When authorities told him he was using his phone for anti-Soviet activity, he countered, "How could you know unless you were listening?"

On the Friday night following our first meeting with him, Lenny and I returned to Ari's Moscow apartment. This time we were met by the smells of Shabbat, the tranquility of candles burning, the sparkle of the prepared table, and Ari's voice lifted in zemirot, the traditional songs sung at Shabbat meals. In the glow of the candlelight, fears of the traps and obstacles laid by men and their governments momentarily disappeared. Shabbat was transporting the Volvovskys into another dimension, and it carried Lenny and me along with it. From my position in Moscow, I imagined the Earth rotating on its axis from daylight to night-shadow, illuminated by successive waves of burning Shabbat candles as it moved westward, one time zone after the next.

On Shabbat afternoon, as pre-arranged, we again met Volvovsky, this time on Archipova Street outside the Choral Synagogue. While the interior of the synagogue, with its state-controlled rabbi, was the domain of the Kremlin apparatus, the street outside was a well-known meeting ground for refuseniks and their western visitors. KGB and militia lurked on the perimeters. Informers, plainclothes KGB agents, hustlers, and black marketeers mingled in the crowd, some posing as refuseniks or activists, angling to snare some naive and unbriefed western tourist.

UCSJ repeatedly warned western visitors to be especially guarded on the street, to speak only to known refuseniks, and to refrain from leaving black market items with any refusenik they didn't know or from depositing books or religious items in the synagogue, where they routinely disappeared.

Ari led us through the crowd to meet Leonid Sharansky, Anatoly's brother, who had a message for us to take home: "The world outcry has to be sustained. The Sharansky trial is a fishbone in the Kremlin's throat. It's your job to see to it that it remains lodged there." Art Tauder, a friend who was traveling with us, took Leonid aside and handed him a sweater he brought from New York. On the front was one word: *Courage*.

Yuli Kosharovsky

Another fateful meeting during that 1978 trip was with Yuli Kosharovsky, one of the men who inspired an exodus. A young man from Sverdlovsk, Yuli had an infectious smile. With his knitted kippah and light blue down jacket, he stood out in the crowd gathered outside the Choral Synagogue.

Yuli came from an entirely assimilated family and, like me, he struggled to come to terms with the trauma of the Holocaust and the killing units that had operated on Soviet soil. Half a million Jews served in Stalin's army, battling the Nazis. Many were decorated war heroes. Regardless of their loyalty, the Kremlin subjected them to the humiliations of state anti-Semitism and sent many to the battalions of slave labor in Siberian prison camps.

When the Six-Day War broke out, Yuli was filled with a desire to be in Israel – despite the danger, despite the threat that Israel may be destroyed. As he told me years later, "My feelings were so strong that I wanted nothing to do with this country – just get out and go to Israel."[2]

In the wake of the Leningrad trials, Yuli had applied for permission to emigrate. Refused permission, he emerged as one of the very first refuseniks to teach Hebrew unofficially. He organized underground summer camps for young Jews to start building Jewish identity. Those who attended learned about Israel, studied the language, and sang Jewish and Hebrew songs around campfires. Yuli also built an underground network of Hebrew teachers throughout the Soviet Union, making himself

---

2.   Yuli Kosharovsky, conversation with Pamela Braun Cohen.

conspicuous to a government that was threatened by any kind of structured connections between groups of people who shared an ideology other than that of the Communist Party.

Yuli worked with refusenik groups that clandestinely published material on Jewish culture and history. This underground self-publishing system, known as samizdat, was vital. In all of the Soviet Union, there were no newly published Jewish books or magazines, much less Jewish bookstores. Yuli and those he inspired were driving the movement with their teaching and by photographing or copying by hand the books that our tourists brought in their suitcases.

On that October afternoon in 1978 when we first met in Moscow, neither Yuli nor I could possibly have imagined that he would be forced to endure a painful, eighteen-year struggle for permission to leave the Soviet Union. Nor could we have believed that our parallel activities on two sides of the ocean would thrust us into the center of the movement's conflicts.

That first trip Lenny and I made to Russia opened my eyes. I met people whose fate I felt I shared. I experienced them as if they were a part of me. Sitting in apartments in Leningrad, Kharkov, Kiev, Odessa, and Moscow, I saw the faces of Jews who looked as if they could have been my uncles or aunts. When I spoke to groups about our trip after returning home, those faces never left me.

No Way Out: Back in Chicago

After our return, as Lorel had requested, Lenny and I prepared a detailed report of our meetings with refuseniks. At a dinner we presumed to be a further debriefing, Lorel announced she was giving up the chairmanship of CASJ. I was flabbergasted. If she thought I was going to take up the mantle of leadership, was she ever wrong. I was only in my mid-thirties, raising three children, I had no connection to the seats of power or finance, and I hated speaking in public.

Then I had a flashback to the questions that haunted me as a teenager. Where were the voices protesting the murder of six million Jews? When the truth trickled in from across the ocean – news of Auschwitz and Buchenwald and Ravensbruck – where was the collective outcry from the millions of Jews who were safe in America? Why did so few answer the call to save so many?

And now, I thought, how could I retreat into our personal lives? If I didn't do something, who would? How could I stand by while this rescue effort died? For me, there was no other option. Sometimes leadership is not dictated by skill but is created by history and circumstance. With trepidation, but determined to play my part in the intergenerational drama of the Jewish people, I accepted the role. And I immediately looked around for support. I enlisted Carole Boron from my letter-writing group and Marillyn Tallman as my cochairs, and Lenny agreed that he and I would pay the rent and phone bills for our first office in Highland Park.

There wasn't much in Lorel's office to move, except a small refrigerator and a couple of boxes of newsletters from the various councils. Our new office, located on the main street in the suburb of Highland Park, was a small windowless space on the basement level of a three-story brick office building. It was crammed with two desks and a donated oversize printer, the size of today's Smart car.

Despite her rigorous speaking and teaching schedule, with her son still at home, Marillyn agreed to come to our first tiny office to brief tourists going to the USSR and to help us raise the funds to operate. Marillyn was my partner, but for others, she was "the General."

From the first day, I was obsessed with data collection. Yellow highlighter in hand, I mined every council's published newsletters for information, cataloging names and systematically detailing refusenik histories. Lynn Singer's phone calls to Russia brought fresh information. In a short time, I had compiled a refusenik card-file database, detailing addresses, phone numbers, family members, and dates of first application and refusals for refuseniks in Russia and Ukraine. It also reflected whether or not the refuseniks wanted publicity, tourist visits, and phone calls, and it chronicled their history of harassment. I carted this file back and forth between the office and my home for years – until my computer database made it obsolete.

In those early days, everything had to be created from the ground up, from designing CASJ's logo to assembling our honorary board of directors. We designed stationary and went to work publishing a newsletter, *The Refusenik*, which would be edited by another volunteer, Linda Opper. In the midst of any storm that blew through the office, Linda was always composed, her long fingers and manicured nails rifling through the stack of news and periodicals, faxes, and bulletins looking for new data.

One dreary fall afternoon, I was at my desk alone in CASJ's office, worrying glumly and cataloging individual refusenik cases. I was also steeling myself. Carole, Chicago Action's third cochair, had resigned, and I felt the weight of her job. As a 501(c)(3) nonprofit organization, our office required fastidious bookkeeping. I was entirely incapable of fastidious bookkeeping.

The door opened and in walked a curly-haired, clear-eyed, rosy-cheeked woman in a dark skirt, white blouse, and cardigan. Before I could greet her, she scrutinized both the office and me. She had a high, cheery voice and an accent I couldn't identify. With a tinkling laugh that exposed her no-nonsense sense of irony, she asked, "You're worried about keeping your books? How many bills can you possibly have? I was a bookkeeper for an import-export firm in Holland for years. I think I'm capable of handling your checkbook." It was Hetty Deleeuwe, the person who, years earlier, had first alerted me to the work others in Chicago were doing on behalf of Soviet Jews. And that was that: Hetty was part of the crew.

Hetty's progenitor was an advisor to Charles V of Spain in the Middle Ages. Hetty had survived the Holocaust, saved by righteous gentiles who hid her in the farmland of the Netherlands. Her accountant's matter-of-fact mind locked onto a problem with precision and reduced it to manageable units. Just as she did that very first day she appeared in the office, for the next thirty years Hetty solved every logistical problem we encountered.

Hetty became CASJ's systems analyst, bookkeeper, accountant, banker, purveyor for tourist goods, communications specialist, and technical expert. As CASJ grew, so did her responsibilities. Whatever the technical or logistical problem, whether it was transferring money to Israel or England, getting a lift of kosher food delivered to Lvov, purchasing a dozen kosher tefillin, or procuring instruments for *brit milah* or *shechitah*, Marillyn and I looked to Hetty to solve it. And she always did.

As the movement grew, Hetty enlisted her husband Al, a Sabbath-observant pilot for United Airlines and a computer expert, to help us with software, file backups, email: all the technical know-how CASJ demanded. Hetty herself handled the growing lists of our new members and our press and government contacts. She arranged for the distribution of *The Refusenik* newsletter, removing me from the responsibility of painfully typing and copying hundreds of addresses on sticky labels with my less-than-satisfactory typing skills.

Other dedicated women gave themselves over to our rescue activity. Betty Kahn came on board as a photographer and our one-woman public relations department. She also crafted a Soviet Jewry curriculum that could be taught in schools. There were others, like Jean Freed, CASJ's liaison to the Illinois congressional delegation, who pushed synagogues and organizations into advocating for refuseniks and their relevant legislative issues with their congressmen. Others represented our interests outside the office. Bob Mednick, for example, a senior partner in a prestigious international accounting company, presented our refusenik case biographies to government leaders worldwide.

An Interlocking Activist Network

Our interlocking network of activists, then and in the coming years, extended far beyond our small Chicago office. Each person brought individual style, abilities, and talents that were essential to the growth of our movement; had even one of these determined activists been missing from the picture, our movement might have failed.

David Waksberg wasn't too long out of college when I met him in the early 1980s at his first UCSJ Annual Meeting in Boston. Tall and lanky, with long curly hair, his reserved but honest smile was worth winning. He didn't speak much, but when he did, I listened. He was the director of the Bay Area Council on Soviet Jewry and later became a UCSJ vice-president. He had the technological savvy of his generation, and when I visited him at the Bay Area Council, I was blown away by the systems they had developed to efficiently process and store a massive amount of constantly changing data and anecdotal information. The streamlined efficiency was equal to Lenny's advertising firm. It was an activist agenda run on a business model, the model I was determined to build for Chicago Action.

David's reasoning was incisive and logical. His writing was journalistic, and he was a strategic thinker. When the executive board would become mired in complicated issues or policies, David had the insight and patience to help others, especially me, to verbalize their strategic rationale.

The Union could not have existed without the powerhouse efforts of people like David and the many others who ran councils all over the country. For every one of these people, the fate and destiny of refuseniks had become enmeshed in their own fate and was tied to their own identity. It had become impossible to separate us. Rae Sharfman was in the Detroit area fighting for Ari Volvovsky and the Poltinnikovs, a family of refuseniks in Novosibirsk. Steve Feinstein at the Minnesota Dakotas Council built UCSJ's first refusenik database. In South Florida, Margery Sandford and Adele Sandberg – and later, Hinda Cantor – published booklets for the US Congress, documenting refusenik cases and separated families as evidence of Soviet emigration violations. Ruth Newman took over the Washington Committee, which specialized in postal issues, monitoring Soviet's non-delivery of mail. Lil Hoffman, head of the Colorado Committee and a friend of Bibi Netanyahu, headed our effort to press the Kremlin to divulge the fate of Raoul Wallenberg, the Swedish diplomat who was arrested by the Soviets and disappeared after issuing thousands of visas to Hungarian Jews during the Holocaust. Omaha Committee's Shirley Goldstein's bubbly personality and warm smile masked a dynamo with strong legislative muscle and ingenuity. Sandy Spinner and Alan Riga in Ohio had the support of Ohio's legislative representatives, and Sandy built and operated a reliable channel to refuseniks in Kharkov, Ukraine. Judy Balint, at Seattle Action for Soviet Jewry, headed UCSJ's campaign to expose the Soviet Sister Cities and peace initiatives as propaganda and disinformation tools to weaken US military defense. Judy Patkin at Boston Action trained the media's attention on the "littlest refusenik," thirteen-month-old Jessica Katz, who suffered from malabsorption syndrome and whose parents were struggling for permission for years until Massachusetts's senator intervened. More than thirty council chairs were running expert advocacy rescue operations, media campaigns, educational programs: some out of offices, some out of their kitchens.

Student Struggle for Soviet Jewry (SSSJ), based in New York, was a vital part of our grassroots network. Their founder, Jacob Birnbaum, was a German-born refugee who grafted the tactics of the civil rights movement onto the emigration movement. Glenn Richter infused SSSJ's press releases with his quick-witted, wry humor and his gift for compressing information into soundbites. While UCSJ assembled and analyzed documentation for testimonies and briefings, Glenn condensed the essence into a few words, making it accessible to the public and the press alike. When the catastrophic Chernobyl explosion occurred at Passover time, Glenn's press release poetically stated: "Mr. Gorbachev, Let My People Go." Throughout the struggle, SSSJ mobilized hundreds of students to demonstrate at the Soviet Mission in New York.

David Selikowitz, from Paris's Comité des Quinze (committee of fifteen), influenced the French government. The London-based 35s, also known as the Women's Campaign for Soviet Jewry, played a vital role in England. Rita Eker, a founder of the 35s,[3] was a tall, attractive woman with a ready laugh who transmitted clarity and focus in her clipped English accent.

Michael Sherbourne, a British Russian-language teacher, found a home with the 35s. He manned the calls to Moscow from London. Michael was the source of data and anecdotal information that traveled across our phone lines, day and night: from London, to Lynn in Long Island, and then in a westward geographic relay across the country, according to protocol. In the days before faxes, let alone computers or cell phones, our home phone rang every night, usually at dinnertime.

I got to know Michael when Lorel brought him and his wife Muriel to Chicago. After Michael's speech at our synagogue, Muriel admired my hand-cut ivory heart that dangled on a gold chain. Instinctively I reached behind my neck, unhooked my necklace, and placed it around her neck. Long after Muriel died, Michael told me, "During all these years, the carved ivory necklace you gave Muriel is still hanging on the lamp where she last left it."

Years later, I learned how their lives had been enmeshed in Jewish history. Michael and Muriel, after having trained in rural England for two years in a Zionist agricultural program, received British certificates allowing them to go to Palestine. They arrived in Paris on September 1, 1939, the first day of World War II. Adventurously skirting through Europe, they eventually came to Kfar Blum, in the Galilee. For health reasons, they later returned to England.

These people made up an international network of the foremost advocates for Soviet Jews, forged by direct person-to-person connections: phone calls, correspondence, and face-to-face meetings with refuseniks.

Of course, when it came to the USSR, these connections were anything but simple. But refuseniks depended on that contact, and the desperate nature of their situation soon became apparent.

---

3. The 35s was also founded by Doreen Gainsford, Zelda Harris, Barbara Oberman, and Sylvia Wallis.

CHAPTER 3
Nuts and Bolts

Adopt-a-Family

I looked around the Highland Park living room, scrutinizing the faces, scanning my memory for pertinent details: profession, family members, city of origin. The man in the front row was a psychiatrist. He would be the ideal match for a refusenik who had been forcibly committed to a punitive psychiatric institution. A woman sitting on the side worked for a Jewish studies program. I would pair her up with a refusenik Hebrew teacher.

Our list of refuseniks asking for support and publicity continued to grow. We simply couldn't handle all the casework from our offices. Marillyn and I began speaking in synagogues and elsewhere to harness members and social action committees to "adopt" refuseniks, reaching out to them by mail and phone, garnering publicity for their cases in the media, and soliciting support from Congress. The Adopt-a-Family programs distributed responsibility by connecting individual American Jews directly with refuseniks. We reached out to those individuals, as well as to groups and institutions like Spertus College of Judaica, and provided them with the data they needed to approach their legislators on a case-by-case basis. Like a physician for a patient, I created refusenik case sheets with the relevant documentation to keep the adopting groups updated.

Yitzchak Kogan and Harvey Barnett

One evening, Lenny and I were speaking about our trip to Russia at a meeting with a group of emerging Jewish leaders. As if scripted, a young attorney, Harvey Barnett, asked what he could do to help. I immediately thought to give him the case of the Kogans: Yitzchak, an engineer, and Sophia, a dentist, and their small daughters. We had met the Kogans in Leningrad and witnessed firsthand their efforts to hold the refusenik community together. They were taking their first steps in a life of Torah, steps that would take them in unimagined directions. Their apartment, walls draped with oriental carpets, was a center for an emerging Shabbos-observant refusenik community. It also served as a meeting ground between activists and Western tourists.

Harvey became the point person, the national case manager, for the Kogans. We relied on him to reach out to the Kogans by phone and mail, to collect information and generate publicity, to urge his representatives and senators to intervene, and to do whatever else required to get the Kogans their visas. I kept him supplied with information as I received it. Harvey threw himself into the cause and ultimately helped win the release of the Kogan family. He also became a major CASJ fundraiser, traveled twice to the USSR, and served under my presidency on the UCSJ board of directors, where he made invaluable contributions to the movement.

With an extensive grassroots infrastructure, CASJ's adoption program intersected with those of other UCSJ councils around the country. It was an effective instrument to win congressional support for individual cases and also to influence governmental policies that supported the emigration movement in general. After all, it was the House and the Senate that held the carrots and sticks that could change Soviet policy.

There was additional logic behind our adoption policy. We might have been a group of feisty and dedicated women, but in reality, we were no match for the Kremlin. Our best chance was to work case by case, fighting for each refusenik, each prisoner of conscience, each family. Every Jewish soul we succeeded in extracting from the prison that was the USSR was a victory. We gave the campaign a personal quality that pulled on people's heartstrings. We were dealing with real people, not an amorphous number. They were people with jobs and families, treasured books and medical conditions; they were people with humor and sorrow and childhood photographs. Adopt-a-Family stood against the cry of despair and bewilderment that echoed out of Auschwitz: *six million!* Six million, that unfathomable figure of destruction and, for second-generation Jewish Americans, disillusionment. Our ammunition against the attempted annihilation of Soviet Jews was not the ubiquitous cry of "never again." Rather, it was a focus on the individual. Jewish tradition states that he who saves one life is considered as if he has saved an entire world. And so, we focused on one world, and then another, and then another.

All Marillyn and I needed was one Harvey Barnett, one synagogue, one Jewish organization; we needed one physicist motivated to work for a single refusenik physicist, one psychiatrist ready to champion the issue of Soviet psychiatric abuse, one Hebrew school to adopt a refusenik Hebrew teacher. Just one. These combined ones then had the potential to enlist the political muscle of the eighteen congressmen and two senators from Illinois alone. All of UCSJ's councils were operating on the identical strategy.

This grassroots mobilization strategy demonstrated CASJ's political muscle to the congressional offices. A deluge of postcards or a barrage of phone calls made clear to the legislator that we had access to their voters. For the congressional office, advocating on behalf of the refuseniks was not a difficult way to please their Jewish constituency.

Sometimes, the Adopt-a-Family program resulted in an emotional reunion between adopter and adoptee. Harvey Barnett's reunion with Yitzchak Kogan was a memorable example. Immediately after I assigned him the Kogan case, Harvey began to write to the family. Mail to refuseniks was a purposeful technique in our campaign. Despite censorship – and non-delivery – correspondence put the Soviets on notice, letter by letter, that Americans were watching. Inexplicably, KGB permitted delivery of Harvey's letter that included a *New York Times* article reporting the release of Leningrad trial defendant Yosef Mendelevich from labor camp. In a world devoid of news, the Kogans never forgot that Harvey's letter and the article made it through the censors.

Marillyn and I corralled Harvey to make the trip to Russia, in part to meet the Kogans, but also to bring him closer to the center of the movement. Though I was far away in Chicago, what happened when Harvey showed up in Leningrad is permanently seared in my memory.

Along with Harvey, we sent Betty Kahn, a crack photographer and a key part of CASJ's volunteer staff. She was in the back seat of the taxi as it drew up in front of the Kogans' building. As Marillyn instructed, she ostentatiously fingered an unopened pack of Marlboros, a valuable black-market commodity, to induce the cabby to wait while Harvey scouted for the right building in the enormous apartment complex. A man in a karakul hat noticed an obvious American wandering around. He approached Harvey and, to avoid being heard speaking English, whispered, "Kogan?" Under instruction not to speak English on the street, Harvey nodded in silence. He motioned to Betty, who released both the cigarettes and the cabby, and they both followed the man with the karakul hat into the building. Wordlessly, they climbed the unlit staircase. The man with the karakul hat reached his apartment, unlocked the door, ushered them inside, and took their coats.

In code, Harvey and Betty identified their role in the movement, "We were sent by Pam and Marillyn." The man's face lit up. "Ah, you're from Chicago! By any chance, do you happen to know Harvey Barnett?" The man from Chicago declared, "Yitzchak, I *am* Harvey Barnett!"

That night over a bottle of vodka, Yitzchak wanted to know where Harvey's family came from.

"Russia, of course."

"Do you know where?"

"Sure. Vitebsk."

"Really? My family was also from Vitebsk. What's your family's name?"

"Itkin."

"Itkin? Harvey, my family's name was also Itkin."

Harvey Barnett and Yitzchak Kogan came from the same family. They were distant cousins. We really are one.

Several years later, we received the message that Yitzchak had become a *shochet*, qualified to perform *shechitah*, the slaughtering of meat according to the halachic requirements of kashrut. He desperately needed a *chalaf*, the halachically prescribed knife, to do his job.

One who is not familiar with Soviet customs cannot imagine the enormity of that request. But we never focused on the impossibility of the task. Difficult though it may have been, if a Soviet Jew needed a *shochet* knife for his community, we had to find a way to get it to him. Especially if that Jew was Yitzchak Kogan. The question wasn't whether to get it to him, but how.

Fortunately, we had our own secret weapon, a weapon to defy nearly any challenge, an agent who engineered techniques to overcome the insurmountable. Hetty Deleeuwe came up with the solution. The *shochet* knife was to be inserted into a podiatry kit we purchased for a Chicago rabbi we were sending to Russia. If stopped when going through customs, the rabbi was instructed to claim that he was a podiatrist and that he never traveled without his medical instruments. For many years, Marillyn, Hetty, and I considered that delivery to be one of our greatest triumphs.

About fifteen years later, Yitzchak, who had received permission to leave the Soviet Union and had immigrated to Israel with his family, visited Lenny and me in our Jerusalem apartment. Our lives had been brought together again – this time in the holy city of Jerusalem. We shared memories and family news. In the course of the afternoon, I laughingly reminded him of our victorious delivery of his knife. He looked abashed, and after I pressed him, he confided that the knife he had needed wasn't what we had delivered. He didn't need a knife for *shechting* chickens, he needed a knife for *shechting* cows! Imagine going through the Moscow airport inspection with that in your suitcase.

Many years later, on a frigid night in January 2010, the doorbell of our Chicago home rang. Lenny answered and welcomed the gentleman into our library. He summoned me from the kitchen. The gentleman was from Moscow's Chabad community, seeking funds. "Does he know the Kogans?" I asked. After all, years after moving to Israel and after the fall of the USSR, Yitzchak had been sent to Moscow by Chabad to oversee kashrut. He even koshered the Kremlin's kitchen for an Israeli official delegation and was often involved in negotiations with the Kremlin over the Chabad books they wouldn't relinquish. The gentleman in our library did indeed know the Kogans. He added, "It's very sad about Sophia."

A sick feeling spread quickly through my stomach. "What about Sophia?"

"She died a few weeks ago."

Beautiful Sophia Kogan. That very morning, I had looked through the boxes of materials I was sending to the American Jewish Historical Society to be archived, and I found several photos of Sophia. There was a snapshot taken during our 1978 trip to the Soviet Union; Sophia is putting her earrings into my pierced ears. We're sitting at their dining-room table in their Leningrad apartment. We are both young. There was another of Sophia in that same apartment, koshering glasses in the bathtub; in another, she was tucking her three little girls, all scrubbed and shiny, into their bunk beds. I kept the photo of the two of us; I wasn't able to part with it. It still sits on my desk.

I was heartbroken to hear this news of my friend. Sophia Kogan, may your memory be a blessing for all of Israel.

Terror and Tragedy: The Poltinnikovs

While it was a strenuous battle for our adopters to reach refuseniks in Moscow and Leningrad, it was far more difficult to reach them in provincial areas, where many refuseniks didn't know English. The absence of foreign press bureaus and embassies also limited their contact with the West, and the resulting isolation heightened the potential danger. Still, we made every effort to keep refusenik activists under our umbrella of protection. For this, we depended on our Hebrew- and Russian-speaking volunteers, and on refuseniks in Moscow and Leningrad who monitored the provinces.

Novosibirsk was one of those places it was better for a Jew not to live. Early on we associated it with tragedy. The Poltinnikov family was one of the first to apply to emigrate from Novosibirsk. Rae Sharfman, in Michigan, spoke enough Hebrew to be UCSJ's point person with the family. Rae and Michael Sherbourne, in London, were the source of all information on the case.

Dr. Isaac Poltinnikov was a handsome, refined-looking man, an accomplished physician and a former colonel, retired from military service. He had chaired the Ophthalmologic Disease Department at the Novosibirsk Medical Institute and was recognized as the top eye surgeon for high-ranking officers in Siberia. But when he applied to emigrate, the authorities unleashed their vindictive fury at him and his wife Dr. Irma Bernstein and their daughters, Victoria and Eleonora.

"You'll rot here!" threatened Colonel Gorbunov, the head of the KGB-operated OVIR, the Soviet office of emigration visas. Summoned by KGB to demote Isaac from his military rank and deprive him of his pension, his former colleagues screamed, "It's a pity Hitler didn't finish with all of you!" and "If I had a pistol, I'd shoot you myself."[1]

When Victoria applied to leave, she was summarily denounced and fired from her job at the Research Institute of Tuberculosis. Eleonora, though threatened with arrest after applying to leave, was given permission and left for Israel with her elderly grandfather on assurances that the rest of the family would be allowed to follow shortly.

Instead of a reunion, there was tragedy. Victoria and her mother were arrested in Moscow in 1972, along with other refuseniks, for attempting to hand in a petition to the Supreme Soviet requesting exit visas. Victoria,

---

1. Eleonora Poltinnikov-Shifrin, "A Monument to My Family," unpublished report sent to author, 1994.

who had tuberculosis, and her mother, a diabetic with a history of heart attacks, were forcibly transported from Moscow back to Novosibirsk by freight train. There, they were sentenced to six months in prison, where their fragile health deteriorated quickly. From our new Highland Park office, we exerted all of our political muscle to support their struggle, and Eleonora traveled from Israel to America to campaign for her family. After three months, the Soviets relented, releasing the two women from prison but continuing to persecute them relentlessly. Authorities warned them to find jobs or be prosecuted for parasitism. Spinning a diabolical web, they instructed the city's medical institutions not to hire either of them.

Meanwhile, having been refused visas to attend the funeral of Irma's father in Israel, the family launched a hunger strike. Eleonora simultaneously went on a hunger strike in London, and UCSJ's Adopt-a-Family network pressed Congress and the State Department to urge the Soviets to release the family. Ever hopeful, the Poltinnikovs ended their hunger strikes, but a month later, they were refused exit visas again – this time, on a new pretext: for having "access to classified information."

The KGB snare of isolation was in place. Mail didn't reach them. Their apartment phone was disconnected. A car swerved off the street and onto the sidewalk, ramming into Isaac, who had a heart attack. Even their guard dog was stolen. It's no wonder the women's minds gave way. The KGB wolves bred paranoia. Irma and Victoria barricaded their doors and stopped leaving their apartment. Every day, they lowered a basket with some rubles from their fourth-floor apartment window, asking passersby to bring food in exchange.

Deliberately isolated by authorities and starving, they still held on to their dream of Israel, their walls covered with maps and pictures of the Holy Land. They studied Hebrew. Isaac wrote poetry. But their last letter to Eleonora demonstrated their mindset: "Either we get our exit papers, or we die here."[2]

Afraid that by the time the Soviets finally relented, it would be too late, we were pursuing every avenue to help them. My work with John Anderson, Illinois congressman, chair of the House Republican Conference, and later, a candidate for the US presidency, led to him becoming one of the most

---

2.   Ibid.

outspoken champions for Soviet Jews in the House. I had asked him to take on the Poltinnikov case.

I phoned Mike MacLeod, Anderson's executive aide, and he immediately shot off a cable to General Slanetsky, chief of the Soviet Department of the Interior, apprising him of Congress's concern: "As you may know, many of my colleagues in the Congress of the United States share my intense, longstanding interest in the case of the family of Doctor Isaac (Itzchak) Poltinnikov of Novosibirsk.... I am writing to ask if you will process their papers as expeditiously as you can, in view of the perilous state of the family health; their many friends in the United States...anxiously await word that the Poltinnikovs are safely on their way."[3]

But all our efforts couldn't save the family. By the time they got permission in 1979, KGB had destroyed Irma and Victoria. Convinced of a KGB plot to induce them to leave their apartment in order to kill them, they refused to go out to pick up their exit papers. Desperate, Isaac broke out of their apartment, determined to demonstrate to his wife and daughter that the visas were real; he ultimately was able to leave for Israel, arriving there on May 31, 1979. But Irma and Victoria were afraid to leave the apartment and instead went on a hunger strike.

On a scorching morning in August, Michael Sherbourne phoned with the grim news. Irma had died of starvation. Despite the direct intervention of Senator Henry "Scoop" Jackson, John Anderson, and the State Department, we couldn't save her. And then, soon after, a destroyed Victoria hanged herself.

The persecution of the Poltinnikovs expanded our view of KGB terror. It clarified how far the state security organs were willing to go to terrorize Jews trying to emigrate. Our small activist contingent was committed to make the public aware and to make the Kremlin pay a price.

The Tourist Program

UCSJ depended not only on our network of adopters, but on our supporters who were prepared to travel into the USSR as tourists, to meet with refusenik activists and return with the anecdotal and documentary evidence of human rights abuses and state anti-Semitism that fueled our advocacy. These trips were also the means through which we channeled

---

3.   Ibid.

crucial material goods and informational resources to sustain hundreds of refuseniks being held for an indefinite term against their will in what was, in reality, a vast holding camp.

Every pending trip was kept confidential to avoid alerting the Soviets in advance of their arrival. It was well known that there was KGB surveillance of Chicago's Polish community, the largest outside Warsaw, and it was a logical assumption that KGB was watching the Soviet Jewry activists as well. Our tourist system was not illegal, illicit, or clandestine. It was protectively and cautiously circumspect. The right of citizen-to-citizen contact was stipulated under the Helsinki Final Act, signed by the Soviets and thirty-four other nations in 1975. By insisting on that right, we were creating a chink in the Kremlin's armor and a cleft in the Iron Curtain.

Marillyn and I designed the briefings for each particular traveler. Hebrew speakers, teachers, observant Jews, rabbis, doctors, journalists, congressional aides, attorneys, writers, students: each had professional or personal assets that we sought to harness. Those travelling exclusively to meet with refuseniks, or who had professional skills or personal resources the refusenik community requested, were given about eighteen hours of briefings.

Marillyn briefed them on the emigration movement's history and on the subtleties and complexities of the various facets of the Jewish national, emigration, cultural, and human rights movements in the USSR. They were briefed on UCSJ's position on the Jackson-Vanik amendment and on the Helsinki Final Act's human rights guarantees. All tourists were taught the Cyrillic alphabet to read street and metro signs. They were instructed on how to make the initial contact from a public telephone booth, how to code their contacts' names into their checkbooks, how to use the Moscow metro, how to pack the goods we gave them, how to answer customs officers in case of inspection, how to find specific apartment buildings in a large complex. They were warned not to speak about anything relevant to their trip in their bugged hotel rooms, not to leave anything "suspiciously Jewish" in their rooms, not to engage in any conversations with unknown people who approached them, and not to drink the water in Leningrad. We briefed them on the current policy issues of the UCSJ.

Tourists were given instructions and subjected to role-playing in case of a KGB interrogation, especially critical for those going to the more dangerous Ukraine. Playing the interrogator, Marillyn verified that their voice tones, verbal responses, and attitude demonstrated that these American tourists were not intimidated and had in fact gone on the offensive. Marillyn was always calmly reassuring in the face of a tourist's apprehension, teasing the fainthearted: "If you're arrested, don't worry, we can always get another tourist."

Once they had a grip on the underpinnings of the movement, I gave our travelers their refusenik itinerary – the case histories for each of the Jews they were to contact in the cities they were visiting. The case sheets were designed to bring refuseniks to life; they detailed application and refusal histories, and each one told a story of persecution and resistance. The case sheets also noted a refusenik's role in the activist community – if he or she were an underground Hebrew teacher or ran the refusenik pharmacy or the unofficial Moscow kindergarten. The sheets indicated if the person participated in the Moscow Refusenik Scientific Seminar, was involved in underground publishing, or provided help to refuseniks who were arrested and sent to hard labor camps in Siberia. The most critical aspect was my list of questions customized for each refusenik, together with our answers to questions they had asked. Some questions were case-oriented, some policy-oriented. In addition to knowing the refuseniks they were seeing, tourists also needed to be familiar with the leaders of the movement; Marillyn and I didn't want any of our travelers to embarrass themselves or us by not knowing identities of prominent refuseniks.

Finally, we gave the travelers the material goods they were to deliver. Hetty purchased Nikon cameras and film, jeans, and down jackets that refuseniks could sell on the black market. For Hebrew teachers, she bought tape recorders, Hebrew books, Hebrew-Russian dictionaries, Hebrew-language cassettes, kosher mezuzah *klafim*, kosher soup cubes. She acquired Magen David necklaces for gifts, microcassettes for activists to surreptitiously tape their meetings with officials, and maps of Israel. For the unofficial refusenik pharmacy in Moscow, Hetty and Frances Peshkin obtained requested medicines in such quantity that our small pharmaceutical department threatened to take over the CASJ office. Hetty also bought items Moscow refuseniks could package and send to our men languishing in Siberian prison camps: black tea, long underwear, and children's chewable vitamins that looked like candy, being that vitamins were forbidden.

By the end of their briefings, loaded with information and the items Hetty had purchased, our tourists were ready for any eventuality.

We left nothing to chance. Although a slipup wouldn't endanger the tourist, it could be a dangerous trap for the refusenik he or she was visiting.

For our effort, Marillyn and I (and the briefers from our councils around the country) had one quid pro quo. We expected all tourists to write a detailed report of their interactions with each refusenik; we then circulated these trip reports confidentially to the network of UCSJ's briefers. I scoured these reports, meticulously recording goods delivered, dates of delivery, and new requests, and I reported that data to each of our councils' briefers for the next trip.

Trip reports contained the most sensitive and vital refusenik information. Their pages outlined the continually changing skeletal framework of the movement, the activities, the names of activists, the configuration of groups, proposals for action, and requests for material aid. Unfortunately, sometimes they also carried inaccuracies or false allegations that could destroy reputations, credibility, and, consequently, support. Because of their highly sensitive nature, trip reports required accurate "decoding," a task performed only by experienced briefers who could deconstruct nuance and had a deep understanding of the structure of the refusenik community. Our briefers could sift the wheat from the chaff and the resulting refusenik data was invaluable.

Our briefers in councils everywhere had up-to-the-minute information on when travelers were leaving the States or England; the effectiveness of our system astounded refuseniks. Refuseniks asking a tourist from one UCSJ council for urgent medication were supplied within days by travelers briefed by another UCSJ council.

Witnessing the Extraordinary

On one occasion, Natasha Khassina, the prominent Moscow refusenik who was supporting our Jewish prisoners of conscience, sent us a request for bear fat. She had arranged for a Chinese homeopathic practitioner to treat Yaakov Mesh, who had been brutally beaten in prison. The practitioner wanted bear fat.

Bear fat? Where were we going to get bear fat? Marillyn called UCSJ's council in Alaska; indeed, bear fat was an available commodity. Amazingly, the Alaska Council happened to have a tourist going from Alaska to Vladivostok the following day. And they happened to have a contact in

Vladivostok who would transport the bear fat across seven time zones and deliver it into the hands of Natasha Khassina in Moscow.

As the complicated and unusual arrangements fell into place seemingly on their own, Marillyn and I looked at each other. The way this episode played out was virtually inconceivable. It was like a roadmap had already been prepared for us, and all we had to do was follow it. I received confirmation of delivery shortly after. Within a few days, they had received the bear fat. Yaakov Mesh recovered.

Marillyn and I had no doubt that this remarkably unlikely sequence of incidents, far from being coincidental, was coordinated by a higher force. Over the years, Marillyn often remarked that there had to be an otherworldly connection between what was needed and what was provided. Refusenik Tanya Zunshine once told me a relative needed a replacement heart valve for surgery at a Riga hospital. Shortly after that conversation, a doctor phoned Marillyn offering to donate a heart valve should it ever be needed. This kind of providential oversight assured both of us that we were doing something right.

One dark, cold Chicago afternoon in 1983, the phone rang as I was getting ready to meet Lenny downtown for the opera. I picked up the receiver to hear the unmistakable echo of the transatlantic cable that delivered international calls.

I was a little surprised. I didn't have a messenger call booked at 4:00 in the afternoon, and a refusenik had never initiated an international call. So I was already on high alert when I heard the voice of Natasha Beckman, who worked with Natasha Khassina on behalf of prisoners. Calling from Khassina's apartment, her tone was uncompromising. "Pomella. We need you to send Alan Dershowitz or Irwin Cotler to Moscow as soon as possible."

Dershowitz? Cotler? My mind reeled. I would do anything for refuseniks, and these two women were key leaders of the movement. Nothing was too hard. But Dershowitz or Cotler?[4] These prominent attorneys had schedules. Even if they agreed to travel to Russia, it took time to organize visas. My mind raced. Beckman and Khassina needed an attorney,

---

4.   Irwin Cotler is a former professor of law at McGill University and was the director of its human rights program from 1973 until his election as a member of Canada's Parliament in 1999. Alan Dershowitz is a scholar of US constitutional and criminal law.

obviously a good one, and they needed someone of stature, someone who could deal directly with Soviet authorities.

I knew the solution was on its way, but I couldn't say anything on an open line. I had to leave it at, "I'll see what I can do."

What I didn't tell them was that an attorney was already on his way to Moscow, via London. We had arranged that CASJ's Harvey Barnett would call me from the London airport for any last-minute instructions. Not long after Beckman and Khassina had called, Harvey checked in from London. I told him they urgently needed a lawyer and asked him to go directly to Khassina's apartment from the airport.

So, roughly eight hours after they had called me in Deerfield, Harvey knocked on Khassina's door in Moscow. When she answered, he started panting dramatically as if trying to catch his breath. "Hello. I'm the lawyer you wanted, Natasha. Sorry I'm late but I got hung up in traffic."

Natasha Beckman called one other time. The unborn baby of a refusenik woman had died. The woman was traumatized by her loss and hospitalized. To her dismay, she had been told that, as there were no labor-inducing drugs in Moscow, she would have to undergo a cesarean. It turned out Lynn Singer had a tourist leaving imminently from New York. The medication was delivered to the refusenik woman in Moscow the next day.

As remarkable as these seeming coincidences were, they were not unusual. Refuseniks needed and the Almighty provided.

Creative Solutions

Although we had closed the distance between the refuseniks and UCSJ, I was aware of what was lacking. In the years before my second trip to Russia, the information we sent through tourists gave the refuseniks only a partial view of what we were doing to help them. They couldn't see the breadth and scope of our work. I wanted them to understand the sophistication of our advocacy and that we were pulling out all the stops on their behalf. I wanted them to know the positions and policies we were developing so they could give us their input. I wanted them as partners, not beneficiaries.

Betty Kahn solved that problem. Assembling professional lighting equipment and cameras in our office, she photographed UCSJ's policy and position statements, press releases, news articles, position papers, and statements in the *Congressional Record*: everything we wanted refuseniks to know. She photographed congressional letters, my speeches, CASJ's

Refusenik newsletter, and relevant op-eds. She meticulously repacked the exposed film cannisters in their original packages, and Hetty had them professionally resealed to appear like new, unused packages of film. Then we gave them to our tourists, who carried the exposed film along with the cameras we had given them.

The drop-off address for the film was the home of refusenik Yakov "Yasha" Gorodetsky. He handed the rolls to another reliable refusenik in Riga, who developed the photographs, which were then copied and distributed throughout the refusenik community. Over the years, I learned that those photographs traveled hand to hand, from refusenik to refusenik, across the expanse of the USSR. Our advocacy lifted morale, brought hope, and unified our geographically fractured movement. The photos of us in CASJ's *Refusenik* newsletter made us as real to them as they were to us.

This process gave birth to another. Hetty and her husband Al repackaged Hebrew audio tapes in generic clear plastic cassette boxes and shrink-wrapped them to look like unopened, blank tapes. Our travelers were able to slip them freely through customs, delivering tape recorders along with hundreds of audio tapes of Torah and Talmud lectures, Hebrew-language classes, lessons to learn the tropes (the cantillation signs used in the reading of the Torah), and Hebrew songs.

CHAPTER 4

Cracking the Communications Barrier

Messenger Calls

Our information channels were a vital conduit that carried the evidence of a frightening crackdown. Once the authorities had, in 1980, arrested the prestigious, internationally recognized scientist and academician Andrei Sakharov, stripped him of his honors, and exiled him, it showed that the Kremlin's gloves were off. They would strike increasingly greater blows on the Jewish movement. Flexing their muscle, authorities arrested my phone contact in Kiev, Yelena Oleinik, for the fourth time, this time for speaking with tourists from the West. Her brother Ivan was sentenced to one year of forced labor. All the news pouring into CASJ was bad: Mosei Tonkonogy was arrested for parasitism; Igor Guberman was given five years; Vladimir Korniev in Odessa was sentenced to one year of prison for parasitism; Valery Pilnikov was given a five-year sentence after presenting a joint petition to the Central Committee. Alexander Magidovich, already in refusal for seven years, was forcibly committed to the nightmarish and punitive Serbsky Institute of Forensic Psychiatry after being charged with Article 70, anti-Soviet activity. Igor Kushnirenko was also interned in a punitive psychiatric hospital.

The arrests went on and on. I greeted each day knowing there would be another victim. Grigory Geishis was charged with draft evasion under Article 80 of USSR Criminal Code, and, after having been sentenced earlier in the month for hooliganism, Vladimir Kislik was forcibly consigned to a Kiev mental institution for punitive psychiatry. As the situation in the Soviet Union deteriorated, KGB increased surveillance on refuseniks. They blocked our conversations with electrical interference and cut the refuseniks' home phone lines. We responded by reaching them through

previously arranged messenger calls made to a call center in either
Moscow, Leningrad, or Kiev. KGB monitored messenger calls, but at least
they couldn't accuse refuseniks of using their home phones for anti-Soviet
activity.

The messenger call process was complex and usually maddening. A
week in advance, I would schedule an appointment for a messenger call at
a specific date and time through telephone operators in the United States
posted to AT&T'S international switchboard for the Soviet Union. These
operators registered the appointed call with their Soviet counterparts, who
theoretically were to notify the intended recipient in Russia of the date and
time of the scheduled call. *Theoretically* is the operative word.

At the appointed time, the recipient went to the post office, the central
call center. If all worked as planned, the Soviet and American operators
would connect as scheduled. The American operator would notify me that
the call was ready, the refusenik's name would be announced at the call
center, and he or she would be directed to a phone and connected to my
call. But too often, the call was obstructed by the KGB-controlled Soviet
operators.

Time and again, I impatiently waited by the phone. When it finally
rang, I would pounce on the receiver, but I was frequently disappointed.
On the line was our American operator, and I could hear her Soviet coun-
terpoint tell her that "Moscow had no record of the call."

The excuses offered by the Soviet operators were endless. I would hear
the Soviet operator say, "Your party didn't come to the phone, dearie." Her
voice always struck me as being an octave above normal range, dripping
with cloying sweetness, registering off-the-chart duplicity: "I'm so sorry,
honey, your party didn't come to the phone."

There was little likelihood of that. I had always preempted that possibility by notifying the refusenik independently, either by way of a message
through tourists, or via calls with other refuseniks. I knew he or she was
there at the call center. This was a microgame of geopolitics.

The Soviet operator was adamant.

No way was I backing down.

Stalemate.

One day, I had had it. My frustration flared at my powerlessness in the
face of the insidious manipulation by these KGB-run operators, undermining our connections with activists. Chicago Action embarked on an

education campaign for our American operators, to convince them to remain tough when their Soviet counterparts were trying to persuade them to give up.

Miss Alma was the training manager for operators at the International AT&T switchboard, located in Pittsburgh. After a couple of attempts, I got through to her, and identified myself, Lynn, David, and UCSJ's other callers. I proceeded to give her a discourse on the status of Soviet Jewry, our advocacy with Congress and the State Department, our right to contact assured by the Helsinki Final Act, the absolute necessity of the flow of information and the documentation of human rights abuses that our messenger calls provided.

I asked her to brief the operators in the department assigned to connecting calls with the Soviet Union. They needed to understand that KGB controlled all departments in contact with the West and our citizens. The Soviet operators were doing their job by controlling and limiting contact with the West. We needed the support of our American operators. After all, it was in the interest of the United States, and part of its commitment to the freedom of contact guaranteed by Helsinki, to keep a free flow of information through those phone lines.

Miss Alma listened intently and asked pertinent questions. Hetty put Miss Alma on our mailing list, so each month she received *The Refusenik* newsletter, with its updates on the status of Soviet Jewry. When any of the refuseniks we called finally received permission to leave, we made sure Miss Alma knew about our victory.

Miss Alma became our first line of defense. Unfailingly, her army of operators backed their Soviet counterparts up against the wall, insisting that our party was at the call center, demanding that the operator call him or her to the phone. I booked all my calls through Miss Alma.

Hetty made sure that, on national holidays, our team of operators received big tins of popcorn from Chicago Action. I only regret that I never honored Miss Alma and her team of operators at a UCSJ Annual Meeting. Their invaluable defense went far in getting those calls through.

But even with the support of the AT&T operators, the Moscow operators found ways of hassling me and the refuseniks directly. They would intentionally summon refuseniks to the call center and then ring my home phone twelve hours before the appointed time, usually about 4:00 a.m. The ringing of the phone was a scream in the night's silence, awakening my family and making my heart race. Had something happened to Mom? Dad? Had there been an arrest?

I'd race down to the kitchen phone, its tape recorder securely attached to the receiver. There it was: that obsequious, high-pitched voice, oozing feigned warmth. No amount of dripping endearments could masquerade the inherent KGB brinkmanship. In perfect English, the Moscow operator would announce: "Dearie, I have your party on the line." A momentary connection, and then the call would be cut off, leaving me to spend a sleepless night struggling to reconnect through the AT&T operators in Pittsburgh. I was sure that on the other side, my party was there at the call center, under the scrutiny of KGB watchers, waiting.

When I did successfully connect with a refusenik, I consciously tried crawling into the mind of that person to understand exactly what he or she was trying to convey. I paid close attention to the accented, deliberately nuanced words, the attempts to transmit information while eluding eavesdroppers. I taped each call and then transcribed it word for word, editing only as necessary to smooth out the English. I sent the transcripts, using our first-generation fax machine, to UCSJ, our councils, SSSJ, and international affiliates – to all our core activists, who were on high alert, day and night. Within hours our grassroots strike force would have the information in the hands of congressmen and at the State Department, National Security Agency, and Helsinki Commission.

Alla Praisman

I understood that these calls were important to refuseniks, but hearing directly from them of the risks they took just for a phone call gave me a much deeper understanding.

After a difficult period of refusal, Alla Praisman got permission to leave, and UCSJ brought her from Israel to speak at our annual meeting in Washington. She told us, "We were afraid to use our private phones. KGB was listening and could disconnect our phones. There were several post offices where we could accept international phone calls. I instructed Pomella how to call the post office and she called at the appointed time. But it didn't stop the authorities disconnecting our telephone several days later."[1]

---

1. Alla Praisman, speech at UCSJ Annual Meeting.

She said she never went to the central calling station by herself, knowing a refusenik woman alone could be easy prey for KGB. Once, already on the way to the post office for my call, she learned that the person who was to meet her was unable to come. Anxiously, she called her husband Leonid to ask him to find someone to meet her there. "Then I rushed to the post office to be on time and not miss your call. I was alone and frightened, and when I entered the building, I saw my five-year-old son with Leonid."[2] How could Leonid bring him? He apologetically explained that he couldn't find anyone to meet her; he couldn't let her go alone but couldn't leave their son alone either.

Alla continued, "The place was crawling with KGB." Leonid recognized one of the plainclothesmen, a KGB agent who had once tailed him. "I froze. I could have turned back," she later told me, "but I was ready to risk almost anything, because your call was my only direct contact with the West. At the end, they didn't stop me."[3] This nightmarish scenario was the price refuseniks paid for their contact with us.

KGB's goal was to isolate refuseniks from the West, and they marshaled creativity and resources to that end. If we could not overcome their effort to block our telephone connection, those who had inherited Joseph Stalin's mastery of psychology would detect our weakness and conclude we lacked the resolve to protect our people. Such a signal would make the recipient of our call vulnerable. Therefore, every phone call was a battleground, a test of will between us and our combatant, the Soviet apparat.

I placed messenger calls in hotel rooms, public phone booths, and even one from a Phoenix shopping center. There were messenger calls to refuseniks in the presence of reporters, members of Congress, and several Chicago mayors. I made calls in front of television cameras, in synagogue meetings, always waiting anxiously for that moment of connection, and all the while reporting the progress of the call to those standing around me. The convoluted process of messenger calls was as educational for our audience as the phone call itself.

Tatiana "Tanya" Zunshine

In March 1984, on one of my regularly scheduled calls with Leningrad refusenik Yasha Gorodetsky, he brought Tanya Zunshine to the phone. In

---

2.   Ibid.

3.   Alla Praisman, conversation with Pamela Braun Cohen.

clipped English, she introduced herself. "Pomella. I am Tatiana Zunshine. My husband Zachar has been arrested. We applied to leave in 1980. Please, please can you help him?"

Tanya, an indefatigable activist, was herself standing up to the intimidating scrutiny of KGB, who tried to silence her defense of her husband by harassment and threats of arrest. From then on, in my regular calls to her, I heard the pain in her voice as she described Zachar's trial, his transport to Siberia, and his incarceration in prison camp. I conspired with her to defend them both. After asking her for his photograph for our publicity, one of our tourists returned from Moscow with a black-and-white photo of a handsome young man with a determined, angular jaw. We weren't going to have any trouble drumming up publicity for a man who looked like this.

One pre-scheduled call with Tanya coincided with a meeting in Washington with my congressman. From our first meeting after his election, John Porter, a tall, distinguished-looking, gray-haired man, was an outstanding spokesman for Soviet Jewry, serving as the cochairman of the House Human Rights Caucus. John and his wife had gone to the Soviet Union to meet refuseniks, and at the Moscow airport at the end of the trip, his understanding of the Soviet debasement of human rights became firsthand and personal. Despite his diplomatic immunity, authorities at the airport subjected John's wife to a humiliating body search, intended to intimidate him.

During this meeting in his office on Capitol Hill, I realized that it was the scheduled time for my messenger call to Tanya and requested, rather apologetically, to use a phone in his office. To my surprise, the congressman got up and seated me at his desk. I was soon connected to Tanya in Riga. She was distraught. She had been attacked, knocked to the ground, and beaten by several KGB agents. They stole her identity papers and warned, "Even your dear Pomella can't save you."

I handed the phone to John so he could talk to her. After the conversation, he went down to the floor of the House of Representatives and spoke at length about the Zunshines, reporting the history of their harassment and Zachar's imprisonment, all of which became part of the *Congressional Record*.

Abe Stolar

That wasn't the only messenger call I placed to refuseniks in the presence of public officials. At two different times, with two Chicago mayors, Harold

Washington and Jane Byrne, I called refusenik Abe Stolar from City Hall, alongside Marillyn and Linda Opper, Abe's Adopt-a-Family case manager. Abe's parents had immigrated to Chicago, where he was born. During the Depression, when Abe was still a child, they had returned with him to Stalin's Russia. Then, in the 1970s, after the Leningrad trials opened the possibility of leaving, Abe applied for permission with his wife Gita and his son, Michael. All three were issued exit visas. They sold everything of value, gave up their apartment, and, as required, relinquished their citizenship papers. At the airport, they passed through passport control, crossed the tarmac, and boarded their flight. At that point, militia agents boarded their plane and dragged them off the aircraft.

After that, they were repeatedly denied permission to leave, condemned to a Kafkaesque world, forced to remain in Moscow without citizenship papers but unable to go to Israel. For years, Abe and Gita lived in refusal. In essence, Abe was a Chicagoan held hostage, and we at Chicago Action based our campaign on his American citizenship. Our strategy was to make Abe a cause célèbre in Chicago, the city of his birth. To this end we enlisted the help of Chicago's mayors, who advocated for his release.

Ari Volvovsky

Strikingly memorable was my messenger call to Ari Volvovsky from my hotel room in Jerusalem, where we had traveled for a UCSJ conference in the spring of 1983.

Several days beforehand, I had begun working with the Israeli operators to schedule a messenger call to Volvovsky. Marillyn and I had bought the books he requested at Ben Artza's shop near the Kotel, and we had Hebrew T-shirts printed at a shop on Ben Yehuda Street to dispatch to him via tourists leaving from Chicago. We longed for the day he would walk the streets of Jerusalem with us.

I had planned a surprise for Ari. I invited a number of his closest friends, Hebrew students, and supporters to join Marillyn and me for our messenger call. One by one, they came up to our small room at the Jerusalem Plaza. There was Ruth Block, an activist from Zurich; Sarah Hamel, a supporter living on a kibbutz; Victor Dubin, smoking cigarettes and wearing his characteristic black tam, worn at a slight angle on his head; and Mark Zilbergertz. Victor and Mark were Ari's former Hebrew students from the USSR.

Together, we waited for the phone call to go through. Victor encased himself in a thick cloud of cigarette smoke and talked to us about Ari and his activity. I called the Tel Aviv international English-speaking operators to check on their progress. With our prompts, they contacted the Soviet operators. From the Soviet side came the familiar refrain: "We have no record of your call, honey."

Israeli operator: "It is order #____, placed three days ago."

Soviet operator: "We'll see if we can find it, honey, and call you back."

Hours passed in this way. I instigated a second round with the Israeli operator. Then another round, and another. Excuses and more excuses. I wasn't backing down.

The jarring ring of the phone sent an electric current through the smoke-filled room. I snatched up the phone, but it was only the Israeli operator. She called to report she was going off duty and was relaying our call to her replacement.

How could someone new step into the middle of this? Starting from the very beginning, I methodically explained the Jewish emigration movement to the replacement operator. I told her about the heroic resistance of Volvovsky and the refuseniks, and about the constant, unremitting Soviet policy of harassment and arrest by KGB. I explained that getting our contact on the line was one aspect of the shield of protection we provided, and that the Moscow operator was deliberately intransigent. Our new operator had known nothing about the Jewish emigration movement. After several hours of intermittent conversation, she was with us. She decided not to go off duty until we got the call through.

The six of us waited it out in the hotel room. There were a set of twin beds, a chair, and a lot of smoke and anxiety. Victor rolled his blue jacket into a ball for a pillow and stretched out on the floor against the wall. Zilbergertz found some space on the floor, his back against the door and knees drawn up. We pushed the twin beds together, and the four women stretched out across them. We waited. And waited.

It was like waiting for the obstetrician to emerge from the delivery room with his report. Our thoughts were in Moscow. Did Ari know we were trying to get through to him? If we got through, how surprised would he be? Hours passed.

Then, just as the tip of the sun broke through the darkness outside the window overlooking the Old City, the phone rang.

I picked up the receiver to hear Ari's voice. Together in that tiny hotel room in Jerusalem, his students and colleagues and supporters from Latvia, Russia, Switzerland, and America all shared a joy that was second only to how we felt when he finally arrived in Israel.

Non-Delivery of Mail

Our campaign for the delivery of mail to refuseniks also played a strategic role in this historic drama. Mail to refuseniks from the West informed them as well as the Kremlin that they were being watched. In this surveillance state, the secret police censored incoming and outgoing letters, but refuseniks' and dissidents' mail was under especially intense scrutiny. This was another front on the battleground that we had to win.

Moscow refusenik Victor Yelistratov defined the significance of mail from the West. In his "Open Letter to All Refusenik Adopters," brought back by one of CASJ's tourists, he wrote:

> Our life is measured by intervals between your letters. We are waiting for another letter from you like a human being in the night is waiting for the sun to rise.
>
> A letter from abroad can encourage a prisoner in his jail, labor camp or exile and even protect him from locally initiated persecution.[4]

Yelistratov urged us to resist the tendency to evade Soviet censors by sending superficial "weather letters" that created an artificial picture of our lives.

> Many times during the last decade we asked people in the USA, Europe, and Israel to make the World Postal Union provide us with the freedom of correspondence under the provision of the World Postal Convention. In response, we have been receiving even more over-simplified letters, as if people lived in countries where a person insisting upon his rights exposes himself to persecution. We ask you to send your letter insured and each

---

4.   Victor Yelistratov, letter to Chicago Action for Soviet Jewry, 1982, in Edward Drachman, *Challenging the Kremlin: The Soviet Jewish Movement for Freedom, 1967–1990* (New York: Paragon House, 1991), 319.

time when you do not get back your return receipts with our
signature, always make the robbers pay you your indemnity.…
Naturally…it costs more.… It takes much time and energy.…
Better to send one costly and time-taking straightforward letter
than several small-talk letters.[5]

We institutionalized Victor's guidelines for our adopters. His seven-point
list of instructions for posting mail were designed to provide evidence
of KGB's purloining of mail, in violation of the Helsinki Final Act. We
instructed adopters to send registered letters, which require the recipient's
signature. Any unsigned registered receipts proved Soviet non-delivery
of mail. Ruth Newman, chair of the Washington Committee for Soviet
Jewry, used hundreds of these unsigned receipts as documentary evidence
when she testified before congressional Post Office and Civil Service
Subcommittee hearings in 1983.

Avital Sharansky's brother, Misha Stiglitz, also stressed the importance
of the delivery of letters when we brought him to Chicago to advocate
for his imprisoned brother-in-law, Anatoly. The strongly built, handsome
young man stood before a crowd at North Suburban Beth El and challenged us: "If you can't get a simple letter delivered to a refusenik, how do
you expect to get a refusenik out of prison or prison camp?"

---

5.   Ibid.

CHAPTER 5

Comets in the Night

Dina Beilina

Through the information we gathered, we built up vivid portraits of the character and ethical stamina of our refusenik partners. We knew their biographies, their family members, birthdays, education, where they worked, where they planned to go. We watched their Jewish identity and their resistance activity emerge from the gray uniformity of the Soviet masses. We knew stories of their encounters with authorities. Listening to the taped phone calls, replayed over and over to decipher the Russian-accented English, I began to hear their voices in my sleep. They might not have known each of us, but we knew them, better than they could have imagined.

There are scores and scores of people we came into contact with, people who under other circumstances might have lived ordinary lives in conformity to Soviet society. These Jews, however, whose characters were fired in the refusenik crucible, drew upon their courage to exert an integrity that defined their lives and imprinted them on the history of their people. Once they applied to leave, crossing the invisible line into defiance of the Soviet demand for submission, acculturation, and assimilation, refuseniks' actions lit up the night sky like flashing comets. Every act of defiance reflected their inner liberation, their desire to live in freedom, in Israel – to live as Jews. And we, the UCSJ activists, were the astronomers watching and protecting their trajectory.

Until she left in 1986, Dina Beilina was always in the middle of it all. Dina was pretty, with dark hair, and her distinctive high-pitched voice had a cadence I'd recognize anywhere, at any time. In my mind's eye, I see her in a well-worn, black-and-white photograph with Natan Sharansky and Dr. Alexander Lerner, in a Moscow apartment, before Sharansky's 1977 arrest.

Michael Sherbourne and Lynn Singer called Dina regularly. Her information fueled UCSJ's advocacy, making her an interlocking piece that unified Moscow's emigration activists with the grassroots. Through Dina, we had vivid descriptions of refuseniks' show trials, of the courtrooms KGB packed with their stooges to bar the activists from entering. Through Dina's reports, conveyed to us in Michael's clipped British accent, we heard the outrageous lies and distortions of the prosecutor. Word for word, we heard the staggering final statements of arrested refuseniks – already haggard after months in pre-trial isolation cells – who had refused state-appointed defense lawyers. They stood before the crowd's leering hostility with courage and dignity, reflecting a national pride that came through clearly in far-off Deerfield.

Dina maintained the list of refuseniks and coordinated with Sofia Kalistratov, a senior lawyer and member of the Moscow Helsinki Group, which was founded in 1976 to monitor Soviet compliance with the Helsinki Final Act and report its findings to the West. Dina was active in all aspects of the Sharansky defense. She had worked with Ida Nudel, the refusenik activist known as the angel of the prisoners of conscience, helping them and their families financially and providing everything else they needed to survive. She worked with Moscow refusenik Lev Blitshtein to distribute material aid to those who lost their jobs. She was always present at the meetings of refuseniks with US congressmen.

Dina also understood the complexities of the refusenik and Jewish movement. She knew when an activist's frailties might make him vulnerable to KGB. She knew who to trust and who not to trust, who was cooperating with KGB, who had been broken during interrogation, who didn't distribute the material assistance we had sent. She was wary of those who talked about themselves during our messenger calls, rather than disseminating information about the movement. She knew firsthand the problems involving Israel's Lishka and their lack of support for those Moscow refusenik leaders, including herself, who cooperated with the broader human rights movement. Dina knew everything about everyone, but she was reluctant to reveal information about people unless she had to. After leaving Moscow with her husband Joseph, Dina lived in Jerusalem, and I consulted with her frequently by phone from Deerfield. Several times our phone conversations were inexplicably cut off. I would be left dumbfounded, looking at the dead phone receiver, wondering who had been listening, KGB or the Lishka.

Boris Chernobilsky

Boris was wiry, with a short wispy beard that had a will of its own and defied the contours of his sharply chiseled, refined features. With bright eyes and a warm smile, he carried himself with a quiet gentleness that belied his tough, determined nature. His sense of humor colored even the gravest situations.

Boris had a long history of confrontation with the Soviet Union, starting with his first refusal in 1976. Delivered verbally, that refusal pushed him headlong into a confrontation with the Soviets over their practice of summarily issuing refusals without citing in writing the pretext for the refusal or its period of limitation. This battle of the few against the mighty Soviet state had vital significance for every refusenik.

Time and again, Boris clashed with Soviet officials, but he refused to be intimidated and continued to fight for recognition. In the fall of 1976, after a confrontation with Soviet militia during a peaceful protest, he and fellow refusenik Yosef Ahss were held in secret for three days and then charged with malicious hooliganism under Article 206 of the Criminal Code.

Their wives sent appeals to Betty Ford and Rosalynn Carter, the wives of President Gerald Ford and his Democratic opponent Jimmy Carter, hoping to attract attention to the refuseniks' plight before the election. The strategy worked. Three weeks later, both men were released.

A few years later, on a bright May afternoon in 1981, I called Ari Volvovsky, and the absence of the usual lilt in his voice told me something had happened. He told me that hundreds of refuseniks had gathered in the Ovrazhki Forest on May 10 to celebrate Israel's Independence Day. Among them was thirty-seven-year-old Boris Chernobilsky.

Accompanied by Volvovsky's guitar, the celebrants were singing Hebrew songs when their voices were drowned out by the roar of approaching tractors sent by KGB and militia to disperse them. But the refuseniks weren't running in terror; they held firm.

One of the militiamen pushed Boris and Leonid Tesminitsky, screaming "*Schnell, Schnell, Yid*," the odious words Nazis used when rounding up Jews during the Holocaust. Boris stood his ground and refused to be shoved aside. The militiamen beat him up and arrested him for resisting authority. He was later tried, convicted on the trumped-up charge of malicious hooliganism, and sent to a Siberian labor camp near Mongolia for one year.

After his release, still refused permission on the spurious ground of having access to state secrets, Boris employed a unique dual strategy. He applied for Israeli citizenship, relying on a Knesset amendment to the Law of Return granting Israel the right to issue citizenship to any Jew who wants to immigrate to Israel but is prevented from doing so.[1] The Soviet law, On the Legal Status of Foreign Citizens in the USSR, passed on June 24, 1981, gave a juridical basis for refuseniks to support their claims as Israeli citizens on foreign soil. At the same time, Boris also tried to renounce his Soviet citizenship.

Boris began to conduct himself as if he were an Israeli foreign national. Though Israel refused to give him a passport, he dealt with the Soviets as an Israeli citizen with a right to live in his homeland. He pulled his son out of the school system and tried registering him in the school sponsored by the US embassy; he also registered his daughter in the International School attended by the children of foreign diplomats. He applied for jobs in the Moscow branches of international firms.

Boris led a movement among refuseniks to create their own Israel within Soviet borders – no easy task during the Brezhnev-Andropov-Chernenko period.[2] This development was significant: refuseniks started taking more active control over their lives. If they couldn't get to Israel, they would bring Israel to them. They established underground Hebrew preschools and afternoon schools, in which they would teach their children about Judaism and un-teach them Soviet propaganda. Boris was a leader of this effort.[3]

Throughout Boris's refusal, UCSJ actively supported his activity. The Bay Area Council approached Representative Barbara Boxer for help, and she asked President Ronald Reagan to press his case at the 1988 Moscow Summit. While UCSJ was working on Capitol Hill on his behalf, Yuri Shtern and Sasha Shipov at the Soviet Jewry Education and Information Center in Jerusalem were pushing his case in the Knesset. But all the while, in Moscow, the Soviets harassed Boris. They even lied to former presidential candidate Michael Dukakis and to Senator Joseph Biden, claiming

---

1. The Law of Return grants Israeli citizenship to everyone who was born in Israel, and to any Jew who comes to Israel and expresses the will to become an Israeli citizen.

2. Leonid Brezhnev, Yuri Andropov, and Konstantin Chernenko were successive leaders of the Soviet Union between 1977 and 1985.

3. David Waksberg, unpublished report.

they had given Boris and his family exit visas when they hadn't. I put out a press statement: "This is a clear indication that the Soviets are very much aware of Congressional concern and involvement with the plight of Soviet Jews."[4] Senator Biden kept up the pressure.

I met Boris several times. Amazingly, while still in refusal in December 1988, he was allowed to come to Washington for a visit. During the period of glasnost, when the Soviet government declared a move to more open and transparent policies, authorities permitted academician Andrei Sakharov, founder of the International Foundation for the Survival and Development of Humanity, to travel to Washington for a meeting of his foundation. Sakharov had asked Boris to join him to represent the emigration issue, and he demanded that Boris be given travel documents.

At the last minute, with Sakharov already in the States, the Soviets withheld Boris's visa. Sakharov exerted pressure to force the Soviets to back down. In the end, the Soviets allowed Boris to attend but held his family hostage, ensuring Boris's return to the USSR. It was shocking to see Boris outside of Moscow, ostensibly free but chained to the country he was trying to flee. We spent some hours together, and I saw the sadness in his eyes.

I met Boris again at the UCSJ Annual Meeting in Moscow, in 1989. The hall was packed with scores of Soviet Jewish activists, hailing from the Baltics to Siberia. It was also filled with dissidents who had come to meet with our UCSJ delegation to discuss human rights, emigration, and the status of prisoners. Boris spoke at one of our sessions: "I wish only the best for Russia in the future – a democratic future, with respect for human rights.… And as long as I live here, I will work with others to help you realize that vision. But I hope that this future – bright as it could be – will be a future without Jews.… For our place, our future is not here, but in Israel."[5] He spoke to the heart of UCSJ's mission, the goal we all worked toward on a daily basis.

At a luncheon UCSJ hosted for activists during that 1989 meeting in Moscow, I sat next to Boris. After fifteen years of agonizing struggle and resistance, he and his family had been given permission to leave. Eyes sparkling with excitement, he told me he planned to drive his car

---

4.   Pamela Braun Cohen, press release.

5.   David Waksberg, an unpublished report.

to Israel. And, ever a nonconformist, he did it, ferrying the car across the Mediterranean. Finally, after so many years of struggle, he had achieved his dream. UCSJ continued a close relationship with Boris and later, at a time when visitor visas were possible, hired him to run our Human Rights Bureau in Moscow.

When I got the call from Sasha Shipov in Jerusalem, I was at my desk at home. It was the fall of 1998. Boris had been at the beach, teaching his grandson how to swim, and had been caught by an undertow. He died under the bright Israeli sun, only in his early fifties. Boris left us an indelible legacy, and I'm not sure he ever knew it.

I was shaken by the abrupt finality of Boris's death – the way his big, uncompromising life, and the future in Israel that he had fought for, had been swept away so quickly and seemingly so meaninglessly. After I hung up with Sasha, I wept. Boris lived with rugged strength, but life is so fragile.

Lev Roitburd

Odessa refusenik Lev Roitburd served a two-year sentence of internal exile for attempting to meet American senators in Moscow in 1975. Three years later, Brezhnev assured Senator Edward Kennedy that Roitburd and seventeen others would be given permission to emigrate, but it took another three years for that permission to come. I saw Lev at a UCSJ conference in Israel, our first encounter since we had met in Odessa in 1978. Lev's warmth and charisma were palpable, and UCSJ arranged for him to undertake a national tour to the States. Of course, his tour would include a stop in Chicago.

Marillyn and I were at the CASJ office with Betty Kahn, Linda Opper, and Hetty Deleeuwe, picking through possible solutions for a serious liability: Lev didn't speak English. Enticing Americans to come and hear a speech given by an English-speaking Russian was one thing; inviting them to listen to a speech through a translator was another. We needed a translator fluent in Russian and Yiddish who could transmit his electric intensity, his vibrant personality. We needed someone with pizzazz. Betty suggested Dina Halperin, an internationally known Yiddish actress married to Danny Newman, a local impresario.

I responded with cynicism and impatience. How could we possibly get in touch with her? Marillyn shot me one of her practical, imperturbable looks that always reminded me of her remarkable nature. The greater the difficulty, the more enticing the quest. She was not daunted. "Well, I'll just call Danny Newman," she said, picking up the phone.

Dina Halperin was a star in her own right. Sitting next to Lev – in his brown tweed jacket, with his handsome face and sweet, sweet smile – the beautiful and dramatic Dina translated his description of refusal, resistance, and prison with her uniquely stylized flare. The pair mesmerized audiences. It was a love-fest that erased the borders of geography and gave all those present a connection to the path of Jewish peoplehood, past and future.

Marillyn and I chaperoned Lev and Dina to various events around the city: in the evenings, synagogues and parlor meetings. During the day, rounds of interviews at NBC and the newspapers, and a meeting at Spertus College of Judaica for discussions with the Hebrew department about their support for our campaign for Hebrew teachers. On the occasions when Dina was not with us, Marillyn, Lev, and I communicated using a potpourri of words from any of the three languages that somehow might have inadvertently lodged in our mental archives. We rocked with laughter at our mistakes. Communication transcended the limits of language.

Together, we braved the driving rain to meet with a Chicago Jewish leader who eventually would become president of the American Jewish Committee and other major national Jewish organizations. Sopping wet and cold, we were ushered into the office; he sat at his desk, affable and polite, but clearly indifferent.

Introducing Lev and his background as a refusenik and former prisoner of conscience, I explained that we had come to give an exclusive briefing on the status of the three-to-five million Soviet Jews. The hour was late; maybe he had a train to catch, maybe he was still thinking about his previous meeting, maybe he was just hungry. In any case, after throwing out a few irrelevant questions about Lev's current personal situation, he flashed a couple Yiddish phrases and moved on to his next appointment. As we drove home, the windshield wipers trying to beat back the rain, we sought to dispel feelings of emptiness and a growing disillusionment with the Jewish Establishment power brokers, the leaders of the mainstream American Jewish organizations. In that moment, we had to retrieve the power cord that kept us focused and moving ahead.

That evening, I came out from the kitchen to find Lev teaching my son Josh to play chess. The next morning, I drove Lev to O'Hare. As he set off for Israel, he took along much love…and one of our suitcases.

Victor Brailovsky

The Soviets weren't about to let the West tell them what to do. Strategically timed to coincide with the opening of the Madrid meeting of the Conference on Security and Cooperation in Europe (CSCE) on November 11, 1980, the Soviets arrested prominent refusenik Victor Brailovsky. Victor was the editor of the prestigious samizdat (self-published) periodical *Jews in the USSR* and chairman of the Refusenik Scientific Seminar. Organized by refuseniks fired from their scientific institutions after applying to emigrate, the seminar was designed to attract the support of scientists in the West. Many Western physicists traveled to Moscow to present scientific papers, providing a boost in morale and a show of support for their Jewish colleagues stripped of their degrees and their positions. With Brailovsky's arrest, the seminar drew its last breath.

In the post–Afghanistan invasion atmosphere, in spite of the human rights emphasis at the Madrid Conference, or perhaps because of it, the Soviets were demonstrating their belligerence.

In response, Chicago Action would hold the Moscow seminar in exile, in Chicago. A shared vision had created a patchwork of relationships between CASJ (and the other councils) and American-based scientists who were sympathetic to their repressed colleagues in Russia. Physicist Zvi Lipkin and his wife Malka returned to Chicago every summer, exchanging his work at Israel's Weizmann Institute for a stint at Argonne National Labs. Zvi had participated in one of the Refusenik Scientific Seminars and knew Brailovsky and Sakharov as well. George Glauberman, a University of Chicago math professor, Murray Peshkin, a physicist at Argonne, and Zvi worked with CASJ to organize the Moscow Refusenik Scientific Seminar at the University of Chicago. I brought in Tatiana "Tanya" Yankelevich, the stepdaughter of Andrei Sakharov and daughter of Sakharov's wife, Yelena Bonner. Sakharov was in exile and both he and his wife were being subjected to the crushing pressure of the authorities.

It was vital that Tanya be at the seminar, even though the scheduling would be grueling. When I dropped off Lev Roitburd at O'Hare, I picked up Tanya from arrivals. With no time to spare, we hauled her luggage into my car and raced to a press conference with Mayor Jane Byrne and the physicists at 10:30 a.m. Beyond her contact with the scientists, Marillyn and I wanted to expose Tanya to some of the most prominent members of the Chicago Jewish community. To that end, Marillyn had engineered a reservation for a table at the members-only Standard Club. Seated in the corner of the dining room was the same national Jewish organization leader we had just taken Lev Roitburd to meet, along with a member of his board, who happened to be my cousin. Confident they would be honored to meet the stepdaughter of Sakharov, one of the most important figures of the century and a victim of a Kremlin campaign of physical and psychological torture, I brought Tanya over to their table. These distinguished Jewish leaders would unquestionably ask for up-to-the-minute information about Sakharov and the Soviet persecution of Jews, about the condition of prisoners and dissidents – about all the issues vital to the policies of their organization as well as to our country.

They did have a question. One: How long was Tanya going to be in Chicago? Then they resumed their conversation, leaving us incredulous, wondering aloud, "Do you think they don't know who Sakharov is?"

The scientific seminar at the University of Chicago was successful and received attention from all of the Chicago papers, exactly as we had hoped.

Evgeny Lein

In the early 1980s, in Leningrad, Grigory Kanovich, Grigory Vasserman, and Lev Utevsky ran underground Jewish seminars to attract intellectual Soviet Jews who had internalized the pervasive anti-Semitism. Many had become self-hating Jews who knew little about Judaism, which they generally associated with shtetl vulnerability.

KGB didn't like the seminars' success and set about knocking out their nerve center. They got rid of Utevsky in 1980 by giving him a visa, and they did the same to Kanovich a year later.

In May 1981, the authorities brought things to a head. Police and KGB plainclothesmen showed up at Vasserman's apartment during one of the seminars, recorded the identities of the scores of students, and tried to break up the session. Lein reacted by urging them to join hands in a show of civil disobedience, and the authorities reacted by arresting him. Yasha Gorodetsky was standing next to him and said of the incident: "So they took him [away] and then afterward invented the grounds to accuse him."[6] Lein was charged with kicking a militiaman. The doctor who examined the militiaman later at the hospital signed the medical record, but he got word to Lein's wife that the alleged bruise was not authentic. Gorodetsky told me, "The case against him was being made."[7]

The authorities knew Lein as a tough nut; he had continued to host seminars and refused to stop teaching, in spite of warnings. Several months earlier, hearing screams in the street, Lein found his daughter being beaten by KGB agents masquerading as hoodlums. After catching the perpetrators, Lein insisted they be prosecuted. Despite pressure to drop the charges, he wouldn't relent. When the trial opened, the defendants had been replaced by stand-ins. The real attackers were never tried.

So for authorities, Lein was a troublemaker with a KGB record. After the incident at Vasserman's, Gorodetsky told me, "It was impossible to stand by idly while they were lying. They were going to send him to prison for four or five years for a lie."[8] He began collecting written testimonies of the witnesses. Misha Elman, Misha Salman, Utevsky's daughter Genya Utevskaya, and others were a new generation of refuseniks, young people ready to defy KGB, and they joined the effort. All summer they collected testimonies defending Lein, drafted in official legal format, and sent them to authorities. Now in Israel, Utevsky and Kanovich, like me, were calling Gorodetsky regularly for information.

Lein's face showed his character. A goatee and mustache framed his sculpted cheekbones, and his expression, suffused with warmth when it was turned toward friends, revealed a fierce implacability when it turned to meet his oppressors. By autumn, Lein's behavior in prison had already made it clear to KGB that he wasn't going to make it easy for them. Pressuring him to admit even partial guilt had failed.

They tried to co-opt him with promises of an easier sentence. They put him in a cell with antisocial convicts. They subjected him to psychological torture. They saturated him with anxiety about his family. Lein couldn't sleep at night. When he did, he awoke in a cold sweat. Every sound was like the cry of his daughter. But day after day, night after night, Lein demonstrated that his response was unconditional: he refused to cooperate with KGB on any grounds.

---

6.   Yasha Gorodetsky, conversation with the author, November 24, 2002.

7.   Ibid.

8.   Ibid.

Just before Lein's trial, Marillyn and I briefed our tourist Peter Nussbaum, a preppy Russian-language student, and sent him to meet with Misha Elman in Leningrad. Caught up in Lein's case, Peter decided to try to get into the courtroom during the trial. When he got to the Kalininsky District Court, the US consul had already arrived, and refuseniks and Jewish activists, barred from entering the courtroom, had gathered outside. There was also a crowd in the waiting room. The consul was ushered inside and to the front of the courtroom. Peter reported afterward:

> At this point I noticed that the thugs who had been sitting in the back were now well positioned near the front of the crowd. We tried to stay as close to the consul as we could. At a few minutes after three, the door to the courtroom opened. A stampede ensued. I had no control over where I was going. Pushed out of the stream, I ended up near a wall separated from the other three Americans. I [grabbed] a seat in the first of the three rows. There were about 80 people packed into a tiny spectator area. People sat on each other, some stood.... In front of me there were two to three rows of people kneeling.... Then the police started to clear out the room, starting with the row of squatters. Only [refusenik] Lev Furman's intervention prevented them from removing Evgeny's mother. Outside, refuseniks tried peering into the courtroom. The door opened and the low mumbling in the courtroom fell silent as Evgeny entered. To his friends he said in Hebrew, "Shalom, I am glad to see you all, my friends."
>
> It is impossible to convey the impression that this man left on me after only twenty seconds. His heavily bearded face and jet black hair bespeak a silent dignity and pride. His intensity is etched in his face and burns in his eyes. Here was a proud man, a courageous and heroic man, fated to suffer unendurable hardships for following the dictates of his conscience, for standing up. I could feel myself starting to cry and the trial hadn't even started yet.[9]

---

9. Peter Nussbaum, trip report for Chicago Action for Soviet Jewry. Reprinted in *Alert* magazine, September 1981.

In his final statement, Evgeny faced down his accusers: "I am innocent. The…authorities are preparing a reprisal against me and my family for our desire to know the history and the language of the Jewish people, for our desire to leave the USSR for the State of Israel. Three years ago…I submitted…the application for emigration…but received a refusal. My intentions did not change.… They became even stronger. My imprisonment did not make me change.… *Yesh li tikvah she'ani echyeh b'Yerushalayim.* I have hope that I will live in Jerusalem. I demand my freedom."[10]

Even though the defense had five witnesses testifying to his innocence, on August 5, 1981, Evgeny Lein was sentenced to two years' hard labor.

Lein's arrest drove UCSJ's councils and his adopters into a frenzy of political activity in his defense. There wasn't much these adopters wouldn't do for their prisoners. I was always convinced that if money could buy Lein's release, Jean Freed, CASJ's congressional liaison, and her husband Michael would willingly have taken a second mortgage on their home to spring him from prison and get him an exit visa. Short of that, Michael, an attorney, wrote a legal brief on his behalf and submitted it to the Soviet court. He also contacted the *New York Times*, resulting in an article written about Lein's imprisonment. In spite of the efforts by many dedicated volunteers, Lein served out his sentence for a fictional offense.

A Stark Contrast

Even as I collected information, connecting dots and piecing together reports to form narratives of people's lives, I had to maintain a balance between the needs of my family and those of our contacts in Russia. I raced home to make car-pool shifts and shepherd our children to all the routine destinations of Jewish suburbia: Hebrew school, piano lessons, baseball practice, weekly allergy shots, the orthodontist, the library. Our life was rich, with Sunday trips to the country and Shabbat dinners and holidays with grandparents and family, and it was seasoned with Chicago's vibrant culture. We had season tickets to the Chicago Symphony, and we went to the ballet, sometimes the opera, and met friends for dinner. But sometimes in social settings, as I plunged into the stories that trickled out of the Soviet Union, the precarious balance between these different aspects of my life began to wobble.

---

10. *Alert Weekly Update*, September 18, 1981.

At dinners with our friends, with the sound of ice hitting crystal goblets, I chatted with the intensity of a cement drill. "Do you know what UCSJ is doing at the Madrid CSCE conference? We opened a human rights center with the congressman Father Robert Drinan, and on Chanukah, Lynn arranged the Freedom Lights Ceremony, and, with the media watching, the American ambassador called Abe Stolar and Alexander Lerner in Moscow. Did you know that Yosef Mendelevich's sister was there? She lit a candle in honor of her brother, who was on hunger strike in a Siberian prison camp, to mark the tenth anniversary of his trial.

"What? You don't know who Mendelevich is? Do you understand just how hard we have to work to make American Jews aware of what's happening in Russia? I mean, look, we are all so focused on the Holocaust, but our parents didn't do one thing to help the victims. Today we know the names of the Jewish leaders who are resisting the Kremlin. Among them is Yosef Mendelevich, the last defendant of the Leningrad trials still in prison.

"Don't you know that Mendelevich was on hunger strike in his cell in the labor camp, for the right to teach Hebrew to other prisoners? Don't you read *The Refusenik*? Mendelevich, who inspired the movement with his acts of spiritual resistance? How could you not know? Remember, we all said, 'never again!' And you're asking, 'Who is Mendelevich?'"

My words were hammer blows, but they struck vacuous faces and polite, empty smiles.

I was undeterred.

In the car on the way home, Lenny's silence was an accusation. It wasn't that I didn't know when to be quiet: I simply couldn't. Which was worse, my compulsive conscience? My terrible frustration? Or their cool indifference?

Years later, Marillyn speculated, "Why were they indifferent?" But then, the *why* did not concern me. What haunted me, day and night, was one question: How could that indifference be pierced?

What a stark contrast between my dinner companions and my UCSJ colleagues. A five-minute drive to Chicago Action's office brought me into a cadre of people who were, like me, swept up in the momentum. The willful idealism and visionary perspective of Soviet Jews, who in other times and other countries could have lived ordinary lives, was contagious.

CHAPTER 6

Spiritual and Moral Resistance

Letters from the Gulag

The growing number of arrests intensified our focus on the prisoners of conscience. For these prisoners, or *zeks*, advocacy and publicity could be a matter of life or death. Details of the horrific conditions they faced leaked out of our underground channels.

The two thousand forced labor camps were documented and exposed by Avraham Shifrin (husband of Eleonora Poltinnikov), after he had served ten years in Siberia's labor camps. His book, *The First Guidebook to the Prisons and Concentration Camps of the Soviet Union*, published in 1980, bears witness to the transports, the columns of prisoners in striped uniforms with numbers across their chests, the attack dogs, the punishment cells in camps and prisons. Shifrin also wrote of psychiatric prisons that were filled with criminals but also with political prisoners: dissidents, Jews.

Perhaps the lowest circle of hell was the excruciating rail transport, called the Itap, which carried the victims to prison camp. In the case of refusenik Boris Kanievsky, the Itap was three unbearable months of suffering, during which he was locked in a transport with criminals and anti-Semites, with zero contact with family or the activist community.

Grigory Goldstein, a refusenik from Tbilisi, Georgia, served a year's sentence near the Arctic Circle. This is his description of the dreaded transport:

> I spent more than two-and-a-half months in prison trains and transit prisons on my way to the labor camp in the Arkhangelsk region near the Arctic Circle. I traveled in a prison train where a sleeping compartment normally containing four persons was packed with seventeen to twenty persons. The only meal between

the stops in transit prisons, usually located at a two- to three-day distance from one another, was herring and bread. Water was obtained only at the discretion of the guard, as was permission to use the toilet. The guard often refused one or both, which constituted a form of torture.[1]

Salted herring, the former *zeks* told us, produced an insatiable craving for water. Their choice was then hunger or thirst. Goldstein continues his account:

> Several times during this trip I was taunted and beaten by the guards.
>
> In the transit prison, a cell built for twenty-five inmates contained sixty to seventy prisoners. Conditions were extremely unsanitary. The mattresses were full of lice and, as a result, when I arrived at the labor camp my body was covered with bites and I was lice-ridden.
>
> If a prisoner refuses to work, he is subject to incarceration. In such cases, prisoners are held in unheated cells in extremely cold weather and with no sleeping facilities. Prisoners receive one meal a day, the meal consisting of bread and water. Every other day this "meal" includes a bowl of hot soup. Unofficial beatings are also frequent....
>
> Political prisoners are treated more harshly than criminals.... Officially there are no political prisoners at all.[2]

The gradually unfolding information from prisoners' families gave us a keyhole. We peered through, only to see that in the midst of these horrific conditions were the greatest examples of resistance.

Yosef Mendelevich: Spiritual Resistance

When Yosef Mendelevich was released in 1981, after ten years' imprisonment, this recognition became clearer. In prison camp, he reported, people were not killed like they had been at Buchenwald. The prison system did,

---

1. Grigory Goldstein, personal account, archives of Pamela Braun Cohen, American Jewish Historical Society, New York.

2. Ibid.

however, "put a human creature under the press of many years of imprisonment and try to squeeze out, drop by drop, the feelings of love and fidelity, the concepts of gratitude and honor. This is not by a particularly complex method. But it works on intellectual and sensitive personalities." He went on to say: "I'm used to being searched. I'm used to someone else's hands rummaging in my things. They take my mother's picture. They read my father's letter. I watch…but their every touch is a…trauma bringing unbearable pain."[3]

When Mendelevich came out, he fleshed out sparsely sketched reports of the acts of resistance that both inspired and challenged us. "Faith alone may not be able to sustain," he explained. "That is a gift from Heaven. But it is the test of faith under critical conditions which counts."[4] In May 1979, he faced ten days in solitary confinement in Chistopol Prison for refusing to share his cell with a provocateur.

> It was Friday. I put aside a piece of bread, the only solid food allowed in solitary, and prepared to greet the Sabbath. I took a white handkerchief which I somehow managed to conceal in my prison uniform and ripped it down the middle. I used half for a head covering and the second half to cover my "challah." There was indeed cause for celebration, for that day I was informed by the rations distributor that the last of the Jewish Leningrad trial defendants, aside from me, had been suddenly freed. I began to sing the Sabbath songs that I once heard from my father.[5]

His guards stopped him from continuing.

Mendelevich told the details of what now has become legend – how in a place governed by absolute evil, he refused to allow his beard to be shaved, demanded the right to observe the Sabbath by going on hunger strike, fastidiously saved a few raisins his father had given him ten years previously to make "wine" for his Passover Seder, and taught Hebrew to other Jewish inmates. He also managed, with the help of Moscow activists,

---

3.   Yosef Mendelevich, "The Meaning of Faith," *Present Tense Magazine*. Reprinted in *Alert* magazine, September 1981.

4.   Yosef Mendelevich, "Tales of the Gulag," *Soviet Jewry Action Newsletter*, March 1981.

5.   Ibid.

to get a pair of tzitzit, which he attached to the edge of a self-made shawl to function as a tallit for use in daily prayer.

Astoundingly, in his prison camp, in a place where any religious books and ritual objects were denied, he davened Shacharit, the morning prayers. In the far-flung bleakness of his cell, Yosef Mendelevich said words of praise and appreciation to his Creator.

Hillel Butman, Mendelevich's co-defendant in the Leningrad trials, recalled the time he heard a mysterious thumping from the prison cell above him. Later on, he found out that Mendelevich, as part of his observance of Purim, was carrying out his obligation as a Jew to stamp out the name of the wicked Haman.

When he was free, Mendelevich revealed the secret system of communication between prisoners. One would initiate a conversation by tapping lightly on the wooden lid covering the toilet, and in all the cells, prisoners removed their toilet covers, held their noses to minimize the stench, and listened furtively. The prisoner would call out a name and, with the sound traveling along the pipes, the two would engage in conversation, safe from the armed guards at the end of the corridor.

When Mendelevich and his underground Hebrew students were thrown into solitary for studying Hebrew, the holy tongue, they continued their lessons through the toilet "intercom." Many years later, in Jerusalem, Mendelevich advised me to expand my Hebrew vocabulary using the method he used in prison. He wrote words on scraps of paper and tucked them beneath his belt. Every morning, on the way to forced labor, guards submitted him to rigorous body checks, but they never figured out what was hidden under his belt.

For a period of time, while at Vladimir Prison, Mendelevich was joined by Anatoly Sharansky, and the two men communicated through the toilet pipeline. Sharansky updated him on the state of the emigration movement and its activities on behalf of the Leningrad trial defendants, and Mendelevich briefed the celebrated newcomer on life in the prison.

Separately, both Mendelevich and Sharansky were later transferred from Vladimir to Chistopol Prison. There, inmates were permitted half an hour of exercise in a walled yard. One day, the guards made a mistake and let both men in the yard at the same time. Although they had never met face-to-face, they recognized each other and emotionally embraced before the guards separated them.

In the spring of 1979, Mendelevich was transferred by prison train to Perm labor camp. The locomotive ground to a halt at the railway station and pairs of guards took each prisoner to a holding cell. Mendelevich recalled:

> Two beds, really just bare wooden boards, one on top of the other, filled the cell. I lay on the bottom one, my face to the wall. My eyes wandered aimlessly over the many names carved into the walls by prisoners like me. What do I suddenly see? Hebrew writing, and not just anything, but our slogans, of the Prisoners for Zion: Next Year in Jerusalem, April 18, 1979, signed by my comrades Anatoly Altman and Wolf Zalmanson, who were…on their way to a sudden release to Israel. I study the wall and carve into it a small addendum: "Next year in Rebuilt Jerusalem."[6]

Especially in the prisons and labor camps, but also in the world of refusal, every Jewish act, every act of compassion, every stance in support of truth, every defense of another innocent person, was an act of defiance and resistance. Sharansky's unrelenting work strike after camp officials confiscated his Tehillim, King David's Book of Psalms, was met by repeated contiguous punitive sentences, amounting to a staggering 186 days in the PKT, the solitary confinement cell in Perm.

The message was clear: in the worst of circumstances, Jews in the USSR wouldn't abandon their Jewish identity. They were heroes, and our first commitment had to be to help them. Only later did I realize that, for me, helping them was only a beginning.

Judith Ratner: Moral Resistance

It was not only the prisoners of conscience who exerted moral resistance against authorities; it was refuseniks as well. The Kremlin and the authorities forced refuseniks into a constant tension between accommodation and resistance. They exerted pressure on them to forfeit their intent to emigrate, or worse, to become an informant.

But for most, accommodation wasn't an option. Resistance was the price of the visa.

---

6.   Ibid.

The Soviet system was based on lies, the denial of objective truth in favor of official definitions of right and wrong. Refuseniks and dissidents were engaged in a struggle for moral consciousness. It was a lesson refusenik behavior taught us again and again.

Judith Ratner was equipped with unyielding determination. A short woman with twinkling eyes and a set jaw, she organized refusenik demonstrations, met with tourists to transmit information, and took messenger calls. When she went on hunger strike in 1987 on International Women's Day to bring attention to the plight of women in refusal, she was denounced in the Moscow press. I had developed a special connection with her elderly mother, Kessia, who was waiting for her in Israel.

One of Judith's sons, Misha, was a gifted mathematics student who wanted to enroll at Moscow State University, though it was virtually impossible for Jews to gain admission to the math department. Jewish applicants were given far more complex problems than non-Jews.

The systematic purging of Jews from higher mathematics had been exposed by Grigori Freiman, himself a professor of mathematics and a refusenik from 1977 until he emigrated in 1982. The Soviets did not want this information leaked to the West. When two dissident mathematicians, Boris Kanievsky and Valery Senderov, released results of their research proving anti-Jewish discrimination in the math and mechanics departments of Moscow State University, they were arrested and punished with long sentences.

In spite of the obstacles, Misha was determined, and dissident teachers helped him prepare for the rigorous exams. The first exam consisted of six extremely complicated problems. Misha and some of the other students answered correctly but failed the exam. Having failed the first test, they weren't permitted to take the second, an oral exam.

Judith and her husband Leonid were ready to expose the department, but they didn't have indisputable evidence. On the day the university designated for meetings with parents of applicants, Judith was scheduled to meet with academician Kastritsin, dean of the math department. Waiting in the reception room, Judith struck up a conversation with another mother, who was holding a packet of papers for her meeting with the dean. These documents, she told Judith, would reverse the decision on her son's candidacy. They were her family's genealogy. She had incontrovertible evidence that there were no Jews in her family, proof that there was no reason for her child to have been rejected. She showed the papers to Kastritsin, and he admitted her son.

Next it was Judith's turn. In her bag, she hid a tape recorder. It was already recording when she confronted Kastritsin: "Why were some of the best students blocked from the math department?"

"It's not only Jews," he replied candidly. "I don't want to take Crimean Tatars, either."

She had him on tape and called a press conference. The recording of Kastritsin's admission was broadcast the following day on the foreign radio networks. It was an embarrassment for a country that had officially outlawed anti-Semitism.

Within days, Judith and her husband received a call from an unidentified source, calling to inform them that the university had decided to permit students who had failed the first test to retake it. Misha passed and entered the math department at Moscow State University.[7]

A Jewish Reawakening

Over many years, we knew of countless acts, both large and small, of bravery and resistance: Lev Blitshtein's trip to visit Ida Nudel, condemned to exile in the frozen reaches of Siberia; the help and support wives of imprisoned men gave each other; refuseniks in terrible straits who asked for help only on behalf of others and not themselves; everyday acts of loyalty our travelers witnessed. All of this impacted us. From ten thousand miles away, these acts inspired and imbued our own lives with meaning and purpose. In a letter to his adopter in Chicago, Riga refusenik Alexander Mariasin related a story:

> In 1944, in a train which was loaded with Hungarian Jews and was being led to Osventsim, to the place of death, someone remembered that it was the day of Simchat Torah. There happened to be a rabbi in the boxcar. So they turned to the rabbi and asked him whether they, being led to death, should celebrate this holiday. The rabbi thought a little, then answered affirmatively, because it is written that a Jew should sing and dance around a Torah on this day.

---

7.   Judith Ratner, interviewed by Pamela Braun Cohen, June 5, 2002.

"Yes, Rabbi, but we don't have a Torah."

The rabbi responded, "Then take a little baby and it will serve instead of a Torah."

So they took a baby, a holy Jewish soul created in the image of G-d, and danced and sang at the same time, when the train could stop any minute near the furnace.

"It's a wonderful story," Mariasin reflected in his letter, "about a wonderful people. That's us.… And so, we celebrated Simchat Torah and were merry, too."[8]

Simchat Torah?

How many of us in Deerfield took Simchat Torah seriously, or even knew what or when it was? The letter triggered in me what was becoming a familiar reaction: a nostalgic longing for something I never had, an inheritance that had disappeared somewhere on the boat between Lithuania or Poland and new lives here. The growth of the refuseniks was inspiring my own.

The irony was not lost on me that a rich Jewish reawakening was pouring out of the state intent on stamping it out.

In a letter, Grigory Vasserman wrote: "We are fighting…a battle…and our weapon is *avodah*, service of the Lord. When we look toward Heaven, Israel overcomes. The regime does not see it and because of this, the regime is doomed."[9]

---

8.   Alexander Mariasin, letter, October 20, 1981. Reprinted in *The Refusenik,* November–December 1981.

9.   Grigory Vasserman, letter, March 5, 1983, archives of Pamela Braun Cohen, American Jewish Historical Society, New York.

CHAPTER 7

Conflicts and Controversies

Confrontation or Quiet Diplomacy

The public perception of the struggle for Soviet Jewish emigration is that it was a united movement to persuade the USSR to "let my people go." In reality, the movement in the West was fractured, complicated by the differing perspectives and objectives of, on the one hand, the Israeli government and its proxies in the American Jewish Establishment, and on the other hand, those of the grassroots movement: UCSJ, SSSJ and their international affiliates.

Our differences were rooted in the aftermath of the Six-Day War in 1967, when Moscow broke formal diplomatic relations with Israel. Without an official presence in Moscow, Israel's relations with Jews in the USSR had to be covert and were reliant on contacts made by the Lishka. Founded in 1952 by Shaul Avigur as a clandestine extension of the Mossad, Israel's intelligence agency, the Lishka was established to bring Eastern European Holocaust survivors to Israel. By the time we encountered it, it was a satellite agency, working directly out of the prime minister's office, representing Israel's interests in the Soviet Union and making undercover connections with refusenik leaders whose activities they supported.

To understand the need for this backdoor strategy, let's zoom out to the world stage, where the Kremlin's global ambitions played out in microcosm in the Middle East.

While UCSJ activists were creating grassroots command centers to support a growing number of Soviet Jews seeking to emigrate, the Kremlin was making its presence known in the Middle East, militarizing its Arab client states and training Palestinian terrorists in Moscow. The threat cast a dark shadow over the region. It had the makings of an apocalyptic showdown on Israeli soil, with the USSR and the United States moving the chess pieces. In order to protect national security, Israeli governments, whether left or right, would bend over backward to mollify the military giant in Moscow. That meant not interfering in what the Soviets considered to be their internal affairs.

Jews wanting to leave the USSR were caught in the middle of a geopolitical struggle. The young Jewish state had to pick its battles; its national security took priority over the needs of Soviet Jews. Israel simply didn't have the geopolitical muscle to tackle the issue of Soviet Jews along with its mandate for survival.

But it's also true that some founders of the Jewish state harbored a lingering affection for the idealism of Lenin's revolution, an affection that influenced their attitudes toward the Soviet Union even when Soviet policies were expressly anti-Semitic.

National security and survival were legitimate reasons for Israel's political establishment to pursue a policy of nonconfrontation with the Russian Bear. The issue was that UCSJ refused to condone sacrificing refuseniks and Jewish prisoners of conscience on the altar of Israel's security. Both objectives, equally nonnegotiable, could be achieved if they were strategically bifurcated, with Israel ensuring its security and American Jewry protecting Soviet Jews' right to emigrate. Soviet Jewry was already a function of US-Soviet bilateral relations due to the Jackson-Vanik amendment, which made the improved relations and trade benefits the Kremlin sought contingent on freedom of emigration. American trade held the key to Soviet concessions. The United States had leverage. It didn't have to make any trade-offs. Together, Israel and the UCSJ could play a united game on separate fields.

But that's not what happened.

With its own objectives in mind, the Lishka initially backed the creation of the National Conference on Soviet Jewry (initially named the American Jewish Conference on Soviet Jewry), which was funded and supported by the Council of Jewish Federations. From the get-go, under the influence of the Lishka and firmly in the realm of the American Jewish Establishment, the National Conference eschewed any degree of cooperation with UCSJ and SSSJ.

To exert control of the movement, Lishka officials and foreign ministry representatives could be brutally combative. An Israeli representative of the Foreign Ministry, Dr. Yoram Dinstein, had suggested that early

Soviet Jewry activists Yasha Kazakov and Dov Sperling were KGB and that UCSJ had CIA connections.[1]

As part of its policy of nonconfrontation with the USSR, the Lishka sought to suppress information and publicity about Soviet Jewry, claiming that publicity would endanger Soviet Jews. Israel's prime minister, Golda Meir, told a group of activists in 1969 that "anyone who succeeds in emigrating must have seven locks on his lips."[2] The Lishka could control information as long as they had a monopoly on the comprehensive list of refuseniks. Denied access to their list, we compiled our own refusenik database both to support our activity and to share with Congress and the State Department. Early on, we understood the vital significance of our role to disseminate all confirmed refusenik information.

The very first cracks in the Lishka's information monopoly were made in the 1960s by an American who'd made aliyah. Ann Shenkar and her small group collected refusenik data from recent Soviet Jewish emigrants and distributed it to an international network of grassroots activists. Her refusenik sources, not the Lishka, were determining the information they wanted released for public consumption. But they ran headlong into the imperious paternalism of Israeli officials. She was told by a foreign ministry official, "If the government officials have decided there is no Jewish problem in Russia, then that is the truth. Who are you and your group...who dare to defy this political line established by our statesmen?"[3]

With newfound access to some of Ann's data, early UCSJ activists organized a massive greeting-card campaign from American Jews in 1970. Lishka head Nechemia Levanon warned Lou Rosenblum, UCSJ's progenitor and first president, that mail from America would place refuseniks in grave danger – they might even "be shot."[4] But the UCSJ had been assured by refusenik family members in Israel that, far from endangering these

---

1. Geoffrey Martin and Natan Herzl [Martin Gilbert and Natan Sharansky], *A Matter of Priorities: Labor Zionism and the Plight of Soviet Jewry, 1917–1996* (Jerusalem: Diamond Books, 1996).

2. Ibid., 94.

3. Ibid., 97.

4. Jeffrey Herf, *Anti-Semitism and Anti-Zionism in Historical Perspective: Convergence and Divergence* (London: Routledge, 2007).

refusenik relatives, the cards provided a shield of protection from the authorities. The grassroots campaigns would eventually result in a bombardment of tens of thousands of cards from the United States, England, and Canada to Soviet Jews. Each card carried the message: *We have not forgotten you.*

As advocates of refuseniks, UCSJ called for a public campaign but found that our policies were distorted and discredited by the Lishka and the Establishment, which churned false information through their rumor mills for two decades. Refuseniks told me their emissaries were sent to Moscow to dissuade them from working with UCSJ. Soviet Jewish activists were also warned not to trust Michael Sherbourne. Ironically, the Lishka accused him of not passing on the information he received from refuseniks.

Instead of being coerced into silence by their repressive government, Soviet Jews had been struggling to break the isolation imposed on them. The real "Jews of silence," revealed Elie Wiesel in his book of the same name, were Western and Israeli Jews who had abandoned their people behind the Iron Curtain and minimized their plight. In spite of the significant risks, some Soviet Jews tried to tear through the silence, crying out for help in the form of open appeals to the West. Among the first of these was an appeal from a group of twenty-six Jews from Vilnius, Lithuania, in February 1968:

> We are confronted by a paradox here. We are not wanted here, we are being completely oppressed, forcibly denationalized, and even publicly insulted in the press, while at the same time forcibly kept here.[5]

The twenty-six noted within the text why they did not sign their names: "We know very well how people who had protested against flourishing anti-Semitism in the Soviet Union at one time or another were summarily dealt with."[6]

The Israelis, however, favored quiet diplomacy over public advocacy and protest. Their response to grassroots protests or advocacy campaigns

---

5. Shivaun Woolfson, *Holocaust Legacy in Post-Soviet Lithuania: People, Places, and Objects* (London: Bloomsbury, 2014), 159.

6. Ibid.

on behalf of refuseniks was *sha shtil* (keep quiet). It was a refrain we would hear for decades. Don't make waves. Don't engage in confrontation.

Avi Weiss personified the antithesis of this approach. Avi, the Modern Orthodox rabbi of Hebrew Institute of Riverdale, in New York, was national chairman of the SSSJ. Avi's activism flew in the face of the right-wing Jewish religious organizations that opposed participation by American Jews in demonstrations and repudiated nonviolent acts of civil disobedience for fear of harsher consequences by the Kremlin. Avi wasn't alone in advocating for activist tactics. In Jerusalem, Rav Tzvi Yehuda Kook agreed. When Avital Sharansky arrived in Israel, she was taken to talk with Rav Kook about the plight of her husband. The rabbi, surrounded by his students, cried, "Our brothers in Russia are in danger. We must fight for them."[7]

Others also rejected the Lishka's stance. In 1983, former prisoner of conscience and Leningrad trial defendant Yosef Mendelevich met with Rabbi Moshe Feinstein, the world-renowned authority on Jewish law. Yosef asked the esteemed rabbinic authority whether yeshiva students had permission to demonstrate. Rabbi Feinstein said, "Look, Yosef, I am also from Russia, and such demonstrations only provoke the sleeping bear, making the situation much worse, more difficult for Jews to survive." Yosef answered, "Rabbi, everything is already destroyed.... This situation needs a kind of shock therapy. If not, there will be nothing at all left."[8] Rabbi Feinstein deferred to Yosef's assessment, as he understood the situation from the inside.

Because refuseniks themselves called for public protest, the UCSJ interpreted policies of the Establishment that overrode that agenda as paternalistic and condescending. Refuseniks' lives were on the line. They understood that public protest offered protection. Further, the Soviets had never before had greater inducements to make concessions. The Jackson-Vanik Amendment and other bilateral and multilateral agreements with the Soviets, even nuclear disarmament discussions, factored in the West's demand for Jewish emigration. That Jewish Establishment organizations were appealing to the Kremlin's "humanitarianism" to intercede on behalf of Jewish prisoners, and discouraging public protest, smacked of ingratiating powerlessness. It ignored the reality of American strength and the

---

7. Rachel Sharansky Danziger, "Thirty Years After Glienicke Bridge," *Times of Israel* Blogs, https://blogs.timesofisrael.com/30-years-after-glienicke-bridge/ (accessed April 7, 2020).

8. Yosef Mendelevich, conversation with Pamela Braun Cohen.

American government's commitment to Soviet Jewry. Besides, media coverage of public protests and civil disobedience was an effective way to awaken a somnolent public.

UCSJ's open activism and independence went against the Lishka's grain. The Lishka paid us back by trying to delegitimize us and sideline our efforts, both nationally and at the local council level. For example, acting on behalf of the Lishka, Jewish Federations in several cities – including Chicago – made concerted attempts to take over the independent UCSJ councils. The Chicago Federation approached us through some of their funders, who were also supporters of CASJ, urging us to work within the Federation's framework. It was out of the question. Marillyn and I understood that if we were operating under the Federation umbrella, CASJ would lose its independence and would be required to conform to the policies of the National Conference on Soviet Jewry and the Lishka. Without autonomy, CASJ would lose our ability to act as the voice of Soviet Jewry, compelling us instead to be a mouthpiece for the Jewish Establishment. I was blunt. "I'd rather see Chicago Action shut down than silenced, compromised, and made ineffectual," I declared. In the end, Marillyn's stature in the community and her people skills enabled us to maintain our independence while avoiding a rupture with the Federation emissaries who were also our supporters.

Although the Lishka attempted to marginalize and discredit us, UCSJ was unwilling to criticize the Israeli government publicly. Our council leadership kept our heads down and focused on the next challenge.

The Question of Dissidents

With their exclusive focus on aliyah, the Lishka and the American Jewish Establishment were averse to supporting Soviet Jews who were not primarily Zionists. They were particularly wary of Jews in the dissident movement, those who focused on the fight for democracy and human rights.

Anatoly Sharansky was not a man for whom the Establishment was prepared to fight. Sharansky bridged the refusenik movement and that of the dissidents. Dissidents expected that the Kremlin wouldn't live up to the Helsinki Final Act's human rights commitments that it, along with thirty-four other nations, had agreed to in 1975. In reaction, Sharansky and others formed the Moscow Helsinki Group to monitor and publicize the Kremlin's violations of the Helsinki Final Act, also known as the Helsinki accords. By documenting human rights violations – and passing on this information to foreign governments – they put international pressure on the Kremlin. It was risky. Yuri Orlov, prominent physicist and dissident, understood that the consequence of their activity could be the death penalty or life imprisonment for high treason under Article 64 of the Soviet Criminal Code, but Sharansky assured him that, because of Western pressure, they would "only" get seven years for anti-Soviet activity under Article 70.

Sharansky was right: Orlov was arrested and charged under Article 70.

Sharansky asked UCSJ to disseminate news of Orlov's arrest. The ensuing publicity triggered a barrage of criticism from the Lishka and the Establishment. UCSJ president Irene Manekovsky was summoned to the Israeli embassy and ordered to cease supporting dissidents. Israeli officials had even warned Avital that if Anatoly were arrested, nobody would touch his case because of his work with dissidents. Irene told us that Nechemia Levanon "wanted everything to be kept quiet – nobody should make any noise. This was why the Union of Councils always had so much trouble with him, because he never wanted us to do anything he didn't have control over."[9] The Israelis and the Jewish Establishment downplayed the Sharansky case, signaling that they weren't supporting movements or activists intent on democratizing or liberalizing the country. "What came through from Jerusalem was an attitude, which was that when Sharansky was arrested, he got what was coming to him," said SSSJ's Glenn Richter, "because he hadn't conformed to their warnings about his cooperation with the Moscow Helsinki Group."[10]

Renowned lawyer Alan Dershowitz, who, along with Canadian jurist Irwin Cotler, served as Sharansky's advocate, found the Israelis were setting up roadblocks to his advocacy by withholding information. UCSJ, however, was able to deliver the information he needed from our own contacts. The Israelis accused us of bringing Sharansky into the spotlight and relegating other cases to the periphery. Dershowitz's track record, though, contradicted the Establishment's charge; he provided legal advocacy for many other refuseniks and prisoners.

9.　*Jerusalem Post, Anatoly and Avital Shcharansky: The Journey Home* (San Diego: Harcourt Brace Jovanovich, 1986), 192.

10.　Ibid., 193.

Some refusenik leaders were aware of the ideological gulf separating the grassroots UCSJ from the Israeli Lishka over the Sharansky case. On November 11, 1977, eight months after Sharansky's arrest, Avital and leading former Soviet Jewish activists in Israel – including Alexander Luntz, Vitaly Rubin, Dan Roginsky, and Alexander Goldfarb – wrote to Irene Manekovsky and sent copies to Israeli officials. They recognized the importance of the UCSJ's public campaign on behalf of refuseniks, especially Sharansky:

> As the events of the past few years have shown, there are certain kinds of activity which can be carried out successfully only by the Union of Councils….
>
> It would be impossible to list all your contributions to the cause. Your activities on behalf of many refuseniks and former refuseniks surely helped to save them from prison terms. Your assistance and the information you fed to the American Helsinki Monitoring Committee was invaluable. Finally, your handling of the Sharansky case – mobilizing support in the Congress, those involved in government administration and the Jewish communities, participation in establishing the International Sharansky Committee, arranging the appearance of Avital Sharansky on national television and her meeting with AFL-CIO President, George Meany – was the most important contribution to campaign on behalf of Sharansky, which is now the central issue of the entire Soviet Jewry movement….
>
> It was extremely pleasing to know that your work has been highly acclaimed by President Carter in his message to you in October.[11]

Irene laid out the crux of the Sharansky affair in an internal memo titled "Jewish Organizational Hardball: Score, Jewish Establishment 1 – Sharansky 0." At the time, I wondered if she deliberately wrote it for the historical record.

---

11. Letter to Irene Manekovsky, November 11, 1977, archives of Pamela Braun Cohen, American Jewish Historical Society, New York.

> We knew, here in the West, that many Jewish organizations were backing off [Sharansky's] case since he was working with the "dissidents." This made him "treif" [unkosher] in the eyes of those guarding the fate of Soviet Jews.
>
> We were horrified when we learned that the Jews of Moscow also knew. We were further horrified that they felt they had to write the appeal, begging for support for Anatoly....
>
> Early in Sharansky's terrible plight, an Establishment Soviet Jewry personality told Avital Sharansky: "Your husband is finished. No one will work for him." Later, this same person told two activists: "The Soviets really do have something on Sharansky."
>
> I am proud to say that our record was, and is, 100% in support of Anatoly Sharansky – even when he was not such a public figure as he is today....[12]

We weren't just up against the Soviet apparat. We weren't just up against the apathy of the American Jewish community. We were up against the harassment and opposition of the Israeli and American Establishment.

Freedom of Choice and the "Dropouts" Issue

One of the central – and most problematic – conflicts between the UCSJ and the Lishka concerned the eventual destination of Soviet Jews. The Israeli Foreign Ministry defined the movement exclusively in terms of aliyah and supported Zionist refuseniks. UCSJ, however, supported the full spectrum of the Jewish emigration movement, including Jews intending to come to the United States. Soviet procedure demanded that, as a first step to emigrating, all Jews were required to have an invitation from Israel, a *vysov*. As the Soviets didn't permit flights direct to Israel, Jews flew first to Vienna and then on to Israel. Some, however, opted to go from Vienna to America. The Lishka – and the American Jewish Establishment – strongly opposed this practice, derogatively dubbing these people *noshrim*, or dropouts. UCSJ held that, with no other option but to emigrate on Israeli *vysov*s, Soviet Jews should still have freedom of choice in terms of where they settled. The fact that the Lishka denigrated Soviet Jews who chose

---

12. Irene Manekovsky, memo to UCSJ, 1977, archives of Union of Council for Soviet Jews, American Jewish Historical Society, New York.

America rather than appropriately blaming the USSR for requiring them to apply with a *vysov* from Israel was maddening.

With extensive surveillance networks, KGB had enough information about refuseniks, especially the activists, to know their intended destination. Letters, telephone conversations, English or Hebrew-language study, and the location of their émigré family members – all revealed probable destination. While the Israeli Foreign Ministry sought an exclusively Zionist-based emigration, their neighbors, the Soviet Union's Arab clientele, were unalterably opposed to an influx of Jews to Israel. It was likely these states would press the Kremlin to dam the flow to Israel, but the United States could influence the USSR to open the gates in return for trade benefits. In that case, to appease the United States, the Soviets could direct emigration to American shores by giving permission to Jews they suspected were going to America. Given the manipulations perpetrated by the Soviet government, and despite the legitimacy of the Israeli claim of a Jewish national home, it was troubling that the Israelis were demeaning Jews who chose not to go to Israel.

UCSJ's position favoring freedom of choice reflected the broad spectrum of refuseniks. The emigration movement comprised Zionists, religious Zionists, refuseniks advocating Jewish cultural rights, and refuseniks focusing on emigration rights within the context of the broader democratic or human rights movement. All were Jews living under a viciously anti-Semitic government; they wanted to leave the USSR, and they were condemned to the Kafkaesque purgatory of refusal. We supported them all.

Keeping the doors to America open went beyond the principle of freedom of choice. For UCSJ, it was critical that America must never close its doors to persecuted Jews. The memory of the *St. Louis* had been seared into our collective consciousness. Never on our watch would Soviet Jews be subjected to the travesty of those doomed 937 passengers, most of whom were Jews. Denied entry to the United States during the Holocaust and forced to return to Europe, most perished in death camps. The situation in the Soviet Union was dangerous and unpredictable. We were determined to keep the American escape route open and provide a safety net for all eventualities.

Although strenuously opposed to closing America's doors, UCSJ favored the development of a vital underground Zionist movement in the USSR. A fundamental aspect of our mandate was to support refuseniks in their quest for Jewish identity and ties to Israel.

The Vysov Crisis

In addition to conflicts over the direction of emigration was the ongoing issue of an insufficiency of Israeli *vysov*s. Sent by family members or proxy family members in Israel, delivery of *vysov*s constituted the precious first step in the complicated application process. Tourists sent by UCSJ to the Soviet Union brought back long lists of people who were asking for *vysov*s. After forwarding these lists to the Israeli Foreign Ministry, we relied on them to arrange delivery. Time and time again, however, refusenik leadership complained of insufficient *vysov*s to fill the need.

There was much speculation as to why the Israelis dragged their feet. Were they deliberately slowing down emigration because of insufficient housing and infrastructure to absorb thousands of immigrants? Cynically, refuseniks even wondered whether there was concern that an influx of Soviet Jews could affect the political landscape, as Soviet Jews were generally right-wing voters. Perhaps it was bureaucratic inefficiency, but it was generally acknowledged that Israel loved emigration but not the emigrants.

While the Israelis seemed to be smothering the *vysov* process, the number of Soviet Jews impatiently waiting for the invitations was increasing dramatically. These people, known as "waitniks," constituted another category in the emigration movement. They weren't refuseniks, as they had not even begun the process of applying to emigrate and thus had not yet been refused; instead, they lived in limbo. At the urging of refuseniks, the Union continually pressed the Israelis to expedite the process, one more source of contention.

The Jackson-Vanik Waiver Controversy

One of the most intractable, enduring conflicts between the grassroots and the Establishment involved the criteria for the United States to award trade benefits to the Kremlin. The Jackson-Vanik Amendment to the Trade Act of 1974 legislated the linkage between Jewish emigration and trade relations. Sponsored by Washington senator Henry "Scoop" Jackson and Ohio representative Charles Vanik, the Jackson-Vanik Amendment was the hallmark of America's commitment to human rights. By denying normal trade relations to countries with non-market economies that restricted freedom of emigration, the amendment was a bastion of support for Jews and other religious minorities struggling to escape from the Soviet Bloc. Only when a non-market country removed its barriers to emigration could Congress recommend that the president grant a one-year waiver of the restrictions and award that country coveted most-favored-nation trading benefits. In such cases, the president would be required to report to Congress twice a year that the country in question remained in compliance.

Whenever the emigration numbers climbed, the Jewish Establishment called for a reciprocal gesture – a nice fat carrot in the form of US trade concessions. In 1979, with numbers on track to exceed fifty thousand for the year, the Establishment endorsed a waiver of the Jackson-Vanik Amendment. This fiery debate would be my first foray into ongoing skirmishes over Jackson-Vanik.

An editorial in the *Washington Post* in June 1979, "A Big Win for Scoop Jackson," supported the Establishment position. With the monthly emigration rate reaching four thousand people, the *Post* recommended that the president extend the coveted most-favored-nation status to the USSR. It urged Senator Jackson to approve the trade concessions. But numbers never tell the whole story.

Glenn Richter reacted with a letter to the editor, revealing fundamental facts the *Post* had overlooked: "The reality is that only a fraction of the growing number of those applying receive exit visas. In several cities – such as Minsk and Odessa – thousands of Jews stand in line at emigration offices just to hand in applications to officials who work at a deliberate snail's pace. Refusals on arbitrary, spurious ground such as 'state secrets' are common."[13]

UCSJ's refusenik sources reported the reason for the long lines at emigration offices in Ukraine and other places not easily accessible to the Western press: the Soviet government had ordered the closing of many OVIR offices. Many were only open a few days a week, compelling Jews to wait in enormous and ever-growing lines just to submit applications to emigrate.

---

13. Letter to the editor, *Washington Post*, June 7, 1979.

UCSJ held tight to our opposition to a waiver and worked closely with Congress. Ultimately, in spite of the Establishment's efforts, the amendment wasn't waived in 1979, and the Soviets were not granted most-favored-nation status.

Such attempts to award Moscow most-favored-nation status abandoned the thousands of Jews still stuck behind invisible bars. Support of a waiver indicated either a lack of information or willful ignorance of documented evidence that the Soviets were not living up to their international obligations. UCSJ argued in each instance that it was entirely premature to surrender our leverage and reward gestures in the absence of high, sustained numbers and an institutionalized emigration process.

Questions of Ethical Leadership

Our problems with the Jewish Establishment and the Lishka did nothing but prompt questions. My questions about the nature of leadership were an outgrowth of questions that had dogged me since I was a teenager. How could power be used both morally and responsibly to help our people?

Why, in 1942, did it take four precious months for the preeminent American Jewish leader, Stephen Wise, to publicize Hitler's plan to annihilate all Jews?

How was it possible that President Franklin Roosevelt, so beloved by American Jewry, didn't make a single public statement for a year after the State Department knew about the mass killings?

With 90 percent of the US emigration quotas unfilled, why did the United States' doors remain closed, even to the *St. Louis*, the ship bearing Jewish refugees, which was turned away from American shores in 1939?

Why didn't the United States bomb the train lines to Auschwitz?

Why? I asked, struggling to comprehend the incomprehensible. *Why?*

Where were our leaders? Where was the Establishment? Where was the public outrage? Looking back, I could see that a lethal mix of passivity, fear, and lack of information contributed to a tragic and shameful silence.

Six million Jews taught me to be skeptical of Jewish leadership who did so little.

UCSJ's council chairs shared my aversion to the traditional Jewish leadership. To us, there were parallels between some contemporary Establishment Jewish leaders and a certain type of Jew in pre-twentieth-century Europe: the *shtadlan* (intercessor), or the court Jew. Used by monarchs for their financial resources, *shtadlanim* were given exceptional status at a time when their fellow Jews had no political status, no rights at all. Theoretically, the *shtadlan* might have used his position to ameliorate the suffering of his people; in reality, he was only a pawn in the hands of the powerful, who manipulated him to fund their treasuries and wars. The *shtadlanim* had access to power but had no real power themselves. They did what they had to do to survive.

Even well into the twentieth century, the pattern of wealthy Jewish intercessors continued. It seemed to have been absorbed into the orientation of the Jewish Establishment and was on display during the Soviet Jewry movement. A few Western Jewish entrepreneurs had ascended to such a level that they could access the upper echelons of Soviet power. They used this access to negotiate on behalf of their beleaguered brothers and sisters, but did so without consulting refuseniks or compelling the Soviets to deal with them directly. Furthermore, these intercessors hoped to use these Kremlin contacts to help them gain access to the Soviet market. The UCSJ saw this approach as a flagrant form of paternalistic self-interest.

There was one striking difference between the Soviet Jewry movement and historical scenarios. The refuseniks and other Jewish activists in the Soviet Union were not the anonymous Jewish masses of the past. They were people who were known and empowered by us.

We believed that the strength of our small army against the Soviets' might was simply right. Our campaign had a moral basis, a Jewish basis. As written in Leviticus, "Do not stand by the blood of your brother."[14] And in the Mishnah: "He who saves one life, it is as if he has saved an entire world."[15] We were impelled by an imperative to rescue, and it came from our collective gut. We were Jews. We were one people. They were ours.

Our small battalion was determined to do whatever we could, no matter how difficult, to save one single Jewish soul at a time. Just one, then another, and then another. We were prepared to muster every possible political, economic, and social resource for each Jew in need. We weren't going to let Soviet authorities get away with any KGB action against a refusenik or prisoner; we would make their authorities answer for such

---

14. Leviticus 19: 16.

15. Mishnah, *Sanhedrin* 4:5.

actions at US-Soviet bilateral meetings, punishing them with constraints on their economy.

None of us could have predicted the far-reaching results of our determined effort. Every single letter that was delivered, each messenger call completed, each book delivered, created infinitesimal cracks in the Iron Curtain, cracks that ultimately formed the fissures that brought down the entire structure.

PART TWO

Jews of Silence No More

CHAPTER 8

International Tensions, 1979–80

The Soviet Invasion of Afghanistan

The headlines of the morning papers screamed: *USSR INVADES AFGHANISTAN!* Overnight, the nuclear arms race escalated, and the Cold War threatened to metastasize into something far worse. President Jimmy Carter recalled the US ambassador from Moscow and asked the Senate to terminate the SALT II nuclear arms talks. He signaled new trade restrictions against the Soviets and threatened that the United States would boycott the 1980 summer Olympics, to be hosted by the USSR in Moscow.

The spike of international tension increased KGB's internal surveillance to solidify their system of lies, propping up their bulwark against information that might leak through its borders. KGB blocked our phone calls to refuseniks, cutting off activists' home phone lines or interrupting calls with either the sound of deafening static or the roar of a train engine through the receiver. Sometimes they just cut the call. With US-Soviet relations at their worst and the doomsday clock moving closer to nuclear confrontation, American tourists canceled their trips to Russia.

The communication blockade imposed a silence that was unquestionably dangerous for refuseniks. The information blackout and downward spiral of US-Soviet relations further isolated the refuseniks and activists, removing them from our protection. The secret police could quietly engineer the disappearance of any refusenik into the gulag archipelago, the vast system of hard labor and prison camps scattered over the USSR, and without contact with the West, the incident would go unreported. In the absence of phone calls and tourist contacts, there would be no information. No information meant no publicity. No publicity meant no pressure on the government, which meant no support for activists and refuseniks.

Lev Blitshtein and His Three Angels

It was a cold and sunless Chicago winter afternoon, and I was alone in Chicago Action's second-floor office in Highland Park, now with five desks. Membership was growing and so was our volunteer staff. Hetty, Linda, and Marillyn had already gone home, and I was packing to leave, glumly reconciling myself to the new challenges facing us in the wake of the Soviet invasion of Afghanistan. Suddenly, three young women appeared at the door. Sherry Peller, Carol Port, and Fran Kaplan had been part of the letter-writing group I had started years earlier, before learning of the existence of CASJ. In those days, we had met in my Deerfield living room to write to refuseniks and brainstorm, and these women had taken on the case of Lev Blitshtein, coming up with a creative campaign we dubbed "Americans United for Lev Blitshtein." With an official letterhead, in envelopes emblazoned with a red-and-blue star superimposed over our slogan, they sent letters to Lev and to Kremlin officials, the Soviet embassy, and the US Congress and State Department on his behalf. The cascade of correspondence made it impossible to guess that "Americans United for Lev Blitshtein" consisted solely of the trio of Lev's angels, Sherry, Carol, and Fran.

Over the years, Marillyn and I worked closely with Lev. He distributed our financial aid to the families of the prisoners of conscience and was the drop-off contact for the material assistance our tourists carried to Moscow. His role made him a particularly important case for us, given the dangers incurred by handling goods from the West.

Lenny and I had met Lev in 1978. We were meeting with refuseniks at the traditional gathering place outside Moscow's Choral Synagogue, when I unexpectedly heard: "Pomella?" At my side was a middle-aged man with an impish smile that betrayed neither anguish nor worry. I was incredulous that he knew who I was. "Pomella?" he repeated in astonishment. Lev, making his way over to introduce himself to us, the only Americans in the crowd, must have been shocked to recognize my voice from our many phone calls.

Denied permission to emigrate on fabricated grounds of having access to state secrets – though he worked in a meat plant – Lev divorced his wife, an act of love, to enable her and their son Boris to get their visas and emigrate. Marillyn and I brought Boris, a charming young man with curly red hair, to Chicago to publicize his father's refusal and the plight of all refuseniks. One day, as Boris was being interviewed by a journalist at a synagogue, a woman approached to ask if she could talk to him. I explained that he was busy but asked if I could help. There appeared to be a branch of Blitshteins in her family tree, and she wanted to explore possible family connections.

I reacted with indignance. Boris was working the press to help free the father he hadn't seen in years and to publicize the plight of hundreds of other separated families. And she wanted to interrupt him to ask about his family tree? It was outrageously selfish.

There were Blitshteins in my family too, but given Lev's activity in the movement and isolated as he was from his family, I wouldn't have mentioned it to him. Intent on shielding Boris, I diverted her by asking to see her family tree. And there, in black and white, was the name of my own grandmother: Anna Rosenstone, my Nanny.

And there, on another page, was Lev's. I was learning – there were no coincidences. The Talmud teaches, "*Kol Yisrael areivin zeh la'zeh*" (all Jews are responsible for one another).[1] We are all connected. We are all part of each other's family trees. We just have to look a little to see it.

On that dark, depressing, winter afternoon in the CASJ office, Sherry, Carol, and Fran had come to talk about the Blitshtein campaign. What more could they do for the only sausage-maker in Russia denied a visa because of state secrets? (Blitshtein used to quip that the reason the Kremlin was holding him was because he knew what the Soviets put in their sausages.)

I told the women, "The Soviets have invaded Afghanistan. Phone lines into the USSR have been cut, trips canceled. We're losing contact with activists and we need travelers. But who in their right mind is going to travel to the Soviet Union now?"

As if volunteering to pick up some coffee, they looked at each other and answered, "Us. We'll go."

So they went home, told their husbands, and made plans for their small children. They reassured each other, it was just for a week. They would be among the first to chart the new waters of post-invasion USSR.

Their trip, like those of all the travelers Marillyn and I briefed, was conducted in absolute secrecy. We insisted that only their immediate families be told where they were going. The best security we could

---

1.   *Shevuot* 39a.

provide both our travelers and the refuseniks was to eliminate all possible leaks. We didn't want KGB waiting for their flight to arrive at Moscow's Sheremetyevo airport.

Of course, Lev didn't know they were coming either. He never dreamed he'd see them on his side of the Iron Curtain. Their first stop in Moscow was to Lev's apartment. For weeks I pictured his delighted astonishment when he opened his door in Moscow to find the three women he only knew from their letters, his three angels. The truth was, they weren't just Blitshtein's angels. They were mine, too. On their return, I made them describe again and again his reaction when he saw them standing before him.

I struggle even now to describe my joy as I devoured reports of the meetings between Jews who lived across the world from each other, separated by what seemed like insurmountable barriers. I was blessed not only to be a part of many of those meetings, but also to have orchestrated reunions between so many people who had never met, but who had meant so much to each other.

The Moscow Summer Olympics

Even before the Soviets had invaded Afghanistan, when Lenny and I were in Moscow in the fall of 1978, Jewish activists and dissidents had already begun expressing grave concern regarding the 1980 summer Olympic Games due to take place in Moscow. Outside the Choral Synagogue, Moscow professor Alexander Lerner, one of the leading refusenik activists, told us that the games would give the Kremlin exactly what it has been seeking since the revolution – they would confer legitimacy on the totalitarian axis of evil and repression. Restrictions on the number of foreign visitors and controls over their movement would allow the Kremlin to stage-manage a hideous deception. The Union of Councils had to prevent that from happening.

The lead-up to the Moscow Olympics marked the start of a new phase in the Soviet Jewry movement. "Now," wrote Irene Manekovsky in a memo to UCSJ councils and the 35s, "we are in another stage. We have, for the next two years, something to focus upon, and that is the Olympics. We must use this as an educational tool and as a pressure point to illustrate Soviet Jewry."[2]

---

2.   Irene Manekovsky, memo to UCSJ, SSSJ, and 35s leadership, June 22, 1978.

We spent those two years gearing up, deliberating, consulting with refuseniks, considering tactics. It wasn't easy to decide on a uniform UCSJ policy. The only question was whether we should advocate boycott or relocation. In the early stages, some of us were concerned that pressing for relocation would cast us in the mold of "disrupters," at the cost of our credibility; furthermore, many felt that relocation was impractical and too idealistic.

After the invasion, the gloves came off. The Kremlin expelled Andrei Sakharov from Moscow, exiling him to suppress his outspoken support for an Olympic boycott.[3] On our phone calls, refuseniks repeatedly emphasized that their political leaders were masters of deception who were staging a performance. They were "beautifying" Moscow for the Olympics by cleansing it of unwanted elements, like Sakharov. Lynn, David, and the rest of UCSJ were getting the same kinds of warnings:

If they got rid of Sakharov, the academician of the Soviet Academy of Sciences, hero of socialist labor, laureate of the Nobel Peace Prize in 1975, physicist and father of the Soviet hydrogen bomb, what do you think they will do to us?

The Kremlin is using the Olympics as an excuse to expel us from Moscow. There will be no one, no dissident, no refusenik here to talk to the reporters about what the authorities are doing to us.

Before and during the games, the authorities will do everything to prevent contact between the international press and refuseniks and the human rights leaders.

Every phone call underscored the refuseniks' fear that, under cover of the games, they would be imprisoned, banished, or held under house arrest without media coverage. Refuseniks also were concerned that the Kremlin would exclude Israel as they did for the Baltic regatta in 1978; there were already rumors that Israel would be excluded from the pre-Olympic Spartakiad Games.

Refuseniks knew the games would give the Soviets the same legitimacy it gave the Nazis when Berlin hosted the 1936 Olympic Games.

---

3.   By 1980, the Kremlin had crushed the dissidents of the Moscow Helsinki Group, which had monitored Soviet compliance with the Helsinki human rights doctrines. Now, by driving the chief spokesman of the dissident and human rights movement out of Moscow, they further crippled the dissident movement, making refuseniks all the more vulnerable.

Additionally, while the Olympics would be a debacle, they would bring in a flood of hard currency the government desperately needed. For broadcasting rights alone, NBC paid the Kremlin $85 million.

The UCSJ executive committee floated all kinds of recommendations. Could we enlist athletes as advocates? During the games, they could wear T-shirts emblazoned with names of prisoners of conscience. What about filling a stadium with tourists who would remove their jackets and reveal shirts with prisoners' names? Maybe we should consider hosting a "Freedom Olympics" outside the Communist bloc? Ultimately, the UCSJ returned to its guiding principle and consulted with refusenik activists regarding our strategy.

Dr. Lerner and other prominent activists wanted us to urge President Jimmy Carter to officially sanction the removal of the games from Moscow. In response, UCSJ and our affiliates established the International Monitoring Committee for the 1980 Olympics and mobilized a petition and advocacy drive in five countries[4] to relocate the Olympics to a site outside of the USSR.

Lynn enlisted Congressman Jack Kemp, a New York Republican congressman and former player for the Buffalo Bills, as honorary chairman of our International Monitoring Committee. Kemp and Senator Wendell Anderson, a Democrat from Minnesota and a former Olympic hockey player, filed resolutions in both the House and Senate calling for relocation. Representative Robert Drinan, acting on behalf of UCSJ, presented the White House with petitions signed by more than sixty-five thousand people, urging the removal of the Olympics from Moscow.

I wasn't surprised that some groups opposed moving or boycotting the games, but when the Jewish Establishment opposed relocation, I was incredulous. The Jewish Agency chairman said that "the Presidium did not believe in the campaign to boycott the Olympics; instead, it should insist on the Soviet Union strictly observing the regulations of the admission and treatment of all participants."[5] According to a memo from Michael Sherbourne, Lishka representatives both in Washington, DC, and in London claimed that "leading activists in the USSR are opposed to a

---

4.   The drive would take place in the United States (via the UCSJ and SSSJ), France (via the Paris-based Comité des Quinze), England and Canada (via the 35s), and Israel (via the activist group Shomer Achi Anochi).

5.   "Daily News Bulletin," Jewish Telegraphic Agency (JTA), September 29, 1978.

removal."[6] At the UCSJ Annual Meeting in September 1978, Sherbourne characterized that claim as a bald-faced lie, disinformation created by the Lishka to undermine our position. I personally had brought out of Russia endorsements for relocation from leading activists. Even after the Soviet invasion of Afghanistan and after the exile of Sakharov, Israel was still against boycotting or moving the games. Even worse, Israel was pressuring Jewish communities in the West to oppose our attempts at relocation.[7]

Against the backdrop of these internal politics, I suddenly found myself cultivating an interest in the personalities that dominated the American athletic world. If I could convince someone with the stature of, say, a Walter Payton of the Chicago Bears to sign a petition advocating relocation, it would be a significant step in forming a critical mass of public opinion.

The person who had formerly expressed unequivocal disdain for the Bulls, Bears, Hawks and other carnivores that devoured a perfectly good Sunday afternoon did a complete turn-around. I tackled the world of athletics with a vengeance, culling sports pages, interviewing the male game-watchers in my family, scanning "who's who" listings in the sports world. How could I get to them? My family watched with amusement. I sat with my brother, and we chiseled out a list.

I brought Avital Sharansky to meet with the vice president of the Chicago Bears, Ed McCaskey. Avital maintained that the Soviets had calculated the timing of her husband's trial to suppress dissident voices before the Olympics. Avital was a mixture of indomitable strength and timid fragility that everyone wanted to protect. She was an eloquent speaker for the repressed, the imprisoned, and those in fear. How could anyone refuse her? Ed was on her side.

Owner Bill Veeck was an icon of the Chicago White Sox. A gravelly voiced chain-smoker, he sat, listening carefully, his arm draped over the table in the Sox dining room at Comiskey Park, sympathetic to what we were trying to do. I wasn't hitting homers, but I believed that if I could just get one sports personality to sign on, the climate could change.

Like so much of what we did, it was difficult to tell how much our efforts had moved the needle. But the protesting voices grew louder. The

6.   Michael Sherbourne, memo to UCSJ, September 17, 1978.

7.   Maurice Samuelson, "Israel Appears to Be Opposed to Boycotting the Games," Jewish Telegraphic Agency (JTA), January 17, 1980.

cacophony was amplified in early January 1980 with Sakharov's call for a boycott and the Carter administration's support of his appeal. President Carter urged the International Olympic Committee (IOC) to move the games, not only due to the Soviet invasion of Afghanistan, but also because the safety of visitors and athletes couldn't be guaranteed in light of the Kremlin's aggression. Though the IOC opted not to move the games, the United States, along with sixty-four other countries, boycotted the Moscow Olympics. While the games went ahead, the untiring efforts we had invested in our campaign were not wasted. Irene was right. The games had given us a platform to educate the public.

CHAPTER 9

Consultation and Crackdown, 1980–81

UCSJ Conference in London

To solidify our strategy to focus the British and Israeli governments on our issues, UCSJ and the 35s hosted an international conference for our grass-roots affiliates. The meeting opened on March 15, 1980, the anniversary of Anatoly Sharansky's 1977 arrest, and Marillyn and I flew to London for the first segment.

The London sessions got off to a rousing start when, at the opening reception in the House of Lords, Greville Janner pledged Parliament's support for the movement. The meetings were dominated by the towering presence of former dissident Vladimir Bukovsky, who had lived through twelve years of grueling punishment in the psychiatric units, labor camps, and prisons of the Soviet Union. Bukovsky had been released in 1976, in exchange for the imprisoned general secretary of the Communist Party of Chile, Luis Corvalán.

Late one night, Marillyn and I retreated to the St. Basil Hotel after a long day of sessions. Exhausted but exhilarated, she recounted some of the stories that illuminated her life and, by vicarious extension, my own. As a teacher of Jewish history, she had knocked on the doors of the homes where historical figures like Sigmund Freud, Franz Kafka, and Albert Einstein had lived. Her authentic interest in Jewish history charmed whoever answered the door, and she was ushered into richly decorated rooms to speak for a few minutes with the remaining family members, documenting their personal stories that would later pepper the classes she taught.

For the second stage of the conference, Marillyn and I flew to Israel to meet with government representatives and interview recent arrivals, many of whom were separated from relatives still refused permission. From the airport, we took a taxi to Jerusalem. The sun beaming from a cloudless blue sky, blossoming almond trees, and verdant orange and olive trees pushed the damp, gloomy grayness of London into the past. The green fields lining the highway changed to scrub dotted with a few cypresses, and then to patches of newly planted forests, as we climbed the rocky hills to Jerusalem.

The first time Lenny and I had been to Israel was shortly after our marriage, before the 1967 war, when much of the Old City of Jerusalem was under Jordanian control. The Kotel could only be glimpsed by standing on a metal platform outside a building on Mount Zion. Ten years later, we returned with our three small children. On the road to Jerusalem we recognized that, finally, after two thousand years of soulful longing, with the words "next year in Jerusalem" on the lips of each generation, Lenny and I were privileged to be able to take our children "home."

At the plenary session at the Van Leer Institute, recently arrived refuseniks Grigory Kanovich and Lev Utevsky, along with other leaders of the Jewish cultural movement, prevailed on us to support the dissemination of Jewish culture. Emigration was not enough, they said. We had to provide Jewish spiritual and cultural assistance to tens of thousands of Jews waiting for permission in the vast Soviet holding camp.

Former Moscow correspondent to the *New York Times* David Shipler spoke about the dissident movement. Levi Ulanovsky, a refusenik activist who had just arrived from Moscow, described the discouragement of the long-term refuseniks in Moscow, only two of whom had been given permission to emigrate in the last year. Levi also expressed grave concern about rising anti-Semitism: Jews had to be taken out as quickly as possible.

The high point of the conference was the celebratory reception held on Mount Scopus for the former prisoners of the Leningrad trials, released after nine years in a prison camp. They had been the focus of our activity for so many years: Wolf Zalmanson, Anatoly Altman, Boris Penson, Leib Knokh, and Hillel Butman. Conspicuously absent was Yosef Mendelevich, the only remaining Leningrad trial defendant still in prison camp.

The counterweight to the Mount Scopus event were heart-wrenching meetings with those who had immigrated to Israel but whose husbands, wives, parents, or children were being held in refusal. Lynn had arranged for debriefings with these separated families in Jerusalem, Tel Aviv, and Haifa.

Our UCSJ activists sat at long tables, taking notes, debriefing new émigrés. There were so many of them, so many tears, so much anguish. We divided into teams to cover the scores and scores of people waiting to be heard.

There was the beautiful young Aviva Gendin, separated from her husband Lev. Rivka Drori, sister of Yosef Mendelevich. Ida Nudel's sister. Vladimir Slepak's sister. Mark Nashpitz's parents. Lev Shapiro's parents. Kim Fridman's wife. Grigory Vidgarov's father, who told us: "Press the system just as they press our children. They separate families on purpose. It's been seven years for my family."[1]

Broken families, broken lives, family members sentenced to terms without limits. None of them knew when they would be reunited.

"Please, help me."

"Help us."

We taped them, took down every word, exchanged phone numbers and addresses, developed individual strategies for each case, asked if their refusenik family members wanted tourists or phone calls from abroad. We transcribed lists of medicines they needed: insulin, blood thinners, heart medications. We promised to match their refusenik family members with adopters who would advocate for them. We promised congressional intervention, publicity, Hebrew books and tapes, rabbis, financial aid. The needs of each were distinct and needed to be met.

My internal voice whispered: "How are you going to do this?"

And then a louder one answered, "I don't know, but how can I not try?"

Important Conversations

On the tour bus going to Haifa for a meeting with separated families, as the sun dipped into the Mediterranean, Marillyn and I sat with Anatoly Altman. In his thirties, Anatoly was charming, quick to laugh, happy to answer our grilling questions. One of the recently released Leningrad trial defendants, he had spent nine years in a prison camp deep in the Siberian taiga, a place he described as a cancer surrounded by exquisite beauty.

For us, the conversation was a unique opportunity to understand the impact of our work – the effectiveness of our advocacy and of the goods we were sending in with travelers for Jewish prisoners of conscience in

---

1. *The Refusenik*, April 1980.

far-flung regions of the gulag. I had the tape recorder running. "The support from the West kept the anti-Semitic guards from beating us. We know about the relationship from the side of the camp administration and guards. They hate us, but they can't call us dirty Jews because it's against the law and they know that we'll protest. Instead, they use provocateurs, informants to get us."[2]

"How did you know about our support?" Marillyn asked.

"By telephone," he joked. Then he went on to answer seriously: "Through family visits – and special, secret communication. Once, my mother came to the camp for a meeting and told me that she met a visitor who came to Moscow wearing a bracelet with my name on it."[3] He grinned broadly at us. "Every time I have a meeting with people from abroad, I tell them, 'I am the best proof of your success.'" He went on:

> We practically didn't have food in the camp. Yes, we had bread and there was enough for us because the older adults simply couldn't digest it and they gave us theirs. But there was no protein, nothing nutritious, and from this bread came all the diseases….

I couldn't imagine this refined, slightly whimsical man in a Soviet slave labor camp. He described how they made use of what we sent in with our tourists. It was forbidden for them to receive vitamins, anything with nutrients, or chocolate, so his mother made cookies out of the kosher chicken soup cubes we had sent. "For us," he said, "it was a big support."

"What about books?" I asked. "When we were in KGB isolation for interrogation," he explained, "some people had Hebrew dictionaries…. It was a miracle, but after some period they took it from us. Bibles were strictly forbidden."

The conversation shifted. He said, "Emigration now is almost closed. It depends completely on the relationship between the US and the Soviet

---

2. Anatoly Altman, taped conversation with Pamela Braun Cohen and Marillyn Tallman, March 1980.

3. Along with "Save Soviet Jewry" bumper stickers, metal bracelets engraved with the name of a Jewish prisoner of conscience, like the one marked with the name of Josef Begun that sat on President Reagan's desk in the White House, raised the visibility of our issue.

Union. America can save many people."[4] That summed up the entire point of our mission.

On Shabbat afternoon, I met up with fellow UCSJ board members outside the prime minister's residence in Jerusalem, went through the security check, and were admitted into his home. Menachem Begin and his wife Aliza welcomed us warmly, and we exchanged pleasantries. UCSJ's president, Bob Gordon, urged the prime minister to do everything in his power to support emigration from the Soviet Union to Israel.

It was about then that Lynn Singer punctured the gracious atmosphere. Never lacking in courage and with an authoritative bearing that commanded the proceedings, Lynn confronted our long-standing problem with the Lishka. At the time of this meeting, the head of the Lishka was Nechemia Levanon, who, like his predecessors, operated the Lishka like the Mossad, the office from which it sprang, without accountability to the Knesset. Politely but firmly in her Long Island accent, she said, "Mr. Prime Minister, don't you think your office should exert some controls on Nechemia Levanon?"

She spelled out that we clearly saw a need to bring the relationship between Israel and Soviet Jewry under the jurisdiction of the Knesset and hold the Lishka accountable to the government. Well briefed, Begin rebuffed her quickly, simply dismissing the need. He made it clear to all of us. He had known Nechemia for a long time and trusted him implicitly. The Lishka would continue to operate as an independent satellite.

The Promised Land

After the conference, with only a few minor hitches, Lenny heroically managed to fly in with our three children and our niece, and we took a family suite at a hotel near the Central Bus Station in Jerusalem. It was our kids' second trip to Israel, but our first Pesach Seder in Jerusalem. We would be spending it with Lenny's sister, Lessa, and her family, who had made aliyah after the Yom Kippur War.

Our children and theirs sat around the table, together with two former refuseniks who had worked with us in Chicago on behalf of those left behind. From Moscow, Deerfield, Sverdlovsk, and Tacoma, now in the holy city of Jerusalem, we had come together to fulfill the commandment

---

4.   Anatoly Altman, taped conversation with Pamela Braun Cohen and Marillyn Tallman, March 1980.

to remember and tell the story of our exodus from Egypt, a memorial in time. We sang songs of gratitude to the Almighty, who delivered us then and was delivering us now. At the end of the Seder, we intoned the promise, "Next year in Jerusalem." The words echoed with significance.

Before our flight back to the States, I caught up with Lenny and the children at the Museum of the Diaspora in Tel Aviv, Beit Hatfutsot. I was in the ticket line when I encountered Leningrad trial defendant Hillel Butman, whom we had honored the previous evening. He was with his wife Eva after nine years of forced separation. As a witness to his success in reaching the Jewish national home, I was struck by the black-and-white contrast between his life and mine. The cost of Butman's one-way ticket to Israel was nine years in a Soviet prison camp. All we had to do was buy plane tickets. We could keep our bank account and travel freely between the United States and Israel. We didn't have to leave everything behind and didn't have to sacrifice years of our lives in grisly labor camps. Our tickets didn't have to be one way.

Upon our departure, I felt the wrench of leaving Israel. For the first time, I didn't want to go back to America.

It would be four long years before we returned to Israel, but when we did, in the summer of 1984, it was to celebrate Josh's bar mitzvah. Lenny took off a full month from work, and we rented a house in the German colony near Emek Refaim in Jerusalem. We traveled the length of the country in a rented car and spent time with the family. Josh read from the Torah in Jerusalem, in fulfillment of the prayers of untold generations of our fathers and mothers. Two thousand years after the Romans had exiled us and only seventeen years after the Kotel was returned to Jewish hands, it was a miraculous blessing to be able to bring our children to the Promised Land.

That night, at the Jerusalem Plaza hotel (now the Leonardo), there was a joyous celebration. My cousin, Josef Ardon, who had brought his family out of Lithuania and started Tadiran, the Israeli electrical conglomerate; his wife Shoshana; Lessa and Michael and our nieces and nephew; my friends who had emigrated from the Soviet Union: all joined in dancing to pulsating Israeli songs, jubilantly singing along. It was a thrilling and euphoric affirmation of the continuity of the Jewish people, of our unity, of the centrality of Jerusalem in our historic mission.

It must have been about then that I decided we should live in Israel.

I was aware of all the realistic obstacles, but I believed Israel, the main current of Jewish history, solidified and ensured Jewish identity. Aliyah was a safeguard against assimilation, against intermarriage. But Lenny had harnessed his creative and business acumen to the challenges of his independent media company. When I broached the topic, he said that maybe "someday we would have a toehold in Israel."

We would see. Maybe.

Back home after that 1980 conference, CASJ was in its usual perpetual state of urgency. There were new arrests. The situation in Kiev was grave. Authorities closed the Moscow kindergarten after terrorizing the children with their raids. In June, the UCSJ board met in Chicago and confronted a visiting Soviet delegation with a protest. While Jerusalem remained in my thoughts and in my plans for the future, the challenges of the present demanded my energy and attention.

Repression and Resistance in Ukraine and Beyond

After the invasion of Afghanistan, the Kremlin appeared to have given KGB the green light to destroy the Jewish movement by arresting its leaders. Their success in choking off contact between us and the refuseniks made it easier for them to operate with impunity.

The appeal I received in April 1980, addressed to the Jews of Israel and the Diaspora and signed by an astounding eighty-four Kiev refuseniks, confirmed reports of anti-Jewish repression and arrests for emigration activity. The appeal proclaimed that they were "hostages, victims of a moral pogrom."[5] Authorities were aggressively using every method to restrain them, expecting the refuseniks to submit and refrain from fighting back. The refuseniks, however, resisted.

Thirteen young activists in Kiev, representing the group known as the Second Generation in Refusal, appealed to the Communist Party Congress. Their stirring appeal read: "For the past two thousand years, seventy generations of our Jewish ancestors dreamed of going to Israel. To forget this is to betray their goals, their memory, and our history written in their blood. Instead of…permitting us to repatriate, we are subjected to all

---

5.   Appeal to Jews of Israel and the Diaspora, April 1980, archives of Pamela Braun Cohen, American Jewish Historical Society, New York.

means of humiliations and persecution. We are called traitors.... Listen to our words. Let us go to our historic home. Let us go home."[6]

Their resistance was met by arrest.

I had never met Stanislav Zubko, but the events surrounding his case were as real as any other aspect of my life. Zubko had been pushing the frontiers of grassroots activism in Kiev, planning protests on behalf of the thousands of recently refused Jews. Going beyond individual cases, he focused on a collective solution.

Zubko was a chemist in Ukraine. The picture I had of him revealed a bearded face with a broad forehead and intelligent eyes. He had been arrested six times in ten months. While he was behind bars, the militia called his mother in for questioning. In her absence, KGB searched her apartment, planting a gun and narcotics. Another Kiev refusenik who was at the prison trying to get information about Zubko's arrest overheard the militiaman who conducted the search report to his chief that everything was in order: the revolver and the hashish had been successfully planted.

Refuseniks didn't dare to so much as jaywalk. After all, KGB was ready to arrest them on any pretext. But by planting evidence, the Soviets were using a new tactic, and it rang an alarm. Ukraine was well known as a testing ground for new methods to restrict emigration. Previously, emigration activists had either been charged with illegal political activity (often branded as anti-Soviet activity) or with antisocial activity, like hooliganism or parasitism. But the Zubko revolver and drugs accusation made it clear that authorities were taking steps to represent Jewish emigration as criminal activity.

That news, as well as our knowledge of the scurrilous cartoons published in Soviet newspapers that depicted Jews as malevolent criminals, made me fearful that they were establishing a precedent for further arrests on criminal charges. It wasn't long before the Soviets used the same tactics to imprison Lev Elbert in Kiev. Having established a successful trial balloon in Ukraine, authorities later began using this tactic in Russia, with the arrest of Hebrew teacher Yuli Edelstein.

By the summer of 1981, the authorities had convicted some of Kiev's most active refuseniks. Valery Pilnikov was sentenced to five years on a framed charge of hooliganism. Kim Fridman was sentenced on charges of

---

6. Appeal to the Communist Party Congress, archives of Pamela Braun Cohen, American Jewish Historical Society, New York.

parasitism. When Lenny and I had met him in 1978, Fridman had already been separated from his wife and daughter for years, as they waited for him in Israel. Vladimir Kislik, the Kiev physicist arrested after leaving a Purim party, was sent to the psychiatric ward of Pavlov Hospital, then to prison, for malicious hooliganism.

Then Zubko was given four years. Authorities were reigning in activists.

In Odessa, KGB conducted house searches of activists Avrely Koifman and Ida Nepomniashy; similar searches took place in Kharkov as well. The KGB crackdown extended to other republics. In Kishinev, activists waiting for exit visas had gone on hunger strike. Thirty-five hundred Jews were waiting to receive applications from the OVIR emigration office, which issued only three or four a day. There was a six-month wait to make the initial application. In September, after an abortive attempt of refuseniks to stage a protest march outside the Kishinev Synagogue, Vladimir Tsukerman and Osip Lokshin were arrested. Included in the evidence the court used to sentence Tsukerman was Leon Uris's novel *Exodus*. This fictional account of the founding of the State of Israel, deemed anti-Soviet by the government, was cherished by refuseniks, painstakingly copied by hand and surreptitiously passed from one to another, even making its way into prison camps. Even in this dangerous time, refuseniks continued to resist in many forms. Denied a memorial to commemorate the Nazi slaughter, Kishinev refuseniks defiantly gathered to mark the notorious 1903 Kishinev pogrom.

Alexander "Sasha" Paritsky

For the better part of three years, Ukraine KGB tracked Alexander Paritsky like bloodthirsty hyenas. Paritsky had brought down the wrath of the authorities when he discovered the Nazis' mass slaughter of Jews at Drobytsky Yar in Kharkov and brought it to international attention. His yearly commemorations were routinely broken up by the secret police. Later, he helped establish the unofficial Kharkov Jewish University for children of refuseniks.[7]

---

7.   In 1978, activists established a Jewish university in Moscow that attracted scores of Jewish students, but by 1982, the authorities effectively shut it down with the arrest of one of its leading teachers, Boris Kanievsky. The Kharkov Jewish University and Paritsky met the same fate.

Authorities finally arrested him in August 1981. Then they set about attacking his family. They found a composition written by his daughter Dorina when she was thirteen years old. In it, she expressed her longing for the land of Israel, her Motherland. The piece was used as evidence against him. Secret police shadowed his wife Polina, threatening to take custody of their two daughters. They terrified the children with a series of provocations.

The extensive KGB pressure on Paritsky and other refusenik leaders prompted strong reactions from UCSJ. I don't think there was any council that didn't have close ties to Paritsky. Boston Action for Soviet Jewry had assigned the Paritsky case to a Somerville group, which formed the Committee to Free the Paritsky Family. They staged rallies and enlisted the support of Representative Barney Frank and Senator Paul Tsongas, who phoned Polina at a press conference three days before her husband's trial. Three major television news networks, two newspaper reporters, and over 150 activists heard Polina say, "Help me! Help my husband! Help my children!" On the other side of the continent, director of Bay Area Council David Waksberg married Ellen Bob in a wedding ceremony that was designed to focus attention on the Paritsky case.

I had been working on the Paritsky case with Scott Cohen, one of UCSJ's most influential political contacts. Scott was the executive assistant to Charles Percy, Illinois senator and chair of the powerful Senate Foreign Relations Committee. On a Friday afternoon, August 28, 1981, I got the call about Paritsky's arrest, and I immediately phoned Scott. Although it was late in the afternoon and Washington was shutting down for the weekend, Scott went right to the Soviet embassy and leveled an official protest on behalf of the Senate Foreign Relations Committee. UCSJ council heads urged activists, synagogues, and congressional offices to escalate activity. Still, Paritsky was sentenced to three years in a labor camp for defaming the Soviet State – Article 190-1 of the Soviet Criminal Code. At the trial, a policy inspector's testimony that Paritsky received too many visitors and packages from abroad revealed that he was actually punished for being a Zionist who had attracted attention from the West. Even after his release, he remained trapped in the Soviet Union until 1988.

We couldn't take our eyes off Ukraine. In those years, it was unquestionably more difficult to make direct contact with the activists from areas far from Leningrad and Moscow. Language was a barrier, as many activists in those areas didn't speak English. In addition, it was harder to reach people by phone in Ukraine. In the wake of Afghanistan and the anti-Jewish crackdowns, many refuseniks were legitimately concerned about passing information over the open lines to America. Yet we relied on information to determine where to send material help and to identify the most reliable contacts and those who needed the most aggressive publicity and advocacy. We needed a point person. Via one of our travelers, I sent a message to Natasha Khassina and she provided a name: Oleg Popov. Khassina said the authorities knew him as the most dangerous Zionist in Russia, a qualifying distinction.

Oleg Popov

Oleg Popov had a PhD in plasma physics from Moscow State University. He had gotten involved with the human rights movement, including the Moscow Helsinki Group and later the Moscow Group to Establish Trust.[8] He was a dissident and had been drawn into the Jewish movement.

Popov had precision-blade intuition about the quality of the data we needed. Though he knew the threat and that KGB disconnected the phone lines of refuseniks who used them for calls from the West, he insisted that I call him at his apartment in Moscow rather than book a messenger call. I assumed he did so because he simply refused to be cowed into submissiveness.

Systematically, he began monitoring cities outside of Moscow, especially Kiev; he collected data about emigration obstacles and refuseniks – their cases, issues, KGB house searches, demonstrations, arrests. Our weekly calls provided documentation and anecdotal evidence that needed to reach the West, including names of Kiev refuseniks who had put themselves on the front lines by signing appeals for help to America.

I taped the calls and faxed careful transcriptions to the UCSJ and CASJ network. Then I turned the information into press releases and letters to US legislators. Within weeks, the signatories on the Kiev appeals had been transformed from mere names to living and breathing people, struggling against the severe persecution of KGB. The calls with Popov produced an ever-expanding need for adopters and case advocacy. While he told me

---

8. The Moscow Group to Establish Trust was a counteroffensive by refuseniks and dissidents to oppose the Kremlin's propaganda-driven peace movement.

about the plight of Jews in Kiev and other cities, never did he speak about himself.

In the summer of 1981, KGB warned Popov that he could be arrested. In January 1982, KGB threatened to open a file against him, and the next month, KGB agents battered down the door of his apartment, terrifying his wife and baby. For six hours, agents searched the apartment, confiscating forty items, including a Bible, an issue of the newspaper *Israel Today*, Hebrew books and newspapers, postcards, and letters. In April, they disconnected his phone.

Popov had become KGB quarry.

Our first obligation was to support refuseniks and prisoners, especially those whose activity put themselves and their families in danger. By strengthening the strongest links in the chain, we could pull out even the weakest, most fragile links. So with Popov under pressure, Marillyn and I assigned his case to Representative Dick Durbin and to a synagogue in his congressional district.

On the night of Thanksgiving in 1982, the phone rang late at my home. Our guests had gone home, the dishes were done, and we had gone to bed. I jumped out of bed and dragged the phone into our closet so as not to disturb Lenny, who was sleeping. Someone must have been arrested. My heart started thumping in anticipation of bad news.

The receiver carried that distinctive tunnel sound that characterized overseas calls. I heard a voice, familiar but somehow different, laced with the exultation of freedom. It was Popov. He was in Vienna. The Soviets had given him ten days to get out of the country. I was elated, but I couldn't help but wonder who would inherit his role as my contact.

When Soviet authorities let Popov go, they exercised one of the options they used to get rid of troublemakers. If they didn't want to quarantine them in the gulag or in psychiatric institutions, they could dispose of them by giving them a visa. Popov was one of the lucky ones.

Popov sent me a packet from Vienna with lists of refuseniks, Jews who needed *vysov*s, refuseniks in the most severe financial need, and recommendations about who we could trust to distribute material assistance. There were also pleas for help for refuseniks who were putting their lives on the line.

UCSJ brought Popov to Washington for our Symposium on US-Soviet Human Rights, Dissent, and Arms Control the following May, and a few days later, he came to Chicago. Marillyn and I drove him to Decatur, Illinois, so he could meet Representative Durbin, who had adopted him and advocated for him.

For years to come, he called me every Thanksgiving Day. Only later did I learn what our phone calls meant to him: "Being in Moscow, I felt your presence and sympathy for me and my family every day. Your calls and talks encouraged me and many refuseniks. I felt proud and satisfied that I made my contribution to a common and noble cause and to draw your attention to their desperate situations."[9]

A black-and-white photo brought out by a tourist while Popov was still in the USSR contains a pictorial code laden with meaning. Taken in Kiev, the photo shows two young women seated on a park bench flanked by two men: one is fair, bearded, and bare-headed; the other, with a dark, sculpted beard, sports a beret. The first man is Popov. The second, Yasha Gorodetsky. Although I couldn't have deciphered it at first, the picture augured my path from the past to the future. It captures Popov with the man who would be his successor as my phone contact. The transition that I had worried so much about was made seamless by the two men without my involvement.

---

9.   Oleg Popov, letter to Pamela Braun Cohen.

CHAPTER 10

"Do Not Let Them Die in Soviet Russia," 1982–83

UCSJ Conference in Jerusalem

To counter the lack of awareness among American Jews of the bleak situation for Soviet Jews during those years, we desperately tried to bring to life the personalities and the struggles of refuseniks. They were not merely cases in a file cabinet or on a list. We heard their voices and identified with their struggle, even those we had never met.

My desk was littered with newsletters covered with my underlines, red-penciled exclamation marks, and notes. *Call Senator Percy; call Congressman Porter; call Congressman Ed Derwinskii about Kislik; write press release; send alerts to adopting synagogues urging letters and calls to the White House and State Department.*

I was increasingly involved in the desperate situation in the USSR. My waking hours were filled with talk of human rights, strategies, messenger calls, congressmen, publicity. But while my heart was in Moscow and Leningrad and Gorky, I wasn't living in those places. I was in Deerfield: a world of tennis matches and golf clubs.

Driving from the office to the grocery store, or waiting in the line of cars at Kipling school to pick up my kids, I was plunged back into my cushy world. What I saw as suburbia's self-imposed isolation and resulting apathy seemed a delusional fantasy, far from the reality of anti-Jewish oppression – present in every generation, and playing out now in the Soviet Union.

I was trying to operate in two mutually inconsistent worlds. How to connect them?

All too often, our fight felt like we were taking one step forward, two steps back. The Soviets were not giving ground.

Within just a few weeks' time, we had an avalanche of bad news. Refusenik Boris Factorovich, already threatened with arrest, was forcibly drafted into the army so the authorities could later use his military service as a pretext to refuse him an exit visa based on "access to military secrets." Lev Elbert, a refusenik for nine years, was arrested on the fabricated charge of drug possession.

Jewish dissident Alexander Podrabinek was put on trial. In Moscow, KGB broke into the refusenik kindergarten, terrorizing fifteen small children. KGB attacked Purim gatherings, broke into Ilya Essas's Talmud seminar, and forcibly dispersed a Torah class, taking refusenik Natalia Rosenshtein into custody. In Sverdlovsk, Lev Shefer and Vladimir Yelchin were tried and sentenced.

Arrests and KGB house searches intensified: KGB tore apart refuseniks' apartments, searching for Jewish and Zionist materials, going through every book, emptying every drawer, touching every personal item – destroying any illusion of privacy.

As the information continued to flow in, ever-increasing numbers of refuseniks were being condemned to the purgatory of refusal and harassment with no known limit, blocked from the only road that could lead to freedom.

It was in this climate of increasing anti-Jewish repression that Marillyn and I flew to Jerusalem for the third biennial UCSJ conference in Israel. As activists from London and Paris began checking in, the hotel lobby filled with the latest news from the USSR. Like any conference, the doors to the outside world closed, but the intensity of this event was nothing like other conferences. Before us was nothing less than the survival of Jews in the Soviet republics.

We had moments of gratification, like when Yosef Mendelevich, finally released, praised UCSJ's work over the past twelve years, sweet words for a group unused to such recognition. Preoccupied with the specter of the Kremlin, we spent our days and nights chipping away, little by little, at its facade. We had long briefing sessions with Israeli activists and government officials, trying to get a better fix on their sometimes diverging perspectives. Yaakov Roi, a historian from Tel Aviv University, and other academics spoke about Israeli-Soviet relations. In and out of briefing sessions, among our activists there was consensus, but between us and the Israeli government, there was no shared vision.

Our UCSJ activists debriefed what seemed like an endless number of newly arrived Jews who had left behind family members still in refusal. Now separated from husbands, wives, parents, children still held in the USSR, they were desperate for help getting them out. Grigory Kanovich, a recent émigré and former leader of the Leningrad Cultural Seminars, reported a chilling new twist to the effort to stop emigration. Officials had stopped responding to applications, thereby preventing applicants from reaching the stage of being refused. "Now in Russia," Kanovich sardonically quipped, "it's a great privilege to be a refusenik." In Moscow alone, an estimated ten thousand Jews had been waiting for over a year for answers to their applications, adding significantly to the number of those we termed waitniks.

I was interviewed by the Voice of Israel, Kol Yisrael, for a radio broadcast into the USSR. I spoke to Soviet Jews directly, assuring them they were no longer the "Jews of silence." Their courageous activity had made them visible. Their names were known, their attempts to apply were documented, and the restrictions barring their exit were monitored and publicized. They had captured the concern of the West, and especially the US Congress. And I told them that behind the Congress and all other activity stood UCSJ.

There were new faces and new voices at our sessions. Among them were Yuri Shtern and Alexander Shipov, young men who had just emigrated. In Moscow, both had started off in the dissident movement but then turned to the struggle for Jewish emigration. Now in Israel, they were trying to promote activity on behalf of refuseniks they had left behind. Shipov and Shtern wanted to create an independent movement, a center for the collection and distribution of information that could wrest some control of Israel's Soviet policy from the Lishka. They were young, smart, energetic, and motivated, natural partners for UCSJ, which had felt the lack of an activist pool in Israel. Soviet Jews deserved and required an independent grassroots voice in their homeland.

When Shtern and Shipov came to the United States seeking partners for their work, they met with members of the Establishment; they also attended the UCSJ Annual Meeting and then spread out to various local UCSJ councils. They were impressed by the complete dedication of UCSJ volunteers. Yuri told us, "Any group of people that talks Soviet Jewry during their lunch break is an organization we can work with." Along with Lynn in Long Island and Rita and the 35s, the large councils directed financial help to Shtern and Shipov's newly created Soviet Jewry Education and Information Center (SJEIC). Mendelevich would be brought in as chairman, and the organization remained closely connected to the American grassroots movement throughout its existence.

As part of the meeting, we traveled to Tekoa and Hebron to meet new Soviet immigrants. We went to Beersheba to hear from Shlomo Gazit, president of Ben Gurion University. A former head of military intelligence, Gazit explained to us the development of the Lishka as an outcropping of early intelligence activity. We drove to the nearly deserted, pristine town of Yamit, nestled along the Mediterranean; within a week, Yamit was to be bulldozed and given over to Egypt as part of the 1979 Israel-Egypt Peace Treaty. Though heartsick, I felt privileged to see it before it was destroyed.

We met with the sweet-faced, elderly mothers of Moscow refuseniks Judith Ratner and Alla Smeliansky; they were afraid they would never see their children and grandchildren again, and we tried to give them encouragement and hope. Under the photos I had taken of their daughters, published in CASJ's *Refusenik* newsletter, former refusenik Misha Edelman wrote: "Please, do not let them die in Soviet Russia."

Publicity was the first step to saving them.

Trauma at Home

There are times in all of our lives when everything stops. For our family, it was in August 1982, the first day of Scott's freshman year at Deerfield High School. I was at CASJ when Josh called: Scott had fallen out of our weeping willow tree and was lying on the ground. Josh had called 911. An ambulance was on its way.

I don't know how I drove home, but when I pulled up, Scott was unconscious under the tree. The paramedics were lifting him onto a stretcher. Josh was nearby; Brooke, in traumatic shock, looked on from the kitchen. Shaking in fear, holding against panic, I went in the ambulance to the hospital. Lenny raced in from the city and together we waited outside the emergency room. The surgeon reported that Scott had a cerebral hematoma and was bleeding internally. They were taking him up to surgery. One by one, friends appeared. A member of our Reform synagogue reached me in the waiting room, helplessly asking what we needed. Prayers. Please pray. We did the only thing we could do: we waited, watched, and mostly prayed.

Scott pulled through the surgery, but then we had days of hand-wringing anxiety until he regained consciousness. Contrary to the surgeon's conjecture, Scott showed no sign of brain damage. To Lenny and me, it seemed like a miracle. It was a gift from heaven, and it called for more than just saying thank you. In expression of gratitude, we kashered our home.

Poisoned Press

Accompanying what was happening at home was the fear of widespread potential calamity and violence in the Soviet Union, as the state media intensified its incendiary anti-Semitic operation. It generated an anti-Zionist propaganda campaign soaked in Jew-hatred that appeared in books, newspaper articles, so-called academic papers, and television programs. Cartoons and posters portrayed money-grubbing Jews with hooked noses dripping in Palestinian blood. Writing to me from Israel, Lev Utevsky, the former Leningrad refusenik who was an expert on refusenik resistance and Kremlin tactics, said, "It seems that only a lack of initiative (or perhaps the habit to wait for a directive from the government) prevents the Soviet people from making new pogroms."[1] CASJ's fax machine regularly churned out handwritten pages of Utevsky's incisive and detailed analyses that I depended on to steer our course.

Week after week, the state's anti-Semitic drumbeat sounded the crackdown on Jewish activity and identity. On October 23, 1982, the Communist Party newspaper, *Izvestia*, informed the Soviet public that the study of Hebrew language and Jewish culture were "fig leaves, covering unlawful actions."[2] The Kremlin's propagandist Lev Korneyev ignited Jew-hatred, characterizing Jews as a sinister fifth column inciting revolution inside the USSR. In one of the most viciously anti-Semitic books ever published – *Class Essence of Zionism*, published March 1, 1983 – Korneyev equated international Zionism with the anti-Soviet collaborators who helped Hitler seize power. In the newspaper *Komsomolskaya Pravda*, Korneyev wrote, "[the] meaning of Zionism is to turn every Jew, no matter where he lives, into an agent of the Jewish oligarchy, into a traitor to the country where he was born."[3] In all his works, Korneyev's message was that Israel

---

1.   Lev Utevsky, fax to Pamela Braun Cohen, 1982.
2.   Martin Gilbert, *Jews of Hope: The Plight of Soviet Jewry Today* (London: Macmillan, 1984), 194.
3.   Ibid., 116.

is only a part of the conspiracy; it is international Zionism that is a threat to all mankind. His warning to the Soviet public was that international Zionism was bent on the destruction of the USSR.

Class Essence of Zionism ushered in a KGB campaign that stepped up attacks against Jewish culture. My new contact in Leningrad, Yasha Gorodetsky, who along with other refuseniks formed the Leningrad Society for the Study of Jewish Culture, said that he had been summoned by KGB and warned to stop all cultural activity, "or else." Leonid Kelbert, a film director and refusenik from Leningrad, was warned by a senior official that KGB would henceforth tolerate no Jewish cultural activity. They told him that instead of nominal fifteen-day detentions, Jewish activity would be charged under the Criminal Code as anti-Soviet, carrying a far more serious penalty. To underscore their warning, KGB disconnected Gorodetsky's telephone and made his professional life so difficult that he was forced to resign from his teaching job.

A month later, on April 19–20, 1983, *Leningradskaya Pravda* published a sinister two-part article; its title translated as "Culture Smugglers." This anti-Semitic rant targeted refuseniks. Another article, published by one of the most powerful organizations in the USSR, the Leningrad Regional Committee of the Soviet Communist Party, turned accusations against the emigration movement: "We have Philistines, money-grubbers, consumers who strive to enrich themselves by any means. Soviet Jews emigrate to Israel to gain a 'moneybags paradise.'" In language reeking of espionage and collusion, it portrayed refuseniks as martyrs of international Zionism with "plans" and "tentacles" to insinuate "creeping 'cultural' infiltration into socialist countries with support from American senators, congressmen, and anti-Soviet organizations."[4]

The war of words opened a front against UCSJ and our tourists. In the "Culture Smugglers" article, UCSJ's president was accused of being a Zionist infiltrator. In lurid language typical of Soviet propaganda, Lynn was cast as a "character…well known in anti-Soviet Zionist circles." The author accused "Zionist emissaries," traveling to the USSR from the States in the guise of tourists, of bringing "instructions to renegades." These renegades, the article claimed, transmitted to the West "slander and tendentious materials" against the Soviet Union, among which was material

---

4.   Charles H. Fairbanks Jr., "Anti-Semitic Echoes Are Sounded in the USSR," *Wall Street Journal*, July 1, 1983.

about the "convicted criminal Evgeny Lein." Lein, released from exile in June 1982, was still without permission and a continuing target for authorities. The same article accused refusenik Aba Taratuta of being "a tool of foreign emissaries" and Gorodetsky, who testified at the Lein trial, of being one who "treads the path of Nationalism."[5]

All Jewish organizations being the same to an anti-Semite, the article managed to smear two groups by incorrectly identifying Lynn with the National Conference on Soviet Jewry. It claimed that Lynn conspired with well-known refuseniks to encourage mass migration from the USSR to make up the loss of thousands of Israelis killed in Lebanon.

The Martinov Papers

Yasha Gorodetsky was working to publicize the media's vilification campaign. On our calls, he filled my tape recorder with reports from Ivan Federovich Martinov, a non-Jewish Russian academic who wanted to bring a criminal case against Korneyev. Martinov was outraged by Korneyev's article alleging that two Israeli soldiers in Lebanon settled their argument about whether a Palestinian woman was pregnant with a boy or a girl by killing her and slitting open her stomach.

The Soviet prosecutor refused to hear Martinov's case, even though anti-Semitism was illegal and even punishable under the Soviet constitution. Martinov and Gorodetsky refused to back down, hoping to keep the spotlight on Korneyev by pouring information down my phone line to expose the Kremlin's rotting anti-Semitic core.

KGB reacted by trying to stop the reports from reaching the West. They threatened to arrest Gorodetsky and warned Martinov to cut ties with him. But Martinov went on the offensive. Calling attention to the anti-Semitism of the academic establishment, he refused his Candidate of Science degree. KGB then retaliated, threatening to cut off his access to publishers and block his contact with foreign colleagues. To out-maneuver his continued resistance, they threatened to institutionalize him in a psychiatric ward. To make sure he understood, the day after his meeting with KGB, the psychiatric hospital called him in for observation.

Meanwhile, despite *Izvestia*'s smear campaign against travelers, UCSJ councils continued to send in tourists to meet with refuseniks. International

---

5.   B. Kravsov, "Culture-Smugglers," *Leningradskaya Pravda*, April 19–20, 1983. Translated by Michael Sherbourne.

guarantees, careful briefings, and the state of US-Soviet relations reassured us that the Kremlin's interests precluded the arrest of an American. Our tourists, if they held themselves exactly to our briefings, would emerge from the Iron Curtain in safety.

So Marillyn and I sent in tourists to Gorodetsky with instructions to bring out the Martinov papers, the case against the Kremlin's anti-Semitic propaganda. Though Marillyn and I put on a confident show, there was no doubt it was risky, more for Gorodetsky and Martinov than for our tourists. Already under surveillance, the two could be tried for distributing information to the West that defamed the USSR. Or maybe worse. We waited. It was a long ten days.

Our travelers returned with the full dossier of the Martinov's papers. I rushed to have them translated into English. The lurid lies Martinov had documented were nothing less than a throwback to *The Protocols of the Elders of Zion*.

CASJ published the Martinov papers, entitled *Documentary Evidence of Anti-Semitism in the Soviet Union Today*, and printed up five hundred booklets that we distributed to the presidents of the Jewish organizational bureaucracy and to the regulars: the House, the Senate, the State Department, our friends at the Commission on Security and Cooperation in Europe (CSCE) – also known as the congressional Helsinki Commission – and the editorial boards of the major papers. Not only did it spread the word about the toxically anti-Semitic environment in the USSR, it offered the best protection we could muster for Martinov and Gorodetsky.

Although there was no response from other Jewish organizations, Congress reacted. In June, the House of Representative's Foreign Affairs Committee and the Helsinki Commission held hearings on Soviet anti-Semitism. Lynn testified on behalf of UCSJ, and members of Congress gave detailed statements based on our documentation. Importantly, they called out the names of KGB's refusenik targets. On the question of anti-Semitism, Assistant Secretary of State for Human Rights and Humanitarian Affairs Elliott Abrams directly accused Soviet leader Yuri Andropov: "It is quite clear there has been a tightening up in the Soviet Union on human rights questions in general in the last year. One can pretty well note that it coincides with the rise of Andropov." He went on to say, "Such broadcasts and books could not see the light of day without official approval."[6]

---

6.   Assistant Secretary of State Elliott Abrams, speaking on June 23 and 28, 1983, at the Hearings before the Subcommittee of Human Rights and International Organizations,

The media also started to pick up our news. The *Wall Street Journal* published an exposé of anti-Semitism in Soviet media. Thanks to media coverage and the House hearings, I could give an encouraging report to Gorodetsky and Martinov. The dangerous course they had undertaken was not in vain. Word was getting out.

"The Last Train Has Left the Station"

The death of Leonid Brezhnev in 1982 heralded the first change in Soviet leadership in eighteen years, and the Western press was rife with conjecture. American media outlets pushed the image of Andropov, a former KGB head, as a Scotch-drinking closet liberal. They remained determinedly oblivious to the fact that Andropov's accession was accompanied by a virtual shutdown of emigration and a crackdown on the Jewish and human rights movements. Secretary of State George Shultz, however, saw Andropov clearly: "He looked more like a cadaver than the just-interred Brezhnev, but his mental power filled the room. He reminded me of Sherlock Holmes's deadly enemy, Professor Moriarty, all brain in a disregarded body."[7]

Under Andropov, the Kremlin deployed a new strategy in its propaganda war. In April 1983, the Soviet news agency, TASS, announced the formation of a committee of prominent Soviet Jews to fight Zionism. The articles that subsequently appeared in the Soviet newspaper *Pravda* laid new bricks in the ideological base for the Kremlin's war against the Jews.

The Soviet Anti-Zionist Committee (AZC) was made up of thirty-seven Jews and headed by none other than General David Dragunsky. Decades earlier, Stalin had picked Dragunsky, a decorated World War II hero, to head a group of prominent Soviet Jews to endorse his plan for the mass deportation of Jews to Siberia. Fortunately, that plan had died along with Stalin. The 1970s found Dragunsky teaching in a military school that trained, among others, PLO terrorists. Now, in the 1980s, Dragunsky was heading up the AZC, along with his first vice-chairman, Samuel Zivs, a prominent member of the Association of Soviet Lawyers and an unsavory figure I would encounter several times in the future.

Committee of Foreign Affairs, US House of Representatives, and the Commission on Security and Cooperation in Europe.

7. George P. Shultz, *Turmoil and Triumph: My Years as Secretary of State* (New York: Charles Scribner's Sons, 1993).

Other treacherous Jews on the AZC included Moscow's chief rabbi, Yakov Fishman, and his successor, Rabbi Adolf Shayevich. Fishman was one of a line of KGB-appointed rabbis who served the Soviets instead of his people. His complicity with the state made him a corrupted symbol of Jewish religious leadership. In 1982 Fishman closed down a Talmud class for elderly Jews. His statement about Zionism dripped with the language of Kremlin ideologues: "I discovered long ago that so-called Zionists are rich persons who do not go to live in Israel but build in Israel factories and plants for taking advantage of poor Jews."[8] Shayevich, on a 1984 trip to the United States – the first such trip of a Soviet religious leader in eight years – categorically denied reports of persecution and harassment of Soviet Jews. He stated, "No one interferes with the study of Hebrew groups. But there are such groups that are engaged in anti-Soviet activity under cover of studying Hebrew."[9] Feeding the propaganda machine back in Moscow, he characterized a demonstration against anti-Semitism on Fifth Avenue as anti-Soviet.

The truth was that the Soviets only tolerated Jews if they collaborated with KGB against their fellow Jews. The members of AZC were mouthpieces of the Kremlin, the court Jews through whom governments had historically manipulated and ultimately destroyed Jewish communities and Jewish life. Years later, after the fall of the USSR, I expected that the Jewish Establishment and religious organizations would demand Shayevich's immediate dismissal. Soviet Jews, starved for Torah and Judaism, Jewish dignity, and connection to Israel, required a new form of rabbinic leadership. They needed leaders and scholars whose hearts and minds were sculpted by Torah ethics, uncontaminated by deception and betrayal. Entrenched in his role as the chief rabbi of Moscow in the Choral Synagogue, however, an unrepentant Shayevich carried the tainted legacy of Dragunsky beyond communism and into the next century.

After its formation, the AZC launched a new public disinformation campaign with a press conference proclaiming that all Jewish families had been reunified and everyone who wanted to leave had already done so.

---

8. Drachman, *Challenging the Kremlin*, 99.
9. Ibid.

In the words of veteran Kremlin press spokesman, Victor Louis, "The last train has left the station."[10]

AZC chairmen Dragunsky and Zivs accused international Zionists of fabricating evidence that Jews were refused permission to emigrate. Brandishing letters from abroad, Zivs accused Zionists of sending thousands of unsolicited *vysovs*, the Kremlin-required invitations to emigrate, to Jews who didn't want to leave the country. The significant number of unused *vysovs*, he claimed, was a statistic used by Zionists to fuel their anti-Soviet propaganda. According to the AZC, everyone who wanted to leave had already gone.

On a beautiful spring morning, while I was making coffee and waiting for the kids to come down for breakfast, I saw the AZC's lies splashed all over the morning paper. An hour later at Chicago Action, I started calling refuseniks. They were outraged by the sheer audacity of the lies. It was a crippling blow to the movement.

How, I wondered, could the Kremlin think they could get away with such prevarication? Numbers didn't lie. Half a million Jews had already taken the first steps to leave and were either unable to apply or were refused because of the government's deliberate systemic obstacles. The Kremlin had thrown down a new gauntlet. We needed to act quickly. On an emergency conference call, the UCSJ board agreed to place an ad in the *New York Times*. Large councils would swallow the cost. Bearing UCSJ's logo and Lynn Singer's name as president, the ad was designed to challenge the Kremlin and send a message to America not to be deceived.

On Sunday, June 12, the *New York Times* ran our full-page ad with a banner quote from Hitler's *Mein Kampf*: "If you tell a lie often enough, people will believe it." We invited the AZC to travel to meet the thousands of separated families in Israel and the United States, and then we hit back:

> You say that almost all of the Jews who want to leave the USSR have already gone.
>
> We say that hundreds of thousands would leave if given the opportunity. In fact, more than 750,000 have begun to apply for exit visas by asking for invitations from Israel, and only 260,000 of these people have emigrated.

---

10. "Soviet Jews: The Last Train Leaves," *Sydney Morning Herald*, January 7, 1984.

The dispute is easy to solve.

Persuade your government to throw open the doors....[11]

Our friends in Congress also stepped up. Congressmen John Porter, Tom Lantos, and Ben Gilman held a press conference, refuting the Soviets' absurd allegation. Porter, Lantos, and Gilman were among those in the House most committed to the issue. Porter was my congressman. He and Lantos were cochairmen of the Human Rights Caucus[12] in the House of Representatives, and Lantos was one of the people Marillyn had brought to the United States on student visas after the Holocaust. The connections between us were close, and the caucus moved quickly into action.

Then TASS parried, quoting the vice chair of the AZC: "In...fact, it was the three Congressmen who were lying."[13] CASJ's *Refusenik* newsletter reported another TASS statement: "Soviet emigration laws accord with relevant international regulations. Therefore, the American Congressmen's distortion on statements by the Soviet Anti-Zionist Committee is but an episode of another anti-Soviet campaign."[14]

Ben Gilman, the ranking member of the congressional Post Office and Civil Service Committee, using our evidence of Soviet non-delivery of mail, disproved AZC's allegations. The committee's year-long investigation produced more than two hundred pieces of evidence of Soviet interception of *vysovs* and correspondence from Israel in violation of the Helsinki Final Act and Universal Postal Convention. The Soviets were closing down the process by denying people the right to even apply.

---

11. Advertisement, *New York Times*, June 12, 1983.

12. On a trip to the USSR in 1982, Lynn and Representative Porter had come up with the idea of creating a bipartisan Human Rights Caucus in the House of Representatives whose goal was to coordinate efforts to help individuals and groups who were being denied basic human rights. Albeit without the status of a congressional committee, it nevertheless served as the operational human rights center in Congress and became an official home for UCSJ's cases and the documentation of human rights violations. Its mandates were to marshal human rights support in the Congress, influence the administration, and impact European parliaments. It was to maintain a file of human rights cases, publish a newsletter, and hold briefings. Porter had met with Secretary of State George Shultz to focus the Reagan administration on the importance of the issue.

13. *Alert* magazine, July 18, 1983.

14. "TASS Calls Congressmen Liars," *The Refusenik*, August 1983.

UCSJ councils worked the media to counter the fallacious claim that all Jews who wanted to leave had already left. A *Washington Times* report rebutted the AZC's contention, explaining that "As many as 500,000 have [either] applied for emigration and have been turned down or are unable to apply."[15] From Jerusalem, David Shipler wrote a painful description in the *New York Times* of aging parents in Israel whose children in the USSR were prevented from joining them. He concluded "that this is a deliberate Soviet policy to break the will and spirit of Soviet Jewry."[16] At a demonstration in San Francisco, five hundred Bay Area Council activists waved computer printout files naming the thousands of refusenik families they were tracking. Each name gave the lie to Soviet assertions.

I wondered at the polarity between Jews who resisted and these Jews of the AZC who capitulated. Did Dragunsky lose a minute of sleep? Did he ever have a moment of remorse? Perhaps Zivs had been brainwashed when he claimed:

> "Victims of Soviet anti-Semitism" and "fighters for human rights" touted by the Western mass media are persons who have openly flouted and violated Soviet laws and the norms of socialist conduct.... Unable to find objective facts and actual instances...to prove their point, they are all the more eager to engage in all manner of fabrication and provocation. They presented drug addict Yulian Edelshtein as an "active fighter for the rights of Soviet Jews and for their right to emigrate to Israel."[17]

The arrival of Boris, the nephew of David Dragunsky, in Highland Park at this time, when few Jews were getting out, struck me as being conspicuously coincidental – especially when he showed up at the same synagogue Marillyn, Betty, Linda, and Lenny and I attended. I could only presume that such a close relative of the AZC chairman, a highly placed Communist party apparatchik, got his visa on condition of some payback. KGB had

---

15. Glenn Emery, "Mail Intercept Stymies Soviet Jews Waiting for Invitations to Emigrate," *Washington Times*, June 9, 1983.

16. Bernard Weintraub, "The Kremlin Is Said to Seize Mail from the U.S. for Jews," *New York Times*, June 9, 1983.

17. Samuel Zivs, foreword to *The Real Truth: Profiles of Soviet Jews* (Moscow: Raduga, 1986).

informers in Chicago surveilling immigrants from Communist-dominated Poland, so it was conceivable that KGB might plant a mole inside one of our councils. Boris expressed interest in working with Chicago Action, but I deflected all of his attempts.

Some twenty years later, Boris and I were thrown together at a Friday night dinner, at a time when we were separately discovering the Judaism that had been lost to each of us. He knew the world of the USSR that I knew, and I decided to store away my previous unease with him, preferring instead to reminisce about the "bad old days." He told me that before he left, at a family dinner at his infamous uncle's home in Moscow, he raised the issue of his own emigration. Like a guillotine, Dragunsky fired off a judgment, swift and uncompromising. He'd have Boris thrown into a psychiatric institution. Boris wasn't going anywhere. He would die in the Soviet Union. But somehow, Boris did get permission. Many years later, he spoke to his uncle in Moscow just before he died. The infamous anti-Zionist David Dragunsky conceded he was at peace with Boris's emigration. He admitted, "I am from the generation of liars and prostitutes."

He did know who he was.

Finding a Lost Connection

The nineteenth blessing of the Shemoneh Esrei prayer speaks against heretics. The blessing was instituted after the Roman destruction of the Second Temple, as a response to the threats of Jews who used their political power to oppress other Jews and slander them to the Roman government. The prayer was incorporated to warn the people of the danger that faced them, and it has been consistently relevant: "And as for slanderers, let there be no hope; and may all wickedness perish in an instant." The members of the Soviet Anti-Zionist Committee were slanderers, slaughtering truth and betraying their own people.

Few Jews in the USSR knew the Shemoneh Esrei. Neither did I. Like our Soviet brethren, many American Jews had lost the connection to Judaism. But the difference between us was striking. In the USSR, their knowledge of God and Judaism had been forcibly purged by the state, and now Jews were struggling to find it and reintroduce it into their lives at great cost. In America, for many of us, our connection to God and Torah had been thrown overboard on the ships that carried our grandparents to a new world. We American Jews didn't feel the exquisite yearning for a lost inheritance. We didn't even know what we were missing. My generation found other paths of meaning outside Judaism to repair a broken world and address contemporary social issues. But, as I came to realize, the essential truths about purposeful Jewish identity and its imperative for survival were obscured for many in my generation.

For Soviet Jews in the movement, there was good and bad, right and wrong. There were heroes and villains and an evil empire. There were rights that had to be guaranteed to individuals under international laws and covenants. Confrontation with the black-and-white nature of these truths triggered a change in me, and in many of my colleagues.

Most Soviet citizens cowed to the will of the tyrants, with the AZC being one of the most visible examples. To keep their positions in scientific institutes and membership in the Communist Party, "homo-Sovieticus" would abandon moral principle and publicly strip a colleague of his scientific degrees for applying to emigrate. They would inform on neighbors or withhold exit permits, make an arrest, or drive KGB's black Volga in the same way World War II–era Europeans had run the trains and gone about their daily lives as Jews were shipped to their death.

Freedom was the conscience that compelled a person to resist authority or social conformity, and the only freedom in the USSR was among the dissidents and refuseniks. Both Altman and Sharansky said they experienced that freedom to resist in rat-infested frigid prison cells. Drop by drop, their inner freedom, freedom to resist seductive social norms and challenge political and social conformity, enabled the freedom to explore their Jewish identity and question what it means to be a Jew – it all permeated my consciousness, changing my worldview and eventually altering my life.

Against this backdrop, UCSJ activists were trying to live our everyday lives, though with an intensity driven by the monumental struggle of the refuseniks. Lenny and I still laugh when I remind him of the time we were alone on a weekend getaway. We awoke to an especially romantic setting, and I turned to him and said, "Lenny, did I tell you that Lev Blitshtein went to visit Ida Nudel in Siberia?"

That's the way it was.

Their lives were superimposed on our own. The scribbled entries in our calendars were a multicolored tapestry that wove together car-pool schedules and baseball practices with weekly conference calls, birthday parties with messenger calls, piano lessons with trial dates. There was our family. There was Soviet Jewry. For most of us, there wasn't time or space for much else.

Captured on Film

A critical aspect of UCSJ's advocacy was raising the level of consciousness in the public arena, in the media, in Congress, in the international trade sector. Our opportunity to do that in Israel was marginal. But then Beit Hatfutsot, Israel's Diaspora Museum (now called Museum of the Jewish People), announced an international photographic competition called the Jewish Heritage in the Eye of the Camera.

Conspicuously absent from the museum's extensive exhibits of Jewish Diaspora communities was an exhibit on the Soviet Jewish refusenik community. The competition offered us a chance to publicize, in Israel, the refusenik struggle to repatriate. CASJ's Betty Kahn, a crack amateur photographer, submitted pictures of refuseniks taken during a 1980 trip. Competing against more than forty-four hundred photographs from forty-four countries, Betty's pictures won.

Captured on film and exhibited for throngs of Israeli and international visitors were images of refuseniks like Pavel Abramovich. Pictured seated, with his characteristically shrugged shoulders, Pavel was identified as a Moscow refusenik, Hebrew teacher, organizer of the Jewish Cultural Symposium, and founder of the Moscow Gan, the kindergarten for refusenik children. Fired from his job in 1971, Abramovich had been told that his application to emigrate would not be reviewed until 1985, and he was warned that if he did not stop teaching Hebrew, he would be imprisoned. Another photograph featured Natasha Khassina, her intensity jumping out of the picture. That caption read:

> Natasha Khassina, Moscow "Guardian Angel" of Jewish Prisoners of Conscience…carries on the work of Ida Nudel, exiled to Siberia for her efforts on behalf of imprisoned Refuseniks. Khassina continues to work for her exiled and jailed friends despite repeated detentions and beatings by KGB. Natasha and her husband have been denied permission since 1976, in violation of the Helsinki Accords, which allows reunification of families.

Betty's photos exposed the plight of Soviet Jewry to a mostly oblivious Israeli public. The timing was good. Abramovich feared he was going to be thrown out of his job and then accused of parasitism. As for Khassina, KGB hadn't returned her official identity card after they took it during a search of her apartment. She could have been arrested at any time for not having it. We wanted to make it clear that if the Soviets arrested either of them, it would cost them international credibility.

I was especially worried about Khassina. She had taken on Ida Nudel's role after Ida was arrested in 1978 and sentenced to exile in Siberia for hanging a poster on her balcony that read "KGB, give me my Israel." Ida was known as the "guardian angel of prisoners of conscience" both in the States and in the Kremlin, and now Khassina had taken on that responsibility, supporting prisoners of conscience and distributing material assistance to refuseniks.

The suffering of the only Jewish woman sentenced to exile in Siberia was particularly heart-wrenching, and we could never let her out of the public eye. Various refuseniks had traveled thousands of kilometers to visit Ida in exile in the far-flung, frozen steppes of Siberia. They described Krivosheino, the grimy impoverished village, and the mud-drenched road that led past shacks with boarded windows. Kilometers beyond the foreboding forest was a barrack that housed the crudest, roughest of Russian men. They were criminals, murderers who had been sentenced to exile. One of Ida's visitors, refusenik and former prisoner Sender Levinson, found the tiny Jewish woman in that barrack, behind an unlocked door. She was the only woman in the barrack. After a day's labor in the hellish peat bogs, the convicts drank anything available: eau de cologne, furniture polish. There was one shared bathroom. The walls were filthy. Drunken vomit spotted the floor; the water from the faucet ran with rust. Ida slept with a knife under her pillow. Sender brought her everything he could carry, but mostly, he brought her words. All he could tell her was that people were doing everything they could to have her released. Former prisoners like Sender loved Ida like children love their mother and wanted to give her the strength she used to give to them.

One day, Rita Eker called me from London. Ida needed a warm coat. In the next tourist's suitcase was my sheepskin coat. The coat traveled from Chicago to Moscow to Siberia. I never knew how she knew it came from me, but after she was released, I received a letter from her, thanking me, and I framed it.

How could Ida's torment be dismissed from our consciousness? It was increasingly difficult to go out with friends and be satisfied with small talk when my mind was consumed with the next arrest, the next trial. What did it mean, after all, when we said, "never again"? What did we do for Ida *today*? We had to publicize. We had to disseminate. One by one, we all began to lose our friends. Some even began to lose their marriages.

UCSJ's major congressional activity, the Congressional Call to Conscience Vigil, was delivering five statements a week onto the floor of the Congress and was to culminate with "Ida Nudel Week," timed to her fiftieth birthday. The attention of the US Congress was on the Siberian town of Krivosheino and on Ida Nudel.

CHAPTER 11

The Dark Years, 1984–86

The War on Hebrew

By 1984 the Kremlin's campaign of repression, begun in the early 1980s, erupted into a sweeping and terrifying wave of intimidation. UCSJ was working actively on the cases of twenty-four known Jewish prisoners of conscience. Of them, eleven had been arrested and four sentenced in one year alone. Friends and family of the accused were under intense KGB scrutiny, forced to submit to rigorous, humiliating apartment searches and called in to incriminate other Jews. Beatings and threats brought back fears of Stalin's reign of terror.

It looked like the Kremlin was going to shut down the Hebrew teachers and Jewish activity once and for all. The Hebrew language was anathema to Kremlin authorities, and yet, the right to teach, learn, and speak Hebrew was guaranteed under Soviet law and was promoted as a platform of the Communist Party.

Not only was the right to learn cultural and national languages legitimized under Soviet law, it was also enshrined under the Helsinki accords. But to the Soviets, Hebrew was an exception, a component of Zionism, and thus a dangerous underpinning of national identity. It had to be rooted out. So much for legal guarantees.

The war against Hebrew had deep roots. Under Stalin, Hebrew was considered subversive, and anyone connected to it was hauled off to the camps. As an exception, Hebrew was taught in a few top universities to future secret or foreign service agents or to Christian or Islamic leaders – just not to Jews.

Except for a Hebrew-Russian dictionary printed in 1963, no Hebrew books or books on Judaism had been published in the Soviet Union for more than fifty years. No books, no newspapers. Nothing. In a country of more than one hundred nationalities, the sixteenth largest had no right to books in the language of their fathers, their people.

Black humor was a hallmark of the Jewish world of refusal. Refusenik jokes could encapsulate all of reality in a few peppery phrases. This joke was common at the time:

> An elderly man was sitting on a Moscow park bench, study-ing Hebrew grammar, when a KGB agent passed by. The agent looked over the man's shoulder and asked, "What is this book with strange writing?"
>
> When told that this was the language of Israel, the agent said, "But at your time of life, you are not likely to go to Israel."
>
> "Alas," said the old man, "you are right. However, they speak Hebrew in paradise, too."
>
> "How do you know you will turn up in paradise?" asked the KGB agent. "Suppose you go to hell?"
>
> "Well," replied the old man, thoughtfully, "I already know Russian."

Authorities had already been turning the Jewish movement into a criminal activity, as when KGB planted hashish and a pistol in Zubko's Kiev apart-ment and then sentenced him to four years. Spreading their net around Hebrew teachers, the Soviets were criminalizing Hebrew by the same means, planting "evidence" they could later discover in searches.

In Estonia, refusenik Hebrew teacher Aleksander Kholmiansky had been arrested in July 1984 on the fabricated charge of possessing a gun that had been planted in his parents' apartment. Between eighty and one hundred unofficial refusenik Hebrew teachers protested to the Supreme Soviet against the systematic elimination of Hebrew.

But the criminalization process was underway. By fall, the police searched the Moscow apartment of Hebrew teacher Yuli Edelstein and "found" narcotics that had been planted. The future Speaker of the Israeli Knesset was convicted and sentenced to three years of labor camp. KGB continued to search a network of refuseniks' apartments, searching for drugs to create links to the Edelstein case but instead finding Hebrew books, cassettes, and *vysovs* from Israel. Meanwhile, the iconic representation of refusenik Hebrew teachers, Josef Begun, was serving out his third sentence for his efforts to obtain official recognition of the Hebrew language and the right to teach it. The threats kept up: stop teaching or face exile. Ari Volvovsky, Victor Fulmacht, Vladimir Kuravsky, Vladimir Magarik, and Boris Teplitsky, all received this warning.

Away from the spotlight of Moscow's foreign embassies and the Western press bureaus, KGB was moving through Ukraine with vengeance. In Odessa, the boxer Yaakov Mesh was arrested on trumped-up charges and so viciously beaten in prison that, fearing his death, authorities released him to avoid the publicity in the West. Also in Odessa, Yakov Levin was sentenced to three years in prison on charges of anti-Soviet slander for circulating Jewish religious materials. His future father-in-law, Mark Nepomniashy, was arrested for anti-Soviet slander, and Mark's wife Ida Nepomniashy was warned.

In Kiev, Hebrew teacher Iosif Berenshtein was given three years in a labor camp for allegedly resisting the police. He too was brutally beaten and stabbed, resulting in deep facial wounds and the loss of sight in one eye.

In Chernivtsi, Leonid Schreier and Yakov Rosenberg were arrested and sentenced for anti-Soviet slander. Searches, threats of subversion, defamations, beatings. The pandemic of accusation spread to Moldova, in Tiraspol, Kishinev, and Bendery.

Jewish activists were under attack in Russia as well. Roald "Alec" Zelichenok was warned to stop teaching under threat of arrest, a threat the authorities made good on. Phones were disconnected. Two dozen Jews were called in by the police and threatened they would lose their jobs unless they gave up their plans to emigrate.

The anti-Semitic media justified the crackdown. A Leningrad television program identified refuseniks by name and accused them of engaging in Zionist subversion. In Moscow, a program equated Zionism with Nazism.

My phone rang day and night. There were ever more arrests, and those arrested were tried and sentenced. We felt increasing pressure to get the information out and to protest. We projected the message to the Kremlin that their reign of terror was undermining their political and economic interests. UCSJ pounded the State Department and the White House with demands for action.

Condemning the accelerating campaign in the strongest possible terms, the United States called on the Soviet authorities to end it immediately. Washington urged the Kremlin to live up to the human rights commitments undertaken as a signatory to the Helsinki Final Act and the Concluding Document agreed to at the follow-up meeting in Madrid in 1983.

But every new day brought a fresh avalanche of challenges. Each caller reported new arrests, new threats, new house searches. One by one, every act of repression demanded that our council leaders engineer another high-level response to the Soviet embassy and the Kremlin. We turned to our grassroots advocates, the refusenik adopters – physicists, synagogues, families of children who had twinned bar or bat mitzvahs with refusenik kids. They mounted postcard and telephone campaigns aimed at their congressional representatives, urging them to issue protests to the Soviet embassy or make formal statements from the floor of the House of Representatives. We pressed the State Department to issue statements and protests to the Soviet foreign ministry. In addition, we hit the newspapers, the broadcast media, industrialists seeking trade with Moscow, Jewish organizations; the list went on and on.

My desk was piling high with incoming and outgoing faxes and memos of emergency actions: calling adopters to urge action, updating refusenik case sheets, faxing information to synagogues on their refusenik cases, transcribing my phone calls to refuseniks, drafting reports detailing violations for congressmen or the Helsinki Commission, writing press releases, organizing media events. There was never enough time. The office clamored with volunteers, but by a long shot, there was more demand than we could meet. We could barely keep up before the next call brought more bad news.

In those years, it was impossible to leave the worry and pressure at the office. I'd leave feeling that my face was frozen tight. Seeing my kids' faces instantly melted my tension, and I threw myself into our busy life at home. There were dinners to make and homework to supervise. It was my world, and I was so grateful for it. I had our children and our parents, and my husband wasn't in labor camp. But try as I might, I couldn't establish definitive boundaries.

Ari Volvovsky

In spite of steady repression of Hebrew teachers, I was able to maintain contact with Ari Volvovsky in Moscow by phone and mail from our first meeting in 1978. Those exchanges certainly impacted my life and my family's, perhaps even more than his. When he asked me for *The Book of Our Heritage* by Eliahu Kitov, I ordered two, one for him and one for me. When he asked me to send books on kashrut, I asked Lenny, "if Ari Volvovsky is going to keep the laws of kashrut – in Gorky – how could we not in Deerfield?" For decades, he didn't know that among his hundreds of students was a Jew in faraway Deerfield.

In January 1980, Volvovsky was expelled from Moscow. KGB gave him seventy-two hours to leave for internal exile in Gorky. Just as refuseniks predicted, authorities were getting rid of undesirables before the Moscow Olympics. They had quarantined him in Gorky, away from the media, his students, and the refusenik community.

In Gorky, he still received my messenger calls and letters. His mail to me managed to arrive, some with inspiring messages. When we decided to twin the bar and bat mitzvahs of our children, Scott and Kira, he wrote to Scott:

> Today the…right to choose is before you.… One way is the way
> of Torah and commandments.…The other is the way of growing
> apart from…Judaism. It is all in your hand and G-d will give
> you the strength and courage to choose the right way.… On this
> important day, we should not forget our brothers and sisters
> who sacrificed their lives for the existence of our nation and for
> the establishment of our State, Israel.… We should not forget
> our people in the Diaspora who cannot live in freedom, and it is
> our holy responsibility to help them with all our power.

Scott and Kira were the future of our people, but one was in Deerfield, the other, locked inside the Soviet Union.

Volvovsky's isolation gave KGB an advantage. They could make him disappear for days before we knew what happened and could mount a reaction. My fears materialized in the spring of 1980. Mila came to the Gorky post office to take my messenger call. She told me Ari had gone to Kishinev to celebrate Israel's Independence Day with other refuseniks. He hadn't been seen for more than a week. Though the militia denied having him in custody, he had in fact disappeared behind the walls of the Kishinev prison. I fired off a battery of alerts to the UCSJ regulars in the government and reached Scott Cohen, who immediately left the Senate office building and went to the Soviet embassy to issue a demarche. The Soviets backed down. Volvovsky was released. But that was only round one.

They made their next move in 1984. Six of his former Hebrew students were picked up and pressured to substantiate KGB's accusation that Volvovsky was indoctrinating them with Zionist propaganda and inciting anti-Soviet activities.

The need to generate publicity to protect Volvovsky triggered a wave of council-inspired media events. In downtown Highland Park, Volvovsky Day brought out a concerned community. Television cameras filmed children launching hundreds of colorful helium-filled balloons, each emblazoned with Ari Volvovsky's name. CASJ's actions were a microcosm of the grassroots activities throughout the United States and England.

Then, after another search of his apartment, Soviet police turned up a large quantity of Jewish books, including a copy of Leon Uris's *Exodus*. On June 26, 1985, he was arrested.

After months of pretrial isolation, he was to stand trial in October. I asked Gorodetsky to go to the Moscow courtroom to be our eyes and ears.

We knew the outcome. The only question was the length of the prison term.

Gorodetsky reported back in a messenger call. In the courtroom, before those who condemned him, in the country that had stigmatized Jews for centuries, he identified himself with his Hebrew name, Ari, and asked for a translator to conduct his defense in Hebrew, the language for which he was being tried, the language of his people and the Jewish State. I was told that my correspondence was among the evidence used in the courtroom. He was sentenced to three years for teaching Hebrew, convicted of anti-Soviet agitation and propaganda.

But I wasn't finished yet.

In Lima, Ohio, during our visit with Lenny's parents for the Fourth of July weekend, a telephone call interrupted our game of Rummikub. It was Tom Needles, a California congressman's foreign affairs assistant who was working with me on Volvovsky's case. He had a problem. A California woman, while visiting Moscow, was hit by a troika crossing a street and had been hospitalized. Her husband was already on a flight to Moscow. But the American embassy had closed for the holiday and Tom couldn't reach anyone from the embassy to meet the husband at the airport. Could

I be of assistance? I told him that of course I could arrange for help. I called Moscow refusenik Leonid Stonov, who magnanimously agreed to meet the distraught husband and deliver him to the hospital. When Needles called back, he asked, was there anything he could do for me?

Well, yes, actually, there was. Could his boss arrange for President Reagan to send a letter to Ari Volvovsky at the labor camp where he was imprisoned?

Twenty years later, when I saw Laura Bialis's film *Refusenik*, I learned the outcome of that request when Ari himself told the story.

He had been ordered to the office of the commandant of the labor camp. He expected to be interrogated for some manufactured infraction of the prison regime. To his surprise, the commandant asked whether President Reagan was Volvovksy's friend. Volvovsky demurred, with a shrug of his shoulders: "Well, if President Reagan wants to be my friend, I don't mind."

Volvovsky was released from prison camp early. Within a few months, in December 1987, he received permission to leave.

Resistance and Protest

In the midst of those dark years, refuseniks were confronting a tidal wave of intimidation and suppression, and we felt it every day, in and out of our offices. The world's most fearsome nuclear power had mobilized its militia and secret police to crush the Jewish movement. Even physical violence against Jews was sanctioned. Authorities zeroed in on Purim celebrations and *shpiels*, the comical theatrical sketches that accompanied the holiday. Vladimir Kislik was arrested after leaving a Purim party. The film director Leonid Kelbert was imprisoned for two weeks for staging a private performance of the play *Masada* in Riga, Latvia.

The Soviets were intent on stamping out Judaism. Officials told this explicitly to Sharansky after he lit Chanukah candles in his prison cell and then was sent back to the punishment cell he had just left. However, the Kremlin underestimated the tenacity of Jewish resistance. Jews have held on for four thousand years. The memory of Auschwitz burned. The movement was showing its mettle.

It was war. The Soviets moved. The refuseniks resisted, and so did we.

The Union and the European grassroots movements watched and reacted, waiting for the Kremlin's next response. It was becoming increasingly difficult for us in the West to see beneath the blanket KGB was using to suffocate the Soviet Jewish resistance movement. It was more and more dangerous for activists to pass on information, but from cryptically worded telephone messages and letters, we understood refuseniks were resisting. Activists continued to monitor arrests and refusals. Over open lines, two beacons of the movement, Professor Alexander Lerner in Moscow and Aba Taratuta in Leningrad, gave us information about arrests, persecution, the situation with prisoners. Their prominence didn't guarantee their safety, but it did offer some level of protection against the Soviets. At least, we hoped.

Newer refuseniks without name recognition in the West might have been legitimately reluctant to play such a role. In the face of arrests and repression, new leaders had to emerge, but who were they? What were their concerns? Little by little I started to see new names: Salmon, Nilva, Sud, Yusefovich, Rochlyn, Akhiezer. Something unmistakably vibrant was coming out of Leningrad through a network of young Jewish activists led by Grigory Vasserman, who worked closely with Gorodetsky. There were other names, too, but Vasserman's came up again and again. I was intrigued. He seemed to be an engine driving new ideas and activities. He had become religious – which was in itself an act of resistance – but his behavior didn't conform to that of other religious activists, some of whom, it seemed to me at the time, justified inaction by casting the full burden and responsibility of history onto God alone. Confident in the power of the Almighty, Vasserman didn't seem to eschew man's duty to resist oppression.

Messenger calls to Yasha Gorodetsky brought evidence of the Kremlin's intention to repress the Jewish movement at any cost. We harnessed every resource to urge the Reagan White House and the State Department to express their outrage in the strongest possible terms. But human rights abuses were just one of a number of factors contributing to tense US-Soviet relations, especially after Russia downed a South Korean airline that killed more than 250 people. Reagan, who saw the Soviet Union as the evil empire, was in a balancing act of trying to be tough on the USSR while also avoiding a Soviet arms buildup and military confrontation.

With presidential elections ahead, Lynn pushed the platform committees of both parties to commit to supporting Soviet Jewry. UCSJ's South Florida Conference on Soviet Jewry staged a three-round boxing match with fighter Joel Levin on behalf of Yaakov Mesh, the refusenik boxer who had been arrested and seriously beaten. The SSSJ and the Long Island Committee for Soviet Jewry held a rally at the Soviet mission to the United Nations during which 120 rabbis and nearly two hundred protesters were arrested. Rabbi Avi Weiss, chairman of the SSSJ, was insistent, describing a spiritual genocide in Russia aimed at the Jewish people. His message to the Kremlin was, no more business as usual, and to the White House, we want action now.

Looking for new strategies, we adopted the methodology of the civil rights movement and turned to civil disobedience. In May 1985, UCSJ's councils coordinated acts of civil disobedience at Soviet consulates in Washington, New York, and California. Twenty-five rabbis, adorned in prayer shawls and carrying six Torah scrolls, deliberately encroached the legal limits protecting the Soviet embassy in Washington, DC. They were searched, handcuffed, arrested by Washington police, and taken away in paddy wagons.

Appeals from Leningrad

Much of my time during those years was spent furiously transcribing increasingly urgent protests and appeals that Yasha Gorodetsky fired off on our calls.

Typically, refuseniks' collectively signed letters were directed to their own government, calling attention to their violations of Soviet and international law. This new battery of open letters to the West was different. They were written to American and Israeli Jews, accusing them of being impervious to the plight of Soviet Jewry and of being lulled into inaction by Western comfort. These letters, intentionally shocking in their confrontational nature, urged American Jews to come to the defense of their Soviet counterparts.

In 1984, Gorodetsky dictated one of the refuseniks' first collectively signed letters to the Jews of the West. In this letter and many that followed, the signatories made no pretense of masking their smoldering contempt for the American Jewish Establishment's complacency. The 1984 letter was addressed to about a hundred prominent Jewish personalities and Establishment leaders: heads of rabbinic organizations, elected officials, writers, journalists, actors, artists, scientists, corporation heads, heads of professional and human rights organizations, and Soviet apologists. It was also addressed to the media, naming television news anchors and newspaper editors. The letter was signed by about fifty refuseniks, all of them well-known activists, from Leningrad, Moscow, Riga, Odessa.

The letter was openly confrontational, opening with "We address to you our words of accusation and trust."

> We call on you, the Jews of the West, those who spend their efforts on the paperwork of endless conferences and races and picnics on the grass in defense of Soviet Jewry…and we say, "Enough, brothers and sisters, of chewing over our despair while lunching at Lindy's."[1] Enough of flaming cocktail parties, declarations…. The time has come to sound the alarm…. The time has come for practical action. Has not past experience been enough for you?
>
> Do you need facts?
>
> But how can we show you the bloody larynx of Anatoly Sharansky [after being force-fed] during his hunger strike in prison?
>
> Is it possible to let you touch Zachar Zunshine's ribs, broken in the Siberian Gulag?
>
> Or the blind eye of…Joseph Berenshtein, which was gouged in prison?
>
> Who could go through the walls of psychiatric clinics, guard rooms, and prison cells and the barbed wire of labor camps to show you the pain and the anguish of Nedezhda Fradkova, Joseph Begun, Yan Mesh, Yuri Tarnopolsky, Alexander Kholmiansky, Yakov Levin, Mark Nepomniashy and Yuli Edelstein?
>
> You Jews of the West are patient when General Dragunsky[2] said the process of emigration has ended.
>
> Open your papers and ask yourselves where and how much space have you devoted to our plight in your programs and publications?
>
> Would it be too much for you to scrape together some dollars, francs, pounds and shekels to publish on the front pages of

---

1. Manhattan restaurant in the 1980s frequented by celebrities and personalities.
2. Dragunsky was cochairman of the Soviet Anti-Zionist Committee, the Kremlin's anti-Jewish, anti-emigration propaganda mouthpiece.

leading newspapers and magazines the list of those who have been unable to see for years their near and dear ones?

Is it really necessary for you to collect drop by drop the tears of all the Jewish mothers separated from their children and to place this vat of tears in front of the Soviet embassy...so that they understand that the process of reunification of families started not from the 1970s but 2,000 years ago?

Our appeal is not meant to be an expression of ingratitude or a reproach against your passivity, but a call for concrete action since Russia has always understood only concrete deeds and practical approaches....

We appeal to all those...who have not forgotten the ancient lands with Abraham, Isaac, and Yakov and to those who have turned to national nihilism – after all, Jewishness is not a club from which one can leave. We in the East and you in the West have the same roots – no matter how different the currents of the river which come together and move apart...the river keeps flowing...this river of Jewish blood.[3]

Gorodetsky instructed UCSJ, SSSJ, and the 35s to demand a response from the American and European governmental and nongovernmental leaders.

That week, on the UCSJ executive committee's weekly conference call, we considered whether or not the letter's provocative, in-your-face political incorrectness could backfire. It was, after all, scathingly critical of the very same prominent personalities whose energies and resources we were struggling to marshal. The executive committee decided that our overriding responsibility to publicize the refuseniks' positions easily superseded other considerations. We sent the letter to the press, to each addressee, and also sent it out in mass mailings. Chicago Action published it in a double-page ad in the left-wing Chicago Jewish Sentinel as a Passover appeal. I don't remember receiving one response.

Refuseniks were also trying to shake the Israeli government from its policy of silence. They introduced a striking new initiative, calling for the repatriation of Soviet Jews.

---

3.   "Letter to Jews of the West," 1984, archives of Pamela Braun Cohen, American Jewish Historical Society, New York.

We, the Jews residing in the USSR but craving to live in Eretz Yisrael, appeal to you, the President of the State of Israel, the Knesset, and the Israeli government, to take urgent political steps for the repatriation of Soviet Jews.

We have the right, after all, to count on your devoted help.

We have the right to remind you about your and our historic Jewish duty.

We have the right to appeal to your national feelings.

And we have the right to expect from you serious and responsible practical action.

Remember, there is no time to be lost.

Tomorrow might be too late.

The responsibility for delay and inaction also will fall on you.

Moscow: Dmitri Khazankin, Dan Shapiro, Igor Kharakh, Inna Brokhina

Riga: Leonid Umansky, Svetlana Balter

Odessa: Mark Nepomniashy

Leningrad: Grigory Vasserman, Mikhail Tzivin, Yakov Gorodetsky, Nikita Dyomin, Evgeny Lein, Evgenia Utevskaya, Alexander Yudborovsky, Mikhail Vinaver[4]

The appeal was brought out by a tourist on tape and broadcast over Kol Yisrael Radio, heard over shortwave radios by Jews and dissidents in the USSR. Refuseniks were afraid that authorities had found a "final solution" to the Jewish problem. They warned that the threat extended beyond frontline activists. Jews who simply wished to remain Jewish were being ousted from jobs and universities. They warned that there could be large-scale deportations to outlying areas.

A month after affixing his signature to the repatriation appeal, Mark Nepomniashy was in prison. As the months passed, refuseniks' patience wore thin. Gorodetsky, Vasserman, Lein, Utevskaya, and other Leningrad refuseniks signed another appeal, this one addressed not to the government, but to the Jews of Israel.

---

4.   Appeal to Israeli government, September 5, 1984, archives of Pamela Braun Cohen, American Jewish Historical Society, New York.

Israel, the center of the Jewish world, should have been at the forefront of the activity for the defense of our national interests by mobilizing the tremendous potential of world Jewry.... For these last several years, each of our initiatives was met with lack of concern on the part of the Jewish State, the indifference of the officials and profound indifference of the Jewish people of Israel to our fate....

Few of our friends repatriated from the Soviet Union.... One after another they despaired, as a result of the impermeable deafness and the secrecy with which official Israel has masked its refusal to act.[5]

Refusenik disillusionment with America was also at a breaking point. From Israel, Lev Utevsky dictated an appeal that was signed by more than sixty refuseniks from Odessa, Leningrad, Tbilisi, Riga, and Moscow. The appeal spoke of the apathy of Jews of the United States and the United Kingdom:

Recently many of our friends have been arrested.

We do not know who will be the next....

Do not be deaf to our fates.

The fates of many of you could be the same...if your grandfathers and grandmothers hadn't left Russia....

When you send your children to Jewish schools, Remember: we have no Jewish schools.

When you take in your hands a Jewish book, Remember, we have no Jewish books.

When you touch lovingly the mezuzah, Remember, our mezuzahs are stripped during house searches.

When you study our beautiful and ancient language, Remember, our Hebrew teachers are imprisoned...on false charges of Hooliganism, harboring weapons or drugs.

---

5. Appeal to the Israeli people, 1985, archives of Pamela Braun Cohen, American Jewish Historical Society, New York.

Every Jewish mother: Remember, the mother of prisoner Zachar Zunshine…could not stand the burden of the ordeals of her son.[6]

Remember Anatoly Sharansky, Joseph Begun, Yuri Tarnopolsky, Moshe Abramov, perhaps they begin this day in a punishment cell or internal isolation.…

Remember, 40 years ago you were silent. So, speak about us and for us.

Call out about dangers threatening us.

We are deprived even of this possibility.[7]

One of the appeals Gorodetsky dictated to me was aimed not just at American Jews but at Secretary of State Shultz, timed to coincide with a meeting in Geneva with his Soviet counterpart, Andrei Gromyko, on January 2, 1985. UCSJ, SSSJ, the 35s in London, and Comité des Quinze in Paris scraped together funds we didn't have and purchased a full-page ad in the *Wall Street Journal* to publicize the appeal. Addressed "To the Jews of the U.S.A.," the appeal concluded with a list of the seventy-three refuseniks signing the appeal. The headline called out: "Secretary Shultz: Seventy-three women and men are risking their lives by running this ad today." The message continued:

It is difficult for us in New York or Washington or Los Angeles to comprehend the heroism it takes to sign such a document by those who live in Moscow, or Riga, or Leningrad.…

So when you meet with the stewards in the Kremlin…carry with you the list of the brave people who signed this plea. Let your counterparts know that these 73 men and women are your special charges.[8]

---

6. Hearing reports of her son's arrival in prison camp, Dora Zunshine collapsed and died of a heart attack.

7. Appeal, October 1984, archives of Pamela Braun Cohen, American Jewish Historical Society, New York.

8. "To the Jews of the U.S.A.," appeal, 1985, archives of Pamela Braun Cohen, American Jewish Historical Society, New York.

Before leaving for Geneva, Shultz met with Avital Sharansky and promised to press Anatoly's case. He also had taken our latest refusenik and prisoner lists with him. But still, his affiliation with Bechtel Corporation, a global corporation with Arab ties, left us skeptical of how energetic the new secretary of state would prove himself to be on our issue. Besides which, the State Department had never been our greatest ally. But the secretary proved us wrong. He took note of the grim oppression, singling out the Soviet war against Jewish cultural activists and the arrests of Hebrew teachers, and noting that "Soviet persecution of Jews and other minorities has not only not diminished, it seems to be getting worse."[9] He worried about Sharansky, whose health in Chistopol Prison was deteriorating. He recognized that emigration was at a standstill and that the Soviet authorities wanted us to believe that everyone who wanted to emigrate had left. Though the Reagan administration was trying to stabilize relations with the USSR, Shultz was committed to calling them to account, saying, "among human rights issues, none has more urgency than the treatment of Soviet Jews."[10]

After I became UCSJ's national president in 1986, Secretary Shultz told me something about himself that I found revealing. I was at the White House for a meeting with President Reagan, the secretary of state, and a handful of Jewish leaders. The meeting was largely a ceremonial expression of gratitude for President Reagan's support for Soviet Jewish emigration. We were seated around a large boardroom table in the Roosevelt Room, and the president opened the meeting in welcome. Referring to the emigration of Soviet Jews who were coming to America, he noted that an American can immigrate to Japan but never become Japanese. An American can immigrate to Italy but never become Italian. An American can immigrate to Sweden but never become Swedish. But when people from Japan and Italy and Sweden immigrate to America, in their own lifetimes, they become American. I never forgot those words.

When we were grouping for pictures, Secretary Shultz told me the following story. When he was a dean at the University of Chicago, he and his

---

9. George Shultz, Reading 23, "Soviet Jewry and U.S.-Soviet Relations," US Department of State, Bureau of Public Affairs, Current Policy No. 628, October 22, 1984, quoted in Drachman, *Challenging the Kremlin,* 461.

10. Ibid., 462.

wife became particularly attached to a brilliant young Jewish student, who often came to their house for meals. After Israel was attacked in the 1967 Six-Day War, the student, against Shultz's advice, left school to join the Israeli army. Not long after, he was killed. Shultz was devastated. He told me he felt like he had lost a son. I thought the story was his way of telling me he was on our side.

Reagan was also on our side, but the Soviets weren't in a mood to compromise, and the situation continued to deteriorate.

Bystanders or Participants

The appeals we had been receiving from refuseniks painted a graphic image of a world that was confronting me every day. I was determined to keep our family's life flourishing, but the phone rang day and night with news of arrests and house searches that demanded immediate reactions. Endless calls announced urgent needs I couldn't ignore.

One such call came on a winter evening, as I was preparing dinner. Avital Sharansky phoned from California. She wanted to come to Chicago the following morning. She needed to publicize Anatoly's declining health in Chistopol Prison, where he had been placed on a strict regimen with reduced rations and exercise. I frantically launched into action, and, as unlikely as it was, somehow the pieces came together. Only twelve hours later, Avital and I were on our way from the airport to her television interview with Irv Kupcinet, a prominent Chicago television and newspaper journalist, followed by an interview on Lee Rodgers's influential news radio program.

Then there was the time when, just hours before the start of Rosh Hashanah, the kitchen in pre-holiday chaos, the phone rang. It was Yuri Shtern, urging that we stop everything and inundate the Israeli embassy with phone calls to pressure the Israeli prime minister to address Soviet Jewry at his upcoming speech in New York. I put the pots on simmer and started making calls before the embassy closed.

One night, already late, I got a call informing me that a delegation of Soviet procurators[11] were arriving in Chicago in the morning. One of them had sentenced refuseniks to prison and labor camps. They were coming at the invitation of the Chicago Bar Association to meet with the city's most

---

11. Procurators were prosecutors who operated with the full authority of the state behind them rather than as part of a democratic legislative process.

prominent attorneys, including many Jews, who would wine and dine their celebrated guests. It was intolerable. As late as it was, I got on the phone, corralling people at the last minute to come downtown to picket them. That meeting was not going to happen in silence.

We had a regular stream of former refuseniks flowing through our home, temporarily taking over our children's bedrooms. Lenny and I felt this exposure was a counterweight to suburbia's suffocating insulation. How did the kids react? Once, Josh was sick and home from school. To cheer him, I rented the newest James Bond film, *To Russia with Love*. He burst into tears. "Does everything have to be about Soviet Jews?"

Nevertheless, Lenny and I hoped our children's hearts would open to what they were witnessing: their people caught in the rushing torrent of Jewish history. These refuseniks were in history's vortex, and American Jews could be either bystanders or participants in this monumental struggle. Lenny and I wanted our kids to understand they were part of a much larger Jewish world that existed beyond their own pristine suburban atmosphere. We were bringing that world into our home.

Looking back, I wonder if there was a degree of vicariousness in my drive. An ally, accomplice, partner, I fused myself into a narrative that the refuseniks were living out, not me. But it seemed to me like the two worlds had blended into one shared experience. My involvement with what was going on behind the Iron Curtain was so vivid, I used to quip that if a refusenik sneezed in Leningrad, I'd say "God bless you" in Deerfield.

Eyewitnesses: The Journalists and Chroniclers

If an event didn't get media coverage, it was as if it never happened. While councils sought publicity from US-based journalists, nothing replaced the work of the Moscow press corps, reporting behind the Iron Curtain. Refuseniks and dissidents found they had sympathetic allies among these reporters, who were attracted to them as the only representation of freedom of thought and expression in Moscow. These journalists recognized that the struggle against a repressive government was a story worth telling.

There were many significant journalists, like David Remnick of the *Washington Post*, Thom Shanker of the *Chicago Tribune*, Bill Keller and David Shipler of the *New York Times*, Bob Gillette of the *Los Angeles Times*, who helped to pierce the fog of the Kremlin's propaganda.

I had many interactions with Kevin Klose, Moscow bureau chief for the *Washington Post*, and found him to be particularly sensitive to and interested in our issue. Klose later became the director of Munich-based Radio Liberty, which played a vital role broadcasting Russian-language news into the USSR. Returning from a conference in Israel, Micah Naftalin, national director of UCSJ, and I deliberately stopped in Munich to further our already solid working relationship with Klose. Like so many other relationships in this movement, my relationship with Kevin went beyond the purely professional, and when he was in Chicago with his wife Aliza, we had them to our home for dinner.

Like Radio Liberty, broadcasts from Voice of America and Kol Yisrael provided refuseniks and dissidents with coverage of their own resistance activities. Refuseniks huddled together over their shortwave radios, eager for any Jewish news. Vladimir Matlin, a Voice of America reporter, covered several of our conferences, informing Jews who wanted to leave of the work being done on their behalf.

At a UCSJ conference in Jerusalem in the 1980s, Marillyn and I struck up a relationship with *Jerusalem Post* reporter Louis Rapoport and offered to underwrite his trip to meet refuseniks. We brought him first Chicago to brief him. On returning from Leningrad and Moscow, his riveting twelve-page spread in the *Jerusalem Post* brought to life the struggle of the young Leningrad refusenik Chaim Burshtein and others. The article launched a weekly column on Soviet Jews with information furnished by Enid Wurtman.

David Satter of the *Financial Times* was close to Sharansky and was with him just before he was arrested. At an event at the Chicago Action office, standing around my desk, Satter told Avital about the last minutes before her husband's arrest, sharing details she had never heard before. He also told her that her husband had been shadowed for weeks by four plainclothes KGB agents, two in front and two behind.

After I read Anthony Barbieri's piece on Volvovsky in the *Baltimore Sun*, I decided to seek him out, hoping he might be a willing go-between. My problem was how to reach him while avoiding the surveillance of Soviet mail. The *Baltimore Sun* wasn't helpful, so I decided to try reaching him through the US embassy's diplomatic pouch, though its use was highly restricted. I was uneasy about starting a relationship on the wrong foot, though, and had to tread with caution. The Soviets suspected the Moscow-based American press corps of having ties to the CIA. It wouldn't be much of a stretch for them to go from the CIA to the international Zionist conspiracy. Who knew what the Soviets would allege? I wanted to avoid embroiling Barbieri in some far-fetched, unforeseen accusation.

Nevertheless, with some assistance from a well-placed party, I sent my cautiously worded letter to Barbieri through the pouch. I was a friend of Volvovsky's, I wrote. I wondered if he would pass along my greetings and (innocently) maybe a book or two.

I had lost hope of his answer when Barbieri's three-page letter finally arrived with news of the Volvovskys. He wrote that I couldn't send Hebrew books through the pouch, but he was willing to pass along some messages, as long as they weren't illicit or sensitive instructions, like staging a demonstration by lying in front of Brezhnev's car.

He confided that there was a surreptitious "telegraph service" operating within the foreign correspondent community. Hardly a week passed when someone didn't leave Moscow for a few days in Helsinki. When they went out, they carried mail. He'd keep me in mind.

He did more than keep me in mind. Sometime after that initial letter, I began receiving mail from him postmarked Helsingfors. In one he wrote, "Since you have a good pipeline to what's going on here, I feel better that I'm not out in left field about what I'm finding here."[12] From then on, he often called our home when he was in Helsinki. It was the epitome of irony that this accomplished journalist had to go to Helsinki and then call Chicago, just to find out what was happening in the city where he was based.

From time to time, Howard Tyner, the *Chicago Tribune*'s Moscow bureau chief, did the same thing. When he was in Helsinki for a weekend, I'd call him at his hotel and supply him names of refuseniks who wanted contact with the press. He reported the Edelstein and Kholmiansky arrests, among others.

While the refusenik struggle was documented on a daily basis by journalists, it was written into history by Elie Wiesel and Sir Martin Gilbert.

In the mid-1960s, in the earliest days of the Soviet Jewry movement, Wiesel had published *The Jews of Silence*, his report of the oppression of Jews in the Soviet Union. This powerful account was a rallying cry, a plea for Jews in the West to speak out on behalf of their brethren in the USSR.

---

12. Anthony Barbieri, letter to Pamela Braun Cohen, March 21, 1980.

During the Gorbachev period, Micah and I went to New York specifically to deliver messages from refuseniks to Elie Wiesel in his Manhattan apartment. Refuseniks had asked us to deliver documents to him and urge him to make a return visit.

My friendship with Martin Gilbert, the British historian and Winston Churchill's official biographer, began at a UCSJ Annual Meeting. It was shortly after his trip to Russia in 1983 and the subsequent publication of *The Jews of Hope*, the first major work on Soviet Jews to appear since Wiesel's book. Martin's work boldly brought to life the heroism of its protagonists, several of whom I had been working with – Grigory Vasserman, Yasha Gorodetsky, Evgeny Lein, Eugenia Utevskaya, and many others. Martin brought prestige and an Oxford historian's authority to the movement. Martin's involvement extended well beyond professional concerns. Before long, our correspondence and phone calls carried news back and forth between us, adding to the flow of information between Leningrad refuseniks and Lev Utevsky in Israel. I have dozens of handwritten letters and notes from Martin, including a cryptically coded postcard from Leningrad to "Dear Auntie Pam."

To Move Heaven and Earth

In addition to the media magnifying the voices of refuseniks, UCSJ's councils and grassroots network were effective, high-powered instruments, carrying the voices of refuseniks and their agenda. There was continual pressure from refuseniks to keep their issue in front of not just the media but also influential organizations, the American people, and especially the administration and Congress.

In spite of (or maybe because of) the Jewish rancor he raised when he claimed Yasser Arafat, leader of the Palestine Liberation Organization, was a "moderate," my senator from Illinois, Chuck Percy, chairman of the influential Senate Foreign Relations Committee, was a strong advocate for Soviet Jews. I attributed his cooperation to Scott Cohen, an ally of the Soviet Jewry movement who had worked for Percy for twenty years.

In the fall of 1984, Percy drafted an appeal on behalf of Soviet Jewry to Soviet Premier Konstantin Chernenko, signed by former Presidents Gerald Ford and Jimmy Carter, as well as a prestigious group of former secretaries of state and Christian religious leaders. Adding to the voice of Reagan, a stronger defense couldn't have been made.

UCSJ pushed Congress on both sides of the aisle. Congress had given birth to the Helsinki Commission and the House Human Rights Caucus. Sensitive to their constituents' concerns, key members of Congress responded to our councils' grassroots pressure; they held hearings, lambasted the Soviets' jamming of the broadcasts of Radio Free Europe and Radio Liberty, met with refuseniks in the USSR, and welcomed former refuseniks into their offices on Capitol Hill. Significantly, they also continued to support the Jackson-Vanik Amendment. Through UCSJ's initiative, the Congressional Vigil, representatives and senators regularly entered statements about refuseniks into the *Congressional Record*.

For example, the *Congressional Record* of Thursday, March 15, 1984, the anniversary of Anatoly Sharansky's arrest, featured statements of support. Tom Corcoran of Illinois summed it up in his written statement:

> We, the Members of Congress of the United States and our fellow supporters of Soviet Jewry all over the world, take this opportunity to urge the governments of all free nations to join in compelling the Soviet Union to relent in its policy of denying the Jews their every human right.... Through demonstrations like today's International Day of Concern for Soviet Jews, the entire free world sends a strong message of solidarity with the beleaguered Soviet Jewry and of outrage at their reprehensible treatment at the hands of the Soviet tyrants.[13]

Councils also enlisted their local governments. Time and again, Mayor Harold Washington of Chicago opened the doors of City Hall to CASJ and the former refuseniks. When Mayor Washington received the visiting deputy mayor of Minsk, he urged him to intervene on behalf of the refuseniks in his city and handed him our Minsk refusenik list. Once, I was in his office when my messenger call to Tatiana Zunshine was scheduled. I put the Chicago mayor on the phone to hear firsthand about her husband, who had been brutalized in the labor camp.

I struggled to bring my two worlds together: the world of the refuseniks and the world of the apathetic Jews that surrounded me. Keeping the issue in the media was the key. The education of the public, our elected officials,

---

13. *Congressional Record* (March 15, 1984): H 1703.

and the Jewish community depended to a great degree on press-worthy events we could orchestrate. Some were dramatically imaginative. On one crisp Chicago winter day at the end of 1984, Marillyn, Hetty, Linda, and I, along with Skokie's mayor Albert Smith, led a morose procession of CASJ activists behind a horse-drawn hearse carrying a casket, draped in black. The long cortege snaked its way through the suburban streets the police had closed to traffic. We were protesting the arrest of refusenik Hebrew teacher Yuli Edelstein, who was being tried on a trumped-up charge of illegal drug possession. We marched to "bury apathy": our message was that the public's indifference to the arrest of innocent Jews was a rotting body to be buried. Our event was covered in print and broadcast media and was picked up by the Soviet embassy. With the light we shone on his case, it suddenly became harder for Yuli Edelstein to disappear.

The Soviet embassy was a natural focus for our protests because it reported to the Kremlin. Frequently we arranged batteries of calls from across the country to tie up their phone lines for hours at a time. For a young religious refusenik denied a Hebrew prayer book in an Odessa prison, we barraged the embassy and consulates with hundreds of siddurim sent by mail in care of Yakov Levin in Odessa. The Soviets got the message.

It was about this time that Marillyn and I sent David Weinstein to Moscow and Leningrad to hold Hebrew seminars. A Judaic studies scholar fluent in Hebrew, and president of Chicago's Spertus College of Judaica, David conducted seminars and then, upon his return, certified refusenik Hebrew teachers as registered Hebrew teachers. He also arranged for Spertus to mail an official invitation to Ari Volvovsky to teach Hebrew at the college. If the Soviets wouldn't recognize their Hebrew teachers, American institutions would welcome them, and it would be publicized in the media.

To publicize the plight of refusenik Vladimir Feltsman, the world-famous Moscow pianist who had been barred from performing in public, CASJ orchestrated a solo piano recital by Israeli concert pianist David Bar-Ilan in a Highland Park home. Our event was cosponsored by journalists David Satter and Kevin Klose. It was a stirring performance, and it made the news, putting Feltsman's name before the public and letting the Soviets know that we were watching what they did and to whom they did it.

We instigated one response after another. The mayor of DeKalb, Illinois, gave Yasha Gorodetsky honorary citizenship; Chicago mayors sent Abe Stolar, the Chicago-born Moscow refusenik, proxy ballots to vote in mayoral elections. UCSJ initiated the effort to rename a section of 16th Street, in front of what was then the Soviet embassy in DC, "Sakharov Plaza," in honor of persecuted academician Andrei Sakharov.

Irkutsk, Eastern Siberia

One especially memorable initiative involved a labor camp in the far reaches of Siberia. I had been working closely with Tanya Zunshine since her husband had been arrested in March 1983 after demonstrating for his right to a visa. An indomitable spirit with a high-pitched voice, Tanya fought relentlessly on behalf of her husband, who had been severely beaten in his prison cell by his jailers. They wouldn't permit her to visit him.

But Tanya had other plans. She was going to cross the breadth of the USSR, 3,797 miles from Riga to Zachar's labor camp in Irkutsk, Siberia, just north of Mongolia. And she was going alone. With outrageous courage, this young woman intended to stage a sit-down strike on the floor of the commandant's office to gain a meeting with her husband.

She wanted me to call the commandant's office to signal that I knew she was there petitioning for a meeting. Before she left, she gave me the phone number and the precise time she wanted his phone to ring.

It was impossible to imagine disappointing her, or more importantly, allowing her to expose herself to the danger of a nonviolent protest in a labor camp without support. She'd be a woman alone, without a protective spotlight, isolated in the far reaches of Siberia, in the maw of the camp's commandant. Working with Miss Alma, our partner at AT&T, I scheduled a direct call. All that long night I waited in a semiconscious state. With the phone's first ring, my body levitated out of bed and to the phone. It was the AT&T operator, connecting me to the commandant's phone in Siberia.

I was flooded with relief. The call I had arranged had reached Siberia, directly to the commandant's office, and he was waiting for it. She had warned him that he was getting a call from Americans who were watching him.

Tanya scored a win. The commandant relented. She got her meeting with Zachar. It was one of those small victories that defined my days. But what she witnessed was beyond deplorable, beyond comprehension. She told me that Zachar spent half his time in a damp, dungeonlike punishment cell about four yards square, where he endured torture by cold. He considered himself lucky to have some paper to wrap around his feet to prevent frostbite, but even so, he could only sleep about fifteen minutes at a time between exercising to stay alive. The only way he could tell night from day was by the warden's visit. He told her that in solitary confinement, prisoners were given meals every other day and, on off days, a piece of bread, which would have to be snatched up before the rats got it.

There were no eating utensils, and inmates were forced to eat like animals. All prisoners were deprived of water, forcing them to drink from radiators. Untreated tubercular inmates mixed with the rest of the prisoner population. Cells were massively overcrowded. Each of these horrors occurring in the camp violated Soviet law.

Over the three years Tanya fought for her husband, KGB kept her under unspeakable psychological pressure. KGB followed her, threw her into jail, beat her, and threatened her with a long prison term if she didn't stop her activities. Over and over, on the phone, she insisted that we keep up the level of support, despite KGB threats. Her actions were guided by the principle that whatever KGB told her not to do, she had to do more of it, every day. It was a position shared by other activists.

Considering an actionable response to the issues of overcrowding, tuberculosis, and lack of water, UCSJ decided on a tactic that would symbolize the inhumanity of the labor camp. Addressing the lack of eating utensils, we sent out a national emergency alert to our members, calling for thousands of plastic spoons to be sent to the Soviet embassy in care of Zachar Zunshine in Irkutsk. At the same time, we pulled every lever we could for our government to protest the conditions. A few weeks later, Tanya told me the head of the camp administration was fired.

A Confrontation

Not every effort to enlist support on behalf of refuseniks paid off, however.

One day Marillyn and I were waiting in the outer office of one of the Chicago newspapers for a meeting with their editorial board. With us was the former refusenik and prisoner of conscience Alec Zelichenok, whom we had brought to Chicago from Israel.

When the door opened, out walked the civil rights activist and politician Jesse Jackson, along with one or two of his assistants. Earlier, Jackson had traveled to the USSR. He had not come to us to be briefed beforehand, but while there he met with four refuseniks and promised to help them. The refuseniks told Marillyn about their encounter with him and urged us to follow up.

Marillyn had subsequently called Jackson's office repeatedly, and his assistant continually assured her that he was "working on it." Nothing came of it, so she doggedly kept up her calls and met continued stonewalling by his staff.

Now in a face-to-face encounter, Marillyn introduced herself and confronted him directly. What was he doing to help the four refuseniks he met? He avoided eye contact, engaged in shaking the hands of everyone in the waiting room while loudly broadcasting, "Don't worry, we'll get them out.... We'll get them all out."

He didn't notice that Zelichenok was wearing a small pin on his lapel with an image of Martin Luther King Jr. Before leaving, Jackson told Marillyn to phone his assistant. Again, she called, and again, there was no result.

One day, Jackson called the CASJ office and asked Marillyn what was happening with the four refusenik cases. Marillyn countered: "Why are you asking me? What is your office doing?" Jackson responded with a proposition: "Listen, if you agree to hold a national press conference for me, then we will really move to get these four guys out...."

It didn't take a second for Marillyn to answer him, her face mirroring her sense of outrage. "We can't do that. Do you mean to tell me that you will help these four people only if we make a national press conference for you – even before they have permission to leave?"

Jackson was candid: "Yes, that's how it is."

There was no way we were giving Jackson a platform for something he didn't do.

Striking a Balance

Increasingly my brain was operating in Moscow and Leningrad and Odessa, in prison cells and labor camps, and it was hard to shut it down on the seven-minute drive between the office in Highland Park and our home in Deerfield.

Lenny and I were raising three children who were too quickly growing up. They no longer needed me to read to them before bedtime or sit on the bathroom floor and sing silly songs during bath time, ready with a big warm towel to wrap them up. Every mother sooner or later reluctantly gives that up. Now they were playing football, having concussions, breaking fingers and windows and wrists, falling nearly catastrophically from a tree. Now my home life played out in the splendid cacophony of slamming doors, ringing phones, the dog barking in mad frustration over an unreachable squirrel, Brooke's arpeggios on the piano, Scott's guitar strumming upstairs in his room, Josh's blasts on his tuba, the car-pool horn in front of the house, the punctuated dribble of the basketball on the driveway and the vibrating resonance when it hit the backboard and dropped into the hoop. There were glowing logs in the fireplace where we occasionally roasted marshmallows, Sunday outings, weekends at Alpine Valley and Door County, Wisconsin. There were baseball practices and neighborhood games in the cul-de-sac in the front of the house. There were the annual Braun Labor Day barbecues, dinners in River Forest at my parents', and long weekends to Lima, Ohio, to visit Lenny's parents.

There were always Friday night dinners at home, sometimes with Uncle Chip and his family, sometimes with Uncle Michael who came from Israel, often with my parents. I lit candles before we sat down to dinner in the dining room, and Lenny said Kiddush. He would make a blessing over the challah and throw a piece to our dog, Falafel, who waited expectantly in the hall, ready to catch it on the fly. We had extended visits with aunts, uncles, cousins. We went to Bermuda and to Amelia Island and Switzerland.

Lenny was building his company, and I was determined to provide a family life that was increasingly enriched with Jewish culture and values. I tried to balance my attention on the needs of our family and on the needs of refuseniks. I was trying to do it all without compromise, baking cookies and putting a freshly cooked dinner on the table every night, trying to be Super Mom. Without question, husband and children came first, but I knew I was stretched between competing claims. I had no idea how any of it would turn out. The world in which our parents had raised us had changed, and Lenny and I were struggling to carry our past's nourishing Jewish values into the present. We couldn't know where it would lead, but we were holding on as best we could.

CHAPTER 12

The Finnish Connection and Other Adventures, 1985

An Informal Contract

Little by little, we had broken through to the isolated refusenik community. The next step forward was about to come.

A small group of young Finnish Lutherans had heard about the plight of Jews in the Soviet Union and wanted to cross the border to make contact. In the early 1980s, these religious Finns had passed themselves off as tourists crossing the border to drink cheap Russian vodka. At the Leningrad Synagogue, they met with refusenik Misha Elman, who took them to meet Evgeny Lein and Yasha Gorodetsky, my messenger phone partner. A few of these Finns had also traveled to Israel and were in contact with former Leningrad refuseniks Lev Utevsky and Eduard Usoskin. They were prepared to carry information to and from Leningrad. Given the surveillance of KGB in Helsinki and tight security at Russia's border, it was a dangerous business for the Finns.

For eight months, Gorodetsky had been trying to connect me to these Finns, a difficult task since he couldn't talk about such a highly sensitive matter over the phone. The UCSJ's conference in Israel was the answer.

I was sitting in the lobby of the Jerusalem Sheraton on break from a session of a UCSJ conference when Marillyn brought Eduard Usoskin over to meet me. This extraordinarily energetic man aggressively put his yellow legal pad onto my lap and scrawled his name in large letters as if to engrave it on my consciousness. "My name is Usoskin, Eduard. I come from Leningrad." In the same bold staccato, he listed the names of his refusenik friends in Leningrad with whom we were already working: "Vasserman. Lein. Gorodetsky."

Yasha had found us.

Usoskin and Utevsky in Jerusalem offered us the Finnish channel to deliver financial aid, vital data, and anecdotal information. They had the channel but lacked financial resources. We had access to financial potential but were desperate for reliable channels. Our partnership was mutually beneficial.

Although Marillyn and I welcomed it as a windfall, our connection to the Finns upped the ante. It wasn't hard to imagine an article in *Leningradskaya Pravda* alleging an "international Zionist conspiracy," accusing conscripted Christian Finns, CASJ, and Soviet Jews of anti-Soviet activity. However, Utevsky was a man of seasoned experience and took a rational, scientific, and legal approach to all refusenik matters. He encouraged us to move forward.

We moved quickly. Usoskin immediately arranged a meeting with the Finns, and a few days later, Marillyn, Usoskin, and I flew to the Netherlands to meet our new partners.

Usoskin, Marillyn, and I were anxiously waiting in an Amsterdam bar having coffee when Maya Kemppi and her colleagues walked in. Maya and Eduard greeted each other warmly, like old friends. Maya was from Kormu. In her mid-thirties, she was slight, with crisp diction, her English breaking through a thick Finnish accent. Marillyn and I sat, astounded, while the former Jewish refusenik from Russia, now an Israeli citizen, and three Christians from Finland briefed each other on the most recent refusenik events in detail. Maya was so well informed. Any hesitation we had dissipated.

First on the agenda was a mechanism for cooperation, engineered by Usoskin. The underground channel would connect four geographic activity centers: Utevsky and Usoskin in Israel, our new Finnish partners in Helsinki, Gorodetsky and Lein in Leningrad, and Marillyn and me in Chicago. Usoskin drew up an informal contract to define our relationships and our expectations.

> To Evgeny Lein or Yakov Gorodetsky,
> We, Pamela B. Cohen, Marillyn Tallman, Eduard Usoskin, and three of our guests are now writing you this letter. First we are sending you our support and love. We are ready to do our best for you, but we need your support too and very reliable, quick information. All information which you are sending…

should be prepared very carefully, photographed, developed and checked, clean and readable.[1]

Head on, he explained our biggest problems with their information. He made it clear that expediency in disseminating the refuseniks' news depended exclusively on the quality of the information and its form. Illegible writing, lack of clarity or specificity, poor translation, anything that required clarifying calls to the USSR meant significant delays in getting the information out. The Finns would bring the contract to the two Leningrad refuseniks.

The Initiative Takes Off

After Marillyn and I finalized our plans in Amsterdam, we headed home. No one at CASJ other than Hetty, Linda, and Betty knew where we had been. And so began the Finnish initiative.

Cryptic correspondence from Helsinki would arrive at my home address so encoded that I could barely decipher it. Maya cryptically referred to Gorodetsky as "the Apple of His Eye" and to Usoskin as "the Boss," and she peppered her lines with references to other colleagues, Timothy and Simon. Maya varied the last line of every letter, but the meaning never wavered: "God Almighty is the only One who can protect His people"; "The Everlasting's arms are about His people." Her actions were guided by her faith.

The Finns' monthly trips to Leningrad produced a surge of activity at CASJ's office. Now on top of scheduled messenger calls, congressional activity, tourist briefings, and the speeches I so dreaded giving, there were funds to be transferred to the Helsinki bank to underwrite the Finns' trips and enable them to purchase goods for refuseniks to sell. Betty intensified her efforts to photograph congressional reports, news articles, and UCSJ proposed policies. Then Hetty packaged the exposed film into the original film cannisters for the Finns to transport back to Russia.

It did not always run smoothly. One time I found a pale blue aerogram in my mailbox at home with a message we had dreaded: "Eric and his friend were caught!"

---

1. Eduard Usoskin, informal contract, 1985, archives of Pamela Braun Cohen, American Jewish Historical Society, New York.

It was the beginning of 1985. KGB had arrested several refuseniks.[2] In the middle of their trials, Maya sent two Finns, Eric and a companion, to Gorodetsky, who gave them film documenting the refuseniks' arrests, court proceedings, and evidence of their innocence.

On their way out, at Russian customs in Vyborg, the two Finns were picked up by KGB and detained. Frightened, Eric buckled and signed a statement implicating Gorodetsky. KGB released them but kept the film. The situation was ominous. Materials like that were likely to turn up as evidence in a courtroom. It turned out that Eric had political connections in Finland, and whether or not that played a role, while we were working hard to prevent Gorodetsky's imminent arrest, KGB decided not to use the material.

Meeting in Finland

The incident with Eric made Maya's repeated request for a face-to-face meeting with us more urgent. Behind the scenes, Yasha had been telling her for more than six months to urge me to come to Finland. Finally, in the summer of 1985, Marillyn and I made the trip. On the way back from visiting day at our kids' summer camp in Wisconsin, I met Marillyn at O'Hare. Only our husbands and a select few in the CASJ office knew about our trip.

In Helsinki, Marillyn and I checked in to the Intercontinental Hotel. Without unpacking, I followed Maya's instructions and phoned her from our spacious room. She didn't answer. I checked the number and called again, but she didn't pick up the phone. Nervous, I repeatedly dialed. Her phone kept ringing, with no answer. The night grew later. Marillyn asked if I had another number for her. I didn't. I had no other way to reach her. I didn't even know Timothy's and Simon's last names, let alone their phone numbers. We had no backup plan. Marillyn and I knew no one else in Helsinki. I kept calling relentlessly. What could have happened? Had Maya led us into some kind of a trap? For what purpose? Ridiculous. We were insignificant. Tension became anxiety. Finally, finally, Maya answered. Without explanation, she coolly and succinctly told me the plan for the next day.

Unable to sleep, we went down to the bar.

---

2.   Leonid Shrayer from Chernivtsi was sentenced to three years in January 1985; Vladimir Frenkel of Riga was arrested after a search; Mark Nepomniashy of Odessa was sentenced to three years in February.

It was as if Marillyn and I had stepped into a movie set. I'd say the
scene was Berlin, 1932. In front of a long, mirrored wall, the dark mahogany bar was set beneath brightly polished brass and cut-glass light fix-
tures. Elegantly dressed people milled around or sat on richly upholstered
sofas surrounding glass-topped coffee tables. The room was filled with the
sound of tinkling ice in crystal.

Like guests at a cocktail party, everyone seemed to know each other;
they looked as if they were writers, foreign correspondents, or spies. An
elegantly dressed gentleman with a mahogany silver-tipped cane, sporting a homburg hat, approached two tastefully dressed women in a booth
across from us. He kissed their hands and joined them. We were dying
to know what they were saying but couldn't understand a word, despite
Marillyn's insistence that she spoke perfect Finnish, which, in fact, she
comically mimicked with unblemished artistry.

That night, we barely slept.

Early the next morning we went to the station and boarded a train that
carried us seventy kilometers northeast of Helsinki, through an immense
forest thick with white birch and firs. There's a snapshot of me in my file
drawer that Marillyn took that day. I'm wearing caramel slacks, holding
on to a hanging leather strap for balance. The face is mine and the photo
proves to me that the whole episode was a novel I happened to have lived.

We got off at the designated stop. It was a small provincial town, an
oasis in the vast Finnish forest. We crossed the street and located the hotel
Maya had described. We were in the lobby having a cup of tea and feeling
very much like spies ourselves when Maya walked in. In no time, we were
in her station wagon, driving into the ever-thickening forest. She turned
onto a narrow gravel road and, after several miles, stopped and turned off
the motor. Timothy and Simon were waiting.

One look at Marillyn and I saw her face reflecting my own incredulity.
Finland. We had come to Finland, to a thick forest of white birch, to a place
so remote that we didn't know exactly where we were. Neither did anyone
else in the world.

We followed them through the forest to a clearing. Suddenly, they bubbled over, rattling off the names that were on our lips every day: Yasha,
Vasserman, Evgeny Lein, Misha Salmon, Tanya and Zachar. They knew
every person, and they knew the details of every situation and had the
freshest of news. It was like a conversation I would have had with Lynn or

Glenn or David, but it was taking place with Christians in an unidentified forest in a remote part of Finland. It was astounding. They were so personally invested in these Jewish refuseniks. It almost couldn't be real, except that it was.

Then they showed it to us.

Across the clearing was a large bunker constructed of wood. They opened the door. It was a barrack filled with cots, pillows, and blankets. Closets brimmed with warm coats, the freezers were stocked, cabinets laden with provisions and medicine. On a desk in one of the rooms was a Bible, open to Jeremiah. They pointed to the verse in Jeremiah (31:7): "Behold, I will bring them from the north country, and gather them from the uttermost parts of the earth."

Indeed, the entire bunker was prepared for the fulfillment of Jeremiah's prophesy that the ingathering of the exiles would come from the North. Marillyn and I were stunned into silence. Then they took us upstairs, and others in their group joined us as we sat around a wood table and relished fresh strawberries and the thickest imaginable cream. We sat among these people who heard God through the voice of Jeremiah.

We got to work. They briefed us extensively, describing the details of meetings during repeated trips. It was clear that refuseniks were equally starved for information about us and our activity on their behalf. With a better grip on what was needed in Leningrad, we figured out a way to streamline the process of sending material aid and information from Utevsky, Usoskin, and us to Maya and her group to carry into Leningrad.

Before leaving, they asked if we could pray together. We gathered into a small circle in their living room and joined arms. Maya led off: "Thank you, God, for bringing us together and for letting us do Your work."

One by one each of the Finns took their turn, speaking in English. Then one rather modest woman began speaking. Her prayer started off in English, but soon her quiet intensity gave way. She closed her eyes and began spouting words in what sounded like a combination of Russian and Hebrew. At the end, an electric silence permeated the room. Neither Marillyn nor I were sure what we had just witnessed. The woman appeared lucid and in control of what she was saying, but when we questioned Maya, she told us that the woman didn't know either Russian or Hebrew. She had been speaking in tongues.

We left Finland with extraordinary memories and increased trust on both sides.

Our Worst Fears Realized

Unfortunately, Eric was not the only traveler who didn't stand up to the Leningrad KGB. Marillyn and I also had one. For some time, Gorodetsky's apartment had been under surveillance by KGB looking for an excuse to haul him in. It was obvious that their presence could easily be a trap for some traveler, not unlike Eric, who could be sufficiently terrified into signing a statement that would implicate Gorodetsky in some fabricated international Zionist, anti-Soviet activity.

As KGB exploited fear, the antidote to their intimidation was a self-assured, even cocky attitude. Safe, successful trips depended on that attitude, and Marillyn and I role-played interrogations with tourists until they adopted the tone and rationale they could rely on if worse came to worst. Traveling in the USSR was not illegal. The Helsinki Final Act guaranteed the right to personal contacts. Most of all, politically, the Kremlin wanted to avoid an international incident. The carrots America offered for most-favored-nation trading status and disarmament progress were pretty dependable incentives for the Soviets to keep American tourists safe. Also, it was conceivable that the Kremlin believed their own propaganda: American Jews controlled the media and Congress, and, paradoxically, American Jews just weren't important enough to warrant the damage that would be created by arresting one of them.

Bottom line: KGB wasn't as much a danger to our American tourists as to the refuseniks they would be visiting. That was front and center for all briefings.

One day, the event that we so dreaded and had tried so hard to prevent happened.

It was disorienting to pick up the phone and hear the voice of our tourist, a doctor, calling from an airport in Europe when he should have been in Leningrad. His voice was shaky. KGB had picked him up at the entrance of Gorodetsky's building, which we had told him was under surveillance. He was brought in for interrogation and threatened, and he panicked. In terror, he did the only thing we warned tourists never to do. He signed a document, written in Russian, not knowing the content. It incriminated Gorodetsky, and KGB was certain to use it against him.

The signed statement required a preemptive strike to protect Gorodetsky. Convinced that negative publicity about the harassment of both an American citizen and a well-known refusenik wasn't in the Soviets' interest, I pursued the very tactic they wanted to avoid. We called a news conference at the CASJ office for Representative Porter, cochairman of the Congressional Human Rights Caucus. With the cameras rolling, he called Gorodetsky.

Seated at my desk, his hand shielding his eyes, Porter told Gorodetsky that the US Congress understood that the American doctor's intimidation was a provocation and assured him that both the House and Senate would be watching closely. Porter had already issued a formal complaint to the Soviets regarding their violation of the Helsinki accords. His message was aimed for omnipresent listeners in Moscow.

With the consent of our tourist, Porter also made a formal statement, published in the *Congressional Record* of September 9, 1985:

> Mr. Speaker, the following statement describes the mistreatment of Dr. X [name withheld] on his recent trip:
>
> Dr. X arrived in Leningrad on Friday, August 9, 1985. On August 10, he and his traveling companion were forcibly taken to a Leningrad police station by three unidentified persons, one of whom was later identified as the Chief of Militia....
>
> Dr. X was taken to a room where there were many plainclothesmen and militiamen. Dr. X was...taken down a long corridor to a small auditorium where all his personal possessions were examined.
>
> An Intourist interpreter[3] arrived and Dr. X's personal possessions from a bag were exposed on a table where they were photographed.... [He] was photographed as well.
>
> His requests to speak with the American Consulate were denied.
>
> Vitamin C, which he was carrying, was confiscated for a drug check with the implied threat that "these people" often bring drugs to our country.
>
> His personal notebook was examined and kept....

---

3. These interpreters were KGB plants.

Their previous day's visit to Leningrad refusenik Yakov Gorodetsky was questioned [and it was] implied that he could be held as a spy and that he lied about being a tourist. Under this intimidation, Dr. X was forced to write a statement which said he did meet with Yakov Gorodetsky and discussed the recent trial of Roald Zelichonek, another Leningrad refusenik and now prisoner. Dr. X signed the statement.

He was told that he was under investigation for speculation. He was removed from detention but was told he had to report his movements to the hotel administration. Dr. X terminated his trip prematurely at great personal expense because he felt he was being followed and watched.

There is no doubt that this tourist was used in an incident designed to manufacture evidence against…Gorodetsky.[4]

Fortunately, this was the only case in which a CASJ tourist capitulated to pressure. We did have another case of tourist intimidation, with a different outcome.

Complications in Kiev

Marillyn and I had prepared three Highland Park couples to travel to the Soviet Union, and she gave them a KGB briefing, role-playing the various scenarios. While in Kiev, Gary and Susie Gurvey had returned to their hotel room after visiting refuseniks when there was a knock on their door. Gary opened it to find a small woman who identified herself as an Intourist interpreter. Some people wanted to talk to him, she said, and she led him to an office where four or five KGB agents – raw-boned, tough-looking plainclothesmen in black leather jackets – waited.

"Mr. Charvey," they began. "Where were you yesterday?"

"I'm not Mr. Charvey," quipped Gary. "You don't want me. You want Harvey Barnett, who is, incidentally, my lawyer. I want my lawyer present. He's right down the hall."

The tiny, clearly terrified Russian interpreter delivered the commandant's response in English.

---

4. *Congressional Record* (September 9, 1985): E 3924.

"No, Mr. Charvey, you can't have your lawyer. This is not America." The interrogator proceeded. "Did you visit an apartment yesterday on Gagarin Street?"

With that first question, Gary did exactly what Marillyn had told him to do. He lied. "No."

"I repeat. Were you visiting an apartment yesterday on Gagarin Street?" Gary continued his denial. The translator delivered the commandant's next round of the fusillade. "The Commandant says he knows you were in the apartment.... We know you were there and what we want to know is, what did you discuss and why are you harassing Soviet citizens. If you aren't going to answer here, we can discuss it at the police station."

It was a game. They knew he was at the apartment. Gary responded: "Oh, *that* apartment. I didn't know what you meant by the word *visit*. In English it can mean an all-day encounter, and we just stayed a few minutes. Well, a friend from Chicago gave me the address…said he ran into this guy at an international conference and asked me to drop in and give regards."

Menacing, the commandant pulled the pin out of the grenade, "Well, then, why did you mention the name 'Orlov' in the apartment?" Advantage, interrogator. Yuri Orlov was a well-known dissident. "Well, are you willing to sign a statement?"

Gary answered: "I am absolutely willing to sign a statement saying that I broke no laws, harassed no Soviet citizens." The Soviet bullies handed him a piece of paper. Gary wrote in English, in big block letters, "Yes, I was in an apartment on Gagarin street on the recommendation of Mr. Brown [a name Gary made up] and I broke no Soviet laws and harassed no Soviet citizens."

They had nothing on him, but they photographed him anyway, like he was a criminal or a spy.

Gary was shaken, but he rose above the fear. He had been transformed, profoundly touched by the refuseniks he had met who were grateful for American tourists, for their concern and their determination to help.

A few hours later, Gary and Susie flew to Leningrad. Gary couldn't shake his worry that the incident in Kiev had endangered refuseniks until he discussed it with Lev Shapiro, a long-term refusenik. Lev told him,

"Look, we live this every day. We'll be all right as long as you don't forget us."[5]

As former refusenik Alec Zelichenok told CASJ activists Mike and Jean Freed, "If not for the foreign visitors, Soviet Jews, particularly refuseniks, would be behind barbed wire by now."[6] As long as refuseniks wanted travelers, we would continue to send them.

---

5. Ibid.

6. Jean and Mike Freed, trip report for Chicago Action for Soviet Jewry, May 21–June 4, 1984.

Steps in the Right Direction

CHAPTER 13

Freedom at Long Last, 1985–86

Glienicke Bridge, Germany

Brezhnev, Andropov, Chernenko came and went with no change in Soviet policy. Fear mixed with disillusion. For refuseniks, it was the darkest period since Stalin. Emigration figures hit rock bottom. In 1984, only 896 Jews were given permission, and the numbers of refuseniks and prisoners of conscience only grew.

The Kremlin was dead set on stamping out any signs of Jewish resistance. KGB raided refusenik apartments and confiscated personal property. Purloined mail was used to convict refuseniks Zelichenok, Lifshitz, Frenkel, Brodsky, and Volvovsky. My phone rang with reports of new arrests: Tarnopolsky, Zubko, Yakir, Shnirman, Shefer, Cherniak, Abramov. Josef Begun had begun serving his third sentence for teaching Hebrew, seven years in Perm labor camp and five years in exile.

Each arrest sent convulsions through the councils.

Meanwhile, Mikhail Gorbachev's accession to power in the Soviet Union and his talk of reform triggered a tsunami of media euphoria. Intent on painting him in the American style of a liberal democratic reformer, the media ignored continuing arrests and trials of refusenik activists.

Occasionally, the Soviets employed the tactic of giving visas to troublesome activists, and in 1985, with fewer than fifteen hundred Jews being given permission, a number of refuseniks in the CASJ-Gorodetsky activist network were allowed to leave. Alla and Leonid Praisman in Moscow, the Balters and Umanskys in Riga, and Boris Vainerman in Leningrad were virtually thrown out.

Then, in early 1986, after years of prison and labor camps, Anatoly Sharansky was abruptly released and sent directly from prison out of the country. Yasha Gorodetsky was also given permission. Along with everyone else, I was overjoyed, but cautiously so. Refuseniks preparing to leave

still faced a minefield of unpredictable hazards, so until the final border was crossed, we waited, watchfully hopeful. After all, Abe Stolar had
already boarded a departing airplane when he was pulled off.

Just as everyone in my generation remembers where they were when
they heard that President Kennedy was shot, UCSJ activists vividly
recall the televised images on February 11, 1986, of Anatoly Sharansky's
astounding walk to freedom. Refusing to conform to Soviet expectations
to the end, he zigzagged his way across the Glienicke Bridge from Soviet-
controlled East Germany to freedom in West Germany. It was a historic
moment of triumph. Finally, finally, after nine long years, it was over. In
just hours, he and Avital would be reunited in Jerusalem.

It happened to be a wintery, blustery day in Chicago. Late in the afternoon, I was making dinner, waiting for Lenny to come home from work,
when the phone rang. ABC News wanted me to come downtown to the
Channel 7 newsroom for an interview about the Sharansky release. Had
he still been imprisoned, I would have been out the door, but now he was
free. There was nothing more I could do for him. I opted to stay at home
with my family, celebrating happily. Thank you, but no. They then said
they would send a driver. I respectfully declined. But they didn't give up.

An hour later, Lenny and I were at nearby Deerfield High School,
watching the ABC helicopter land in the deserted parking lot and disgorge
their TV crew. We drove them to our home. They set up lighting and cameras in our living room and interviewed me for the nightly news. I tried to
encapsulate the years of the intensive campaign we had mounted for him
right here in Chicago, in Washington, and all across the country, but I was
also intent on keeping the spotlight on other Jews still suffering in punitive
labor camps for their desire to emigrate.

The following winter, UCSJ brought Anatoly, now known as Natan,
to Washington, DC, for our annual meeting. Afterward, on December 11,
he was to fly to Chicago, where CASJ had scheduled a city-wide event for
public officials, press, supporters, and the public at the Westin Hotel. I told
him that I'd meet his plane. I wasn't counting on a snowstorm.

It started falling in the morning – large, feathery flakes, the kind of
snow that sticks and drifts. Before long, newscasters were warning driv-
ers to avoid the highways. Midway Airport was about forty-five miles
from our home, a good hour and a half away under normal conditions.
I set out about three hours before his flight was due. After two hours on

icy roads that were becoming increasingly difficult to negotiate, I had to face the fact that I wasn't going to make it. On our car phone, then the size of a B49 bomber, I dialed Lenny at his office and asked him to get in touch with Marty Oberman, who we had sent to Moscow to meet Ida Milgram, Sharansky's mother, when he was in labor camp. A Chicago city alderman, Oberman arranged for a police motorcade to meet Sharansky's plane, which miraculously landed in the storm, and take him to the hotel. I arrived in time to introduce him to a large and fired-up crowd of activists and media. Characteristically, he opened with humor, saying that while he didn't know what to expect in Chicago, he wasn't expecting to find police cars at the plane waiting to take him away.

A few months later, in January 1987, Micah Naftalin and I bumped into Sharansky on the streets of Washington as he was pushing against the wind in another snowstorm. This one was threatening an important event UCSJ had arranged on Capitol Hill. Sharansky, along with former prisoner of conscience and dissident Dr. Yuri Orlov and law professor Irwin Cotler, were to testify at our Commission of Inquiry on Soviet Human Rights. Commissioners included Senator William Armstrong of Colorado and Senator Charles Grassley of Iowa. Washington can shut down with even small amounts of snow, and we were nervously on edge, but the proceedings went as scheduled. Cotler, who had worked on Sharansky's case and later would serve as a member of Canada's Parliament, set the baseline for the meeting and, we hoped, for US foreign policy:

> Soviet law itself, even in the age of Gorbachev, emerges not as a protection of rights, but as an instrument of repression. Speaking the truth is anti-Soviet slander and agitation. Seeking family reunification is malicious hooliganism. Applying to emigrate is circulating a fabrication slandering the Soviet system.... Monitoring human rights…is defamatory. And in the classic Catch-22 of Gulag justice, a person fired from his or her job for desiring to emigrate may then be charged for parasitism for not having a job.[1]

---

1. Union of Councils for Soviet Jews, Commission of Inquiry on Soviet Human Relations Violations, Public Hearing, Washington, DC, January 23, 1987. Archives of Union of Councils for Soviet Jews, American Jewish Historical Society, New York.

Sharansky and Orlov testified on the status of Soviet human rights and emigration. When Sharansky testified, I was astounded at how this man, incarcerated in prisons and labor camps for almost a decade, virtually shut off from the outside world, allowed scarce communication even with his family, was articulating with precision the views, policies, and platforms of UCSJ and SSSJ. On the most contentious issues – freedom of choice and the Jackson-Vanik Amendment – we were in absolute harmony.

A Reunion

Yasha Gorodetsky was an effective activist; authorities saw him as provocative and incessantly irritating. They must have concluded that he would be less of a problem in Israel than in a Soviet prison – either that or his visa was a concessionary gesture to President Reagan.

My partnership with Gorodetsky had paid off in visas. He and Grigory Vasserman understood the mentality of their formidable opponents and together they had formulated strategies to crack the manacles, case by case. Yasha had a good sense of how the Soviets played their game, and he was judicious in terms of both information and material assistance. In February 1986, a few days before UCSJ's conference in Israel, I flew to Tel Aviv to meet Gorodetsky's plane. I expected intensive debriefings and sensitive new information he couldn't have transmitted from the USSR.

My mother joined me on the trip, and we started with a visit with the Praismans and Alla's mother, Berta Schachnovskaya, a survivor of both the Holocaust and a long period of refusal. She and my mother sat together, speaking Yiddish and laughing as if they had always known each other. Their small apartment in Gilo, then an absorption center for new immigrants, glowed with the luxurious warmth of Jewish historical memory. Alla, who had bravely gone alone to take my messenger call at the Moscow post office, surrounded by plainclothesmen, was now here in Jerusalem with her mother, a survivor of Nazism and Soviet Communism, and with my mother, who was in America because her parents left in advance of the Nazis and Communists. Now Alla and her husband Leonid were facing new challenges without financial resources, jobs, or support systems.

The next day, I met Lev Utevsky and Eduard Usoskin, the activists who had engineered our Finnish connection. We buzzed with anticipation over a pizza and taxied to Ben Gurion to meet Gorodetsky's plane. Six hours earlier, they had called the Jewish Agency representative in Vienna to confirm that Gorodetsky had arrived there and was on the flight to Tel Aviv with his family.

We entered the arrivals hall along with a crush of new *olim* (immigrants), who had just landed. We waited. Suddenly, a manifestation of the refusenik on the other end of the phone line for all those years materialized. Like his pictures, he was short, wearing a tam and a leather flight jacket. His wife and daughter were glassy-eyed with exhaustion and anticipation.

I had come to meet my activist colleague who had been so effective, resourceful, and trustworthy. I was grateful to have had a partner who felt responsible and accountable for the material assistance and medicines Chicago Action had sent to him. But freedom brought new realities. Our previous operational structure had been based on mutual dependence. I needed his information and he needed our activism. With Gorodetsky in Israel, we were no longer codependents.

Only after he emigrated did I become aware of the extent to which he and other refuseniks assumed continued emotional and financial support from us once in Israel. I knew that a few felt I had abandoned them. As much as I would have liked to help, it was simply beyond our mandate and our ability to support them past the point of emigration. In truth, our eyes were forever on those who were left in the Soviet cage.

CHAPTER 14

The Reagan Reset and the Reykjavik Summit, 1986

The Evil Empire

By the time of Ronald Reagan's 1980 election, Soviet repression and refuse-nik resistance had been playing out on a much larger gameboard. The nuclearization of the US and USSR was front and center in global politics.

The Left, agitating for a nuclear-freeze, saw Ronald Reagan as the quintessential cold warrior. The truth was that he did have a long-standing antipathy to communism. He was cognizant of the irrefutable differences between repressive totalitarian governments and free democracies, especially in the area of human rights. The two systems had become engaged in a colossal geopolitical and nuclear competition, and Reagan believed there could only be one winner.[1] In 1982, Reagan was invited by Britain's prime minister Margaret Thatcher to speak to Parliament at Westminster Palace. Set against the canvas of repression I looked at every day, his speech really resonated with me.

> If history teaches anything it teaches self-delusion in the face of unpleasant facts is folly. We see around us today the marks of our terrible dilemma – predictions of doomsday, antinuclear demonstrations, an arms race in which the West must, for its own protection, be an unwilling participant. At the same time we see totalitarian forces in the world who seek subversion and conflict around the globe to further their barbarous assault on the human spirit. What then is our course? Must civilization

---

1. Bret Baier with Katherine Whitney, *Three Days in Moscow: Ronald Reagan and the Fall of the Soviet Empire* (New York: William Morrow, 2018), 123.

perish in a hail of fiery atoms? Must freedom wither in a quiet deadening accommodation with totalitarian evil....?

What I am describing now is a plan and a hope for the long term – the march of freedom and democracy which will leave Marxism-Leninism on the ash-heap of history as it has left other tyrannies which stifle the freedom and muzzle the self-expression of the people.[2]

Reagan's simple rhetoric put front and center what previous administrations had overlooked in favor of diplomatic compromises: he recognized the Soviet Union as an enemy of democracy and that their leaders "have refined their instruments of repression."[3]

Then, when Reagan broke from traditional diplomatic constraints and called the Soviet Union what it was, "an evil empire," Soviet Jews, dissidents, and the UCSJ grassroots saw a laser of light coming from the White House.

The president was using the Oval Office as a moral force, a bully pulpit, to get the Soviet Union to change its practices, and Soviet Jewry was clearly on his radar. In 1983, on the fiftieth anniversary of Hitler's accession to power, Reagan said, "Never again can people of conscience overlook the rise of anti-Semitism in silence."[4] He had set a benchmark for Moscow.

And indeed, Reagan did take the diplomatically imposed cover off the Soviet cesspool. His ambassador to the United Nations, Jean Kirkpatrick, condemned the Soviet's anti-Semitic and anti-Zionist campaigns. Most important, she called out refuseniks by name. "For Sharansky and Brailovsky, Ida Nudel and Vladimir Slepak, and for all their brethren in the Soviet Union, I say we stand with you in hearing and honoring their determination to be free."[5]

In his speeches, the president gave voice to an image of the world that we shared. He was tough but ready to pursue a policy of engagement with

---

2. Ronald Reagan, "Address to Members of the British Parliament," June 8, 1982, Ronald Reagan Presidential Library and Museum, https://www.reaganlibrary.gov/research /speeches/60882a (accessed June 20, 2020).

3. Ibid.

4. Pauline Peretz, *Let My People Go: The Transnational Politics of Soviet Jewish Emigration during the Cold War* (Somerset: Taylor and Francis, 2015).

5. Ibid.

the Kremlin, advancing, like UCSJ, the "carrot and stick" approach to modify Soviet behavior. His secretary of state, George Shultz, embarked on a US agenda that included human rights along with arms control, regional issues, and bilateral relations. Reagan's response to the mutually assured destruction of the arms race was the creation of a defensive shield, the Strategic Defense Initiative (known by some as "Star Wars"). Even the threat shook up the Kremlin. Clearly UCSJ had an administration we could work with.

Reagan didn't let up. He accused the Soviet Union of being "the focus of evil." Although his critics accused him of being too confrontational, of upsetting the diplomatic balance, of turning the Cold War into a holy war, Reagan pursued a policy of engagement. While his Star Wars military defensive strategy was putting extreme pressure on Russia's collapsing economy, the president simultaneously moved to engage the Kremlin in nuclear demilitarization, human rights, and other issues. "Trust, but verify" – a statement favored by Reagan, based on a Russian proverb – sounded a lot like what UCSJ talked about.

UCSJ's struggle with the Kremlin was also the struggle between good and evil, right and wrong. In those days, whether one liked the current president or not, America wasn't perceived as the cause of the world's problems. The opposite was true. America's commitment to democratic values demanded that it exert influence to protect against Soviet missiles, end Soviet repression of human rights, and bring a stable peace to the world.

UCSJ Presidency and the Summit in Reykjavik, Iceland

In the fall of 1986, at our annual meeting, I became UCSJ's national president.

It was not a role I coveted. Far from it. As a UCSJ vice-president and a member of UCSJ's executive committee, I was among the small group of the board's leadership, comfortably away from the limelight. My role at CASJ had given me the only cache I ever cared about: credibility with refuseniks. Besides, I hated speaking in public.

My problem was Harvey Barnett and Yasha Gorodetsky. They thought otherwise. After Gorodetsky emigrated, Chicago Action brought him to the States for the regular publicity rounds. One night, in our kitchen, I found myself at odds with Harvey and Gorodetsky's pressure that I accept the Union's nomination for president. Gorodetsky then upped the ante, instigating a collectively signed letter from refuseniks calling for me to become UCSJ's president. I simply couldn't stand down. My constituents had drafted me.

By the time of the meeting, I had made my peace with it. Although I didn't see myself as a charismatic leader, I did have a clear understanding of the issues and a vision of how to advance our advocacy. I knew how to represent refusenik interests. Additionally, as a team player, I knew I could free up the maximal leadership potential and expertise of my board, a group of supremely capable and dominant personalities.

Having accepted the post at our meeting, I was at the podium in the large, red-carpeted meeting room, when Lynn agitatedly strode in from the lobby to tell us that a meeting between Reagan and Gorbachev had just been announced. It was big news: the first summit between Reagan and the newest premier of the "evil empire." The meeting was designed to be shielded far from world media, almost as far as one could get – Reykjavik, Iceland.

The controlled pandemonium that initially broke out in the room quickly transformed into a unified, spontaneous resolution. UCSJ would have a presence in Iceland. We weren't going to let the location be a barrier, but it would present a significant logistical challenge, to us and to the media. Reykjavik had no international news bureaus. All the crews and equipment would have to be sent in from abroad and set up well in advance of the arrival of Air Force One and Gorbachev. We conjectured that while the news teams were awaiting their arrival, they would be hungry for news stories – and UCSJ would be there to feed them.

Instantly, our agenda turned to Reykjavik. My first job as president was to make sure that our issues were integrated into Reagan's Iceland statement. It was crucial for Reagan to make clear that the new US-Soviet relationship was dependent on verified trust, and for that, Gorbachev would have to comply with the USSR's human rights commitments.

I assembled our Reykjavik team: David Waksberg, Marillyn, June Daniels, her daughter Dani, and Scott Cohen, Senator Charles Percy's former executive assistant whom I hired as UCSJ's temporary director. We also brought our Israeli colleagues, Yosef Mendelevich and Shmuel Azarch from the Soviet Jewry Education and Information Center in Jerusalem. Of course, SSSJ's Glenn Richter and Avi Weiss were going as well.

Before we left for Reykjavik, Senator Chic Hecht – who was related to Marillyn by marriage – asked her for a list of the most desperate refusenik cases for Reagan to present to Gorbachev. She gave him UCSJ's list of the twelve hundred longest-waiting refuseniks. Senator Hecht passed the list on to President Reagan, urging him to present the list to the Soviets.

It was a cold and windy October evening when David met Marillyn and me curbside at O'Hare. Tall, lanky, already rumpled from his flight from San Francisco, David was schlepping outsize cartons housing an early-generation computer, a monstrous printer, and a modem – a feat for an NGO in 1986.

We arrived in Iceland with high hopes. David had rented a van, and we all moved into several rooms in a Reykjavik family's home. David found a kiosk-sized space to rent in the hall of a downtown office building, and we arranged for our press credentials.

As we surmised, the international press corps was already on-site. Now fully credentialed, we accessed the media center and distributed the press release announcing SSSJ's first event. Looking for news, print and television crews showed up to cover Mendelevich deplaning with a Sefer Torah in his arms. We were all on the tarmac, and when his feet touched the ground, we spontaneously encircled him and the Torah scroll, singing in Hebrew. The photos, splashed on papers from Tokyo to New York, introduced us and our Jewish agenda to the media.

Mikhail Shirman

The 35s brought Mikhail Shirman to Reykjavik. A young Soviet Jewish refugee, Mikhail was critically ill, and his survival depended on a bone marrow transplant from his sister. But his sister, Inessa Fleurov, was in Moscow, and the Kremlin wouldn't let her leave.

UCSJ's kickoff event was a press conference focusing on the gravity of Mikhail's condition, and we rented a large hall in town that could seat a couple hundred journalists. I booked a messenger call for Mikhail to speak with Inessa in Moscow, and we prepared background papers, objectives for the summit, and press releases for the media. I also wrote a speech.

An hour before our press conference, I had just put the finishing touches on my speech when the printer's transformer blew. I panicked. Unless I was giving a fact-based briefing, I always relied on prepared text to deliver an impactful, motivational message. Now I had no text. On top of that, it was my first press conference as UCSJ's national president – and I was addressing the stars of the international press corps. My heart was racing, and I looked beseechingly to David, who I confidently believed could surmount any technical obstacle. His expression told me differently. He hauled the enormous, heavy printer into our van and went in search of a computer store, sending me off in a taxi to get started.

I had no idea what to expect. I was at war with my nerves, trying to set my body language to appear confident and professional as I got out of the cab.

I entered at the rear of a large hall planked in blond wood and filled with rows and rows of tightly packed card chairs flanking two sides of a single aisle. At the podium, UCSJ's emblem hung prominently. The room was already packed with reporters, their notepads, microphones, and television cameras at the ready. Summoning a pretense of authority, I walked down the long center aisle to the podium. All heads turned. I took the microphone, introducing myself and the Union. Then I talked about Mikhail and his desperate situation. By the time David came in and handed me my speech, I was already on a roll. I knew what I had to say. When I was done, I turned to Mikhail – young, unmarried, hairless from chemotherapy – and brought him to the podium for questions.

"Why have you come to Reykjavik, Mr. Shirman?" asked the *Chicago Tribune* reporter, notepad in hand.

Mikhail answered in six fiery words: "I've come to meet my murderer."

The next morning Mikhail's story was on the front pages of the world's press. That night when I called Lenny, he told me that one of his business contacts had heard my speech on the radio as he was driving through the cornfields in southern Illinois. We did it. Mikhail's story was out.

Mikhail camped outside the summit meeting hall for two days, sometimes in heavy rain, carrying a chilling poster intended "to remind President Reagan that I am meeting the man who is murdering me." Mikhail knew he was facing death. His pall and resignation were etched on his face. At night, he disappeared from our shared residence for a walk, leaving the rest of us anxiously aware of his tragedy.

He had come to fight and fight he did. But by the time Gorbachev let his sister leave, it was too late for Mikhail. Sometime later, in Jerusalem for a conference, I went to the cemetery for Mikhail's *shloshim*, the month after his heart-wrenching passing. His death could have been avoided. Gorbachev had in effect murdered him.

Pandemonium at the Airport

Reykjavik was a contest to attract media coverage. To get his share of the limelight, Gorbachev brought his propagandists, among them Samuel Zivs, the cochair of the notorious Anti-Zionist Committee. It was also a combat arena where Ida Nudel's sister, Elana Freedman, former dissident Alex Goldfarb, other former refuseniks, families of refuseniks, and former prisoners of conscience could confront the Kremlin.

While Reagan and Gorbachev were setting the agenda for their relationship and future meetings, our activists circulated through the jammed media center, engaging the press and supplying them with evidence of Gorbachev's machinery of repression – refusenik case sheets and documentary proof of State anti-Semitism – all the while insisting that Soviet Jews be on the summit's agenda. While the two leaders clashed over Soviet Jewish emigration and other issues, the Reykjavik summit was later seen by some as a turning point in the Cold War.

After the summit ended, Marillyn and I packed up and boarded the airport shuttle. On the way, we were stopped by a police barricade that had closed off access to Reykjavik's airport for Reagan's and Gorbachev's cavalcades. We were assured our flights would be held for us. I hoped so. Yom Kippur was in two days.

Finally at the airport, we were met with pandemonium. The flight to New York had departed, leaving everyone stranded, media and government officials alike. A sinking desperation slowly took root. I wasn't going to make it home for Yom Kippur.

Lines for the public telephones were unbearably long. Finally it was my turn. At the sound of Lenny's voice, I couldn't hold back the tears. I was sobbing. I couldn't even tell him when they would get us out.

We were all put up at the nearby Keflavik military base, and Marillyn and I were installed in one of the bleakly sparse dormitory rooms. I spent Yom Kippur fasting, lying on my cot, trying to pray without a siddur, a prayer book, and asking for forgiveness for missing the mark, for my uncorrected character flaws. I was abject in my feelings of separation from my family, from my people. Tearfully I imagined my husband's and children's faces in front of me, wondering if they felt abandoned, worried, or angry. How could I convey the primacy of family to our children when I had put myself in a position where I could be separated from them? They would break the fast at my brother Chip's house, and I was thousands of miles away.

The pain of separation was torture. I counted the hours. No, the minutes.

The chartered flight that eventually rescued us was a cocktail party on wings. Everyone was euphoric to be going home. Flight attendants pouring free drinks tried to make their way around the passengers who were milling in the aisle. Joan Baez, the folk singer, was in the first row, a *Time* magazine reporter sat two aisles behind me, and reporters from all the major newspapers stood around, drinks in their hands. I was working the crowd when I glanced around and saw the Soviet ambassador to the United States seated across the aisle.

He didn't rebuff me when I handed him my UCSJ business card. Then again, there wasn't too much he could do to escape, as I had deliberately blocked his access to the aisle. Anatoly Dobrynin was middle-aged and dressed in a typically diplomatic dark suit. I suppressed my contempt and distrust for this official member of the apparat of repression and state anti-Semitism and told him about UCSJ – as if he didn't already know who we were. Curtly, he denied linkage between Jewish emigration and Reagan's Strategic Defense Initiative. In the next breath, he said that without progress on arms control, there could be no real progress on human rights. The Kremlin wanted to use us to pressure Reagan to compromise on his Strategic Defense Initiative.

Dobrynin also suggested a troubling new linkage: progress on Soviet Jewry depended on progress in the Middle East conflict. He told me that American Jews could benefit refuseniks and Soviet Jewish emigration by pushing for a Soviet presence at a future Middle East conference.

That last point reminded me of the danger UCSJ saw in moving the Soviet Jewry issue out of the US-USSR bilateral relationship and into the Israeli sphere. Only the United States could stand firm against the Soviet Union effectively. Any concessions Israel might give the Kremlin to increase emigration would necessarily threaten its national security. Only the United States had the carrots, primarily economic advantages, the Kremlin sought. For years to come we would continue to oppose the Israelis on this issue.

At the end of our conversation, Dobrynin said I was always welcome to come to the Soviet Union. "I'll remind you of that the next time I'm refused a visa. By the way," I added, "I had tried to get a meeting with you in Washington but was turned away." Next time, he said, would be different. We would see about that.

CHAPTER 15

The Union Goes to Vienna, 1986–87

Micah Naftalin: A Paragon of Leadership

Immediately upon returning from Reykjavik, I began the search for a new national director. The process took six months of flying back and forth to Washington for interviews. Working with Scott Cohen, our acting director, I interviewed several middle-aged people who were still riding high after working in the Kennedy White House or staffing a congressional office. We spent months meeting people who had either peaked in their twenties or who were looking for a springboard to something greater. We didn't see UCSJ as a springboard to anything other than free emigration for Soviet Jews.

These candidates typically exuded an impenetrable arrogance that probably was a cover for insecurity. I met a lot of people and learned that early stardom isn't a guarantee of future success. I was reminded of a lesson from my grandmother, Nanny. She told me about a corporate president who, when interviewing for an assistant, kept a large phone book on the floor at the entrance to his office. Most of the candidates walked around it. He hired the one who picked it up. I was looking for someone like that: someone without arrogance, with strong convictions, who shared our worldview. Someone who would argue with the board when he was right and stand down when he wasn't.

It wasn't surprising that, in those years, UCSJ national directors didn't last long. After all, we were a tough, hands-on board. Each member headed his or her own council, making it a board of bosses. The "wish list" of qualities we wanted in a national director made the role practically impossible for anyone to fill. We wanted someone strong, but not too independent; a powerfully strategic thinker; a persuasive speaker who could articulate and sell our program to the highest levels of government. We wanted someone whose priority would be building the public identity of UCSJ, not their personal resume. We needed someone who believed in the power of the grassroots and in what we were fighting for. We needed someone who could work with our board, handle the direct mail campaigns, instigate a development program, manage the budget and fiduciary responsibilities, and forge important relationships on the Hill, and in the State Department and White House. If that wasn't enough, we needed someone who could oversee our publications, organize our national meetings and conferences, and handle the media so we could get our story out to the press.

That someone was Micah Naftalin.

Scott was at his desk in our DC office, and I was sitting across from him, ready for the next interview. At the doorway appeared a big pillow of a man in a rumpled blue shirt with lots of little notes stuffed in the pocket, an open warm smile, kind eyes, and maybe a little spot on his tie. He kind of eased back in the chair next to me and peered over his glasses, and we just started talking. He had been working with Elie Wiesel at the Holocaust Council, had previously practiced law, had worked for a congressman, and was ready for a change. He was at ease, thoughtful, funny, and clearly smart, and when I described what we did, he just seemed to get it.

I told Micah that, though the Washington office needed to operate professionally, the UCSJ saw itself less as an organization and more as a strike force, like Peter Bergson's Emergency Committee to Save the Jewish People of Europe.[1] Was he familiar with this committee that tried to save Jews during the Holocaust but was sabotaged by the Jewish Establishment? When he told me that his mother was involved with the Bergson committee and had been burned by one of the Establishment organizations, I knew it was a done deal.

Peter Bergson was my role model for rescue. Dynamic, articulate, and intense, Bergson was motivated exclusively to save Jews. He changed his name from Hillel Kook to protect his highly respected uncle, Rabbi Abraham Isaac Kook, the first chief rabbi of Palestine.

In the 1940s, as Europe was slaughtering its Jews, England blocked Jewish entry to Palestine and America blocked Jewish entry to the United

---

1. Bergson also founded the Committee for a Jewish Army of Stateless and Palestinian Jews.

States. As reports of the systematic annihilation of Jews became known in November 1942, Bergson's committee used every available tactic, including full-page ads in major newspapers, to demand that the American people, and especially American Jewry, pressure the government to open the gates to Jewish refugees. Much of the American Jewish leadership, however, undermined his efforts, accusing Bergson and his committee of recklessness, sensationalism, and even gross effrontery for having the audacity to speak for an American constituency.[2]

Jewish organizational heads were afraid that the Bergsonites would seize the leadership of the languishing rescue effort. Aware of the Bergson committee's plans for a March 9, 1943, premiere in Madison Square Garden of *We Will Never Die*,[3] a musical performance to convey to the public the enormity of the tragedy, Rabbi Stephen Wise and the American Jewish Congress tried to preempt them by scheduling their own separate mass meeting a week before at the same location. With the extermination machinery running at full capacity, Rabbi Wise and other Jewish leaders sought ways to undermine Bergson, in part due to his criticism of the Roosevelt administration for not doing enough. But Bergson pressed ahead with congressional intervention, keeping up steady pressure for the government to take action, a tactic emulated years later by UCSJ.

The first lesson I took from this contemptible and tragic history was to view the Jewish Establishment leadership with a pervasive cynicism and lack of trust. The second lesson reaffirmed that even the best of democratic governments cannot be relied upon to guarantee Jewish rescue or

---

2.   Bergson also incurred the wrathful opposition of the Establishment as an adherent of Vladimir Jabotinsky's Zionist Revisionism. The Establishment was averse to Jabotinsky's militarist self-defense approach to Jewish survival and autonomy in Palestine. The basic tenets of Zionist Revisionism were a Jewish state based on a Jewish majority in Palestine, a Jewish Legion, and Palestine as a refuge for the suffering masses of European Jewry. For more information, see Shmuel Katz, *The Lone Wolf: A Biography of Vladimir (Ze'ev) Jabotinsky* (New York: Barricade Books, 1996).

3.   This stage performance featured top stars of the day, including Paul Muni and Edward G. Robinson. It was written by screenwriter Ben Hecht, scored by Kurt Weill, produced by Billy Rose, and directed by Moss Hart. The opening performances were attended by more than forty thousand. When it was performed in Washington, DC, the pageant was attended by First Lady Eleanor Roosevelt. For more information, see David Wyman and Rafael Medoff, *A Race against Death: Peter Bergson, America, and the Holocaust* (New York: The New Press, 2002).

survival. Only the actions of the independent public, a vocal organized swell of grassroots resistance, could bring moral and political force to bear on the government.

The Bermuda Conference underscored my conclusion. In April 1943, the United Kingdom and the United States met in Bermuda, sequestered from the press, to address the public question of Jewish refugees. The govp ernments only agreed that the war must be won. The United States did not increase the immigration quotas, nor did they even fill the allotted refugee slots. The British did not lift their prohibition on Jewish refugees seeking refuge in Palestine. It was an ominous signal, conveying to Hitler: *Do what you want with your Jews.*

The Bermuda Conference will stand in perpetuity as a monument to the dishonor and shame of those governments.

The Bergson committee was my prototype for rescue. They enlisted famous Jewish and non-Jewish personalities; engineered well-pub-licized events to attract an unresponsive public and press; organized a demonstration of Orthodox rabbis in Washington; and ran news-paper ads that printed what the press failed to report. The Jewish Establishment reacted with a campaign of delegitimization and vili-fication, eventually influencing Bergson's contributors to withdraw financial support.

I explained to Micah that, like Bergson, the UCSJ and our coun-cil leaders operated outside the mainstream and were confronted by the Establishment's overt efforts to silence, vilify, and sabotage us.

The Establishment also undermined our credibility by whitewashing the Soviets' behavior. There were leftist Jewish organizations and media that were overt Soviet apologists. They squelched UCSJ's information about Soviet repression in favor of promoting so-called peace initiatives, ignor-ing the warning of the exiled Soviet academician Andrei Sakharov that a nation that makes war against its people cannot be trusted to make peace with its neighbor. Prestigious Chicago Jewish attorneys warmly welcomed and lavishly entertained the very same Soviet functionaries who had sen-tenced Jewish refuseniks to labor camps and prison. Corporate heads were seduced into becoming Soviet apologists so that they might advance their commercial interests in the USSR. There were prominent Jewish leaders with access to the highest reaches of government who saw our movement as a threat to their authority, access, prestige, and fundraising. In fact, some

Jewish and religious leaders viewed our open opposition to and nonviolent confrontation with the Soviets as dangerous.

The Union of Councils opposed them all.

Micah Naftalin's worldview made UCSJ a perfect outlet for his abundant personal resources. He understood that UCSJ wasn't seeking a national director to do organization-building; rather, we wanted a streamlined rescue force. After all, those who cannot remember the past are condemned to repeat it. And the Union never forgot the past and the tragedy of the Holocaust.

And now Micah Naftalin was on board to move our efforts forward.

The last question I asked in the interview was, could he handle the strong personalities on our board?

He quipped, "You kidding? You ever worked with Holocaust survivors?"

In truth, he was everything the movement needed him to be and what we all needed him to be. He was undefeatable. When his mother passed away, Micah sat the traditional seven days of shivah and then jumped on a plane to meet me in Vienna for a conference. Later, though weakened by chemotherapy, he insisted on going through with our plans to go to Russia.

He was an attentive listener who grasped the core of complex issues and formulated strategies to deal with them. He was a superb advocate and consummate negotiator. In the most intractable conversations, he patiently picked his way through an argument, point by point, until he managed to turn things the way he saw it.

Micah always pulled it off. It was never too late, he was never too busy, nothing was ever too hard. He always found the time, energy, and resources to do whatever was needed to mount a response to the perpetual crises.

He touched and changed the lives of hundreds, if not thousands, of people who are now in America and in Israel. I am overcome by an avalanche of memories of what he did and what he accomplished, the people he helped, the lifelines he created. He fought for prisoners of conscience and refuseniks, for the right to leave a country and to return, for the right to identity, and against the ominous currents of anti-Semitism and fascism in the Soviet Union. He forged organizational relationships and built coalitions.

And through it all, he was optimistic and superbly undefeatable, like a big sturdy engine that just keeps steadily rolling down the track, never disappointing people waiting at the station.

Even his illness backtracked in the face of his quiet determination, but in December 2009, his body finally gave out. Although I had been present for his surgery years before, I was home with a bad case of bronchitis when he died, and I was unable to fly to the funeral. The closure I needed never came.

Micah Naftalin, may your memory be a blessing for all of Israel, just as your life was. It was a privilege to have known you, to have worked with you, to have been your friend. You will always be missed.

The Helsinki Final Act and the Vienna Follow-Up Meetings

The Union was operating in Washington with increasing effectiveness, but we never missed an opportunity to use the international framework to further our cause. The 1975 Helsinki Final Act, also known as the Helsinki accords, gave us a brilliantly strategic venue for advancing the Soviet Jewry issue.

In simple language, it gave us international leverage.

The grassroots Soviet Jewry movement was well underway when thirty-five nations, flags waving outside Finlandia Hall in Helsinki, signed the final document of the Conference on Security and Cooperation in Europe (CSCE) in the summer of 1975.

The Helsinki Final Act created an unprecedented structure to deal with global problems. It created four categories, or "baskets," of issues that were separate but linked. The first basket covered political and military issues like territorial integrity, international recognition of national borders, and the implementation of confidence-building measures between military adversaries. The Soviets were especially interested in this basket because they sought international recognition for their incorporation of the Baltic nations seized during World War II. This basket provided a strong incentive for them to sign the agreement.

The second basket focused on economic issues, like trade and scientific cooperation. This aspect was very much in our interest, as it legitimized contact between scientists outside the USSR and refusenik scientists, who had been fired from their institutions and were convening the Refusenik Scientific Seminars.

It was the third basket, though, which fired up our struggle. It officially recognized individual human rights, including freedom of emigration, reunification of families, and cultural exchanges as legitimate principles and objectives. It called for the respect for human rights and fundamental freedoms, including freedom of thought, conscience, the press, and religion or belief. The third basket thrust our agenda onto the front burner.

The Helsinki Final Act involved a straightforward process: progress in one basket required equivalent progress in the others. What it meant for us was that, if the Soviets were interested in achieving their goals in one of the baskets, they would have to make concessions in the area we cared about: human rights.

On the practical side was CSCE's process for implementation and follow-up review meetings, which were international venues to measure compliance by the signatories. This provision provided a mechanism for UCSJ to present evidence of Soviet noncompliance regarding Jewish emigration. Review conferences were held in Belgrade, 1977–78; Madrid, 1980–83; and Vienna, 1986–89. The Union played a role in each.

During the several trips I made to Vienna for CSCE follow-up meetings, I never got to know the city. My daylight hours were occupied with meetings with governmental delegations. Besides, for me, the magnificence of this city – the cradle of Mozart and Strauss, with its glittering opera house and palaces and stunningly dressed women – was overshadowed by a history I couldn't forget. I couldn't cross a boulevard without hearing Gestapo sirens blaring, tires screeching, boots clomping, and the screams as they dragged Jews out of their apartments. Images of thousands of swastika-waving Viennese welcoming Hitler's army just refused to leave me. All Vienna had for me was in the CSCE meeting halls.

Ambassador Warren Zimmermann was the US delegation head at the CSCE Vienna conference. I always found Warren to be warm and straightforward, sympathetic and responsive, despite being a State Department official. He related to refuseniks as people, not just as names on case sheets. Over the years, I met with him in several international venues.

I have one singular memory, a precious cameo of Warren, a story within a story. A momentary frame in Laura Bialis's film *Refusenik* contains a hint of the story, though hardly anyone would notice it.

After seventeen years of refusal, seventeen years of resistance against the state's organized brutality and repression, after arrests, prison cells, hunger strikes, demonstrations, meetings with American dignitaries, and abasement, Masha and Volodya Slepak, in desperation, hung a sheet on their balcony, printed with the words "Let us go to our sons in Israel." For this crime, they were sentenced to five excruciatingly painful years in Siberia, exiled from their friends, exiled from the most essential physical comfort, even further exiled from their sons than they had been before.

Finally, in October 1987, it was over. They were on a flight to their sons in Israel with a short stopover in Vienna. Laura Bialis had her camera waiting, focused on the large doors that would open for arriving passengers.

Suddenly the doors opened. Masha and Volodya were the first ones out, and in front of them were the two sons they hadn't seen for many long years. Parents and sons clung to each other in a tearful hug that didn't end. While Laura was filming the emotional scene, her camera happened to catch a glimpse of Ambassador Warren Zimmermann, who had arranged the emotional reunion. By the time the film aired, Warren Zimmermann was no longer alive.

Shortly after the opening of the 1986 Vienna conference, Warren honored Micah and me as special guests at a luncheon he hosted at the ambassador's residence. He afforded us an extraordinary opening, an insider's forum, where we could work on building consensus with the heads of the European delegations.

Warren ushered Micah and me into the elegant dining chambers of the residence and seated me next to the Dutch ambassador, who was smartly dressed in a crisp striped shirt. By the time lunch was over, he had rapidly reviewed UCSJ's extensive compilation of evidence of Soviet noncompliance with the human rights basket of the Helsinki Final Act. He was looking for this kind of specificity and planned to raise these critical issues directly with the Soviet delegation later that afternoon. Warren's luncheon established our credibility with the European CSCE ambassadors and paved the way for our follow-up meetings with their delegations. He helped advance the United States' interest in gaining consensus with our European allies on Soviet human rights violations.

Still, I wasn't immune to the incongruity of the circumstance. Here I was in Vienna in my well-tailored suit and three-inch spiked heels, carrying the new MCM bag given to me by my mother for my fortieth birthday, seated at a meticulously set table with calligraphed place cards, gleaming silver, sparkling crystal, and white-jacketed waiters. Around the table were cultivated European diplomats in fine suits, smelling of aftershave. In this world of refined elegance, I was representing a world of brutality, of incessantly frigid cold, insufficient food, and anti-Semitic cruelty – a world where Jews held on to their humanity in labor camps, prison cells, and transports. The Jews we had come to represent were barely surviving, and all the luxurious splendor couldn't chase away the brutal visions that were always in front of my eyes.

Micah and I had come to Vienna well prepared. For weeks in advance of every CSCE meeting, UCSJ's council leaders prepared extensive data, documenting state-sponsored anti-Semitism and anti-emigration policies. The Washington office assembled thick spiraled briefing books with our updated refusenik list, case sheets, appeals, and position papers. As a fully registered nongovernmental organization (NGO), UCSJ functioned as an operational facilitator, providing delegations and the press our briefing books as evidence of Soviet noncompliance. We had unrestricted access to delegations – including the Soviets.

In Vienna, Micah and I sat down with Ambassador Richard Schifter, assistant secretary of state for human rights and humanitarian affairs, to confer with him about our strategy. In a letter to Secretary of State Shultz before the closing of the Vienna conference, he warned against ignoring Soviet violations. He wrote, "continued failure on our part to relate our human-rights concerns to concrete measures, combined with continued expressions of appreciation for the few acts of Soviet 'kindness,' will cause the Soviets to conclude that our statements of concern are largely for public consumption. They will further conclude that these statements are either not sincerely [meant] or, if they are, that we are satisfied with the small steps they have taken."[4]

Although we saw Schifter as an advocate in the government, it would take decades until I comprehended the depth and sincerity of his commitment to Soviet Jews.

By the end of the first Vienna meeting, I returned home utterly drained, but hopeful. While there, I had presented facts, argued, and persuaded. I had been completely absorbed in every interaction, alert to nuances or doublespeak that might be easily missed. I hadn't realized just how much energy it took. On the flight back, Micah and I methodically scrutinized our interactions. Which delegations needed ongoing consultations? Which required more work or a fresh approach? Where were we strong? Where

---

4.   Anatoly Adamishin and Richard Schifter, *Human Rights, Perestroika, and the End of the Cold War* (Washington, DC: United States Institute of Peace Press, 2009).

was our weakness? Exhausted, I just wanted to submerge myself in my family life and try to delay the pressures waiting for me. But Vienna wasn't over. Micah and I would have to return over the next three years.

In the summer of 1987, as the second Vienna conference was coming to an end, a concluding document was in the works. Warren Zimmermann said the US goal in assessing the USSR's compliance was to compare their promises to their actions. Exactly right. Although the Kremlin had reunified some separated families, given exit visas to some former prisoners of conscience, and stopped some jamming of the radios, it had a long way to go.

Before the final document was approved, in a preemptive strike to defuse international criticism, the Soviet delegation floated a proposal to host a human rights conference in Moscow. "And will Soviet citizens be prohibited from attending these sessions?" Zimmermann questioned the Soviets.

UCSJ objected immediately. A Moscow human rights conference was a ludicrous contradiction in terms. UCSJ and the 35s proceeded with a parallel campaign, urging President Reagan and Prime Minister Thatcher in the strongest possible terms to prevent Moscow from hosting the follow-up CSCE human rights conference. After all, whatever improvements they had made were not sufficient to give Moscow the legitimacy that would come from hosting a human rights conference.

In a letter, President Reagan assured Micah and me that there were preconditions for his agreement to a Moscow conference. Rita Eker had similar assurances from Thatcher, and we were confident they would hold the line. Then, late in 1988, both of them caved. Moscow's last-ditch effort to look like a credible partner on the world scene won out. Maybe Reagan was trying for an end run before the new president, George H. W. Bush, would be sworn in a few months later. In any case, the final document of the Vienna conference included a reference to a Conference on the Human Dimension to be held in Moscow in 1991.

The question was, what were the assurances that Reagan had referred to in his correspondence to us? What did the United States get in exchange for this conciliatory gesture? OVIR offices were still refusing exit visas based on "access to state security." Emigration procedures were still not institutionalized. Jews were still currency for barter. Nothing had changed. I believed Reagan and Thatcher had lost an opportunity to encourage real reform at an optimal time for success, and they had sanctioned an intolerable legitimization of the Soviets' repressive policies. It was now just a question of how many Jews and dissidents would be held under house arrest or dragged off trains and planes while the Soviets sat in plush chairs in a conference room, professing concern for freedom.

Reagan's worldview of the "evil empire" had brought us hope. But in the end, his support of the Moscow conference sorely diminished the capital the United States had stored up, and that left all of us in the movement deeply disappointed.

CHAPTER 16

Dupes and Pawns, 1986–87

Reagan's public recognition of the "evil empire" reaffirmed America's commitment to human rights. Soviet Jews, dissidents, and the UCSJ endorsed his words, hoping they'd be followed by action. Even if they weren't, the rhetoric was indispensable. After all, the first step in winning a war is identifying the enemy.

Reagan's view wasn't unanimously accepted. Some, on the far left, were idealistic utopians, duped by the notion that all peoples are imbued with liberal and humanitarian values. Perhaps less naive were those hoping to gain some legitimacy or advantage from dealings with the Soviets. Motivated by self-interest, wittingly or unwittingly, these pawns became apologists for the Kremlin, which moved them around on an international chessboard.

The Dupes

Shrugging off the lessons of Hitler and Stalin, and ignoring Andrei Sakharov's warning that a nation that makes war on its own people cannot be trusted to make peace with its neighbors, many ideologues believed peace could be achieved by citizen diplomacy, by regular people just talking to each other.

The resulting "citizen summits" allowed the Kremlin to present a human face to the gullible American public, duped by sophisticated Soviet propaganda. Distortions and egregiously false claims spread in the media like wildfire, and UCSJ was desperate to stamp them out. Reverend Billy Graham, during his 1982 visit to the USSR, claimed there was "a measure of religious freedom"[1] in the USSR. Reacting to this outrageous fabrication, Marillyn and I called on CASJ activist Marty Oberman, a highly

---

1. Kenneth A. Briggs, "Billy Graham Back Home Defends Remarks," *New York Times,* May 20, 1982.

visible Chicago alderman, to write a rebuttal, which was published in the *Chicago Sun-Times*.

One of the most stunning examples of media distortion was Mike Wallace's soft-pedaled interview on *60 Minutes* of Viktor Afanasyev, the chief editor of *Pravda*, then one of the world's most widely circulated newspapers. It was an obvious and shocking failure for Wallace not to have squarely questioned Afanasyev about the paper's vicious anti-Semitism. He also neglected to question the editor about his direct role in publishing defamations about specific refuseniks and vilifying the emigration movement as anti-Soviet. His omission, intentional or not, whitewashed *Pravda*'s role in disseminating these poisonous articles, the very articles we were giving to the Congress and State Department to use in protests to the Soviet government.

Initiatives like the US-Soviet sister city programs and Ted Turner's Moscow Goodwill Games were manipulated by the Soviets to whitewash their image. The educational Chautauqua Society, the trade unions, even the American Bar Association seemed to operate under the illusion that the nuclear threat would magically disappear through a citizen diplomacy that turned a blind eye to repression and rule by fear. They were duped by the Soviets' masterful manipulation, which extended even to doublespeak. Both sides used the same words – such as *truth* or *peace* – but meant different things.

Among the most flagrant examples of Soviet propaganda and American naivete were the "space bridge" telecasts linking Soviet and US audiences, co-hosted by Phil Donahue in New York and Vladimir Pozner in Moscow. In their respective studios, the hosts discussed issues and took questions from the audiences. The problem was that these programs gave voice to free-speaking idealistic Americans in the US studio and to scripted Soviet apologists, KGB plants, in the studio in Moscow. It was a farce. It created the illusion of equivalency between the two societies and, as such, betrayed every truth-loving Soviet citizen yearning for freedom.

Pozner, a smooth-talking Soviet commentator, was Jewish, raised in the States by Russian émigrés who had returned to the USSR in 1952. He was the ideological antithesis of refusenik Abe Stolar. Abe's parents had also brought him back to Russia from the United States, but Stolar, fighting the Kremlin for his visa, was caught in the Soviets' web of lies. Pozner, in contrast, was a Soviet apologist consulted by the US media for his "objectivity," seducing millions of Americans with his affable warmth and unaccented English.[2] He was so influential that ABC gave him eight minutes of uninterrupted airtime following one of President Reagan's speeches. (The network later apologized after receiving a sharply worded complaint from the White House.)

Donahue protected the agenda from questions of human rights and Jewish emigration. Attempts to alert the program's producers that the Soviets would pack their studio with propagandists went unanswered.

Caught on Camera

Even as Donahue and Pozner were airing their space bridge telecasts in 1987, the Kremlin was violently cracking down on refusenik protests.

It was February 13, the day of one of the Donahue hookups. That snowy evening, I'd stopped to pick up something to make for dinner after work. Anxious to get home, I was oblivious to the news blasting from the store's wall-mounted television. Suddenly I stopped cold. Did I hear the broadcaster say "Natasha Beckman"?

Turning to the screen, I saw KGB agents beating up Moscow refuseniks demonstrating on behalf of longtime activist Josef Begun, who had been sentenced three times for his emigration efforts and Hebrew teaching. About a dozen uniformed police officers and some eighty plainclothesmen were waiting for more than a dozen Jewish protesters when they arrived at Arbat Square for the fifth straight day of demonstrations. Paralyzed, I watched twelve plainclothesmen kicking Beckman on a Moscow sidewalk after they had thrown her to the ground.

Then the unidentified agents turned on Western reporters covering the protest, assaulting them and destroying their camera equipment. CNN correspondent Peter Arnett said he and his cameraman and producer were pushed to the street and kicked in the face and groin.

Uniformed police officers watched and did nothing while plainclothes agents jumped Josef Begun's son, Boris, pinning his arms and dragging him screaming from the square while other men punched and taunted him. He and other protesters were sentenced to fifteen days in prison for hooliganism. One activist was hospitalized with kidney injuries.

---

2. In 1987, Donahue and Pozner happily accepted an award from the Better World Society, a Ted Turner organ that also supported the left-wing Sandinistas in Nicaragua.

TASS smeared the Western correspondents as anti-Sovieteers who had made dissidents and Soviet Jews their pet projects. The Soviet news agency also reported, refuseniks told me, that many of the demonstrators had been urged to organize the rally by long-distance phone calls from Pamela Cohen.

Donahue never referred to the incident on his space bridge broadcasts.

The Pawns and the Firestorm over Jackson-Vanik

In addition to naive, idealist dupes, there were also the pawns, those who allowed their personal interests to make them vulnerable to manipulation by the Soviet apparat. We knew that kind of manipulation well. It was the kind our prisoners of conscience fought every day in Soviet prisons and labor camps, where KGB interrogators told them: "Just recant and we'll set you free." And refuseniks were promised, "If you just cooperate with us by giving us a little information about other refuseniks, you'll get your visa."

Against this backdrop, two prestigious public figureheads took center stage.

UCSJ and our council leaders had managed for years to keep our simmering controversies with the Israeli government and the Jewish Establishment away from the public. We refrained from airing our differing policies on Soviet Jewry in public lest that undermine the administration's and Congress's support for Israel. Nevertheless, the controversy exploded, and we were drawn into the center of a public storm.

In the mid-1980s, the escalating numbers of Jews choosing the United States over Israel was increasingly troubling for the Israeli Foreign Ministry. Jews emigrating from the Soviet Union to the United States did so as refugees, but for Israel, the existence of the Jewish homeland made the concept of Jewish refugees obsolete. Furthermore, Israel maintained that Soviet Jews, emigrating with Soviet-required *vysovs*, invitations from Israel, were obligated to go to Israel.

UCSJ supported refuseniks' aliyah-driven activity, but we couldn't claim the movement was exclusively Zionist. We supported their freedom of choice, and for that reason, the Lishka accused us of "diverting" Jews to America. Worse, they characterized us as anti-Zionists.

We earnestly believed that, with the support of the Lishka, UCSJ could do more to foster Zionism in the USSR. We delivered to the Lishka refuseniks' requests for information and questions about absorption, jobs, and housing, and we urged them to follow through with answers. More of an immediate issue was our concern that refuseniks' complaints about the lack of *vysovs* were not being addressed. Israel wasn't sending a sufficient number of *vysovs* to accommodate the constantly growing demand for exit visa applications. This issue was a source of contention for years.

UCSJ's briefers were sending tourists to refuseniks with information on Israel, but we lacked the materials and resources of the Sochnut, the Jewish Agency, and of the Lishka. We sought to advance their objectives and urged them to supply us with information to help facilitate aliyah. Our willingness to cooperate went nowhere.

In March 1987, Moscow refuseniks reported that two prominent Jewish Establishment leaders were in Moscow at the behest of the Israeli government. Their brief was to negotiate a direct-flights agreement with Soviet officials, an agreement that would cut off the emigration route to America. As their discussions became public, it was clear that the emphasis was on the direction of emigration rather than the number of Jews who were leaving.

The two men were powerful representatives of the Jewish bureaucracy. Morris Abram was chairman of the organizational octopus, the Conference of Presidents of Major American Jewish Organizations, and simultaneously the chairman of the National Conference on Soviet Jewry. Canadian-born billionaire Edgar Bronfman was president of the World Jewish Congress and also the CEO of Seagram's Company. Seagram's had long advocated a waiver of the Jackson-Vanik Amendment to facilitate whiskey sales to vodka-soaked Russia and to import Stolichnaya to the United States. After their negotiation with the Soviets, Abram and Bronfman had called a group of refusenik leaders, including Yuli Kosharovsky and recently released prisoner of conscience Josef Begun, to their hotel room to inform them of their proposal.

Word spread quickly, and I phoned Yuli. In the background I could hear raised, emphatic voices. On behalf of the Israeli Foreign Ministry, the two men had suggested that a Soviet agreement for direct flights[3] to Israel, and assurances of visas for ten to twelve thousand emigrants per year, could be linked to a waiver of the Jackson-Vanik Amendment and possibly even a seat at a future Middle East peace conference.

---

3.   The proposed direct flights from the Soviet Union to Israel were not strictly "direct"; they necessitated a stopover in Romania, where El Al had landing rights.

The heads of the American Jewish Establishment, colluding with Israel's Foreign Ministry, were offering a possible waiver of Jackson-Vanik's trade restrictions without demand for a commensurate quid pro quo. In exchange for an insignificant number of Jewish emigrants, including permission for some long-term refuseniks – barely a dent in the half-million Jews wanting to leave – they were ready to concede our most powerful weapon. It was a sellout. Whatever assurance they thought they had extracted from the Soviets, it came nowhere near the refuseniks' criteria for a waiver of Jackson-Vanik.

Infuriated, Yuli told me that Abram and Bronfman "were negotiating their futures" without having first consulted refusenik leadership. He bitterly noted that the two emissaries and the Soviet officials shared common ground in their complicity to sideline the leaders and spokespeople of the Jewish movements in the USSR.

From Israel, Lev Utevsky faxed me the response of two of the most prominent refusenik activists, Natasha Khassina in Moscow and Inna Mizruhina Elbert in Kiev. "You can't imagine the indignation in this connection. There was never such surprising unity.… For me, it was the same kind of a betrayal as the sell-out in 1938. He sold those on whom Jewish culture, Hebrew teaching, Torah studies, etc., were built. On this was built the bones of the people who were refused 10–17 years. What right has he not to take us into consideration? Will we be ransomed one by one as it was before?"[4]

The inflammatory contempt of refusenik leaders and former prisoners like Yosef Mendelevich in Israel sent shock waves throughout the grassroots in Israel, America, England, and Canada. In and out of the Soviet Union, activists were outraged by the highly publicized negotiations and by the *shtadlan* model – the intercessor, the court Jew – we all rejected.

I was stunned and outraged. Jackson-Vanik was sacrosanct until the Soviets met our criteria for a high and sustained level of emigration, and they were nowhere close to that.

Controversy between Jewish organizations and UCSJ erupted from time to time about where to set the benchmark for the presidential waiver of the amendment and how to ensure steady emigration rates should the Kremlin meet our demand. In 1986, just a year before the Abram-Bronfman

---

4.   Fax, 1987, archives of Pamela Braun Cohen, American Jewish Historical Society, New York.

proposal, numbers had plummeted to just 914 emigrants, after exceeding fifty thousand in 1979. The World Jewish Congress and other organizations blamed the amendment's restrictions and started pushing President Reagan to implement the waiver in an effort to increase the numbers. Under Morey Schapira, UCSJ's president, we took out a full-page ad in the *New York Times* telling the president that Soviet Jews and prisoners of conscience were calling on him to "hang tough," keeping the amendment in place until the Soviets released every Jew who wanted to leave. Assured that a direct approach to Morris Abram, president of the National Conference, would go nowhere, Morey exercised his good relations with Ken Bialkin, then chairman of the Conference of Presidents, who accepted the UCSJ- and SSSJ-approved document. Bialkin then got Abram to agree. On May 30, 1986, without significant changes, the Conference of Presidents released the statement Morey had crafted and sent a unified signal to the Kremlin that all the Jewish organizations stood together. Behind us stood our allies in Congress. The Jewish organizations' unity defied the Kremlin's active measures to separate us.

But now, only a year later, when the Kremlin was promising permission for only ten to twelve thousand Jews, the Lishka and the Establishment were ready to squander our strongest asset.

Numbers don't mean much unless they are compared to the larger picture. The increased number of emigrants, on track to reach eight thousand for the year, only reflected the dramatic increase in applicants, due to the increasing anti-Semitism in the public arena. By this time, an estimated four hundred thousand Jews had already applied to leave. If emigration continued at its 1987 rate, it would have taken fifty years for every Jew who had already applied to get a visa. And that number didn't include the "poor relatives" who couldn't get the required permission to emigrate from parents or spouses. It also didn't include a growing number of Jews who hadn't been able to receive a *vysov*. Additionally, there were no assurances that the Kremlin would hold even to this marginal number on an annual basis. It was astounding that the Jewish communal organizations were prepared to give the Soviets most-favored-nation trading benefits on the basis of some meager assurances.

To promote the stabilization of high emigration rates, UCSJ advocated the institutionalization of emigration rights. Changes to Soviet law would certainly not provide guarantees, but they would be a barometer of intent.

Another significant flaw with the agreement involved the closing of the American option for Soviet Jews. Until this point, all emigrating Soviet Jews first flew to Vienna, which served as a processing center. There, Jews opting for Israel were handled by the Jewish Agency, and Jews choosing America were processed primarily by the Hebrew Immigrant Aid Society (HIAS). Under this new proposal, Soviet Jews would be flown from Moscow to Bucharest. From there, El Al would immediately fly them to Israel, where they would be given Israeli citizenship. As Israeli citizens, they would be ineligible for US refugee status and subjected to normal immigration quotas. Abram and Bronfman were setting into motion the Israeli government's long-term goal: denying freedom of choice by effectively closing America's gates.

The negotiations for direct flights to Israel engineered by Abram and Bronfman triangulated the shared interests of Israel, big business, and the Kremlin – and were a powerful threat to Jackson-Vanik. The agreement signaled that the little the Kremlin was doing was sufficient, as long as it would change the direction the emigrants would take upon leaving.

UCSJ recognized that these secret negotiations and their implications were seriously problematic and could not go unanswered. Micah flew to Chicago, and we worked well into the night, drafting a statement of UCSJ's position. The next morning, we caught an early morning flight to meet with a member of the *New York Times'* editorial board. An editorial or an op-ed could help us hold the line on the amendment, but I was skeptical that the *Times* would publish a position that deviated from that of the Jewish bureaucracy. Karl Meyer grilled us for an anxiety-ridden couple of hours, and we walked out depleted and without much hope.

About three weeks later, as my morning coffee percolated, I opened the *New York Times*; opposite the editorial page, I caught sight of a sketch of the Kremlin. Below, a bold headline read, "Give Soviet Jews a Choice." The authors were Pamela B. Cohen and Micah H. Naftalin. They published our position paper.

The piece laid out UCSJ's criticism of the secret agreement. Our primary objection was that the Israeli plan disconnected the waiver of Jackson-Vanik's trade restrictions from free emigration and instead focused on the direction of emigration. This plan "distracts world attention from the chief issue facing Soviet Jews, which is to pressure the Soviet Union to allow more Jews to emigrate."[5]

The destination of airplanes out of Moscow was irrelevant, we argued. Jackson-Vanik was concerned with the number of Jews given permission, not the direction of the flights. Equally outrageous was their contention that an annual emigration rate of ten to twelve thousand – only one-fifth of the emigration figure in 1979 – was adequate.

Israel's attempt to end its troublesome *noshrim* (dropout) problem was not our only objection. Our op-ed piece laid out a far more critical consequence of their negotiations: the emasculation of American leverage. By restricting Jewish emigration to Israel, the proposal would effectively take the Soviet Jewry issue out of the bilateral relationship between the United States and the USSR and drop it into the Israeli-Soviet sphere of influence. But in the absence of diplomatic relations and without sufficient political-economic leverage to induce the Kremlin to make concessions, Israel's negotiating posture was marginal. America was strategically far better positioned to attract the Kremlin's desire for trade advantages, scientific and technological exchange, and disarmament. Soviet Jewish interests demanded that emigration remain a function of American-Soviet bilateral relations.

UCSJ's positions didn't coalesce in a vacuum. While there were refuseniks, like Yuli Kosharovsky, who viewed the movement as exclusively aliyah driven, there were also refusenik leaders, like Leonid Stonov, for whom emigration was a function of the broader human rights agenda. Regardless of the differences, both groups, like us, expected substantive performance from the Soviets before Jackson-Vanik could be waived.

The op-ed explained that two separate bilateral agreements could fulfill the aspirations of both groups.

It cited our call for an Israeli-Soviet agreement for the voluntary repatriation of Soviet Jews to Israel, just as Grigory Vasserman and Yasha Gorodetsky had advocated. A repatriation agreement, eliminating the Soviet-required Israeli *vysov*, would encourage aliyah.

Simultaneously, we advocated a US-Soviet agreement confirming the broad principle of family reunification. Such an agreement would affirm

5. Pamela B. Cohen and Micah H. Naftalin, "Give Soviet Jews a Choice," *New York Times*, June 18, 1987.

America's insistence that high levels of Jewish emigration would continue to be the preeminent benchmark for the waiver of the Jackson-Vanik Amendment.

A Tense Encounter

When the Jewish Agency's World Conference on Soviet Jewry met in London a few months later, UCSJ, always pariahs to the Establishment, was relegated to observer status. Seated in the auditorium were the Establishment heads of the Jewish communities representing Israel, France, England, America, and Australia. Micah and I unobtrusively took our seats in the rear.

One speaker after another made it clear that they had scrapped their formal agenda. Each of them gave vent to anger about the "insidious" *New York Times* op-ed, uniformly defaming UCSJ leaders as anti-Zionist, publicity-seeking renegades perpetuating their own selfish organizational interests.

It was an unabated harangue even before Morris Abram took the podium. Morris was an accomplished attorney with an Oxford University degree. He was a former president of Brandeis University and had contributed to civil rights legislation. He was a commanding figure, the leader of the American Jewish organizational structure. He was a formidable opponent, but he was wrong, and we had called him on it.

Finally taking the podium, Abram declared the Soviet Jewry movement to be exclusively an aliyah, not a human rights, movement. This was a legitimate, if controversial, point of difference between the Israeli government and UCSJ. However, he crossed a line by going on to say that Soviet Jews were not going to America because they were refugees fleeing anti-Semitism, but because "they wanted two refrigerators." That accusation debased every Jew fleeing Soviet Jew-hatred. (Not much later, at a press conference with Secretary of State Shultz in America, he hypocritically articulated the exact opposite position, saying that the Soviet Jewry movement was a human rights issue.)

I could barely keep seated. After numerous unsuccessful attempts, at the end of two days, I was finally recognized and permitted to respond.

I got to my feet, my mind racing with retorts and corrections to their fallacious accusations and defamation. But before I could begin, in what was clearly intended as an ostentatious protest, the prominent leader of

French Jewry, a short, pompous, gray-haired gentleman in an elegantly tailored three-piece suit, slowly rose from his chair. The room fell silent as his silver-tipped cane and the heels of his shoes clipped deliberately on the wood floor as he walked the length of the room to exit.

When he finished, I began. Step by step, I explained the rationale for UCSJ's categorical opposition to the Establishment's denigration of Jews who emigrated to the States rather than to Israel. Their criticism of these so-called dropouts placed blame on the victims of Soviet repression while at the same time excusing the Soviets for tactics that influenced the direction of emigration. Anticipated concessions from Washington motivated the Kremlin. We didn't underestimate the capacity of KGB surveillance to trigger opening the gates wider for Jews going to America than to Israel. Besides, UCSJ was not prepared to advocate any policy that might close America's doors. I then went through the laundry list of criticisms that the refuseniks leveled against Abram and Bronfman's dealings with the Soviets and the concessions they proposed.

Morris Abram and others fumed, but no one else walked out.

David and Goliath

The London conference wasn't my only altercation with Morris Abram. Shortly afterward, in his position as head of the Conference of Presidents, Morris was asked to put together a small delegation to meet with President Reagan and Secretary of State George Shultz. It was clear that the White House, not Abram, put UCSJ on the list of attendees, but he called to inform me of the meeting and took the opportunity to berate me. He was furious. First, he claimed that Micah and I should have consulted with him before submitting our article to the *New York Times*. Then, in reference to the upcoming meeting at the White House, he threatened me. He said that if I said anything at the meeting that would damage his relationship with the Secretary of State, he would "destroy" my husband.

Following the meeting with Reagan, I complied with Morris's demand for a consultation. Micah and I met him at his richly appointed New York law office. In one of the board rooms, I briefed him on the factors that had contributed to our assessment of the state of emigration and Soviet intent. It was shockingly apparent that Morris, the chairman of the National Conference for Soviet Jewry, had only a superficial understanding of the issue he was representing.

I watched his reaction to data that I could not have imagined he didn't already know. The refusenik number he was using to negotiate for a waiver of Jackson-Vanik didn't take into account the rapidly expanding number of Jews trying to leave. An untold number were unable to get the *vysovs* they needed even to begin the application process.

Furthermore, regarding his accusation about our lack of consultation before going public with criticism, I reminded him of our letter detailing UCSJ's position. In it, we had cautioned him about the danger of negotiating away Jackson-Vanik for a small proportion of Jews seeking to leave. He said he never received our letter. With that, I confronted his executive director, Jerry Goodman, seated directly in front of me, inquiring why he never gave our letter to his boss. Jerry snaked out of the room.

I went on: Abram and Bronfman had negotiated their Moscow plan on the bones of people like Lev and Inna Elbert. Earlier that year, the Elberts had gone on a hunger strike for over forty-five days to protest the twelve refusals they had received since 1976. When we talked on the phone at the time, Lev was weak and could barely speak. He said, "The last weapons we have to use are our own bodies."[6] Before hanging up, he said that when Steny Hoyer, chairman of the congressional Helsinki Commission, and the rest of a congressional delegation questioned Gorbachev about Lev and Inna's case, he said that "their term of refusal [on grounds of state secrets] was from five to ten years." If that were true, Lev and Inna's refusal would have already expired. Then Gorbachev exposed the lie of these alleged secrecy refusals, saying that a resolution of "broader issues" between the US and USSR would lead to the resolution of the Elberts' case.[7] That was exactly our point. The fate of Soviet Jews was in the hands of the American government – not in the hands of the Lishka.

Micah and I felt we had made our case, and we left Morris's conference room feeling more than a little like David after overcoming Goliath. My first thought was my Uncle Shel. Our emotional political debates when I was in my twenties usually drove me from family dinners in tears, but eventually I learned to be clinically factual. I owed the day to him.

Decades later, I learned that Morris Abram had come to regret his role in these negotiations with the Soviets and his lack of consultation with

---

6. "Lev and Inna Elbert Hunger Strike Leaves Refusenik Couple Weak and Ill," *Jewish Telegraphic Agency* (JTA), April 17, 1987.

7. Ibid.

refuseniks. Early on he came to doubt "that Gorbachev's policy of glasnost would provide any significant benefit to Soviet Jews."[8]

Our confrontation with Morris wasn't a personal vendetta or a case of one-upmanship. It was a matter of principle that went to the very core of who were the legitimate spokespeople for Soviet Jewry. Was it the court Jew, the *shtadlan*, the head of the American Jewish bureaucracy? Or was it the refusenik leaders, those with the most at stake but who were being patronized or ignored in negotiations that moved them like pawns on an international chessboard? To me, it was a matter of abolishing the old stereotypical form of intervention. It was about confronting the infamous legacy of the Reform rabbi, Stephen Wise, who had become America's most influential Jew.[9] While six million of his people were being slaughtered, he had unparalleled access to President Roosevelt. Instead of urging FDR to intervene, to open the doors to Jewish refugees, and to inform the Jewish public about the atrocities, Wise was an apologist who sought to protect both the president and his access to him.[10] Wise actually identified himself in terms that we used pejoratively. In a 1942 letter to Supreme Court Justice Felix Frankfurter, he wrote: "I don't know whether I am getting to be a *Hofjude* [court Jew], but I find that a good part of my work is to explain to my fellow Jews why our Government cannot do all the things asked or expected of it." Asked to stay silent about news from Europe that the Germans were planning the mass murder of all European Jews, Wise told Frankfurter, "I have kept the thing out of the press up to this time, thus accepting a great responsibility if the threat should be executed."[11]

---

8. David E. Lowe, *Touched with Fire: Morris B. Abram and the Battle against Racial and Religious Discrimination* (Lincoln, NE: Potomac Books, 2019), 208.

9. Stephen Wise was the head of the American Jewish Congress, the World Jewish Congress, and the American Zionist movement as well as the Free Synagogue in New York City and the Jewish Institute of Religion (later to merge with Reform Judaism's Hebrew Union College).

10. Regarding a proposal to admit European Jewish refugees to the Virgin Islands, Wise explained his opposition to a colleague in the autumn of 1940, shortly before the presidential election: "Cruel as I may seem, as I have said to you before, his re-election is much more important for everything that is worthwhile and that counts more than the admission of a few people, however imminent be their peril." David Wyman Institute for Holocaust Studies, *Encyclopedia of America's Response to the Holocaust*, s.v. "Wise, Stephen S.," http://enc.wymaninstitute.org/?p=543 (accessed June 10, 2020).

11. Ibid. (accessed April 14, 2020).

After leaving Abram's office, Micah and I felt that by standing up to the Jewish Establishment in the present day, we were also standing against a shameful history. And so we made our stand and won this round in the battle for Jackson-Vanik.

CHAPTER 17

A Diplomatic Victory and Freedom Sunday, 1987

Linking Emigration with Arms Control

Despite the widespread optimism about Gorbachev's policy of glasnost (openness), UCSJ recognized that the release of Soviet Jews was motivated by Soviet self-interest, not by humanitarian principles. Gorbachev's need for cash to restructure the Soviet economy gave the West and America a historic opportunity to encourage real and substantive change, if only we could seize it. The USSR was borrowing billions from US banks in the form of untied loans – cash that could be used in any way the Soviets wanted, including arms buildup. Banks were also granting extremely favorable interest rates on these loans, based only on the full faith and credit of the Soviet treasury. UCSJ launched a new campaign to impose restrictions on these untied loans, linking them to Soviet progress on human rights as well as to national security.

While holding firm to Jackson-Vanik, we were looking to reinforce the construct of linkage. We hoped our untied loans strategy, which garnered significant congressional support, would be an impetus for substantive change. Representatives Toby Roth and Jack Kemp proposed the Kemp-Roth bill, or the International Financial Security Act of 1987. This bill would authorize the president to restrict untied bank loans to any Soviet Bloc country that failed to make progress in human rights, including emigration, and to verify that such loans did not threaten US national security. Seizing the opportunity to publicize our initiative and effectively advocate for Soviet Jews, Micah and I wrote an article published in *Moment* magazine,[1] explaining UCSJ's initiative and the importance of linking American bank loans to concrete reforms in the Soviet Union.

---

1. Pamela Braun Cohen and Micah Naftalin, "Will Tying Up Untied Loans Free Soviet Jews?" *Moment* 12, no. 6 (October 1987): 42–46.

I first became aware of the Soviets' interest in another linkage, one between arms control and emigration, on the flight home from Reykjavik after the 1986 Reagan-Gorbachev summit. Anatoly Dobrynin, the Soviet ambassador to the United States, told me then that without progress on arms control, there could be no real progress on human rights.

Years later, in 2019, Ambassador Richard Schifter, former assistant secretary of state for human rights and humanitarian affairs, shared with me behind-the-scenes diplomacy from that period that had been completely shrouded at the time: "It was December 1986 that we got the first inkling that Gorbachev was changing things, when Sakharov was told to come back to Moscow.... [Secretary of State George] Shultz decided to put together a delegation to go to Moscow to see whether we can discuss a new relationship. I was invited to join the delegation to discuss human rights."[2] Schifter had preliminary meetings with his assigned counterpart, Deputy Foreign Minister Anatoly Adamishin.

The delegation's trip, in April 1987, overlapped with Pesach. The Jewish deputy chief of mission had arranged a Seder at the ambassador's residence, Spaso House, and invited a number of long-term refuseniks, including Vladimir Slepak, Josef Begun, and Lazar Yusefovich, who was in the twenty-sixth day of his hunger strike and was speaking regularly with David Waksberg. News of the Seder raced across our phone lines, especially reports that Secretary Shultz had left the arms negotiations to attend the Seder. He spoke emotionally to the refuseniks, urging that "they should never give up. " He promised to raise their cases whenever and wherever US diplomats met with Soviet officials. "You are in our minds. You are in our hearts. You can be sure we will continue to struggle on your behalf."[3]

Meanwhile, Schifter's first meeting with Adamishin hadn't produced a concrete agreement. In the following months, without much progress on emigration and with arms-control talks scheduled for September, he wanted to "get the Soviets to move on refusenik cases."[4] Back in Moscow, he told Adamishin he wanted to discuss emigration policy and to get

2. Richard Schifter, conversation with Pamela Braun Cohen, 2019. For more information, see Adamishin and Schifter, *Human Rights.*

3. William Eaton and Robert C. Toth, "Attends Seder Dinner with Them: 'Never Give Up,' Shultz Tells Soviet Refuseniks," *Los Angeles Times*, April 14, 1987.

4. Adamishin and Schifter, *Human Rights.*

action on the refusenik list he had brought. Expecting that was the case, Adamishin had set up a meeting for him with OVIR, the emigration office. Ambassador Schifter related, "OVIR was prepared to talk to me about the cases of people who had relatives in the US and wanted to emigrate to the US. As for other cases, they told me it was none of my business and refused any discussion of those cases."[5]

Schifter affirmed what we had long understood. As Micah and I had told the World Conference on Soviet Jewry in London, the Soviets knew where refuseniks intended to go and deliberately exploited the bifurcation of intended destination. They opened the gates in one direction or the other, depending on their self-interest, pitting Jew against Jew, Israel against America, the Establishment against the grassroots. The dropout controversy played into Soviet interests and they manipulated it with diabolical expertise.

Schifter was displeased with OVIR, and he expressed his dissatisfaction to Adamishin, informing him of his intent to report to Secretary Shultz, who would be gravely disturbed. There was no doubt "this development would cast a shadow over the [upcoming] September arms control talks."[6] Adamishin didn't respond.

At the airport the following morning, Ambassador Schifter was unexpectedly met by a Foreign Ministry representative who steered him to the VIP lounge, brought him a cup of tea, and urged him to sit down to talk. Schifter recalled that he "turned to me and said 'that list that they didn't take at OVIR yesterday, please give it to me.'"[7] When he landed in Warsaw, he sent a cable to Shultz's chief of staff, paraphrasing the quote from Secretary of State Dean Rusk about the end of the Cuban missile crisis: "I think the other side just blinked."

On the Soviet side, in his report to the Kremlin's Foreign Minister, Adamishin emphasized the damage unresolved refusenik cases would have on the progress of arms control. Then, just before the talks began, the Soviets issued a significant number of visas to refuseniks on Schifter's list, including those emigrating to Israel. The issue of Soviet Jews was inextricably linked to US-Soviet foreign and economic policy. The linkage held.

---

5. Ibid.

6. Ibid.

7. Ibid.

A Quiet Giant

Just as his negotiations with the Soviets were revealed to me decades after the fact, only after a long period of time did I grasp the depth of Ambassador Schifter's sensitivity and commitment to our cause. Despite having many briefings with him, I found Schifter difficult to read. During the dark years, when there was no movement on the refusenik cases, his formality and stoicism prevented me from getting a fix on how much he internalized the dangers we were describing or the depth of his concern for the cases we brought him.

Whether in the Old Executive Office Building in Washington or at human rights meetings in European capitals, he never failed to pay close attention to our documentary evidence of the Kremlin's anti-Semitic policies, their human rights violations, and their abuse of prisoners and refuseniks. He always politely listened, but he remained impassive, seemingly unmoved. Sphinx-like, his composure never crumbled. It would take several decades before I was to understand him better.

In November 2010, I was asked to represent the American movement for Soviet Jewish emigration at a hearing of the Knesset Committee on Immigration, Absorption, and Diaspora Affairs. Richard Schifter was my counterpart, representing the American government. Together we encompassed the totality of the movement from the American perspective: the grassroots and the government. It was our first meeting since 1989.

The Knesset auditorium was filled with former Jewish refuseniks and activists, and Schifter and I were seated together in the first row, together with the other speakers. The future president of Israel, Reuven Rivlin, took the podium and was followed by Yuli Edelstein. Like the biblical Joseph, who rose to become one of the most powerful figures in Egypt after being imprisoned by Pharaoh, Yuli, a former refusenik and underground Hebrew teacher sentenced to prison camp, was then deputy speaker of the Knesset.

While I fidgeted, nervously shifting in my seat, next to me, Ambassador Schifter was characteristically immobile. Then he took the podium and told his story.

Born in Vienna, he was fifteen when the Nazis invaded. His parents had applied to leave, but the United States issued only one visa to the family. He explained to the packed auditorium that his parents insisted that he use it. The audience was hanging on his every word. He went on with an openness I had never seen before. He told the audience that his parting promise to his parents was that he would do everything he could to get them out. Then the facade crumbled. He stopped, regained control, and then, restraining emotion, told the assembled former refuseniks, "I failed. I couldn't get them out. But I swore I would get each one of you out."[8]

His commitment to them had been seeded by personal and national catastrophe. He was trying to redress our history.

What he didn't say was that after he arrived in the States, he was recruited to the famed Ritchie Boys, a special intelligence team of young, German-speaking immigrants trained at Camp Ritchie in Maryland to interrogate German prisoners of war.

I also learned many years after the fact that, while Schifter was negotiating with the Soviets to resolve cases of refuseniks, prisoners, and victims of psychiatric abuse, he was also fighting an internal battle within the State Department. Some believed the State Department's defense of human rights had become an impediment to improved relations with the Soviets, but ultimately, Schifter won over key players, scoring a major victory in terms of the US commitment to our issues.

After leaving the State Department, he went on to create and head the American Jewish International Relations Institute to work with congressional figures and national and international officials on behalf of Israel at the United Nations.

Richard Schifter was an implacable lover of the Jewish people and Israel – a quiet giant.

Capitalizing on the Summit in Washington

The third Gorbachev-Reagan summit was scheduled for December 1987, in DC. The General Secretary's new policies of glasnost and perestroika, a restructuring designed to loosen the Kremlin's shackles on its moribund economy, had electrified the media. Those of us scrutinizing Soviet behavior felt the elation was premature at best. Ambassador Richard Schifter had it right in his letter to Secretary Shultz in November 1986, when he wrote, "no meaningful improvements in the Soviet human rights performance are now in evidence. That does not mean that meaningful improvements could not occur if we keep pressing for them.… But it does suggest that no

---

8.   Richard Schifter, speech at hearing of the Knesset Committee on Immigration, Absorption, and Diaspora Affairs, November 2010.

such improvements will take place if we are prepared to characterize these make-believe or token steps as the real thing."[9]

I couldn't have said it better. After all, the new proposed emigration law the Soviets had heralded at the end of 1986 allowed some emigration, but it also codified some restrictions. As Schifter wrote, "it would appear that for the time being, this is the definitive answer to our appeals for free emigration.... It's *nyet* on the basic question, *da* for a relatively small subgroup."[10] He thought it would be *da* for about thirty thousand Jews – still a small subgroup, considering the half million Jews waiting to emigrate.

Meanwhile, refuseniks organized demonstrations and hunger strikes in Moscow and Leningrad timed to the summit, aimed at piercing the media's euphoria. One hundred refuseniks signed a letter of protest to the Supreme Soviet.

Natan Sharansky[11] had a plan, and he came to the States to sell it. He wanted a massive gathering in Washington to coincide with Gorbachev's arrival. He was calling for four hundred thousand American Jews to march in solidarity with the four hundred thousand Jews Gorbachev was holding as bargaining chips. It would be a colossal undertaking.

Then, as Soviet leaders traditionally did before summits, as if to smooth the way, Gorbachev gifted Reagan with a number of well-known, long-term, "celebrity" refuseniks and prisoners of conscience. Two months before the summit, Ambassador Schifter was notified of an incoming call from Jerusalem. He wrote: "At 3:18 p.m., the call came through. 'This is Ida Nudel. I'm in Jerusalem. I'm home.'"[12]

Ida Nudel, the "guardian angel of the prisoners of conscience," herself sentenced to a nightmarish term of Siberian exile, had been granted permission to leave after a sixteen-year struggle. Dick Schifter's eyes filled with tears. He finally had won her freedom.

Masha and Volodya Slepak also received permission, after seventeen years of refusal and a sentence of exile in Siberia. Former prisoner Josef Begun also received permission to leave, as did Yuli Edelstein, who had

---

9.   Adamishin and Schifter, *Human Rights*.

10. Ibid.

11. Sharansky changed his first name from Anatoly to Natan after arriving in Israel.

12. Ibid.

served a labor camp sentence on a trumped-up drug charge and would later become Speaker of the Knesset.

I was ebullient. The waiting, suffering, intimidation, humiliation – the wasted years for these Jews – all were finally over. The Kremlin had deliberately molded their lives by turning them into hostages, pawns, currency on the US market. Now, the Kremlin's strategy was playing intentionally into the elation surrounding the summit.

Historical events look different with time, but then, in 1987, with nearly half a million Jews still struggling to get out, long-term refuseniks still waiting for visas, Jews still in labor camps, and punitive psychiatric abuse unrestrained, we believed the euphoria to be counterproductive. The public would conclude the Soviet Jewry problem was resolved. Except, it wasn't. The Council of Ministers still hadn't delivered on their promised emigration law, and the Kremlin could turn off the emigration faucet as quickly as it had turned it on.

Sharansky's Freedom Sunday mass gathering would reinforce Reagan, Shultz, and Schifter's human rights stance by sending an unambiguous public message to Gorbachev that America was demanding that he release all Jews who wanted to leave.

When Sharansky talked to Micah and me about his plan, we unhesitatingly endorsed it, but we were frank about UCSJ's limitations. We couldn't drive the numbers he wanted. He needed a commitment from Jewish Establishment organizations to fully mobilize their professional staffs to handle logistics and transportation.

Thirty years after the event, Sharansky recollected in the *Jerusalem Post*, "It's a battle that American Jewry should proudly be known for. But what is less known is that from the moment Elie [Wiesel] and I proposed the March in 1986, shortly after my release [from prison], there was a lot of resistance to it from Jewish organizations.... [Wiesel told me] 'Natan, don't waste time on meeting with Jewish organizations. Only students can do this. They will convince the Jewish organizations.' This was the best advice I ever received."[13]

Sharansky spoke with fifty different Jewish organizations in America, and Wiesel worked with the World Union of Jewish Students in France and England.

In the end, they convinced everyone to play their part.

---

13. Kelly Hartog, "Sharansky's Debt of Gratitude to Elie Wiesel," *Jerusalem Post*, November 21, 2017.

Freedom Sunday

It was a crisp, sunny winter day when cars, buses, trains, and planes disgorged an astounding quarter of a million Jews from all over America for Freedom Sunday. They were bundled against the cold, carrying placards and posters, their T-shirts blazing, "I went to the summit for Soviet Jews." The sea of people merged on Constitution Avenue and amassed on the National Mall. Among them were Lenny, Scott, and Josh.

On the Mall, enormous screens projected the program, which opened with the blowing of the shofar. Each speaker lit a candle of freedom on the menorah on the dais to symbolize the upcoming Chanukah holiday.

Morris Abram read a supportive statement from President Reagan. Pearl Bailey sang the spiritual "Let My People Go." Vice President George Bush demanded, "Let's not see five or six or ten or twenty refuseniks released at one time, but thousands, tens of thousands. Mr. Gorbachev, let these people go!"

I introduced Sharansky, whose vision had brought out 250,000 Jews, unified, speaking with one voice. Still so averse to public speaking, I was now standing before a quarter of a million people, my picture broadcast on several gargantuan screens. From the podium in front of the Lincoln Memorial, I saw an ocean of Jews stretching endlessly across the Mall, expressing an extraordinary unity and purpose.

The crowd was intoxicating.

One by one, the recently released prisoners of conscience and refuseniks took the podium, our generation's heroes – Ida Nudel, Josef Begun, Vladimir Slepak, Felix Abramovich, Yuli Edelstein, Misha and Ilana Kholmyansky. After each introduction, the massive crowd spontaneously broke out, roaring, "Am Yisrael Chai!" The people of Israel live!

But on the podium, I couldn't help thinking about those left behind: Leonid Stonov, David Charney, Boris Chernobilsky, Professor Alexander Lerner, Yuli Kosharovsky, Vladimir "Zeev" Dashevsky, Boris Kelman, and so many more. Only six months before, twenty-seven-year-old cellist Alexei Magarik had been sentenced to three years' labor camp. His father was in Israel, his wife in Moscow with their infant son. Grateful for the successes, I still worried that they were a fireworks display that eclipsed the brutality inherent in the Soviet system. Gorbachev was giving repressive, totalitarian communism a human face, but even the most hopeful of us knew enough to be deeply skeptical. Successive bursts of thunderous applause for each Soviet Jewish speaker expressed an exultation I feared would play to the euphoric media. I wondered how the White House and the Kremlin would interpret what looked like a jubilant celebration of victory, when the road ahead was still unclear?

Yosef Mendelevich had the same concern. He had been excluded from the speakers' roster, this man who had opened the doors to emigration through the doomed 1970 hijacking plot. But a man who wasn't defeated by the Kremlin wasn't about to be intimidated by either the Jewish Establishment or protocol. When Sharansky finished speaking, Mendelevich took the microphone. He lashed out against false optimism. He warned against the concessions Reagan might be willing to make in the coming days. He called on the president not to deal with Gorbachev on a case-by-case basis, urging him to stand fast in the linkage of trade with human rights until sixty thousand Jews could emigrate each year. He urged a complete ban on trade with the Soviet Union and called for an end to American bank loans to the Soviets, the initiative proposed by UCSJ. Mendelevich wasn't one to subvert what he saw as truth. He had fought his captors for eleven years and was not about to abandon his principles in freedom.

Elie Wiesel took the podium and warned Gorbachev against sacrificing human rights on the altar of a nuclear disarmament agreement. Peace and human rights are inseparable. While he was speaking, I looked across the Mall at a quarter-million Jews and wondered how many millions could have been saved in 1942, had American Jews mounted a demonstration of this magnitude? I wasn't the only one who had that thought.

"Too many were silent then. We are not silent today,"[14] Wiesel told the gathering.

Why were we silent then? My thoughts went back to the organizational rivalry that dampened and ultimately shut down the pageants Peter Bergson engineered to mobilize the public and the White House in 1943. The Establishment undermined them at every turn, suffocating them altogether, thwarting Bergson's efforts to demonstrate the catastrophe occurring in Europe.

But in Washington on that crisp Sunday morning, Sharansky's vision and his ability to push the Establishment had made the unthinkable

---

14. "More Than 200,000 Rally on Behalf of Soviet Jewry in Massive D.C. Gathering," Jewish Telegraphic Agency (JTA), December 7, 1987.

happen. Each member of the communal orchestra brought together an event of harmony no one thought possible.

Then Mary Travers, of Peter, Paul and Mary fame, was at the microphone, her voice soaring over the mall. She sang "Light One Candle," singing for the Maccabee children, whose freedom and very existence have been threatened for hundreds of generations. Repeatedly, the refrain exhorts us not to let the light go out.

We were all Maccabee children, both here and in the Soviet Union. We were the surviving remnant. Our forefathers had all heard the same voice at Sinai. We were one people, and a quarter of a million of us were standing together for those who weren't with us but were an integral part of us. It was the right song for the right place and time.

The reception that followed in the Capitol rotunda for the event's speakers brought me face to face for the first time with Volodya Slepak. It was as if we had always known each other, and in a sense we had, especially as I had worked with his sons, Leonid and Sanya, for many years at several national and international venues. The Slepaks had been at the helm of the refusenik leadership. Their Moscow apartment served as unofficial headquarters for visiting tourists and congressional delegations. Day and night, it was a magnet for refuseniks from all over the country seeking advice, help, and consolation.

Volodya had a broad smile and twinkling eyes, with distinctive muttonchops that had gone gray and a presence that couldn't be ignored. The son of a highly placed communist, he defied his father by applying for a visa in 1970. A founder of the Moscow Helsinki Group, he had brought the Jewish emigration movement into the context of the broader human rights and democracy movement, which didn't find favor with the Lishka. I was heartsick to learn, decades later, that a tourist sent by the Establishment to Moscow actually told the Slepaks that Nechemia Levanon himself – head of the Lishka – had said that the Slepaks' "arrival in Israel is undesirable."[15]

Slepak attributed his problems with the Lishka not to his ties to the human rights movement but to his aversion to quiet diplomacy and his open support for Jackson-Vanik. Years later, in an interview with Yuli Kosharovsky, he revealed, "We were constantly pressured from Israel. When I was told that Levanon himself thought it was necessary to act quietly and

---

15. Yuli Kosharovsky, "*We Are Jews Again*": *Jewish Activism in the Soviet Union* (Syracuse, NY: Syracuse University Press, 2017), 99.

we would be brought out by means of quiet diplomacy, I couldn't contain myself and said on the phone to Israel that if Levanon adheres to such an ideology, he should be driven from the leadership of the organization. At that time I didn't even know what kind of organization."[16] The Lishka, he added, was not against Jackson-Vanik but felt it shouldn't be advocated for openly. The Slepaks were seen as dissidents by the Kremlin. They were also seen as dissidents by the Lishka.

After being refused for ten years, in 1978, Volodya was sentenced to five years of exile in Siberia after he and Masha hung a banner from their apartment's balcony, reading: "Let us go to our sons in Israel!"

Now, he was here in the rotunda. Finally, our paths had crossed. I was overcome with emotion.

Sadly, I wouldn't see either Volodya or Masha again until I bid each one separately a final farewell at their funerals in Jerusalem. At Masha's funeral in 2017, Dan Roginsky[17] recalled that Volodya and Masha were always fueled by optimism and unity and were exemplars of the movement for identity and emigration. Masha, he said, took all the pain and bitterness refuseniks brought her and absorbed it into her sweet and loving smile. They were both remarkable people, hidden heroes.

Sharansky's Freedom Sunday did give Reagan the leverage he needed. Reportedly after the initial formalities, the two leaders sat down together to discuss arms control. But before their talk commenced, the president turned to Gorbachev and asked, "Have you heard about the rally on the Mall last Sunday?" Obviously Gorbachev couldn't have missed it, but he didn't respond, anxious to get on with their talks. Reagan, however, wouldn't let go. Like a pit bull, he talked about the size of the turnout, how vital Jewish emigration was to the American people, and how critical it was that the Soviet Union respond positively. The more Reagan talked, the more impatient Gorbachev grew, but the president didn't relent. He delivered the message that the issue of Soviet Jews was an integral part of

---

16. Ibid., 100.

17. A physicist at the Hebrew University in Jerusalem, Roginsky had been an activist in the Zionist movement and an underground Hebrew teacher in Moscow in the early 1970s.

the US-USSR relationship, and that the issue had to be positively resolved for the relationship to flourish.[18]

Sharansky's plan had worked.

---

18. This story was shared by Secretary of State George Shultz in a speech given on the occasion of receiving the Emma Lazarus Statue of Liberty Award from the American Jewish Historical Society, at the Waldorf Hotel, New York, April 25, 2007.

CHAPTER 18

An Unexpected Sequence of Events, 1988

Protest and Advocacy in Helsinki

I hadn't been to Russia and Ukraine in eleven years, and as anxious as I was to get back, having been labeled a "Zionist anti-Soviet agitator" by the Soviets, I was worried that my meetings with refuseniks could give KGB a pretext to entrap them. But Gorbachev's invitation to Reagan to a summit meeting in Moscow, timed to the thousand-year anniversary of Christianity in Russia, might give us the cover we needed. It was unlikely the Soviets would do anything that might sabotage the veneer they were putting on their public image at so visible an event, so Micah and I went to see Sandy Vershbow with a proposal. Head of the State Department Soviet desk at the time, Sandy went on to have a distinguished career as a diplomat.

We knew Sandy to be a good man. He was also young and sympathetic – and he liked us. We briefed him on the newest information from Russia, and then Micah and I floated our proposition: the two of us wanted to go with the president's delegation to Moscow. Sandy liked the idea but thought it was doubtful that we could join the official delegation. He did suggest that we could travel independently but at the same time as the official delegation. He would see what he could do to have us included wherever appropriate. So, Micah and I applied for visas and waited on pins and needles. I had still heard nothing about my visa when Micah called to tell me he had received his. A few days later, however, he was summoned to the Soviet embassy, where he was summarily informed that his visa had been canceled. The Soviets had mistakenly thought he was still employed by Elie Wiesel at the Holocaust Council. As he was now director of an "anti-Soviet" organization, they were retracting his visa.

Even Micah, a genius negotiator, couldn't convince them otherwise. We held a press conference with Senators Chuck Grassley and Dennis DeConcini in the Senate Press Gallery. I spoke to the point: by keeping American citizens out of Moscow during the summit, the Soviets made it clear they were going to isolate refuseniks and dissidents, preventing their contact with Western media during the meeting. I continued, "How do we expect that American nongovernmental organizations…will be able to gain visas for an international Moscow human rights conference as the Soviets proposed at the Vienna follow-up meetings of the CSCE?"[1] This very circumstance was one of the chief reasons we opposed that conference in the first place. A human rights conference in Moscow was a contradiction in terms, and by refusing to issue us visas, the Kremlin gave us another arrow to shoot it down.

At the State Department, Sandy Vershbow protested the issue of our denied visas to the Soviet embassy but made no headway. Conferring with us at a follow-up meeting, he proposed that Micah and I go to Helsinki instead, where Reagan was stopping on his way to Moscow.

So Micah and I left for Finland, prepared with briefing papers on the status of emigration and state anti-Semitism for the press. I also hoped to catch up with our Finnish friend Maya and her colleagues.

We focused our activities on the Helsinki Press Center. The world's television and press correspondents had set themselves up in lines of long tables that filled the cavernous hall. Micah and I went up and down the tables, speaking to the press corps, supplying them with documentary evidence of the Kremlin's flagrant human rights abuses, talking about refusenik cases and prisoners. The media coverage of any given issue depended on how much news on that issue was available, so we kept supplying them with fresh details and organized events.

An ad hoc organizational umbrella we named Helsinki Action for Soviet Jews pulled together the grassroots forces. The indefatigable duo, Student Struggle for Soviet Jewry's Rabbi Avi Weiss and Glenn Richter, orchestrated a Freedom March, joined by the London 35s, the evangelical Helsinki groups, and UCSJ. The procession, led by a Torah scroll carried by Yosef Mendelevich and a "Helsinki Action for Soviet Jews" banner, marched from the American embassy to the Soviet embassy. Chains

---

1. Pamela Braun Cohen, speech at a press conference, Senate Press Gallery, May 19, 1988.

stretched along the procession, symbolizing the imprisonment of all Soviet Jews locked within their borders.

I spoke at the start of the Freedom March, warning President Reagan about an ominous phenomenon. The commemorations of the thousand-year anniversary of Christianity in the Soviet Union had awakened Russia's historic, endemic Jew-hatred. Jewish graves had been vandalized throughout Russia. Posters and leaflets in Moscow, urging patriotic Russians to stage pogroms, had left Jews afraid to leave their apartments. This intimidation, I warned, was a Kremlin-backed provocation to suppress contact between refuseniks and the media during the summit.

"Therefore, Mr. President," I said, "a case-by-case resolution of the Jewish issue is insufficient – 385,000 Jews have taken the first steps to leave and thousands more are seeking visas every month. Their only hope for repatriation is you." I concluded: "Mr. President, as we did in Reykjavik, we again call upon you to negotiate in Moscow a comprehensive exit visa settlement to secure the orderly evacuation, retroactively by year of application, of all Jews who wish to leave the Soviet Union, beginning with the prisoners of conscience."[2] It was the first time the UCSJ called for *evacuation*, a potent word that, years later, would raise the ire of the Lishka.

In a speech days later, Reagan did address the issue of human rights, claiming there could be no "true international security without respect for human rights." However the Kremlin may have internalized the message, it publicly reacted with a statement by the Soviet Foreign Ministry spokesman, Gennadi I. Gerasimov, who accused the president of lecturing the Soviet people: "We don't like it when someone from outside is teaching us how to live." Not surprisingly, it was the same message they regularly gave us.

While in Helsinki, I had contacted Maya with our plans for the Freedom March, but suddenly and without explanation, she cut contact, leaving me baffled. I conjectured that either we were blacklisted, or she had become afraid.

Meanwhile Avi and Glenn attracted the television news media in their inimitable style. They set up a prison cage in the center of the city and showed up in striped prison-issue uniforms. Avital Sharansky, Micah, and

---

2.   Pamela Braun Cohen, speech, Helsinki, May 25, 1988.

I also caged ourselves for the press. SSSJ conducted public outdoor Shabbat services and read from the Torah in front of the Russian airline office.

In what the Kremlin considered a provocative move, Reagan invited refuseniks from across the Soviet Union to Spaso House, the ambassador's residence, for an official reception. Still in Helsinki, in a call to Leningrad I learned that some refuseniks had been put under house arrest and others were dragged off trains as they tried to make their way to Moscow for the reception with the president.

Micah and I immediately went to the press center, to the American correspondents, who were all lined up at a long table. I told them I had just learned that refuseniks were being forcibly stopped from going to Moscow. In a flash, reporters put down their coffee cups and newspapers, and I found myself barraged with questions. "How do you know?" "What's your source?"

I pointed to the phone at the end of the table. "Give me that phone and I'll call Evgeny Lein, a refusenik in Leningrad." In an instant, wheel-mounted cameras shifted toward me, microphones were shoved in my face, and I made a direct call to the one and only apartment phone number in the USSR I knew by heart.

I prayed the call would go through. I prayed the Soviets wouldn't block the call. I prayed, *Please let him be at home; please, let him pick up the phone.* The phone seemed to ring forever. Then, suddenly, Evgeny was on the line.

Though he certainly was unprepared to be on a live line to the Helsinki press center, he kept his cool and described the situation in English to the *New York Times* reporter I put on the phone. Elena Keiss-Kuna and Alec Zelichenok, among others, had been forcibly removed from a Moscow-bound train. Even though they had been warned by KGB, refuseniks were still trying to get to Moscow by any means. Twenty-eight Leningrad refuse-niks planning a demonstration in Moscow were hassled by KGB. Some had been warned that if they persisted in demonstrating on the eve of the summit, they would "live to regret it."[3] The story ran on the front pages of the *New York Times*, the *Washington Post*, and the *Chicago Tribune*. It was one of those rare publicity grand slams, revealing Soviet repression of refuseniks to a massive readership. I was euphoric.

---

3.   Jerome R. Watson, "Soviets Relent on Dissidents' Reagan Parley," *Chicago Sun-Times*, May 27, 1988.

Later, after the adrenaline had worn off and I was half asleep in my Helsinki hotel room, suitcase packed for the morning's flight home, the phone rang. I jumped. It had to be Lenny. But no, it was Micah, and he was uncharacteristically excited. Our office had just called. Reagan's national security adviser, Colin Powell, had raised our visa issues at a White House briefing, and after that, the Soviets relented. Our visas would be ready for us at the Soviet embassy in the morning, on the condition that we agreed not to be in Moscow while Reagan was there.

We were going to Russia! I phoned Lenny, who was as surprised as I was. The morning couldn't come soon enough. There was one problem. I wasn't at all prepared. Except for Evgeny's, I didn't have one other phone number with me. Everything, every refusenik meeting, would hinge on reaching him.

Once in Leningrad, I got a kopek piece for a public phone I located away from our hotel and called the same number I had called from the Helsinki press center. And once again, Evgeny answered. I shouted into the receiver, "Evgeny, it's Pomella! I'm here!"

By the time Micah and I got to Leningrad from Helsinki and I made that call from a telephone booth to Lein, seven years had passed since his arrest. He had served out his two-year term of hard labor in Siberia. Five years after his release from Siberia, Lein was still in refusal.

Reunion

Micah, new on the job and on his first trip to the USSR, was astounded by what that single phone call brought in its wake. Lein and the refusenik leadership set into motion a systematic process of specialized briefings day after day, first in Leningrad and then, after President Reagan's departure, in Moscow.

At our first session, refuseniks jammed into a small apartment; on the wall was a blackboard with "Welcome Pam!" written on it in large block letters. Although it was our first face-to-face meeting, it was more of a reunion for all of us.

They certainly weren't strangers. I knew each of them, their families, their cases, their stories. And they knew me. They all knew the Union of Councils and each of the councils' leaders. These refuseniks had been indelibly inscribing their values on me, slowly altering my worldview, my political orientation, my definition of what it means to be a Jew, my ever-growing identification with Israel.

Micah and I were shepherded through continuous meetings from morning until late at night. In apartments with more people than seats, we clustered with Jews who identified themselves by the category of the pretext for their refusal. There were "poor relatives," whose parents or spouses refused to give them the required permission to leave; those who couldn't even apply because they didn't have the required *vysov*; and Jews refused on the pretext of having access to state secrets. In English or with a volunteer translating, men and women of varying ages struggled for words to explain their strategy for getting permission, to describe KGB's intimidation of them and their children, or to convey their anxiety that aging parents waiting for them in Israel wouldn't live long enough for the family to be reunited. The most unbearable were the pleas from the wives and parents of refuseniks who had been sent to hard labor and prison camps, and from the refuseniks responsible for the material aid to support both the prisoners and their family members. Micah and I groped for words of assurance.

All of these people were looking to find partnership and support for their work. They were struggling against all odds to build a semblance of Jewish life and systems for self-preservation and stability in what they perceived as a vast transit camp within Soviet borders. Injustice galvanized them, and, gravitating into orbits of special interest, they became specialists in their field. A few secrecy refuseniks took a brazenly adversarial position by creating the Public Committee to Monitor OVIR, providing invaluable documentation on refusals. Mika Chlenov and Roman Spector, trying to get official recognition of their Jewish Cultural Association, wanted to rebuild, as Mika told me, "the golden chain that connects us to the majority of our people." An ethnologist and Jewish culturalist, Chlenov was one of the earliest underground Hebrew teachers.

Huddled together in small groups or large gatherings, information poured out, and I scribbled notes, coding names in case KGB picked us up. The refusenik pharmacy distributed medicine we sent in through our tourists. A group with ties to Yad Vashem wanted to lift the official veil off the suppressed information about the Holocaust on Soviet soil. The Women for Emigration and Survival in Refusal described what it was like to try to hold demonstrations. Often, they would emerge simultaneously from separate subway stations, only to find KGB waiting for them, ripping the placards from their hands and forcing them to disperse. The Moscow Refusenik Scientific Seminar had a worldwide network of scientists that publicized their scientific work; a group of Hebrew teachers struggled for official legitimization of Hebrew and the right to teach; and Yuli Kosharovsky's secret underground steering committee coordinated various wings of the Jewish movement.

In one meeting, we were told books had to be clandestinely produced inside the Soviet Union because Moscow's Jews were afraid to pick up a book that had come from the West. Seven journals were being published, including Sasha Smukler's *Information Bulletin* and *Problems of Refusal*.

Moshe Greenberg, a Chasidic Jew with permission to leave, brought us his map of the graves of *tzadikim* (righteous ones) that he had discovered. He wanted help in restoring these graves. Later, from Israel, he would author an important book documenting the discovery and locations of graves that might otherwise have been lost to history.

The totality of need was staggering, but there was not one activity that did not contribute significantly to the whole. As people poured out their objectives and the barriers they encountered, I understood that they were looking to us as partners in the development of a strategy and framework for international support and material assistance. They gave us a mandate, and Micah and I resolved to move heaven and earth in our efforts to support them.

At one meeting, we were particularly impressed by one refusenik's obvious political acumen, insightful worldview, articulate expression, and selflessness. Micah turned to me and said under his breath, "That's our new leader."

That man was Leonid Stonov. Neither Micah, Leonid, nor I could imagine at that moment how our lives would enmesh for years to come.

Leonid Stonov

Leonid was an agrobiologist who had studied law; he had been refused permission on secrecy grounds. He later became the leader of the Moscow Refusenik Legal Seminar, was connected to the Moscow Helsinki Group, and had good relations with all wings of the movement, all of whom respected his juridical, fair, nonjudgmental abilities.

Leonid was a man of extraordinary personal substance and character. The subsequent years of his leadership showed him to be quietly intelligent, with the political and legal skills of a diplomat and lawyer. He could relate to everyone: refuseniks, dissidents, officials, congressmen, ambassadors, tourists. He had an affability and genuineness that attracted people. A self-made expert on international human rights law, Leonid wrote several proposals for the law on the right to exit and enter a country. He also drew up conditions for the US waiver of Jackson-Vanik's trade restrictions. After he emigrated, he always referred to my dad as "the senator," but I think it was a case of psychological transference. Had Leonid been born in America, he could have been one.

Stalin's anti-Semitic, anti-intellectual reign of terror permeated Leonid's life as it did millions of others. When his father, a writer, was arrested and sent to labor camp, Leonid was only a child, but he remembered his mother standing in long lines trying to get word of him. He was released after five years, and by then, Leonid could already read between the lines, and he wanted out: away from the lies, away from the hatred, away from the repression.

When Micah and I met Leonid, he had already started the Public Committee to Monitor OVIR, advising new emigration applicants of their rights under Soviet and international law and preparing appeals for refuseniks. Pressure from us on the State Department and Congress provided some protection for their work.

Leonid and his wife Natasha lived in his father's apartment on Lavrushinsky Pereulok, in the building Stalin had given to writers before the Great Purge. In their living room was a dark mahogany upright piano with an ornate silver candelabra mounted on each side. Their library, shelves packed with books stretching from floor to ceiling, was warmed in a soft light. Oriental carpets covered the floors.

Leonid's and Natasha's mothers could usually be found in the kitchen when guests from the West started to arrive, as they did most nights. Refuseniks never had the luxury to have a quiet night in their robes – guests were always expected. In a country wracked with shortages, everyone spent hours in long lines hoping to find something in the way of food, shoes, and clothing. Refuseniks bought whatever they could find among meager supplies, for themselves and for their friends. But somehow, in the Stonov apartment, there was always plenty. Their small table seemed to expand magically to accommodate the many unexpected guests who knocked on their door: congressmen and diplomats, tourists from America, England, France. On my first visit, their mothers brought out so many dishes, I assumed the appetizers were the main course.

Up from the cold, danger-fraught streets of Moscow, where everyone was watching, I was enfolded into Leonid and Natasha's glowing warmth. That apartment on Lavrushinsky became my home away from home.

Vital Documentation

We went from meeting to meeting, taking in whatever refuseniks wanted us to know, though some information was difficult to hear. A well-known Leningrad refusenik confidentially related that the Jewish Establishment had sent him tourists conveying the message that contact with me was "dangerous" and warned him not to work with me. The same tourists told a different refusenik that I wanted refuseniks to demonstrate until "there was blood on the streets."

While these accusations were deeply disturbing, I recognized them as a typical attempt by the Lishka and Jewish Establishment to discredit UCSJ. They did trigger a much-needed discussion with refuseniks of the policies that distinguished UCSJ from the Establishment – policies that did not, God forbid, call for blood on the streets.

At a meeting with refusenik leadership, Micah and I went through the gamut of issues, explaining the differences in approach and substance between UCSJ's grassroots movement and that of the Establishment. Perhaps the most significant difference, we noted, was the grassroots' partnership orientation. UCSJ, SSSJ, and the 35s operated as part of *their* movement, eschewing the paternalism and patronization of the Establishment. To make that partnership concrete, I invited the various refusenik groups to be official members of the UCSJ honorary board.

By the end of the trip, Micah and I had briefcases thick and heavy with stacks of papers from refuseniks testifying, documenting, and verifying the Soviets' abusive repression of rights. We had carefully handwritten case histories, appeals, declarations, and lists of Hebrew teachers. We had data detailing Soviet violations of their own criminal and emigration codes and of the Helsinki Final Act. Micah and I were increasingly anxious about getting these papers safely out of the country. In all probability, we would be stopped and searched going out.

We went to the American embassy in hopes that they could provide help. For Frank Vargo, deputy director of the US Commercial Office, and the others in his department, the problems we faced were the same ones they had to deal with. The absence of law in general, and specifically of legal guarantees for freedom of movement and speech, also impeded US commercial interests. Micah had met with Frank several times in Washington, and they found that their thinking on Jackson-Vanik and other trade issues was aligned.

On the sunny morning when we walked into his office, Frank didn't need much explanation. We showed him our reams of papers, and he immediately offered to help us get the documents safely out of the USSR. We later learned that Mike Mears, director of the US Commercial Office, made copies of everything we had, just in case our papers were confiscated.

Everything made it out, and Micah was able to construct a full account of the trip in a detailed council memo, with pages and pages of addenda that the refuseniks provided us. The documentation that we needed to push the refuseniks' cases forward was safe in our hands.

An Extraordinary "Coincidence"

On the day of our departure, activist Mika Chlenov and refuseniks Georgi Samoilovich and Evgeny Grechanovsky, who had been with us for many of our meetings, insisted on taking Micah and me to the airport. On the way, they surprised us by pulling up outside Georgi's apartment building and ushering us upstairs for one last *l'chaim*. The five of us stood around Georgi's dining-room table, drenched in the warmth of authentic affection, as Chlenov poured a round of vodka shots. We lifted our glasses in *l'chaim* and then, surprisingly, Chlenov started to sing, with the two others joining him.

I could hardly believe what I was hearing. The song was part of my family. It was the one and only Yiddish song I ever knew. It had been sung by my grandparents, aunts, uncles, and cousins, also around a dining-room table, in celebration of birthdays, anniversaries, bar and bat mitzvahs. From the time I was a small child in Maywood, Illinois, I grew up with my Braun family's Yiddish song. Our hosts may have been as astounded as I was, when this American sang along with them.

Lomir alle in einem, in einem,
[honoree's name] *mekabel punim zayn.* (x2)
Lomir alle in einem lustig un freilich zayn!
Lomir alle in einem trinken a gleizeleh vayn!

Let us all in unison, in unison,
Welcome [honoree's name].
Let us all in unison be joyful and happy!
Let us all in unison drink a little glass of wine!

We sang a round for Micah. Then for refuseniks. Then all Jews. Somehow, I was in Moscow with men who until a few days before had been strangers, and they knew the words to the only Yiddish song I had ever heard, my Braun family's treasured Yiddish melody. And they were singing in my honor.

Lomir alle in einem, in einem,
Pomella mekabel punim zayn.

Although I have returned many times to Russia, never again did I hear that melody. Not there. Not in America or Israel. Not anywhere. Of course, it wasn't a coincidence. I was around a dining-room table again, ten thousand miles from home, with fellow Jews, with family. I so deeply regret that I haven't held this haunting and beloved melody close to the hearts of our children. Songs transmit what words alone cannot capture.

Back on the Ring Road, we circled out of Moscow. The three men insisted on accompanying us into the large terminal, an extraordinary circumstance. After all, which refusenik even had a car? Torn from their jobs and vocations, they sold their possessions to exist. But that night, these men were with us in the departure area when we discovered our flight had been canceled.

Micah and I were in a bind. With expired visas, we couldn't leave the airport. Had the three men not been with us, Micah and I would have suffered through the nightmare of rushing from counter to counter, waiting in interminable lines to find a flight out. But they hustled us to an out-of-the-way second-floor office that tourists would never have known existed. There, agents were booking flights. Chlenov started negotiating with them, intermittently translating for us. There were no seats available on any flight to Europe. I told Mika, "I don't care where, just get us out of here. Out, to anywhere." I had to get home: to Lenny, to my family. These three activists who had taken on the Soviet apparat weren't going to take no for an answer, and before long, Mika had us on a flight to Amsterdam with a connection to the States.

As I walked through the departure gate, I looked back over my shoulder and saw Samoilovich, Chlenov, and Grechanovsky waving goodbye, locked in the invisible Soviet cage. When would they be able to pass through a gate to freedom? When and where would I see them again? I took a mental photograph of them before forcing myself to turn away, knowing I had left something precious behind.

At passport control, I faced the characteristic scrutiny of the young, pimply-faced official who checked my face, my visa, again my face before finally stamping my visa. As I turned away, I heard him. He had whispered, "Shalom." I could barely catch my breath and suppressed the instinct to turn back. The word, a revealed code, resounded in my ears. This young man, a Soviet border agent and an assimilated Jew, must have seen who I was on his computer screen, and in spite of all the reasons to stay quiet, he reached out to me in a whispered signal. We were one people.

A Partnership, and a Request

I couldn't stop thinking about Yuli Kosharovsky, whom I had first met ten years earlier at the Choral Synagogue. One day during this trip, he had taken Micah and me to meet with Mashka, the secret, underground group that coordinated the various wings of the Jewish national movement. This meeting gave us the opportunity to interface with the points of connection for the many organizations that made up this movement. It was an acknowledgment of our partnership.

A few days later, Yuli, along with three other refuseniks, called an especially secure meeting with Micah and me. Typically, when communicating sensitive information in refusenik apartments, we wrote on children's "magic slates" to elude KGB bugs. Lifting the thin panel of cellophane erased the words without a trace. But for this meeting, they took us outside the apartment building so that we could speak without surveillance.

Yuli told us that the funds he had been receiving from the Lishka to pay for their samizdat, their underground publishing, had stopped. He had urgently requested funds from another UCSJ activist but hadn't received it. The samizdat group needed $10,000 – a small fortune in the 1980s. I was already raising funds for CASJ's tourist program, and as UCSJ president I was also cultivating donors to operate our national office. I was at a loss. Who could I approach for a staggering ten grand?

I reacted with uncharacteristic cynicism. I jabbed Yuli's upper arm with my forefinger and said, "Yuli, I'll get you your money…even though I know you will never do one thing to help us when you get out."

Though our relationship was based on mutual respect and a cooperative interdependency, Yuli and UCSJ represented differing – and at times opposing – perspectives. It was ironic that Yuli was approaching UCSJ to fund a defaulted expense of the Israeli government office, but I wasn't about to let their underground publication efforts falter. Still, the hefty financial commitment was a responsibility I was afraid I couldn't meet.

Landing in Amsterdam, I checked into a hotel before the morning's flight. I was anxious about my assurance to Yuli. I couldn't take such substantial funds from Chicago Action. Where was I going to come up with that kind of money? I had no alternative but to call in the only ticket I had. I called Jay Pritzker, the Hyatt Hotels magnate who was building his $15 billion empire. Before his official trip with mega-builder Albert Reichman to discuss the prospects for a hotel in Russia, I had briefed Jay about the condition of Soviet Jews and urged him to raise the issue and address specific refusenik cases with government officials he would meet. I had also arranged for him to meet with several refuseniks. He walked out of those meetings committed to the issue and to helping us.

From Amsterdam, I got Pritzker's secretary on the line. I told her I had just come out of the Soviet Union and needed to talk to him. He was on a call selling the family's stake in Braniff Airways; would I wait? Of course, I'd wait. I held on, expecting to hear the secretary's voice again, but in a few minutes, Jay was on the line. Yes, he'd give us the $10,000 Yuli needed. A few days later, Yuli confirmed receipt of the funds. He had needed help, and we delivered.

An Unfinished Story

While I admired and liked Yuli on a personal level, as we played out our respective roles, long-standing issues that were bigger than either of us filtered into our relationship. Fast forward to the 1991 Persian Gulf War. Saddam Hussein was launching Scud missiles into Israel. I had just returned from Soviet Central Asia, where there had been a pogrom in the Fergana Valley, and several Jews had been murdered in separate incidents. Central Asian Jews complained that the Israeli government wasn't sending in enough planes to accommodate the people who wanted to leave. They also weren't sending in sufficient *vysovs*, the invitations to emigrate that were still a required part of the process. UCSJ issued a statement calling for the evacuation of Jews from the former Soviet republics. Our dual objectives were to pressure Israel to send more planes and issue more *vysovs*, and simultaneously to urge the State Department to implement an emergency program to accelerate family reunification for the tens of thousands who had already applied to immigrate to the States. The Israeli Foreign Ministry reacted strongly and immediately. The Israelis were not prepared to handle the state of emergency we were suggesting. Furthermore, they were incensed by what they perceived as a call for a mass evacuation to the United States.

The Lishka went on the offensive. Yuli, who had finally received permission and was living in Israel, was dispatched to New York for "damage control." In an article from the Jewish Telegraphic Agency (JTA), he stated, "They [UCSJ] somehow are acting in the same direction as Saddam Hussein.… They don't understand what they're doing."[4] He asserted that UCSJ's proposal would prevent Jews from immigrating to Israel by offering them false hopes that they could immigrate to the States. He compared the outcome as having the same negative impact on immigration to Israel as Saddam's Scuds. I was overwhelmed by a sense of betrayal. My thoughts returned to that cold day, years before, when I told Yuli I'd get him his $10,000.

I knew, even then, that the Lishka would prevent him from crediting our work. But I could never have imagined he would hurt us and malign full-time volunteers devoting days and nights for years to rescue Soviet

---

4. "Ex-Refusenik Opposes UCSJ Plan to Expedite Immigration to US," *Jewish Telegraphic Agency* (JTA), February 27, 1991.

Jews, one Jewish soul at a time. We were partners in the same struggle, operating on two continents, separated by an iron curtain we were determined to crack. Comparing us to Saddam Hussein? I was deeply, deeply hurt.

Now, fast forward again, to 2010, to Sderot, Israel, where Lenny and I were attending the wedding of Laura Bialis, producer of the film *Refusenik*. Yuli, now gray-haired and without a kippah, suntanned and still flashing his infectious smile, greeted me with a rush of enthusiasm, arms extended. "Pomella!"

Mockingly, I looked left and right. "Pomella!" he repeated. I feigned confusion. "Pomella? Oh, you mean Saddam Hussein?"

He failed at hiding his reaction, and I caught a glimpse of recognition. But we both let it pass. Thousands of rockets had bombarded Sderot during the Gaza war, and this wedding celebration was an act of resistance. Somehow, in the midst of it all, our tension dissipated.

Yuli was writing his remarkable work on Soviet Jewry. He asked to interview me, and I agreed. He was a brilliant interviewer. From our conversation, he methodically extracted the multifaceted and ascending levels of our advocacy. Somewhere in the middle, he was aghast. He could not believe we were unsalaried professionals. He hadn't imagined the magnitude of our work, the considerable output of relatively few activists. We openly discussed our conflicting viewpoints. At the end, the intensity of two hours of questions and answers, the vaulting over of animosity and vast fissures of policy and points of view, left me shaking.

"You know," I reminded him, "we go back a long time, to 1978, when we met in front of the Choral Synagogue." During his eighteen years in refusal, Yuli had met hundreds of people, and he didn't remember our first meeting. But I could visualize the photograph of us, he in his blue jacket and knitted kippah, and me very young, with my fashionable newly permed hair. I even knew exactly where that photo was: in my desk drawer. But when I got back home to Chicago, it wasn't there. I searched through my drawers, emptying them of all the scraps of paper and notebooks and photographs, but I couldn't find it. I had so wanted to show it to Yuli as a reminder of the beginning of this exceptional relationship.

The next summer, Lenny and I took our grandson Ezra to New York for his bar mitzvah trip. Family protocol demanded a visit to the American Jewish Historical Society and a guided tour of the Soviet Jewry archives.

Andrei Filomonov took us down to the stacks and showed Ezra the more than seventy boxes of my personal archives, the Chicago Action archives, and the Union of Councils archives, and he asked Ezra what he'd like to see. Ezra wanted to see photos. Of the hundreds of boxes, Andrei picked one and extracted an archival-quality envelope of photos. Ezra pulled out a photo. I peered over his shoulder. There I was, hair permed and wild, standing next to a man in a blue down coat and a knitted kippah. Yuli and I, in 1978: the photograph I'd been searching for. Andrei made me a copy. I planned to bring it to Israel, put it in Yuli's hand, and with it, seal the friendship that had been born out of a long process of cooperation, enmity, and finally, reconciliation and mutual respect.

One more time, let's fast forward, to April 2014.

The first days of Pesach were over, matzah crumbs swept away, and our "Hitler-Stalin" room, named for my library's collection and the setting for our large Pesach Seder, was orderly again. I went to retrieve the messages from our answering machine. There had been an accident. Yuli Kosharovsky, seventy-two years old, in the middle of his exhaustive work on Jews in the Soviet Union, did not survive.[5]

Yuli was gone.

This is the end of a story, but it remains unfinished. It's an incomplete story accompanied by incomplete grief.

---

5.   My friend Enid Wurtman arranged for the publication of Yuli's book, "*We Are Jews Again*": *Jewish Activism in the Soviet Union*, released in the spring of 2017. It is the quintessential work on Soviet Jewry, and I hope that somewhere in the world to come, Yuli has the *nachas* from his achievements in this world. May the memory of Yuli Kosharovsky be for a blessing.

CHAPTER 19

Jerusalem, Vienna, and Moscow, 1989

Paternalization versus Partnership

As 1988 came to a close, Micah and I traveled to Jerusalem to attend a meeting of the International Council of the World Conference on Soviet Jewry. Denied official status, we attended as observers.

Israeli Jewish Agency representatives, Lishka officials, European and American organizational presidents were seated in the front of the room, closest to the podium. Recently released former prisoners of conscience and refuseniks were assigned seats at the back. The optics said everything. Some had paid for the chance to come home to Israel with a term in the gulag. They should have been seated with honor in the front, briefing us on new conditions, evaluating strategies, chiseling new policies, creating new mechanisms and programs. The fact that the leaders of the movement were sidelined was disturbing.

Just before the conference opened, I responded to a message from a refusenik asking me to call Yuli Kosharovsky. Yuli dictated a weighty statement in Russian into the tape recorder attached to the receiver. It was a message to the conference, signed by Yuli and other prominent refuseniks. Micah and I had the document translated into English and printed on UCSJ letterhead. We placed a copy of the statement on every seat at the conference.

Their statement surprised me. On our trip to Moscow earlier that year, Micah and I had called for a non-patronizing, non-paternalistic partnership with refuseniks. Yuli's statement incorporated our terminology, which was central to our ethos. The language of the text was precisely that of the Union. It was ironic that Yuli, whose activity was funded by the Lishka, relied on the Union of Councils, the very group eschewed by the

Establishment, to deliver the refuseniks' statement of priorities for conducting the political, material, religious, and cultural campaign for Soviet Jewry. The paternalistic attitude of the Establishment toward Soviet Jews was the antithesis of UCSJ's approach. We were the refuseniks' partners in the West. We were their voice. The golden age of comic books was over; we had no delusions of being Superman. It was the Jews in the Soviet Union, not us, who were the heroes; their resistance dictated our rescue efforts and lay at the center of UCSJ's ideology and methodology.

Just a few weeks later, another opportunity arose to reinforce our philosophy of partnership with the refuseniks. In late December, Lenny, Josh, and I went to Scotland to visit Scott, who was studying at Edinburgh University. In the middle of the trip, in a call to Moscow, I was told it was important that I meet Moscow activist Mika Chlenov in Vienna. After a visit with Scott and a quick tour of northern Scotland, I went on to Vienna, meeting up there with Micah, who had flown in from Washington.

Chlenov met us at the hotel. He was short, sharp-eyed, broad-boned, with dark hair and a warm smile. He had a way of speaking with his hands that reminded me of a gambler preparing to roll dice. In Vienna for a professional conference, he must have been traveling outside the Soviet Union for the first time.

At the top of my agenda was to clarify the role of UCSJ in the movement. Free from KGB interceptors, we spent hours with Chlenov, speaking frankly about the movement, cautiously outlining the distinctions between the UCSJ and the National Conference on Soviet Jewry, discussing their close ties to the Lishka. I meticulously watched my words, avoiding anything he could interpret as denigrating the Establishment and clarifying the differences in our policies and methodology. I explained the rationale for UCSJ's "freedom of choice" policy and Jackson-Vanik and laid out our broad grassroots relationship with the US Congress. I also mapped out the connections between the UCSJ, the London-based 35s, Student Struggle for Soviet Jewry, and the French Comité des Quinze.

Most of all, I clarified UCSJ's distinctly non-paternalistic orientation. "UCSJ activists are your partners, not your benefactors," I told him. "We are one movement on two sides of the ocean."

It was a watershed meeting. Chlenov took the message back to the refusenik leadership and reinforced our positions.

The Solomon Mikhoels Cultural Center

After returning home from Vienna, in January 1989, I was surprised by a birthday telegram from Yuli Kosharovsky and Sasha Smuckler. When I called Moscow to thank them, Yuli delivered the second surprise. He wanted me to come to Moscow for the opening of the Solomon Mikhoels Cultural Center. He said I should be there.

Using Gorbachev's policy of glasnost for their own ends, refuseniks were pushing the new openness, trying to achieve official recognition for Jewish activity that had operated underground since Stalin. Gorbachev had opened the door by just a crack, but activists intended to shove it open all the way. This center, a significant step toward Jewish cultural legitimacy, was to be named for the Yiddish actor Solomon Mikhoels, known internationally for his stunning performance of King Lear. Mikhoels had become the tragic symbol of Stalin's annihilation of Jewish culture and the murder of the Jews who had created it.

Stalin had recruited Mikhoels during World War II for his Jewish Anti-Fascist Committee (AFC). AFC was designed to use Russia's internationally known Jewish cultural figures to solicit support from their Jewish American connections for Stalin's war against Germany. In June 1943, Stalin dispatched Mikhoels and poet Itzik Feffer to America.

Mikhoels was a genuine rock star. Fifty thousand Americans turned out to hear him speak at the New York Giants' baseball stadium. He met with Albert Einstein, Charlie Chaplin, and Marc Chagall, ultimately raising $16 million for the Soviet army.

Mikhoels, however, soon became a target for Stalin's paranoia, but the beloved actor and remnant of Russia's Jewish intellectual and cultural heritage was too prestigious and well known to be openly arrested and executed. Five years later, Stalin orchestrated his murder to appear accidental, having his body dumped on a street in Minsk, looking as if he had been hit by a truck.

But no one was fooled.

Then, on August 12, 1952, on what became known as the Night of the Murdered Poets, Stalin ordered the murders of the cream of Russia's intellectual Jews, who were shot in KGB's notorious Lubyanka Prison. It was the final blow, the end of Jewish culture in Russia.

Some forty years later, in Switzerland, I heard the tragic story firsthand. Leonid Stonov was just a boy on January 13, 1948, when the phone rang in his family's Moscow apartment in the Writers Compound. His father picked up the phone, listened in absolute silence, and then, putting down the receiver, told Leonid, "Mikhoels was run over by a truck and killed. It's the beginning of the end."

Not long after, Leonid's father was arrested.

And now, thirty-five years later, Jewish activists were trying to jump-start the engine by opening the Mikhoels Cultural Center.

"Of course," I told Yuli. "Of course I'll be there." So the following month, Micah, Lenny, Marillyn, David, and I flew to Moscow for the February 12 opening.

The short winter days only exaggerated the gloomy atmosphere that perpetually hung over the city. Away from the Kremlin and the spectacle of the onion-shaped domes of St. Basil's Cathedral and palaces harking back to imperial Russia, the oversized, crumbling Stalinist-era buildings loomed. Massive apartment complexes, reminiscent of Chicago tenements, graphically diminished the people living there, who were, after all, only insignificant cogs in the totalitarian system.

Unwelcoming, unmarked entrances, unlit hallways, and peeling walls characterized Moscow's apartment buildings. Babushka-clad women with metal-capped teeth swept streets with handmade straw brooms. On a street corner, a raggedly dressed, unshaven old man sold kvass out of a barrel, wiping off the used cup with a filthy rag before handing it to the next person in line. Police and militiamen, wearing long coats with shiny brass buttons and gleaming leather boots, patrolled the streets, watching. Everywhere, there were watchers. Throughout the city, people submitted to long lines, hoping that at the end they could "get," get something, anything. They waited in long lines for their turn to buy bread or, if they were lucky, a chicken. They waited in line to buy shoes, hoping the supply wouldn't run out. If they found shoes in the wrong size, they bought them anyway, hoping they could be traded for something they needed. They waited in long lines for buses. No one smiled. No one talked. Eyes deliberately avoided others. Repression, depression, and fear had snuffed out life. They were the walking dead; I wondered if they became alive in their depressing apartments after a bottle of vodka.

Welcomed by Solomon Mikhoels' daughter and Elie Weisel in the yellow prerevolutionary building on Taganka Square, fifteen hundred foreign guests and refuseniks attended the opening of the Mikhoels Cultural

Center, watching black-and-white clips of Mikhoels' breathtaking performance of King Lear. Seeing him on the screen, we had the sense that
history had converged with the present. In Moscow's bleak atmosphere,
bright Jewish life and values were forcing their way out of the frigid crusty
earth, miraculous as the first fragile spring daffodils.

Foreign guests were more optimistic about the promise of progress
than the refuseniks. Elie Wiesel expressed some optimism after the return
of Andrei Sakharov from internal exile and the release of fifteen Jewish
prisoners of conscience. But he challenged Gorbachev to restore diplomatic
relations with Israel and admit the fate of the heroic Raoul Wallenberg.

Wallenberg's fate was a big agenda item for UCSJ. A Swedish diplomat in Budapest during the Holocaust, Wallenberg saved thousands of
Hungarian Jews by issuing false papers and passports. After the Soviets
invaded Hungary in December 1944, he was arrested and disappeared.

The gutsy, indefatigable Lil Hoffman, chair of UCSJ's Colorado
Committee of Concern, headed the International Committee to Save
Raoul Wallenberg. Working with Congressman Tom Lantos, himself saved
by Wallenberg and brought to America on a student visa by Marillyn and
Abe Sachar, Lil initiated the bill that gave Wallenberg honorary American
citizenship in 1981.

The Soviets continually claimed that Wallenberg died of a heart attack
in Lubyanka Prison in 1947. It wasn't until 1989 that they admitted he was
probably killed by Lavrenti Beria, Stalin's NKVD[1] henchman.

In 1981, Marillyn and I had been privileged to receive the Raoul
Wallenberg Humanitarian Award from Prince Sigvard and Princess
Marianne of Sweden, at an event sponsored by the Raoul Wallenberg
Committee of Chicago, to memorialize "a war hero who never wore a uni-
form or fired a gun."[2]

The memory of the tragic fates of both Wallenberg and Mikhoels
couldn't be swept away by the fanfare of either event, and Micah and I
shared the refuseniks' caution when the Mikhoels Center opened. The
Kremlin's recognition of Jewish cultural institutions steamed along a track
that paralleled the anti-Semitic activity driven by Pamyat, a neo-Nazi

---

1. NKVD was the predecessor to KGB.
2. Jon Anderson, "A Tribute to a Hero of Biblical Proportions," *Chicago Tribune*, April
   5, 1987.

group of chauvinist Russian Orthodox ultranationalists run by a fanatic anti-Semite.

When the Mikhoels Center opened, no one could predict where the new openness was going. Yuri Cherniak, who had finally received permission, told me, "For some people this is just a show. For others, it is very real." Refusenik Valery Sherbaum noted that, at the moment, the cultural center seemed like a *beriozka*, the shops run exclusively for foreign visitors paying with dollars: it was beautiful, but it seemed like it was all designed for others.

The instability ate away at any sense of equilibrium. There was still no emigration law, no definition or term limits on secrecy pretexts, no resolution of "poor relative" cases. Still, I couldn't help but feel that something was changing. At the very least, Jews were allowed to meet openly.

In Leningrad and Moscow

The next day, we went to the Stonovs' apartment to talk to Natasha, Leonid, and Yuri Cherniak about UCSJ's refusenik list. Natasha and Yuri agreed refuseniks could assemble and compile a far more comprehensive list and agreed that they, along with Edward Markov in Leningrad, would undertake the task.

In Leningrad we visited Alec and Galina Zelichenok. Like old friends, we huddled around their small table, relishing fresh greens and sweet garlic from Soviet Georgia. Alec was a self-taught Hebrew teacher who, along with his wife, had been refused permission for over a decade. In 1985, he had been sentenced to three years in prison camp for spreading "anti-Soviet slander." His conviction, like Vladimir Lifshitz, another Leningrad refusenik, was based simply on the evidence of his having written personal letters to the West, mail illegally purloined by KGB. His dangerously high blood pressure had put him at serious additional risk, especially during the perilous transport to the gulag. UCSJ mobilized the US government. In 1988, he was taken from prison camp in Kazakhstan and brought before two separate courts. He was told he had been "reformed" and was released.

US Consul General Richard Miles hosted a reception in Leningrad for Micah and me. Our conversation focused on Leningrad's long-term refuseniks, especially the former prisoners like Evgeny Lein and Zelichenok. Social and political pariahs, they couldn't even walk into our hotel, which was guarded by leather-jacketed KGB goons who fastidiously barred the doors while they checked passports and identity papers, admitting only hotel guests. How could we get people out of the country if we couldn't even get them into our hotel? It was absurdly frustrating, but it gave rise to an idea.

Micah and I arranged a small dinner party at the Astoria hotel with three refusenik couples and Joyce Marshall, the consular officer. I asked her to meet the Zelichenoks, the Leins, and the Markovs outside the Astoria and escort them in. Though KGB would be restricting access, they wouldn't turn away the refuseniks under US protection.

Before dinner, Alec took Micah and me on a short expedition. Almost in the shadow of the elegant Astoria was the foreboding Kresty Prison, where he and Evgeny had been held in pre- and post-trial detention. Kresty held eight thousand prisoners – many of whom were innocent but had been sentenced to long labor camp sentences. Slave labor, Alec quipped, was the country's only dependable labor source.

Once we were together in the Astoria's restaurant, Evgeny and Alec began briefing the consular office about the illegalities of their sentences. A small band began to play, and abruptly Alec left the table. My back to the dance floor, I turned and saw him. He was mesmerized. Curious, I got up to see what had captured his attention.

What I saw terrified me.

A young scantily clad woman was undulating to provocative music on the dance floor while a twelve-foot boa constrictor slithered around her body. I have a deathly fear of snakes. Somehow I made it back to the table and pretended to reconnect to the conversation.

Afterwards, back in my hotel room, my anxieties paid me an unwelcome visit. I could not close my eyes. What if the snake were still in the hotel? What if the woman and snake were staying for tomorrow's performance? My brain spun waking nightmares. The snake was probably caged, but maybe it had escaped. Where was it? Slithering down my corridor? Coming up through the toilet? Every phobic improbability produced spasms of panic. My fear gravitated around one snake in the Astoria Hotel. KGB didn't terrorize me, but that one snake did. I spent an intolerably endless night waiting to escape from the hotel.

Back in Moscow, before we flew home, Leonid arranged a dinner for activists from abroad and from Moscow. Marillyn, Rita Eker from the London 35s, David, Micah, Leonid, a few well-known dissidents, and I sat on thick cushions on the floor, around a large, low, dark wood table, in a typically Georgian restaurant. The walls were decorated with brightly painted Turkish ceramic tiles. Turbaned servers brought tasty dishes, shashlik and pilafs. Mostly, they brought vodka. And the camaraderie, always infectious, brought us to one *l'chaim* after another.

The hour was late when we finally left. Leonid tried to find taxis to take us back to the hotel in Moscow's center, and we installed Marillyn and a couple of others in the one he did manage to secure. The rest of us took off on foot through a dark park. The broad boulevard winding through the park was deserted, and a peaceful quiet had settled in. Leafless branches, moving softly in the wind, shimmered in the moonlight. From around the bend appeared a Moscow city bus. Led by Leonid, the vodka definitely at work, a few of us waved down the bus and blocked its course. The driver opened the door and Leonid began to negotiate our passage. No, the driver's workday was done, and he was taking the bus back to the terminal. But the evening's effects hadn't worn off, and our group of refuseniks, dissidents, and American and British activists were unstoppable. Our sense of unity and our shared goals and values, along with the vodka, had triggered a communal high, and we weren't about to take no for an answer. So we commandeered the bus, insisting the driver take us to the city center. It probably wasn't the smartest thing for a bunch of known anti-Soviet Zionist conspirators to do, but it made for a wonderful memory.

PART FOUR

Riding the Storms

CHAPTER 20

Problems at Home, 1989

A Threat to Jackson-Vanik

Meanwhile, back home, the drive to offer the USSR premature economic concessions broke out again after the welcome but vastly overdue release of some long-term refuseniks. Yuli Kosharovsky, Evgeny Lein, and Yuri Cherniak were finally given visas. Fresh winds that brought the hope of change also revived interest in a waiver of the Jackson-Vanik trade restrictions. Word had it that the amendment would be on the agenda when the new president, George H. W. Bush, met Gorbachev in Malta and that the Establishment was reviewing and reassessing their position. Seagram's CEO Edgar Bronfman, speaking on behalf of the World Jewish Congress, strongly promoted concessions. "The Soviets have gone far toward answering the problems that led the US to put the Jackson-Vanik Amendment into law," he said. "This sea change calls for an energetic and imaginative Western response."[1]

But the Kremlin hadn't gone far enough. Alec Zelichenok and others were still waiting, refuseniks were being given fresh refusals, and there was still no codification of the right to emigrate. Although the emigration rate in 1989 could possibly double the previous year's nearly nineteen thousand, three years earlier only 914 Jews had been given permission to leave. No one could predict in what direction the Kremlin's emigration pendulum might swing.

In April, in a memo to UCSJ councils, I noted, "No Soviet Jewish emigration leader known to us in the USSR or Israel supports a waiver. The terms clearly have not been met. There can be no waiver until the Soviets comply with these preconditions: (a) assurance of high and sustained emigration levels, (b) evacuation of all outstanding refuseniks and

---

1. "U.S. Should Reassess Jackson-Vanik, World Jewish Congress Leader Says," Jewish Telegraphic Agency (JTA), March 23, 1989.

(c) institutionalization of emigration rights through enactment and implementation of reform legislation consistent with the Helsinki and Vienna accords."[2]

Testifying two years earlier before the joint hearing of the House Subcommittee on International Economic Policy and Trade and the House Subcommittee on Europe and the Middle East, I spoke about Jackson-Vanik's psychological and symbolic value. Echoing sentiments expressed by Sharansky and activists in Israel, I said:

> Jackson-Vanik is the symbolic cornerstone of American human rights policy as it affects Soviet Jews. It is the singular, tangible expression of American support for Soviet Refuseniks, and I can assure you that any effort now to dilute Jackson-Vanik, or grant a waiver, would be a devastating psychological blow to the Refusenik community, and one that the Union of Councils for Soviet Jews will resist as a matter of highest priority.[3]

Despite strenuous efforts of past UCSJ presidents Morey Schapira and Lynn Singer, in June 1989 the National Conference on Soviet Jewry announced support for a waiver.

Stuart E. Eizenstat was former chief domestic policy advisor to President Carter and a supportive and influential member of UCSJ's honorary board. Stuart, who attended National Conference's Convocation on Soviet Jewry, told us that, in their internal discussions, the National Conference brushed aside UCSJ's precondition for legal codification as an "unnecessary impediment."[4] Instead, they decided to promote the development of good relations between the USSR and the American Jewish community.

I wrote to Sharansky on June 16, 1989, asking him to weigh in with the Establishment. I explained that our position was supported by some of our

---

2.   Pamela Braun Cohen, memo to UCSJ councils, April 1989.

3.   Pamela Braun Cohen, testimony before US House of Representatives Committee on Foreign Affairs, joint hearing of the Subcommittee on International Economic Policy and Trade and the Subcommittee on Europe and the Middle East, July 14, 1987.

4.   Stuart Altshuler, *From Exodus to Freedom: The History of the Soviet Jewry Movement* (Lanham, MD: Rowman and Littlefield, 2005), 99.

good friends in Congress on both sides of the aisle, but support had taken a toll due to the lobbying efforts of Bronfman and Mark Talisman, the well-connected representative of the Council of Jewish Federations, along with the pro-trade, disarmament Democrats and the Israelis. Once again, the powerful monolith was in a crucial conflict with those they ostensibly represented.

I also reached out to Rabbi Shlomo Noach Mandel, who ran the Canadian Foundation's Community Development Program for industrialist and builder Albert Reichmann. Reichmann was supporting Jewish revival in the USSR and Eastern Europe, and Rabbi Shlomo Noach had helped a number of refuseniks. He had especially earned my appreciation for arranging delivery of some officially prohibited computers to Moscow and Leningrad refuseniks.

In the midst of the 1989 Jackson-Vanik controversy, Rabbi Mandel suggested I meet with Albert Reichmann and Rabbi Moshe Sherer, the highly esteemed head of Agudath Israel of America. Representing Orthodox Jewry, the Agudah had won respect in Washington for their legal and advocacy activity. We met in their New York office, and I related the various factors and positions of the Jewish organizations. Rabbi Sherer was in agreement with UCSJ, and having endorsed our opposition to a waiver, enlisted his Washington representative to lobby the Congress.

Reacting to the Establishment's threat to Jackson-Vanik, our council leaders called on grassroots activists to phone their representatives in Congress to support our position. At the end, with help from Assistant Secretary of State for European and Canadian Affairs Rozanne Ridgway, and, above all, because of the outpouring of support from refusenik leaders who backed us, UCSJ's position prevailed.

We weren't intractable. Acknowledging some progress, Micah had announced an accommodation a few months earlier. Should the USSR fulfill its promise to relax restrictions on emigration and permit the departure of all long-term refuseniks, UCSJ would endorse the repeal of the Stevenson Amendment. That law, passed in 1975, set a limit of $300 million on loans and loan guarantees to the Soviet Union by the Export-Import Bank for the purchase of American goods. "By international standards of human rights, the Soviets are not up to par yet, but we need to recognize the progress they have already made," Micah said.[5]

---

5. Robert Pear, "Some Jews Favor Easing Soviet Trade Curbs," *New York Times*, February 5, 1989.

Calamity and Calumny: Refugee Status

The threats to Jackson-Vanik's linkage were only one of two significant challenges to the movement. The second was the Israeli Foreign Ministry's periodic attempts to close America's gates to Soviet Jewish refugees. That effort reemerged in 1987, building steam and coming to a head in 1989. This time, the US State Department was the dragon that was breathing fire into the controversy.

Israeli prime minister Yitzchak Shamir had asked Secretary of State Shultz in February 1987 to close the doors to emigrating Soviet Jews by denying them refugee status. Israel's position was advanced a month later by the negotiations in Moscow led by Morris Abram and Edgar Bronfman.

Shultz reacted to Shamir's request with concern. If Jews couldn't enter the United States, many might not leave the USSR. He further told Shamir that if Gorbachev were deposed, conditions might worsen, and there could even be mass killings once again. In such a scenario, the secretary told Shamir, "I would never forgive myself, and you would not forgive yourself either."[6]

Pressure to restrict Jewish emigration to America came not just from Israel but from within the United States. At that time, almost 90 percent of all emigrating Jews wanted to come to the States, increasing the Jewish Establishment's resettlement costs as well as the US government's expenditures.

Nevertheless, our activists continued to oppose American capitulation to any proposal that would create a barrier to Jewish emigration. Israel is the national Jewish homeland, but it was incumbent upon American Jews to keep every escape hatch open, even one to the United States.

And Secretary Shultz continued to bolster UCSJ's position: "Soviet Jews are at risk. Let's get them out first and worry about where they want to go. However, they shouldn't go where they don't want to go."[7] He was right not to ignore the risks. Both the anti-Semitic outbreak in the press and the open calls for pogroms in several cities were driving ever greater numbers of Jews to seek permission to leave.

---

6.   Adamishin and Schifter, *Human Rights*.

7.   Frederick A. Lazin, *The Struggle for Soviet Jewry in American Politics: Israel Versus the American Jewish Establishment* (Lanham, MD: Lexington Books, 2005), 264.

In the summer of 1988, Leonid reported with alarm the first signs that Soviet Jewish emigration to America was about to change substantially. At first, ostensibly to satisfy budgetary parameters, US refugee processing from the Soviet Union was halted. When it resumed a few months later, it appeared that America no longer categorically applied a presumption of persecution to Soviet Jews. As the dust cleared, it was announced that the United States was requiring that all Soviet Jews seeking entrance give evidence they had a well-founded fear of persecution. They would be assessed on a case by case basis in an interview at the US embassy in Moscow.

In no time, hundreds of Jews were awaiting interviews at our embassy in Moscow. Soon it was thousands, then tens of thousands. Some Jews left the USSR without refugee status, but they were then held up in Rome, awaiting a status-determining interview at the US consulate there. Before long, thousands of Soviet Jews were in Ladispoli, a small seaside town outside of Rome, waiting to be interviewed, without resources. Panic spread and UCSJ started enlisting pro bono lawyers to go to Ladispoli to advocate for Jews denied refugee status.

What had triggered the change in America's long-standing commitments to Jewish emigration from the USSR, a change that coalesced with Israeli interests? The US had made an ideological concession to the Israelis, and I had a sickening feeling that it was a result of some behind-the-scenes negotiation that would put Israel at risk. In the long run, what price would Israel pay for getting America to back down?

At the end of 1988, the US government announced a stunning reversal of its diplomatic boycott of the Palestine Liberation Organization (PLO). President Reagan and President-elect Bush had agreed to direct talks with Yasser Arafat, based on ostensible assurances that the PLO had "totally and absolutely renounced all forms of terrorism."[8] I couldn't prove the behind-the-scenes diplomatic horse-trading, but I suspected at the time that the price for closing America's doors was the legitimization of the PLO. It might have been the quid pro quo I had feared was coming.

Responding to the announcement that the United States was strictly limiting refugee visas to Soviet Jews, Micah and I explained in a letter to Shultz, "This policy provides to the Soviet Union a public relations bonanza by permitting them to claim that they are now releasing more Soviet Jews

---

8.   Norman Kempster, "US to Talk with PLO," *New York Times*, December 15, 1988.

than the United States is willing to receive."[9] In Moscow, Leonid Stonov told US Ambassador Jack Matlock that just as the Soviets were beginning to let Jews emigrate, America was blocking the gates.

UCSJ was pushing on two fronts, to reverse the decision that Soviet Jews were no longer presumptively classified as refugees fleeing anti-Semitism, and then to raise the number of refugee slots that were allocated for them. Senator Edward Kennedy from Massachusetts and Senator Bob Kasten from Wisconsin helped promote our agenda in Congress by proposing to raise the ceiling on Soviet immigrants from twenty-five thousand to fifty thousand for 1989. Echoing our language, Shultz was pressing hard within the administration. In a letter to Bay Area Council he affirmed that every effort had to be made to take out the greatest number of Jews and that he considered Soviet Jews refugees fleeing persecution.

By the fall of 1989, the United States had restricted immigration to those Jews with invitations from first-degree relatives – parents, spouses, or minor children – living in the States. Even for those people, refugee status would be granted sparingly, determined by interviews at the embassy. I sent a memo to our board summing it up: "Clearly they are responding to predictions of a flood tide of future Soviet emigration permissions not yet realized and by no means confirmed. And, of course, they are working with Israel to try to compel a greater percentage of Soviet Jews to choose Israel over the United States."[10]

Free, open Soviet Jewish immigration to America was over.

At that pivotal moment, New Jersey senator Frank Lautenberg appeared no less than a giant on the stage of history. His bill, passed in 1990, granted presumptive refugee status to Jews from the Soviet Union, requiring immigration officials to take into account a historical well-founded fear of persecution when judging an applicant's refugee status.

Senator Lautenberg himself estimated that his amendment allowed an estimated 350,000 to 400,000 Soviet Jews to enter the United States by lowering the burden of proof for those seeking refugee status. Leonid called the senator a national hero.

---

9.   Micah Naftalin and Pamela Braun Cohen, letter to Secretary of State George Shultz, November 18, 1988.

10. Pamela Braun Cohen, memo sent to UCSJ board, 1989, archives of Pamela Braun Cohen, American Jewish Historical Society, New York.

CHAPTER 21

Shadows on the City of Light, June 1989

Fighting against the Waves

Four months after the opening of the Mikhoels Center in Moscow, Micah and I were in France for the continuing CSCE process, the Paris Conference on the Human Dimension (CHD). Vienna's stately grandeur gave way to Paris' leafy, tree-lined boulevards, a stark contrast to Russia, where the political-social terrain had become unpredictably dangerous, pitted with quicksand. Some long-term refuseniks had been given permission, but as of January, about five hundred scientists were still in refusal, with Leonid Stonov among them. A far more incendiary brand of Jew-hatred had spawned from thousands of newly sanctioned anti-Semitic organizations. Our phone lines burned with the intense anxiety of Soviet Jews, fearing pogroms. Their panic was fueling the ever-increasing levels of emigration.

The Vienna Concluding Document had mandated the Paris CHD to evaluate the spectrum of human rights and humanitarian issues, to hold rhetoric to account – in other words, verify that behavior complied with assurances. Micah and I were to provide the American and European delegations with documentary evidence of the Soviets' continuing human rights violations. The head of the US delegation was Morris Abram. Our contentious history made it unlikely anything productive could result from a meeting other than agonizing discomfort on both sides. But the UCSJ had solid relations with the congressional Helsinki Commission chairmen, Senator Dennis DeConcini of Arizona and Representative Steny Hoyer of Maryland. In fact, the Union had honored them both with our Henry Jackson Freedom Award just a few months earlier. Sam Wise, the commission's staff director, and Janie Fisher, deputy staff director, were also vital liaisons who viewed UCSJ's activity as integral to US interests. My

251

congressman, John Porter, cochair of the House Human Rights Caucus, was also in Paris. Our access to these prominent figures diminished our dependency on Abram to have access to other delegations.

The Paris conference gave me a firsthand impression of the new president, George H. W. Bush. Flanked by the press, he entered the sumptuous hotel lobby and gave what I considered an entirely inappropriate celebratory speech, hailing his vision of a new post–Cold War world order. Because of the activity of Solidarity in Poland, Rukh in Ukraine, and a host of human rights monitors still in prison, Soviet domination over Eastern Europe was in fact loosening its grip. But Bush's orientation seemed more about supporting Gorbachev's view of a new world order and less about a commitment to human rights and the indigenous democratic movements. I didn't like it. Its victorious tone was premature. I feared it could dilute the US commitment to the verification process of the Helsinki principles. It didn't help that the new secretary of state, James Baker, seemed to be sending a message about the strategic significance of CSCE by failing to come to the Paris meeting.

Another discouraging impression of the conference resulted from the appallingly restrictive registration process for nongovernmental organizations. The Helsinki process formally embedded into its operational architecture the advocacy of private citizens and NGOs. NGO monitors provided governmental delegations evidentiary documentation to verify compliance with the principles of the accords. But it quickly became apparent that this Paris meeting would be different.

The grueling registration process made it clear that the organizers were stifling the role of the human rights monitors. On the first day, we lined up on the Rue des Ecoles near the Sorbonne in an attempt to register and receive official passes. Outside the palace where the conference was convened, uniformed guards denied access to NGO participants without credentials. These credentials were issued daily, a procedure never required at previous CSCE meetings. In a Kafkaesque twist, the only place to acquire those credentials was inside the building we were blocked from entering. The city of the Eiffel Tower and the Louvre might as well have been the Kremlin.

Somehow we managed to succeed, but each day we faced a hostile brigade. Even armed with the previous day's credentials, NGOs were turned away by the guards. At the top of a marble staircase leading to the entrance of the conference, Micah tried to face down a guard, who grabbed his thumb, twisting it aggressively enough to nearly cause Micah to lose his balance and fall down the stairs. Eventually we secured permanent passes, but we still had to confront the guards each day.

Once admitted, NGOs were sidelined to observer seating for the plenary sessions, making it difficult to mix with delegates. At various meetings, it became clear that the European delegates' concern about Soviet human rights compliance was evaporating in the blinding glare of the "New Europe." They were sure that a new social order, liberated from the legacy of the past, was being built on mutual respect and cooperation and that it heralded the demise of the era of confrontation and division.

In our meetings with the Soviet delegation, they gave assurances that they were living up to the promises made in Vienna. But in direct violation of the Vienna Concluding Document, the Kremlin had denied Leonid, David Mikhalev, and Yuri Semenovsky temporary visitor visas to Paris. Leonid dictated their statements to me over the phone, to raise with the delegations.

We raised the issue with the chairman of the Soviet Human Rights Committee of the Ministry of Foreign Affairs. He made it clear he had no intention of letting Leonid and the others out for the Paris meeting but dangled hope that he'd let them attend the following CSCE meeting in Copenhagen. A gift, not a right – a suggestion of possible elasticity in the near future. But for now, they denied Zeev Dashevsky a visitor's visa to accept an award by the British House of Commons and refused Mika Chlenov and two other scholars permission to travel to Jerusalem to the World Congress of Judaica.

Besides flagrantly violating the Vienna agreement, these obstructions underscored our concern about the forthcoming Moscow human rights conference. Free access was a precondition for US participation and the Soviets were demonstrating that they wouldn't permit refuseniks free access. Micah and I raised this issue with both the NATO delegations and the Soviets. We also brought them the July 14 joint declaration of the Moscow-based Refusenik Legal Seminar and the Public Committee to Monitor OVIR. It pointed out that in spite of the increasing number of Jews leaving the country, there were no principle changes in the emigration policy and that few long-term cases had been resolved since the signing of the Vienna agreement.

One starry Paris night, along with a corps of international glitterati, Micah and I followed other attendees along a grand, red-carpeted walkway into a dazzling French Renaissance palace for the formal reception for President Bush, the European ambassadors and their delegations, the media, and NGOs. I had come on a working trip, and evening clothes had not made it into my suitcase. Still, I managed to pull myself together. It didn't matter much. There were few other women among the hundreds of guests, and I was just another black jacket in a sea of black.

The large, formal hall was resplendent in a blaze of crystal chandeliers. Somehow, in the crowd, we found ourselves talking to the men who were leading their Soviet-dominated countries to independence. Lech Walesa was the Polish head of Solidarity, the Soviet bloc's first independent trade union, and winner of the 1983 Nobel Peace Prize. We spoke about our mutual interest in the human rights issue, and Micah and I specifically addressed both the issue of Jewish emigration and our deep concern about anti-Semitism. Walesa said he was committed to ensuring a safe future for Poland's Jews. The weight of Solidarity's movement, the work strikes engineered as protests, and the struggle against the Soviets showed in the lines etched on his skin. I could not have known that night that this man was destined to be the first president of independent Poland.

Also in attendance were other leaders of the "captive nations" that had been struggling against the Soviets for decades, republics that were just starting to emerge from under the Kremlin's repressive yoke. These leaders all looked to the West, to the NATO countries, to the Helsinki signatories, to America, to help advance their sovereignty agendas. Some, like Walesa, had spent years in Soviet prisons and camps. Others, in the Baltic nations and Ukraine, would shortly take over as the heads of newly independent governments. For a fleeting moment in time, Micah and I dared to hope that these leaders would bring their emerging nations not only to democratic values but to a cessation of their long-standing and vicious anti-Semitism.

That night, the Soviet delegation mixed freely with those they persecuted. Kremlin leaders of the apparat brushed shoulders with those they had dispatched into the gulag. The faces of the Politburo members showed their most saccharine expressions as they spoke with ingratiating affability: "Yes, of course, Mrs. Cohen, our government is working very hard to resolve all the cases of our refuseniks, and yes, of course, to enact a new law on emigration. Oh yes, it is indeed quite unfortunate about those cases of Stonov and the others who couldn't be here, isn't it, but you do have to understand that there are so many new bureaucratic issues that we are feverishly trying to overcome."

It was madness. There would be no Nuremberg trials in the USSR. Those who sentenced mixed with those they had sentenced – the smiling wolves hiding their fangs, and the sheep, quietly but firmly uncompromising. No one was sure who would prevail, but everyone was playing out their role.

The celebratory mood of the Paris meeting represented a disturbing change. This meeting had been preoccupied with emerging democratic movements in Eastern Europe and was looking for "architecture for a new Europe." Human rights had been sidelined, and NGOs like the UCSJ had been frozen out of the process. Submitting our testimony to the congressional Helsinki Commission, Micah explained that we were suddenly out in the cold. The CSCE excluded from the agenda anti-Semitism, psychiatric abuse, political prisoners, and emigration barriers. He urged the commission to use their influence to reinstate those issues on the agenda for the 1990 Copenhagen conference.

UCSJ struggled to reverse the trend, but we were riding against the waves.

Georgi Samoilovich: A View from Moscow

The frustrations like those of the Paris CSCE conference were offset by the joyful relief when refuseniks obtained their visas. The news of Georgi Samoilovich's release in the spring of 1989 was one of many instances when I knew our hard work was making a difference in people's lives.

Georgi had the looks and bearing of a gentleman who might be seated next to you at the opera. He was tall, slim, and elegant, refined and soft-spoken, with sparkling eyes and a quick smile. It was in Georgi's apartment that I had been stunned to hear him and other refuseniks singing my family's Yiddish song before Micah and I left Moscow in 1988.

A refusenik for eleven years, Georgi was the editor of the samizdat journal *Problems of Refusal*, one of the self-published underground bulletins on Jewish history and culture produced to feed the culture-starved community of Jewish refuseniks. He and his wife Vera were among many long-term refuseniks who still hadn't received permission to leave – not after the Vienna Concluding Document had embedded the right to emigrate, not after Gorbachev's reassurances to the United Nations that secrecy refusals could be appealed, not even after the United States agreed to participate in the Moscow human rights conference. Georgi continued to be in refusal, and he desperately needed to emigrate if he was to save his life.

After he was finally given permission in spring 1989, Georgi presented me with a scrapbook of his memories and photos. It begins with "Words of Gratitude," a reflection that tells his story and reveals how refuseniks saw us when we appeared in their world. It's a perspective from Moscow of the massive rescue movement UCSJ was operating on a multinational scale and simultaneously on a case-by-case basis, one refusenik, one Jewish prisoner at a time:

> The beginning of the summer of 1988 was very hot for Moscow's refuseniks, and not only due to the extreme temperatures. A Reagan-Gorbachev summit was scheduled. It was then that we got to know about the arrival of Mrs. Pamela Cohen and Mr. Micah Naftalin, National President and National Director of the Union of Councils for Soviet Jews. It was decided that we invite them first to a round table of our underground magazine, *Problems of Refusal,* that Evgeny Grechanovsky, Michael Gutman and I published to give them an all-over brief picture and also give us all a chance to know more about the Union of Councils.
>
> So there it was – a sunny, hot morning when Evgeny, Michael, Yuri Cherniak, Volodya Meshkov and I were sitting at a table in Grechanovsky's apartment. A ring of our doorbell and our guests entered the room. A young, delicate-looking woman looked even more fragile next to a big man with intelligent and kind eyes. We greeted them, gave Pamela flowers, and it seemed to me that they constantly felt themselves to be among friends. After my short introduction, Pamela and Micah explained to us goals, structure and activity of the Union of Councils. They explained the linkage between the rate of Jewish emigration from the USSR and the flow of free credits from American banks to the Soviets.

I have seen how Pam and Micah were meeting other groups. They worked each day from morning until night and we all wondered how they carry on under such pressure in this unusual heat. We started to realize the will, the inner strength of this remarkable woman, her devotion to human rights, to freeing her Russian brethren.

At the end on their way to Sheremetyevo airport, we held a small farewell party for them in our home.

But as fate has willed it, Pam and the Union of Councils have played a very special, decisive role in the life of my family.

Later in the year 1988, I was diagnosed with lymphoma. This illness (unfortunately, not the only one) was not treatable in the USSR. As if this alone was not enough I was even denied any treatment in the leading Soviet oncological center. Dr. Richard Rosenbluth, a prominent oncologist, immediately flew to us with an invitation to be treated in the Hackensack Medical Center in New Jersey. But the Soviets have twice refused me permission to go.[1]

Linda had been phoning Georgi regularly from our Chicago Action office. One call left her visibly devastated. Again, Georgi had been refused. Why were these stakes so high? What did they want? Were they going to let him die there? Marillyn, Hetty, Jean, and I sat around the conference table, brewed yet another pot of coffee, and raided Marillyn's stash of M&M's. One thing was clear. Whatever price they wanted for Georgi's freedom, what they were going to get from us was reaction. The four of us put everything we were doing on hold and triggered what had become, after so many years of rescue activity, CASJ's and UCSJ's emergency response network. We fed the fax machine a constant stream of alerts to Georgi's adopters, our councils, SSSJ, and our British colleagues. I notified the congressional Helsinki heads, the State Department, Ambassador Richard Schifter, and the White House. Jean hit all the congressional offices, and Linda stirred up a firestorm intended to make Moscow choke. In a barrage of press statements, she condemned the Soviets for an egregious violation of its signature on the Vienna Concluding Document. That document

---

1. Georgi Samoilovich, scrapbook given to Pamela Braun Cohen, November 1996.

provided that within three working days all participating nations would act on travel applications for those who "have a proven need of urgent medical treatment or who can be shown to be critically or terminally ill."[2] Moscow's refusal to let Georgi travel was "the first known case of noncompliance to the provisions of the Vienna Concluding Document signed by the Soviets and thirty-four other nations. "[3]

First, the Soviets reacted by deliberately twisting the meaning of the Concluding Document. OVIR official Hya Karakulko unceremoniously informed Georgi that the provision "has nothing to do with you. It pertains only to *foreigners* who must enter the Soviet Union in an emergency."[4] Such self-justifying, contortionist maneuvers were typical of Soviet officials, but this one was so blatantly ludicrous that I wondered how Karakulko got the words out of his mouth with a straight face. No sane foreigner would want to go to the USSR for a medical emergency.

Their second reaction was to deny the Vienna provision altogether. The high-ranking Kremlin mouthpiece Yuri Reshetov made a public statement claiming that knowledge of state secrets overrides any permission for ill people to leave.

So much for Soviet obligations under the CSCE Vienna agreement.

Linda, also the director of UCSJ's International Physicians Commission, enlisted its cochairs, doctors Marty Motew and Vic Borden, for a counterattack. Wearing white lab coats and carrying placards with Georgi's picture, doctors and UCSJ and SSSJ activists demonstrated outside the Soviet embassy in Washington, DC, while Soviet officials photographed them from the rooftop. The Russians weren't the only ones paying attention. The Washington police arrested eight of our demonstrators when they sat down in front of the embassy and refused to leave. But coverage in the media of the demonstration and arrests did help publicize Georgi's case.

Georgi continues his story in his scrapbook reflection:

---

2. Organization for Security and Co-operation in Europe, "Concluding Document of the Vienna Meeting 1986 of Representatives of the Participating States of the Conference on Security and Co-operation in Europe," https://www.osce.org/mc/40881?download=true (accessed May 6, 2020).

3. "Two Refuseniks Arrive in Israel; Another with Cancer Remains," Jewish Telegraphic Agency (JTA), January 31, 1989.

4. Ibid.

Despite a big campaign, organized by Pam and Micah, the Soviets have twice refused me even temporary permission to go and get treatment in the United States.

When my case became known in the United Kingdom, Rita Eker, my other savior, head of the Women's Campaign for Soviet Jewry, the 35s, opened another front in the battle to save me. Now Linda Opper was coordinating efforts in America with her British counterpart, Liz Phillips.

But the Soviets twice refused my going for treatment in the UK as well.

Almost every day Pam and Linda were calling me, and you cannot imagine how it felt to feel their support and conviction of the ultimate victory, to hear Pam's voice in a receiver....

In February 1989, Linda and Marillyn came to Moscow with the intent to force the Soviet Ministry of Public Health to lift their objections to my treatment abroad. They succeeded in meeting a deputy minister and bullying him into giving me a letter, stating that the ministry "didn't object to my treatment abroad." We have a picture of Marillyn standing in front of the ministry and threatening it with a fist.

Here's another picture dear to me: Micah speaking in front of a group of people. An American newspaper printed this photo of the meeting, held on my behalf in Washington.[5]

Repeatedly, we raised Georgi's case with the State Department, especially with Ambassador Richard Schifter, urging them to get the Russians to move quickly on a humanitarian basis.

Georgi Samoilovich concludes his reflection:

So this campaign, inspired and organized by Pam, lasted for more than half a year, when one evening in the beginning of April, Pam called me. I was listening to her absolutely excited voice. Ambassador Richard Schifter had just told her about information he received by diplomatic channels. I will be released to go for treatment in London....

---

5.   Georgi Samoilovich, scrapbook given to Pamela Braun Cohen, November 1996.

The next day I received a call from the chief of Moscow OVIR, informing me that my foreign passport was ready and by the end of the same week I was in a hospital in London, leaving my family behind, but assured by authorities that they would soon follow me.

Hours after my departure from Moscow, my wife Vera suffered a severe heart attack, followed by a second one two months later. Vera categorically forbade me to return to Moscow, even for her funeral. All this time, nearly every day Pamela was calling Vera and [our son] Victor, supporting and inspiring them.

Finally in October, Vera and Victor were able to leave the Soviet Union....

Perhaps, I have spoken too much about myself and my family, but we are the one example of what Pamela and the Union Councils have done for real people in real mortal danger.

I know this. I have seen it.[6]

---

6. Ibid.

CHAPTER 22

"Because We Can": Russia, 1989

UCSJ's Groundbreaking Official Meeting in Moscow

It was a new idea, revolutionary and daring, but when I thought about it, it had ancient roots: Jewish chutzpah, the audacity of Jews not to simply survive, but to thrive.

The media euphoria over supposed reforms in the USSR was cresting when UCSJ's board met in 1988, and we sat around the table drawing a schematic of the obstacles we faced. First and foremost was the Moscow human rights meeting, proposed at the 1987 Vienna CSCE meeting and set to take place in 1991. A human rights conference in Moscow was a ludicrous contradiction. This meeting would anoint the Kremlin with credibility even as it cracked down on dissent. With his pencil working as an extension of his fingers, David Waksberg, now with a few grey hairs straggling out of his dark curls, looked up from his legal pad. In his typically thoughtful, weighty tone, he then masterminded a preemptive strategy. "Why don't we test the Kremlin's behavior in advance? Why not host a human rights conference of our own…in Moscow?"

As the words left his mouth, I saw a slow-motion reaction work its way through the room. One by one, the faces of our board reflected the hilarious sense of irony, the preposterousness of an idea that was the only clinical test we could undertake. It was brilliant. Some of us had been denied visas. Some of us, like David, had been tailed by KGB in Russia and Ukraine. Some, like Lynn, had been vilified in the Soviet press. All of us were forced to communicate secretly, writing with magic slates in refuseniks' apartments. We were all persona non grata in the USSR, but we were going to host an open conference for Soviet Jews on their territory. When someone asked why we would do this, David brought down the house with his rationale: "Because we can."

A triumphant giddiness swept the room. It was strategically brilliant. We would make the Kremlin's long-sought Conference on the Human Dimension dependent on whether they would let us have ours. Everyone was talking at once about who we would invite, pulsing already with anticipation of being together with our refuseniks and prisoners, meeting openly.

Then, Harvey Barnett took it one step further. "Why not convene UCSJ's annual meeting in Moscow?" We saw it all in an instant. Already, it was a delicious victory. We would beat the Kremlin at its own game. We had the upper hand. Imagine what a group of students and housewives could do.

The more I thought about it, the more I loved it.

So we scripted "The First Ever Annual Moscow Meeting of the Union of Councils for Soviet Jews" as the grand rehearsal for Moscow's official CSCE human rights conference. Ours would be an open human rights conference with a full discussion of all the refusenik issues – emigration, the right to Jewish identity, a condemnation of the full menu of abuses that plagued their lives. If Moscow infringed on our meetings or denied refusenik access, we would have incontestable grounds for denying them their official conference in Moscow. And the congressional Helsinki Commission would be on our side. Even more than a litmus test, if we could pull it off, we would be creating a historic venue for the first open meeting in memory among Jews from the West, Israel, and the Soviet Union. There would be no surreptitious, looking-over-your-shoulder meetings in refusenik apartments; no communicating by writing on magic slates; no late-night walks to avoid KGB bugs. Everything would be open and public, and the Soviets would have no choice but to go along with our script.

I couldn't wait to tell Leonid. He recognized the potential of the plan, but I also heard what he didn't say. For the first time, I began to have an inkling of the logistical challenges and potential pitfalls that would face him, of the pressure authorities would use to discourage him. I had no idea how we were going to pull this off, but as always, Leonid reassured me, "Don't worry. I'll do everything."

From our side, we needed the government to have our backs. Micah and I had lined up meetings with the State Department. First on board was Sandy Vershbow, the head of the State Department Soviet desk (and, years later, ambassador to Russia). Not only did he endorse the plan, he said he wanted to attend. Given the State Department's role in cutting refugee slots, his presence would make a statement about America's commitment to Soviet Jews. Next was the congressional Helsinki Commission. Its deputy staff director, Janie Fisher, was also excited about the prospect of being there.

With government participants, our plan's parameters were expanding.

In Moscow, Leonid was consumed with logistics. For months, with characteristic determination and diplomatic skill, he negotiated political minefields with governmental and nongovernmental groups alike. He moved forward cautiously. Knowing KGB's capacity to delegitimize or infiltrate nongovernmental initiatives, he relied at first on only a few refuseniks, including David Mikhalev. Only after having some traction did he expand his contacts. Ultimately Leonid crafted our agenda, planned the seminars, and lined up speakers, all the while navigating through complicated logistics and personalities. Costs were covered by money sent by David through a tourist. Leonid prepared a ten-day agenda for October, running day and night in several cities, for eighty-three participants.

Leonid's plans had just gotten underway when Yuri Reshetov, the head of the so-called Soviet Human Rights Committee of the Department of Foreign Affairs, called him in for questioning about the nature of the meeting. Leonid cagily characterized it as a scientific meeting. Reshetov responded, "No, it's a meeting of foreigners." To justify his point, Reshetov asked him, "What if you were in the United States and held a meeting with foreigners?" In a heartbeat, Leonid responded. "America's a free country – foreigners are permitted and do attend meetings there." With Reshetov caught off-guard, Leonid went on to invite him to our "scientific symposium."

Enthusiasm for the meeting spread like wildfire. The Washington office coordinated the trip logistics for our forty councils, from Alaska and Seattle to Florida and the East Coast. Activists from Israel, England, Canada, Holland, Switzerland, and France had registered.

A few days before our American contingent was to leave on a flight from New York, Micah had planned to come to Chicago to fly with me to Moscow. But suddenly it looked like it was all over. Before his flight, a phone call summoned him to the Soviet embassy, where he was confronted by a high-ranking officer, most certainly KGB: they weren't going to tolerate the meeting, and furthermore, Micah should notify our contingent booked on the New York flight to Moscow that the meeting was cancelled. If they disregarded the warning, they would be stopped when they landed and sent out of the USSR on the next flight.

Micah dug in his heels. He told them their expectation for the Moscow Conference on the Human Dimension in 1991 was dependent on them allowing our meeting to proceed without impediments. Arguments and counterarguments flew back and forth. Then the apparatchik, who had been joined by several others, criticized the official nature of the conference. They didn't want us to convene meetings in public venues such as the Soviet Geographic Society and would only tolerate gatherings in private apartments. Then they objected to Soviet officials addressing our gathering. Finally, they rejected language referring to the conference as the "first ever annual meeting in Moscow of the Union of Councils." It was not the first of many future international Jewish meetings in Moscow. We should understand that this was an exception, not a precedent.

Then Micah did what he always did so brilliantly. He offered one single conciliatory gesture that made the embassy believe we had buckled. We would back off from framing it as an annual meeting. In fact, we would remove the word *annual* from all our printed materials. And with that victory, Micah and I flew into Moscow.

Close Calls

Landing at Sheremetyevo International Airport the next afternoon, I could barely contain my excitement, especially to see Leonid, who was meeting us in reception after we cleared passport control. I could hardly wait for his carefully calculated agenda to be set into motion.

There weren't a lot of passengers at passport control when Micah and I separately presented our visas to the official who was waiting for us. With deliberate concentration, his eyes moved slowly from my face, to my passport, to the hidden computer, back to my face, again to the passport. Finally, he motioned me to the side. With a calculated show of authority, he beckoned Micah forward, subjecting him to the same officious procedure. When he thought his attempted intimidation sufficient, he emerged from his passport booth and motioned us to follow him.

He led us to an adjacent waiting room and gestured to unwelcoming plastic seats lining one wall of the large, sterile hall. We were alone. Waiting. There were no other passengers in the hall, no airport employees. We were just waiting. Even our whispers seemed to rebound off the walls. We assumed we were waiting to be interrogated by some KGB agent. Maybe we were being held until they could expel us on the next outgoing flight.

And so, we waited. There was nothing else we could do. I was increasingly anxious about Leonid, who was somewhere in the airport, waiting for us. He must be frantic with worry. What were they telling him?

It seemed like hours passed. We were afraid our passivity would appear as if we had been intimidated into submission. How well did I understand that the more the Soviets threatened American tourists, the greater the need to summon up an authoritative, even strident, show of confidence. Attitude counts. It was a lesson drummed into us by former prisoners of conscience and refuseniks who had been subjected to KGB interrogations. Hold your ground. Know your rights. And we told that to every tourist we ever briefed.

So Micah and I abandoned our designated plastic chairs, picked up our carry-on bags, and made our way through a small area behind a partition, probably prohibited to travelers. Not surprisingly, we were apprehended by an airport official, and we immediately took the offensive. We were outraged by our detention. We demanded that he get us on the phone to Jack Matlock, the US ambassador who, we told him, had been expecting our arrival hours ago. We went on to tell him they were making a big mistake: our detention was going to create an international incident. There wasn't anyone in Congress, the State Department, or the Bush administration who didn't know who we were, where we were, and why we were here.

Without a word, he stamped our passports and visas. It was Tuesday night, October 17.

By himself in the vacant reception hall, Leonid greeted us like a welcoming angel, relief plain on his face. He had waited hours for us to appear.

It was already late when, in the nurturing haven of the Stonovs' apartment, the phone rang with David Waksberg's call. He should have been on a flight to Moscow. What had happened? Wasn't he coming? Was he ill? Leonid held the receiver in silence.

I held my breath, scrutinizing Leonid's expression for some visible reaction. Finally, he put down the phone. At 5:04 p.m. local time, the magnitude 6.9 Loma Prieta earthquake had hit the San Francisco Bay area, killing sixty-seven people. The city was shut down. Bridges and highways were closed. My mind racing, I thought, even if everyone was safe, David wouldn't leave his family. Then Leonid continued, "Only one flight made it out of San Francisco – and David was on it. He was calling from New York and would make his connection to Moscow." *Thank You, God.* David was coming.

With that crisis averted, Leonid returned his attention back to Micah's report of his meeting at the embassy. Deepening facial furrows showed he wasn't so confident that our problem with the authorities had been resolved. "We shouldn't assume they will let the meeting continue. You can't trust them." He pointed out that our airport experience was likely a deliberate warning to our delegation, due to arrive in a few days.

It was nearly midnight when Leonid phoned Petrus Buwalda, the Netherlands' ambassador to the Soviet Union.[1] Leonid had met the ambassador at a concert at the embassy, and they had struck up a friendship. An hour later Micah, Leonid, and I were in his residence, built for aristocracy under the Czars. Vilma, the ambassador's wife, graciously ushered us to a sitting room to wait for the ambassador. I could read Leonid. He was worried. When Buwalda arrived, Leonid recounted the warnings the Soviets had given Micah. No one could predict how far they would go to stop the meeting. Would they harass our delegates? Buwalda was thoughtful. He concluded that we should proceed, but he concurred that we should make a gesture by removing *annual*, the word they found objectionable, from the UCSJ logo that would be mounted behind the speakers' podium.

We were still plagued with worry about our delegation. I was especially concerned about David. He had been refused visas several times. In 1982, he had been picked up in Kiev with Yuri Cherniak and interrogated by KGB. He was released, but Cherniak wasn't. Though KGB tried to stop him, David staged a sit-in strike for Cherniak outside KGB headquarters. After a struggle, four big agents hauled him off and stuffed him in a taxi that whisked him back to his hotel. KGB had a long memory and massive files. With his history, would they let him back into the country for a meeting they didn't want us to have?

After making it out of the earthquake, he was, in fact, pulled out at passport control, where Moscow officials informed him that he wouldn't be allowed into the country and would have to buy a ticket back to the States. David held his ground. After some hours, the Soviets relented, and, exhausted but jubilant, David was on his way to Leonid's apartment.

---

1.   The embassy of the Netherlands also represented the interests of Israel in the USSR; Israel didn't have diplomatic relations with the USSR, and thus had no embassy.

The Sessions

Months of Leonid's planning was finally about to unfold. Converting objectives into ground-breaking reality, he had arranged it all – the agenda and speakers, meals, hotels, transportation. He had invited the refusenik network from Vladivostok to the Baltics, the dissidents, and our embassy officials, and he had informed the press. He even invited members of the Soviet government. His fortitude and cleverness were indispensable in dealing with the inevitable confrontation with the authorities. After Moscow, our conference would move to Leningrad, and from there, each of our eighty-plus activists would fan out to other provincial cities to meet with refuseniks for briefings on local conditions. Finally, we would all meet back in Moscow for a joint debriefing. Logistics alone would challenge a corporate conference coordinator, let alone a refusenik activist maneuvering around a repressive government. It was an audacious plan, the first open meeting of international Jewry, and we surely expected the authorities to flex a little muscle.

Leonid had rented a hall near the Kremlin and the Soviet Geographic Society. As there was no other option, he was forced to rely on Intourist, the KGB-run Soviet tourist agency, for buses to pick up our delegates from the airport. Intourist did try to undermine us, spreading a rumor that our conference had been canceled.

I wasn't at the airport to witness the arrival of the eighty-three UCSJ activists, council leaders, Europeans, Israelis, and our governmental representatives, who had come to the USSR for this historic event. I wasn't there to see them openly board the buses. I didn't see it, but the authorities did, and though they watched, they didn't stop us.

So they came: the State Department's Sandy Vershbow and three members of the US Helsinki Commission – Janie Fisher, Oreste Deichak, and Jesse Jacobs. From the Soviet Jewry Education and Information Center in Jerusalem came Shmuel Azarch and Natasha Beckman, whose beating while still a Moscow refusenik I had watched on a television in a Highland Park store. David Selikowitz and five others from the Comité des Quinze represented French Jewry. A delegation from the 35s came from England and Canada. Andrew Cillen represented the Dutch community. Michael Berenbaum represented the US Holocaust Commission. Genya Intrator of the Interreligious Task Force came from Toronto, Canada. Congressional aides came on behalf of senators and representatives. Fifteen members of the UCSJ national board were there, as well as rabbis, lawyers, émigrés. Of course, Lenny was there.

The unofficial kickoff, on October 20, was Leonid's birthday. UCSJ's executive board members huddled together at Leonid and Natasha's apartment on benches around the small table that magically opened to accommodate us all. Leonid's and Natasha's mothers prepared the parade of salads and appetizers that had surely required a battalion of friends to stand in lines for weeks to procure ingredients in this country of want. We were together, and whatever else was to happen, that night all we felt was exuberant joy.

The next morning's opening plenum was crammed with refuseniks, activists, former prisoners of conscience, and dissidents who had come under the assumed protection of the American delegation. US Ambassador Jack Matlock was next to Leonid, who was to introduce all the speakers and sessions. Scanning the crowded room, I was preoccupied, seeing the hundreds of constituents I would be addressing in the next few minutes. Some had traveled through eight time zones to be here; others had come after sentences in prison or labor camps. This was their meeting. It was convened for them. My heart was pounding. I wasn't paying close attention to whatever Leonid was saying to introduce me until he unrolled a parchment-like document and began reading: "From the Moscow Legal Seminar on Emigration Problems and the Public Committee for Monitoring Visa Office Work, an award honoring Pamela Braun-Cohen for outstanding achievement in support of Soviet Jews." I was shaking when he handed me a beautiful gold metal box. Inside was a medal featuring a Magen David framed with my name. On the opposite side, the phrase "Let My People Go" surrounded the words "The Moscow Legal Seminar."

Standing to the side, I was overcome with gratitude. Though it was my name on the award, it represented the collective efforts of so many. Our people, our refuseniks, were honoring us. They recognized our connection and commitment to them. What I had known from the very beginning was how much these people were giving us. At that moment, when the refusenik community stood, applauding, I understood the power of love, the sheer force of Jewish unity. They understood just how deeply we were invested in them, in their future, their families, their lives. No other recognition or award has ever meant as much to me. It sits on a shelf in my Chicago kitchen.

Each session was led by a refusenik who specialized in a specific aspect of emigration obstacles. In the climate of Gorbachev's glasnost and perestroika, they examined existing legal barriers to emigration, the rule of law, anti-Semitism. They reported continuing obstacles faced by "poor relatives," Jews whose parents or children refused to give the required permission to leave, and by those denied on the pretext of state secrets. Emanuelis Zingeris, a Jewish activist from Lithuania, focused on Soviet psychiatry's punitive treatment of dissidents. Speakers represented the Refusenik Legal Seminar, the Refusenik Scientific Seminar, the women's groups. Boston Action's Donna Arzt, a law professor at Syracuse University and chair of the Soviet Jewry Legal Advocacy Center, emphasized the primacy of international human rights legal standards as the basis for weighing Gorbachev's reforms. Josef Zissels, founder of the Chernivtsi Jewish Cultural Fund and a former prisoner, spoke about the conditions in Ukraine.

Sandy Vershbow explained the new US immigration requirements and participated in dozens of smaller meetings to coach refuseniks on their individual cases. Members of the congressional Helsinki Commission focused on the Helsinki Final Act's requirement for citizen participation, the vital role individuals play in developing human rights standards, and evaluating the state's performance.

It was at this conference that I met Elimelech "Meylakh" Sheykhet, a refusenik from Lvov (now Lviv), for the first time. Meylakh has reminded me many times in our long friendship that, at the plenum session, I spoke about the importance of Jewish identity, history, tradition, and religion. He reminds me of my words, "You can't know where you are going unless you know where you came from." It remains true for all of us, all the time, in every place.

Throughout the sessions, Leonid and I were operating on separate electrical circuits. Mine was so hardwired to our constituents that I didn't sense he was on high alert. He was afraid KGB would lock the doors of the hall from the outside, penning us in. He didn't know what to expect exactly, but he did expect some provocation. Afterward he told me some people had been in the hall demanding to know what we were doing there, warning that a bomb had been planted in the room, and that we had to evacuate. Leonid correctly identified it as a KGB provocation, and the meetings continued.

Leonid, Micah, and I broke away from one of the sessions to meet with Deputy Interior Minister Rudolf Kuznetsov. Kuznetsov was also the director of OVIR, the emigration office. With him was Fedor Burlatsky, a supposed Gorbachev advisor who was director of the Soviet Human Rights Commission.[2] Charged with reforming Soviet legislation, Burlatsky had assured the United States that the long-promised emigration reform legislation was being addressed. But Kuznetsov told us that it wouldn't be on the Supreme Soviet's agenda until 1990. Parenthetically, he added that it should be passed because the government has prepared public opinion in support of it. I heard him: they were seeding the propaganda.

Although Kuznetsov claimed the new law would impose a five-year provision for secrecy refusals, he contradicted himself by adding that they could be arbitrarily increased. It was double-speak. It was all arbitrary even with a new law. Even Burlatsky contradicted him. There was nothing new here; no substantive change was being discussed. The matter was strictly political, and it was being decided at the top of government. We told them their approach was not in the interest of the Soviet government and rattled off our positions, which they, of course, knew very well.

To Leningrad and Beyond

After the Moscow sessions had ended, the delegation boarded the night train to Leningrad, packed into sparsely equipped, dingy sleeping cars. A gray-haired Russian matron with silver-capped teeth sold us vodka that we drank in cheap plastic cups, and we spent a long night sharing our experiences, telling Russian jokes. Encouraged by the vodka, we reacted uproariously to the varying methods the women shared of navigating the filthy wooden toilet seats, too wide for any of us to straddle.

In Leningrad, Boris Kelman and David briefed us on their activities. Working in tandem, Leningrad's Jewish Cultural Society and the Bay Area Council had established a flagship cooperative effort to foster Jewish renewal.

One late night I sat with a group of Leningrad "poor relatives," who suffered double victimization: first by the government, which required close family members to give permission to those wanting to leave, and second, by family members who refused to give permission. I sat with Zev

---

2.   This commission was officially named the Public Commission for International Cooperation in Humanitarian Problems and Human Rights.

Meshkov. Zev was sandy-bearded and soft-eyed, with a sweet gentleness and a strong will. He was wearing a kippah. I sat by closely as he told me his story. His wife's family wouldn't let them leave.

Hundreds of families had been wrenched apart by this requirement, and the situation for these families was complicated. Family members asked to sign these affidavits permitting their relatives to leave were afraid of being castigated as Zionist coconspirators, being fired from their jobs, or losing professional standing or membership in the Communist Party. This onerous requirement was ripping families apart. Ever since Stalin encouraged children to inform against their parents, the Communist state had pitted children against parents, parents against children. Cohesive social unity outside of the Kremlin's intended social order was against its interests. Their idea of cohesion was class unity, as in the phrase "workers unite."

While Meshkov was speaking quietly about "poor relatives," without warning, I found my eyes filling with tears. What, I wondered, had evoked such a reaction? As if outside myself, no longer in the room, I saw this man who, in the face of difficult obstacles, threats, and intimidation, had chosen to resist. He resisted by going on demonstrations and signing petitions, but he also resisted by wearing a kippah, publicly dignifying the nucleus of his identity. In the smoldering firepit of anti-Semitism, Meshkov, like Zeev Dashevsky in Moscow and Grigory Vasserman in Leningrad, made a conscious decision to live as proud Jews and live openly Jewish, observant lives in the USSR. I didn't know Jews who took such a proud stand in the freedom of Chicago. It overwhelmed me and brought the tears that were hovering precariously. They were tears that spoke through the generations, tears that sprang from meaning, from purpose, from vision, from truth. There was something about these Jews who had made their way, against every possible adversity, to the path of our forefathers, to the path of Torah, that touched a deeply buried, inchoate chord with exquisite precision. All I knew was that listening to Meshkov's soft voice, feeling the golden warmth that permeated the small room, I was transported by the beauty of their Jewish conviction in that desolate, harrowing place.

It took many years to understand that Essas, Meshkov, Polonsky, Vasserman, Volvovsky, Mendelevich and others who hacked their way through the thick, secular Communist propaganda were not only creating a path for their own Jewish Soviet people, but also for me, far away in Deerfield. It was in Leningrad that I learned that in my life, unexpected tears always signaled the emergence of a deeply buried psychological or spiritual truth.

After a series of seminars in Leningrad, refuseniks from outside Leningrad and Moscow took our delegates to their provincial home cities: Tallinn, Estonia; Kharkov, Ukraine; Vilnius, Lithuania; Riga, Latvia; and other cities. After several days of on-the-ground briefings in other republics, the delegation reconvened in Moscow to report our findings. Retreating to Malakhovka, a suburb outside of Moscow wrapped in thick forest, we assembled in the villa that had housed the first yeshiva in Moscow, jump-started by Albert Reichmann. There, former physicist Zeev Dashevsky, who stood at the helm of the national-religious group Machanaim, and Pinchas Polonsky reported on the most pressing obstacles to emigration – the inability of hundreds of Jews to even take the first steps, to obtain a *vysov* from Israel that would enable them to apply for permission. Zeev, regardless of his position as a member of the religious Zionist wing of the movement, did not hold back: he accused Israel of not sending enough invitations. Some were forced to wait for two years for a *vysov* before they could even apply. He exhorted us to push the Israelis. It would occupy us for months to come.

In our honor, Ambassador Jack Matlock held a reception for UCSJ and some refuseniks and dissidents at Spaso House, the residence of the US ambassador. Some members of the government and the Central Committee of the Communist Party were included, which strategically put our Soviet Jewry advocates face to face with Soviet officials over cocktails and buffet. Together with Leonid, who now had become a prominent leader of the emigration movement, Micah and I milled among the guests to speak to key people. We brought Leonid over to talk to Vladimir Tumarkin, who was an official dealing with the Soviets' "Jewish problem." It was a moment when time seemed to freeze. As Leonid approached him, I saw Tumarkin recoil with an unmistakable expression of revulsion and turn his back on him. Leonid handled the effrontery with his typical measured composure and calmed my fury. He was used to insults.

One night, before tearing ourselves from each other, everyone, refuseniks and delegates alike, met for dinner in a small private room at the

Cinema Club near Mayakovsky Square. With new friendships and partnerships forged, an irrepressible sense of unity found expression in song:
"*Hineh mah tov u'mah na'im shevet achim gam yachad*" (How good it is
for brothers to sit together). And then we were on our feet, in a single line,
each of us with our hands on the shoulders of the person in front, circling
the room. We were singing, nearly yelling, the words of Rabbi Nachman
of Breslov.

> *Kol ha'olam kulo gesher tzar me'od*
> *gesher tzar me'od*
> *gesher tzar me'od;*
> *v'ha'ikar, v'ha'ikar, lo l'fached klal.*

> The whole world is a very narrow bridge
> a very narrow bridge
> a very narrow bridge;
> and the important thing, the important thing, is not to be afraid.

Over and over, not wanting the magic of the night to end, we sang, with
one voice.

Devised in partnership with refusenik leaders, we came away from this
historic meeting with a comprehensive menu of UCSJ's policies and priorities. The movement was calling for:

- The release of all remaining refuseniks
- Codification under law guaranteeing the right to emigrate
- Reasonable limit on refusal on the grounds of "access to secrecy"
- Positive resolution of all the "poor relative" issues
- Legal right to appeal refusals in courts of law
- Accountability of all organizations involved in refusenik issues
- A dramatic increase in the number of *vysovs* sent from Israel to
  accommodate the backlog

By uniting Jews from the USSR and abroad, we had changed the movement. At those meetings and assemblies and dinners, we were together,
one people, with one past and one destiny, each responsible for the other.

In the process, we forged personal bonds that would span decades. In an uncanny twist, many of us in the West would later come to realize that in the process of rescuing Soviet Jews, we ourselves had been rescued.

Finally, it was the beginning of a new era.

After the meeting, a tourist brought out a letter, dated December 4, 1989, from Leonid Stonov, Boris Kelman, Zeev Dashevsky, and Mark Kotlyar, addressed to Micah, Judy Balint, Hinda Cantor, June Daniels, David, and me – and to everyone who came to UCSJ's meeting:

> The refuseniks know quite well and for a long time the organization which proclaimed itself the voice of refuseniks....
>
> We were happy to see many of you here. You were followed, humiliated at customs, detained at the passport control, refused visas. In this way you also became refuseniks. You found your ways in our life here, not knowing the language, called only from telephone booths, moved from one flat to another. You stayed days and nights discussing our problems. We noticed that passing some places in the cities you exclaimed, "Zev Sheiba lived here, and Evgeny Lein used to live here, and here, Yuri Cherniak lived." And it is to your credit that they live in a new desired world. You helped them and us morally, supported materially, and always did it tactfully, never hurting anyone's feelings. You helped them to survive.
>
> We thank members of your families who patiently withstood your love to us. And mainly we thank God who gave you to us. You who reflect all the best that was stored by Jewish and American tradition....
>
> You gave us courage and strength. You helped us gain human dignity. You helped to survive every Jew and the Jewish people as a whole.
>
> God bless you.[3]

We returned to the States with reams of evidence of emigration and human rights abuses, our council leaders and the Washington office would spend countless hours preparing reports for distribution to the government and

---

3. Letter, December 4, 1989, archives of Pamela Braun Cohen, American Jewish Historical Society, New York.

media. Micah and I flew directly to New York to communicate the concern about the insufficiency of *vysovs* to Lishka representatives, but, exhausted, I succumbed to a ravaging virus that kept me caged in the hotel room until I could fly home, where the real work began.

CHAPTER 23

Winds of Change, 1990

Conferences in Moscow and Copenhagen

New winds blowing through the Kremlin in 1989 brought a mix of skepticism and hope. Gorbachev had provided for the freest elections in Soviet history, sending Andrei Sakharov and other dissidents to the newly created Congress of People's Deputies, and paving the way for Boris Yeltsin to play out his dramatic role first as its member, then as a part of the Supreme Soviet, and later, as president of the Russian Republic.

That year found us struggling to steer an inflatable raft on tempestuous waves, trying to calculate the wind's direction. Despite the election of a number of democrats, the Congress of People's Deputies was still controlled by the hard-liners. And those right-wing hard-liners were allied with xenophobic, anti-Zionist, and anti-Semitic groups, including the ultranationalist Pamyat. Even Gorbachev, the supposed reformer, brought Pamyat leaders into his cabinet. The inconsistencies only augmented the unpredictability of the moment.

Still, it was undeniable that change was in the air. The world was stunned by the fall of the Berlin Wall in the autumn of 1989, and I recalled the prescience of President Reagan who, two years earlier at the Brandenburg Gate, had called out: "Mr. Gorbachev, tear down this wall." No one could imagine that this formidable symbol of the USSR would crumble in a matter of hours.

But we couldn't depend on hope. Our only option was to capitalize on the potential of the moment by continuing to push hard on our demand for Jewish emigration. Still in refusal in Moscow and filled with vigorous commitment, Leonid pulled together a broad spectrum of human rights groups for a legal symposium on freedom of movement in the spring of 1990, cosponsored by the Refusenik Legal Seminar and UCSJ.

A stellar lineup of dissidents and refuseniks congregated in the Cinema Hall at the Central Dom Turista hotel to help us evaluate the state of human rights in this period of extreme uncertainty. Heads of the Jewish cultural movement, the religious Zionists, the democratic and human rights movement – all presented papers. Leonid and Boris Chernobilsky handled the freedom of movement panels. The BBC, Voice of America, and other media covered the event. At its conclusion, the Refusenik Legal Seminar called for the abolition of the *vysov* requirement, and the expiration of the secrecy classification two to five years after the termination of employment in a classified job. Finally, the withholding of permission by family members must be strictly confined to a failure to meet financial obligations.

Every speaker confirmed the lack of progress in their fields of specialization and were unanimously anxious about the rise of ultranationalism and Jew-hatred seizing the anti-Gorbachev reactionary forces. We all were nervously playing a waiting game.

When the Moscow meeting ended, Micah and I flew to Copenhagen for another CSCE Conference on the Human Dimension. Defying all odds, on our flight out to the free world were two long-term refuseniks, Leonid Stonov and David Mikhalev.

Their appearance was the consequence of an unlikely chain of events centering on the first woman in space, the Soviet cosmonaut Valentina Tereshkova. Harnessing her international visibility, the Kremlin requisitioned her into the Foreign Affairs Ministry. Part of her mission was to forge partnerships with independent human rights groups, clouding the distinction between them and the newly created Soviet State Helsinki Commission, a KGB strategy known as parallelism.[1] Tereshkova wanted Leonid and Sergey Kovalev, leaders of the Moscow Helsinki Group, to meet with her. A big woman with thickly applied red lipstick, Tereshkova was unabashedly wooing them. Leonid, recognizing the danger of contaminating his group's authenticity, rejected her proposal for cooperation. He warned the delegations to the Copenhagen conference that Tereshkova's commission was not independent and in no way spoke for them.

---

1. Soviets tried to hijack and represent the activity of the Group to Establish Trust, the independent peace organization started by Sergei Batovrin, Mark Reitman, Vladimir Fleyshgakker, Vladimir Brodsky, Yuri Medvedkov, Valery Godyak, Maria Fleyshgakker, and Olga Medvdkova, as well as our Sister Cities movement and others.

Astoundingly, in spite of their rejection, Tereshkova was ordered by the Foreign Ministry to issue prized visitors' passports to refuseniks David Mikhalev, Sasha Shmuckler, Leonid Stonov, and Mika Chlenov for the Copenhagen meeting.

David Mikhalev was still in refusal, without permission to leave the country. But he had US refugee status, which opened up an opportunity for escape: Tereshkova's visitor's passport could get him out of the country, circumventing the need for OVIR to issue permission and a visa, and his refugee papers could get him into America. UCSJ would buy Mikhalev's ticket to freedom from Copenhagen.

Once in Copenhagen, we checked into the Plaza. Early the next day we made our way to the red-bricked Vartox complex for UCSJ's Symposium on Human Rights. Unlike the Paris meeting, in Copenhagen, the Union commanded the recognition and the attention our cause merited. I was surprised when more than a dozen Soviet officials made their way to seats, scattered among members of human rights groups, American and European NGOs, official delegates, and representatives of the Baltics and Ukraine who were trying to release the grip of Soviet occupation. The Soviets were sporting artificial smiles and conducting themselves with newfound civility purposefully designed to demonstrate their fitness for the upcoming official CSCE Moscow human rights conference.

Ambassador Max Kampelman, the head of the US delegation, opened our symposium, followed by representatives of Estonia and Lithuania who, looking for support for their quest for independence, spoke rather convincingly of their commitment to our Jewish issues. Micah focused on the relevance of the Helsinki process and the mandate for compliance; Leonid drew out juridical elements for the draft of the emigration law and gave an update on the status of refuseniks and prisoners. Steven Cohen, chair of UCSJ's Lawyers Committee, and law professor Ralph Ruebner spoke from the perspective of international law on the draft laws of emigration and freedom of religion, and I did the wrap-up. Steven went over our refusenik list case by case in a meeting with Soviet official Vladimir Babenkov, the Kremlin's deputy chair of the Department of Humanitarian Affairs.

UCSJ had prepared impressive documentation of state and grassroots anti-Semitism in the Soviet press, academia, and media. Leonid placed a copy of our document on the chairs in the main CSCE conference hall, but the Lishka's Sarah Frankel ordered that they be removed. He complied, but then he personally distributed one to every member of the conference.

In the end, Copenhagen produced widely supported, broad-reaching proposals that confirmed the significance of the rule of law and guarantees for the protection of Jews, primarily freedom of movement, religion, expression, assembly, and association, much of which was in the Concluding Document.

During the proceedings, I kept an eye on Babenkov, wondering at what point he would walk out in the face of our intense criticism. Surprisingly, however, he sat through every session. I had met him on several occasions, but this time he was particularly ingratiating. He wanted a meeting with us away from the official venue. A few hours later, Micah, Leonid, and I were at a little outdoor café, waiting for him. He arrived, still on his fawning, best behavior. Forgoing subtlety, he handed me a kilo of expensive, tinned black caviar and then ordered the mandatory bottle of vodka. Babenkov was a caricature of the Soviet apparatchik – big, self-important, wearing a wrinkled suit with the inevitable Communist pin in the lapel of his jacket. After a couple of drinks, he laid his cards on the table. He was soliciting UCSJ's official participation at the Moscow human rights conference.

There wasn't a chance. We might have lost our battle with Reagan and Thatcher, who had finally consented to the Moscow conference, but we weren't about to cave. As the evening wore on, Micah, Leonid, and I kept Babenkov on the defensive, confronting him with every violation of the Vienna Concluding Document, especially the issue of refuseniks. Finally, and at the end of the bottle of Smirnoff, he seemed candid. He admitted that if Moscow couldn't even resolve the cases of a few hundred refuseniks, he didn't see how it could resolve its enormous economic and political problems. Actually, he said, the internal political conflict was much more than just a conflict; it was a civil war.

We gave Babenkov no assurances for our participation, and he gave us no assurances regarding the cases we raised. But one thing was certain from his responses and demeanor: we were chipping away at the fortress.

Mikhalev's exit hung over us throughout the conference. The Soviets presumably knew his plans to emigrate without permission. The question was, would they let him go. We held our breath as we watched his flight roll back from the gate. The nightmare scenario of unmarked KGB agents boarding the plane began to fade.

UCSJ's Moscow Human Rights Bureau

UCSJ's role in the historic rescue of Jews from the Soviet Republics wasn't built on heroics so much as a dogged, day-to-day resolve not to abdicate the "small issues" and to refuse to accept what conventional wisdom said couldn't be changed. But in retrospect, it's nearly impossible to imagine how we did what we did, especially considering the absence of sustained, open communication between our activists and the refuseniks.

In Moscow, Leonid continued to monitor the work of the OVIR. At the same time, he was looking for ways to use the new openness to crack the communications barrier between UCSJ and the movement inside the Soviet Union. We needed regular and dependable transmission of information, documents, *vysov* requests, and the computerized refusenik list.

Leonid asked Ambassador Buwalda to use the Netherlands' embassy to channel information to the State Department in DC, but the diplomatic channel to the State Department was through the American embassy, not the Dutch. Buwalda did agree, however, to permit Leonid the use of their fax machine to transmit information to me in Chicago, and that was a breakthrough.

At about this time, Leonid was visited by Dean Hughson, a wealthy egg producer from the Midwest who had business in Moscow. Hughson had access to a corporate fax machine, and, recognizing Leonid's central role in the movement, he made it available to Leonid, removing his reliance on Ambassador Buwalda. With access to a fax machine in Moscow and the two computers that Rabbi Shlomo Noach Mandel had delivered, UCSJ was slowly cracking the Iron Curtain's communication barrier.

New perestroika-driven joint ventures between American companies and Russia provided a precedent and a framework for UCSJ to make a significant strategic breakthrough. Seizing the opportunity, we used them as a model to create a human rights joint venture that would bring together two partners, UCSJ and Leonid's OVIR-monitoring organization, now known as the Moscow Public Committee on Exit and Entrance and Human Rights.

If we could pull it off, an officially sanctioned human rights bureau could facilitate information exchange and revolutionize the relationship between the movement inside the Soviet Union and outside. It could also support the work of Hebrew Immigrant Aid Society (HIAS), deluged with the rising numbers of Jews trying to enter the United States. A

Russian-American joint venture would legitimize the struggle and unify its parts. From America, though the obstacles still seemed formidable, we were committed to pushing open every slight crack glasnost had opened.

It was Leonid who engineered the complicated tightrope through the bureaucratic maze to register our bureau, with the help of many activists and former dissidents – from Ariel publishing house and the Moscow Helsinki Group, and from former dissidents Father Gleb Yakunin and Valery Borshev, reformers newly elected to the Moscow City Council. It also helped that Moscow City Council was led by two of Russia's foremost reformers, Chairman Gavril Popov and First Deputy Chairman Sergei Stankevich. We officially registered the Joint Jewish Bureau for Emigration-Repatriation, Human Rights and Rule of Law, also known as the Russian-American Bureau for Human Rights, or simply as the Human Rights Bureau. All the players in the human rights community welcomed this milestone event, and Borshev praised the "active collaboration"[2] between the new Moscow City Council and the Human Rights Bureau.

UCSJ launched the bureau, rather ingloriously located in the former annex of a vegetable store on Novoslobodskaya Street, in October 1990. The spartan space was still being remodeled when crowds of supporters and media jammed in for its official opening. "Today is a joyous day for us," said Leonid. "We will assist the current flood of emigrants from the Soviet Union by giving them information about Israel and the United States in advance, coaching them for visa interviews, and compiling a computerized database to match their skills with the needs of their future countries." In Moscow for the opening, David Waksberg said, "We are excited to be the first Western human rights organization to open an office in Moscow."[3]

The next morning, the *Chicago Tribune* carried the article, "Rights Bureau Opens in USSR: New Office Makes Soviet History."

Our bureau soon moved to Rustaveli street, where it became a flagship for human rights in the center of Moscow. The bureau helped and consulted with families of prisoners of conscience, refuseniks, Jews applying for permission, and victims of human rights abuse. Staff dispensed resettlement information in support of those seeking to make aliyah or obtain

---

2. Thom Shanker, "Rights Bureau Opens in USSR: New Office Makes Soviet History," *Chicago Tribune*, October 30, 1990.

3. "Office Opened in Moscow by UCSJ to Monitor Soviet Human Rights," Jewish Telegraphic Agency (JTA), October 30, 1990.

US refugee status. There was even a computer school to train future emi-grants.[4] Most important, they kept us abreast of new refusals, which were camouflaged by the rising emigration rates. Chicago Action's fax machine overflowed with missives and reports from the bureau.

Our focus continued to be on maximizing emigration numbers and facilitating the expeditious exit of Jews who had visas. That included con-tinued pressure on Israel to deliver the thousands of requested *vysovs* and to increase the number of flights, especially from Soviet Central Asia, where there was a prolonged and seemingly dangerous wait for planes to Israel.

Among the first of the joint ventures, we were sailing the Human Rights Bureau in uncharted waters. With perestroika came a threat from Soviet employees and workers to "privatize" government-owned and gov-ernment-operated industries, corruptly seizing assets for personal gain. Because we knew our staff well and believed them to be invested in our work, we were aghast when Leonid discovered a plot to privatize the bureau. They were planning to appropriate the office and all our techno-logical equipment. They tried to cut UCSJ out of the partnership, severing the bureau from its roots. It was a coup d'état, and we were furious. Our national membership had donated the funds to meet the costs of salaries, rent, overhead, and travel. We had a responsibility to our contributors to ensure the bureau's continued work, and we were not going to tolerate this "junta" by paid staff. It was theft, not privatization.

UCSJ's executive committee flew into Washington to formulate a plan. Huddled together in our national office, we looked for an equally wicked response to this attempted takeover. We would fight fire with fire. Lynn, David, Larry Lerner, and Morey came up with some outrageously diabol-ical ideas. Before long, the plan came together. We would stage a dramatic performance in Moscow to terrify the perpetrators.

Greg Smith, a member of the Bay Area Council board, was an open, friendly guy who was committed to the cause. He also was a former cop. The plan was to send him to Russia. Leonid enlisted Ilya Zaslovsky, the newly elected reformist deputy in Moscow's regional council, to arrange for Greg to have a car – a KGB car, actually – and a driver.

---

4.   Later, the successful enterprise moved to Bolshoy Golovin, where we shared space with the Moscow Helsinki Group.

Soon after, Greg was in Moscow, in the back seat of an intimidating black Zhiguli. His driver pulled up in front of the bureau, stopped, and opened the car door for him. Officiously, Greg entered the office, identified himself with his police badge, asked each staff member to identify themselves, and recorded their names. Playing his role to the hilt, he handed each of the mutineers a document, notifying them that, as a consequence of violating the property rights of US citizens, they would be stopped at US immigration and turned back if any of them ever sought entrance to America.

I would have loved to have seen the expressions on their faces. Larry Lerner's strategy was a slam dunk. The crisis was diffused and the staff replaced. The bureau remained in our hands, thanks to Greg Smith's masterful performance.

Jackson-Vanik Under Threat

As so often happened in our "one step forward, two steps back" battle, our victory with our bureau was offset by a new challenge: America's farmers, seeking grain sales to the Soviet Union, were urging the president to waive the Jackson-Vanik amendment's trade barriers. In response, President Bush had announced he was considering a one-year waiver.

UCSJ announced opposition immediately. In a letter to President Bush, Micah and I stressed that the higher number of Soviet Jews leaving the country did not resolve Soviet human rights issues. Reward was premature. The Supreme Soviet seemed ready to vote on a new draft of emigration legislation that didn't even go as far as earlier drafts in eliminating some of the emigration restrictions.

"Earlier drafts," we explained in a Jewish Telegraphic Agency article, "put a five-year limit on visa refusals on the pretext of possession of state secrets. The new version could extend the time indefinitely."[5] Additionally, the proposed law didn't resolve the "poor relatives" problem. It also prevented the emigration of men between ages sixteen and twenty-seven who were reservists or subject to military draft.

I was in Miami, raising desperately needed funds, when Micah called. I had been asked to testify before the House Subcommittee on Wheat, Soybeans, and Feed Grains, at hearings to determine a recommendation

---

5.   "Bush's Reappraisal of Jackson-Vanik Takes Soviet Jewry Groups by Surprise," Jewish Telegraphic Agency (JTA), December 3, 1990.

on the waiver for the president. Dwayne Andreas, the powerful tycoon who had turned Archer-Daniels-Midland Company into the world's largest processor of agricultural products, was also to testify.[6] I had no doubt his opinion would influence Bush's decision.

In the congressional hearing room, the witnesses were seated at two adjoining tables facing the committee members, who peered down at us from the dais. I gave my statement, summarizing the written testimony Micah had prepared. UCSJ's policy was that emigration reform should be codified before we would endorse the waiver, but we had cautiously moderated our position in the interest of American farmers. I announced that we wouldn't oppose a one-year waiver, though we were urging the president to hold off until the Soviets passed legislation consistent with their international obligations.

After all the witnesses gave their testimonies, the congressional panel followed with questions. In response to an inquiry, Andreas defended the Soviets' lack of human rights progress, attributing that lack to bureaucratic cogs in the architecture of the newly created Congress of People's Deputies. His ingratiating answer was accompanied by a just-between-the-two-of-us smile: "As a matter of fact, I believe he [Gorbachev] has tried to get the codification done, but now that they are beginning to feel their freedom in the Supreme Soviet, there are factions developing there that take a dim view of this, just like our Congress."[7]

Though still hesitant to speak in public, I just could not let his comment pass. I knew it was an audacious break of protocol, but I summoned my courage and raised my hand. The chair of the subcommittee, Dan Glickman, ignored my irregular request to speak. But again, I slightly lifted my arm. This time, Representative Bill Emerson noted, "I sense that Ms. Cohen is anxious to jump in."[8]

I said, "I think [refuseniks and dissidents] would take issue with a concept that the problems that Mr. Gorbachev has in passing legislation...are

---

6.   Andreas later stepped aside after the company was found guilty of price-fixing commodities.

7.   House Subcommittee on Wheat, Soybeans, and Feed Grains of the Committee on Agriculture, *Soviet Agriculture and the Outlook for Soviet Purchases of Grain and Oilseeds*, 101st Congress, 2nd session, September 24 and December 5, 1990.

8.   Ibid.

commensurate with what goes on in a free society."[9] To sell his soybeans to Russia, Andreas justified Gorbachev's restraints on freedom of emigration by conflating the legislature of a totalitarian government with the Congress of the United States, which, for over two hundred years, had forged the ideals of democracy, free speech, and representative government.

In the end, President Bush did waive the restriction on extending credit guarantees for American farm sales, but, importantly, he didn't grant the USSR most-favored-nation trade benefits. He said the most-favored-nation linkage would be preserved until they made good on their promise to enact a legal codification for emigration.

Political Advocacy in a Changing Climate

Uncertainty was the order of the day in the Soviet Union. One by one, the long-term refuseniks were leaving, but an untold number of Jews were still waiting for invitations from Israel or waiting for exit visas. Others had family reunification issues with the US embassy and couldn't get refugee status. And still, the Soviets had no emigration law.

Micah and I kept to our regular rounds of meetings with Sandy Vershbow at the State Department, Ambassador Schifter, the congressional chairmen of the Helsinki Commission, and Representative John Porter of Illinois, cochair of the House Human Rights Caucus.

We met periodically with Condoleezza Rice, George H. W. Bush's director for Soviet and Eastern European affairs for the National Security Council (NSC) who later served as secretary of state. I liked and admired her. Unlike most diplomats, who conducted meetings around their desks, Condi always rose from her desk and ushered Micah and me to her informal sitting area, creating a more intimate atmosphere. I briefed her on the status of the Soviets' emigration abuses and updated her on the anti-Semitism unleashed in the glasnost era, and I found her sensitive and responsive. All we could do was arm her with enough documented evidence for her to confront the Soviets.

After one briefing session, the atmosphere especially warm and relaxed, I had the temerity to question, "How does somebody grow up to be Condi Rice?" She answered candidly. She was born in Birmingham, Alabama, when segregation ostracized Americans of color. She related that once, as

---

9.   Ibid.

a young girl, she climbed into her father's truck to drive to a wedding out-side of town. Before setting off, her father reached down under the seat to pick up his rifle and place it across his lap. It was the only way he knew to protect his child, the apple of his eye. He was proud of the little girl who came home from school with her good grades, and he mounted her work on the refrigerator. She had emerged from a climate of racial hatred with a strong sense of self and no trace of victimhood, qualities that I also saw in refuseniks.

We also met with Lawrence Eagleburger, President Bush's deputy sec-retary of state. He was a big, broad-shouldered man with an outspoken personality and round cheeks that gave the dangerously false impression he was the soft, cuddly type. During a meeting with him and a group from the State Department, I raised UCSJ's concern about the administration's policy at a pivotal time, when it had maximum potential to influence the course of history in the Soviet Union. I said it appeared Bush was more interested in stabilizing Gorbachev than encouraging the democratic movements for national independence, which were being supported by the human rights movement and these emerging nations' Jewish communi-ties. The sentence was barely out of my mouth when Eagleburger smashed his hand on the table and, at a surprisingly nondiplomatic decibel level, told me off. How could I question President Bush's commitment to these movements, especially as the administration supports Jewish emigration as part of its priority policy? In spite of the drama, he didn't quell my con-cern. When the meeting broke up, I was making my way out when he caught up with me and, smiling reassuringly, put his hand on my shoulder. I got it: his explosion was a performance not intended for us. Apparently he needed to demonstrate his defense of Bush's position to someone else sitting in that room.

After every meeting, Micah and I would stop for a postmortem. I could never step out of myself to objectively assess how a meeting went. I might have thought we had thrown the perfect pitch, but I could never tell whether the batter would strike out or hit it out of the park.

The Stonovs

At the beginning of 1990, OVIR notified Natasha Stonov that she could leave – but alone, not with Leonid. Their son Sasha had been given permis-sion and left the previous year. This business of separating families, slice by slice, forcing unimaginable choices – who will stay, who will leave – was a demonstration of the vicious power of the state to crush the hopes, plans, and dreams of a family. Natasha refused to leave without her husband.

After further consideration, she agreed to travel to the West to publicize the situation of refuseniks and then return to Moscow. Leonid made the rounds of the embassies to arrange for tourist visas for her to the Netherlands, France, England, the United States, and Israel. By the end of February, Natasha embarked on her itinerary organized by UCSJ, the 35s, and the Comité des Quinze. Crowds jammed into venues to hear her give the latest information from Moscow.

Natasha arrived in Washington to spring's burst of pink cherry blossoms. Most of her life, she had been demeaned in Russia, and now she was stepping into the White House as a guest for its first commemoration of Passover, the Jewish festival of freedom. Ushered into the Roosevelt Room, Natasha was seated between Vice President Dan Quayle and Secretary of State James Baker. For his Passover message, President Bush assured his guests – including Sylva Zalmanson, the former Leningrad trial defendant, and Ze'ev and Karmela Raiz, recently released after eighteen years of refusal, that the administration would continue its support for the exodus of Soviet Jews. Then the president turned to Natasha, and with the press's cameras rolling, extended his profound "regret that another Passover is here with Leonid still in the Soviet Union," asking her to take the message back to Leonid in Moscow that he and other refuseniks "are not forgotten."[10]

Two weeks later, while Natasha was in Miami working with UCSJ vice-president Hinda Cantor of our South Florida Conference on Soviet Jews, there was an unexpected call from Leonid. Bush's statement had pushed the Kremlin over the edge, and finally, the Soviets had relented and given him permission. She was euphoric.

But she soon returned to a Moscow seething with rumors of impending anti-Jewish pogroms. Resurrecting the Russian ultranationalist, xenophobic movement under the czars, the Black Hundreds and other pogromist organizations incorporated vicious anti-Semitic incitement into their anti-reformist program. Fears of anti-Semitic attacks and pogroms were

---

10. George Bush, "Remarks on Signing the Passover Message," April 4, 1990, The American Presidency Project, University of California Santa Barbara, https://www.presidency.ucsb.edu/documents/remarks-signing-the-passover-message (accessed May 26, 2020).

widespread. An organization calling itself Death to the Yids hung up signs calling for "Russia for the Russians." I was told that signs in subways, railway stations, and worker clubs denounced Jews for their penetration into Russian life and called for their removal "one way or another." A tourist brought out film of one such sign:

> Comrades! Russian patriots! How can we accept that the dirty ones have made our wonderful nation into a Jewish mob of sorts.... Why should we – outstanding, intelligent, beautiful Slavs – consider Jews among us to be a normal phenomenon? And why should Jewish cattle be able to acquire Russian surnames and put down Russian as their nationality as do these dirty, stinking Jews, hiding under such heroic and proud names as Russians.[11]

Along with rumors, there were reports of vicious harassment and anti-Semitic bullying. A crowd outside the apartment where several Jews lived chanted: "Soon we will kill you." Some parents were keeping their kids home from school. On the eve of an expected pogrom, a staff member from our Moscow bureau went to the Stonovs' apartment with an ax to protect them from the expected mobs. The number of Jews planning to emigrate skyrocketed.

We waited, anxiously counting the days until Leonid and Natasha and their mothers could leave. Leonid had accepted our invitation to come to Chicago and continue his work, now as UCSJ's official director of foreign affairs. I couldn't have relinquished working with the man who had become my eyes and ears in the Soviet Union. A giddy thrill of excitement and anticipation pulsed through our office. We wanted everything ready for them. The head of CASJ's relocation team, Gail Winston, found a Skokie apartment for the Stonovs, and we equipped it with beds, furniture, linens, pots and pans, down to the fingertip towels in the powder room. And then we waited.

Packages arriving from Moscow to CASJ were proof that Leonid really was leaving. Every day, the postman delivered a few brown paper packages containing three or four books from Leonid's extensive Moscow library.

---

11. Photograph of Russian sign, translated into English, archives of Pamela Braun Cohen, American Jewish Historical Society, New York.

Overwhelmed by deliveries, the post office installed a US mail collection receptacle in our office. Each delivery brought us closer to their arrival.

Meanwhile, in Moscow, Leonid was still working feverishly. In an unprecedented move, on November 22, just a few weeks before his scheduled departure, the USSR Supreme Soviet Committee on Legislation met with him to discuss the draft law on emigration. In an email, he reported that it still fell far short of the draft he had proposed on behalf of the bureau. Particularly problematic was the latitude given to ministries and departments to override a five-year limit on secrecy terms.

Finally, the long-anticipated day arrived. The Stonovs' flight was to leave Moscow on December 7, 1990. I pictured the Moscow apartment I had visited so many times. I had a vivid recollection of everything left behind, possessions of lifetimes forbidden to be taken out of the country. I could see the empty bookshelves, the worn but beautiful oriental carpets, the mahogany upright piano graced with delicate silver candelabras attached on either side of the music stand. I imagined the suitcases and satchels and their two mothers in their eighties, leaving behind everything they had ever known. It takes courage to fight to leave, and then it takes courage to leave. I imagined their door closing behind them one final time. I pictured them having to submit to the final indignities of officials at customs and passport control who still saw Jews as defectors and traitors. I couldn't control my underlying anxiety that, at the last minute, the Soviets were preparing an unpleasant surprise to assert their power and authority over the activist who had monitored them, protested against them, and sent reports about them abroad. To monitor their departure, I arranged eyes on the ground. Throughout the day, my calls to Moscow tracked them, step by step, until I received confirmation they were on the plane, ready to fly to freedom.

At O'Hare, our excited core of CASJ activists were buzzing around members of the press when, abruptly, the door to the reception area burst open to a frazzled Natasha, looking for dollars for luggage carts. Finally, they were all in sight, two elderly mothers who had just taken their first flight, smiling but walking heavily on swollen ankles, exhausted from the long trip, and Leonid, glowing from a childhood dream come true.

We bundled them into our cars and took them to their new apartment where a set table, full dinner, and bottles of vodka awaited. With the memory of the rich, history-laden atmosphere of their Moscow apartment in mind, I was afraid that, despite our detailed, loving preparation, their new apartment looked suburban-tract-housing cheesy. But they beamed in gratitude. Around their new dining room table, glasses were continually refilled with vodka. There was one toast after another, one *l'chaim* after another, tributes to the people and events that led to this family's exodus. Leonid's *l'chaim*s became reflective: he spoke of how, even in the terrible Soviet system, so many found the courage to resist. His last toast, overflowing with emotional gratitude, was reserved for accomplishments of two senators who changed the course of Soviet Jewish history. Soviet Jews, he said, should pray for them every day. They were Henry Jackson and Frank Lautenberg.

The next morning, even my hair hurt.

Certainly, Leonid and Natasha's integration into American life was atypical. Jews going to Israel in the 1970s and 1980s were sent to absorption centers to learn Hebrew and adapt to their new culture with other emigrants who shared their experience. In the States, though Soviet Jews were assisted by a tangle of agencies under the Jewish Federation system, these new emigrants didn't experience a commensurate communal absorption process. However, the Stonovs and their mothers were enfolded in a cushion of supporters who had become friends.

Compelled to sustain the movement they left behind, Leonid and Natasha would continue, but as salaried professionals whose expertise made them invaluable. Marillyn immediately brought on Natasha as a full-time CASJ employee. For Micah and me, Leonid was the third corner of our triangle. Long before they received permission, Leonid and Natasha were in our hearts, and once they arrived, we simply made room for them in our office.

Before long, Leonid, the de facto head of our Moscow bureau in addition to being UCSJ's director of foreign affairs, was at his desk in our office, working overtime to coordinate activity between Moscow, our councils, and the Washington office, just as he had in Moscow. His desk was piled high with transcripts, position papers, analyses. Micah, Marillyn, and I were ecstatic. Instead of placing a messenger call every few days, all I had to do was walk over to Leonid's desk.

CHAPTER 24

"Don't Leave Us Behind": Moscow and Central Asia, Spring 1991

Round Table Hearing on Human Rights

Tumultuous events marked the beginning of the new decade. The collapse of the Berlin Wall and the reunification of Germany at the end of 1989 seemed to be the leak in the dam that started it all. In early 1990, Estonia, Latvia, and Lithuania declared independence from the Soviet Union, and the remaining republics were not far behind.

Closing down my computer one late afternoon in January 1991, I noticed a spurt of emails with Lithuanian email addresses. Before deleting them as spam, glancing from one to another, I realized they were graphic on-the-ground, minute-to-minute reports from Kaunas university students. Before the era of texts or Twitter, they were sending out eyewitness reports of Soviet tanks advancing toward Vilnius in order to force Lithuania back into the Soviet federation. One email read that a column of tanks were heading to the TV tower. Another student wrote that their countrymen were taking to the streets to defend it and other buildings. Then another wrote that shots had been fired, and the tanks were driving through the crowds, killing several protestors. Another posting said that students and university professors were broadcasting in several languages from the university radio station, urging people of good will to broadcast in as many different languages as possible to the world that the Soviet army was killing unarmed people in Lithuania.

I don't how they got my email, but I got on the phone and started calling news services. Moscow was showing its real face. At the end, more than fifty thousand Lithuanians showed up to protect the Supreme Council,

Lithuania's governing body. World pressure forced Gorbachev to back down; the Soviet Union was in the process of dissolution and it was too late for him to stop it.

Our Moscow bureau, meanwhile, was reporting mixed signals. Yes, long-term refuseniks were leaving, but there were new refusals for applications and no law governing the right to emigrate. Unpredictability was an existential reality feeding our anxiety. The uncertainty, in the face of reports of violent anti-Semitic incidents, was compounded by the continuing problems resulting from insufficient flights to Israel and the protracted waits for *vysovs*. Expedited systems had to be put in place to accommodate the wave of Jews trying to escape.

Then our attention turned to Central Asia. Decentralization had turned it into a powder keg since 1990. After decades of Russian domination, interethnic rivalry was pitting Uzbeks, Turks, Tatars, and Kyrgyz against each other, and all against the Russians, some of whom were Jews. Our Moscow bureau had reported rumors of a pogrom in Uzbekistan's Fergana Valley.

Micah queried the State Department, which denied government-backed violence. Israel also rejected the accusation of government complicity. But UCSJ reacted with skepticism to their reassurances. The US position reflected a resistance to raising the refugee ceiling and expediting the backlog of Jews with exit visas. Israel also seemed to resist a dramatic increase in emigration, perhaps due to the ever-growing Russian aliyah's need for housing and infrastructure.

The upheavals in Russia and beyond demanded a reassessment that prompted us to schedule a Round Table Hearing on Human Rights in Moscow. Though it was April, our plane's descent into Sheremetyevo Airport left behind the blinding sun-washed sky and pushed through the thick grayness that perpetually hung over Moscow. It struck me at the time that the only Moscow I ever knew was the grim, gray city below the shining clarity of light above.

Our kickoff event was a meeting with refuseniks and "poor relatives" who were not among the 187,000 Jews who had permission and were leaving. Hundreds of Jews, either denied permission or unable to apply, streamed into Moscow's Shalom Theater, grouping along the walls, unable to find an empty seat in the 250-seat auditorium. Scores of Jews, many from distant cities, surrounded me, handing me their written appeals and case histories, begging us not to forget them. I spoke extemporaneously from the stage, stopping intermittently for Leonid's translation into Russian. Scanning the room, I saw the faces of my people, who were looking to us for assurance that we could get them out to Israel, to the United States, to freedom. I had made that commitment long ago, and I was going to move heaven and earth to ensure that they weren't left behind. I would never have told them that most Americans and the media believed the Jewish problem in the USSR had been resolved.

Leonid, in tandem with the Moscow bureau, pulled together a star-studded panel of Jewish activists and former dissidents and political prisoners to deliver expert reports. These lions of the human rights movement represented the foremost nongovernmental groups operating in the former USSR.[1] I led off the meeting in the conference hall of the Moscow Barrister Association, expressing our objective: to develop a unified strategy in advance of September's official CSCE Moscow human rights conference.

One human rights expert after another documented abuses that had condemned people to a nightmarish existence, emphasizing the rising Jew-hatred in Russia. Those reports were the ominous foreshadowing of a catastrophe we were trying to prevent.

Alla Gerber, a prestigious human rights authority, was an attractive woman with chin-length hair who carried herself with elegant patrician authority. A member of the Russian-Jewish intelligentsia, an attorney and a journalist, she was unequivocally alarmed about the rise of the ultra-nationalist Pamyat, which self-identified as the "people's national-patriotic Orthodox Christian movement." Pamyat wasn't a fringe group. Its pogromist Black Hundreds ideology blamed the "Zionist conspiracy" for Russia's problems, an appealing message for Russian nationalists. It was supported by the government apparatus – KGB, the Communist Party, the Orthodox Church, and the prestigious Writers' Union – which accused Jews of stealing national treasures when they left the country. Reminiscent of the Nazi party in Germany in 1938, Pamyat was distributing the insidious anti-Semitic tract *Protocols of the Elders of Zion*.

---

1.   Participants included the Moscow Helsinki Group, Andrei Sakharov's International Foundation for the Survival and Development of Humanity, Amnesty International, the Memorial Society, and the Soldiers' Mothers Committee.

Alla confirmed reports that Pamyat was also operating armed military camps. The room fell silent when she emphasized the very real threat of anti-Jewish pogroms. Not knowing which way the wind would blow, Jews were scared. She explained that some Jews had internalized the anti-Semitic propaganda. The mixture of guilt and fear was driving the exodus that, she correctly predicted, would continue for years.

As each speaker added to the grim picture, my heart sank deeper and deeper, leaving me more convinced than ever that every Jew who could do so should leave as quickly as possible. As I listened, I worried. How would our small team muster the resources to make good on all the assurances we were giving?

The warnings resounded like a drill on cement. Journalists were being repressed and threatened. An hour after a Radio Liberty correspondent tried sending information to Munich, an anonymous caller warned: "Shut up or we'll kill you." Such threats presaged the murders of journalists under Putin many years later.

There was still no legal right to demonstrate; punitive psychiatric incarceration and political arrests continued; and prisoners were still beaten and tortured by hunger and cold. The magnitude of abuse was staggering.

Then Leonid spoke about emigration. State-secrecy refuseniks were still being held for more than five to ten years after leaving their jobs or otherwise ending contact with their supposed secrecy source. "Poor relatives" were without legal protection. Furthermore, anyone wanting to emigrate collided with economic and technical obstacles. Emigrating Jews were forced to relinquish their Soviet citizenship and then charged five hundred rubles for the honor. Some OVIR offices had quotas for emigration applications, while others claimed not to have applications or denied would-be applicants the right to apply.

Our activist consortium universally decided to convene our own parallel human rights conference in Lithuania timed to coincide with the official meeting in Moscow.

It was both gratifying and heartbreaking to hear participants express sincere gratitude that the Union hadn't given up on them. But our work was far from over. After a reception at the American embassy, Micah, Leonid, and I caught a flight to Tashkent.

On to Central Asia

Rumors and reports about pogroms and murders in Central Asia demanded an on-the-ground consultation with local Jewish leaders. Over the years, Central Asian refuseniks had traveled to Moscow to meet UCSJ's activists; now it was our turn to travel to them. Soon I found myself hurling into the unknown, accompanied by a team of experts: Micah, Leonid, and four of our top Moscow bureau staff.

At Sheremetyevo, we lugged our suitcases across the hot and sticky tarmac for baggage handlers to load. Leonid and Micah were shepherded to the first-row seats of the small commuter jet, while I was being held to board last and seated in the rear. The jet was packed with Tatar men in fur coats, round fur or felt caps with earflaps, and leather boots. The women also wore headgear with what seemed to be mandatory earflaps, as well as colorfully embroidered aprons and leather boots. Everyone had large bags stuffed with cooked food. It was April, unseasonably warm, and the plane, baking in the sun, was stifling. The odor of unwashed bodies in fur coats mixed with the spicy-smelling food of several national cultures. I was suppressing spasms of nausea when a uniformed flight attendant took the empty seat next to me. She pulled out an aerosol deodorant from her bag and heavily sprayed the seats in front of us. It helped a little.

She settled in and abruptly turned to me. Where was I from? Why was I going to Uzbekistan? Was I traveling alone? How long would I be there? Were people meeting me at the airport? No, I was an adventurous and enthusiastic tourist ready to explore the further reaches of the Soviet Union. But my interrogator knew better. I had been deliberately seated alone. Intimidation failing, my impostor attendant, surely a KGB informant, tried the fear factor, informing me in unnerving detail why Tashkent's airport was the world's most dangerous. Nestled beneath soaring mountains, the airport was the site of frequent unpublicized emergency landings. My window view confirmed her description. It was exquisite, a fantasy world of icy spiked peaks and blue sky, but all I could see was danger. Except for my encounter with the python in Leningrad, nothing on previous trips had terrified me as much as that four-hour flight. The hours ticked by, minute by excruciating minute. It was a white-knuckle landing.

In four cities in three Central Asian republics, each of our arrivals followed a consistent pattern. At each airport, we were met by leaders of the indigenous Jewish cultural society. Young and friendly, their views and positions were strangely uniform, and they denied all the reports and rumors we had come to validate: there was no anti-Semitism, no anti-Semitic violence, no pervasive fear. From the outset, we felt our meetings were being controlled, and we were being watched.

Central Asia was an incongruous jungle of subterfuge, intended to distort reality. Nothing was what it seemed to be. I felt like I had landed on the moon.

After that long, harrowing flight, I just wanted a shower, but I was daunted by the primitive hotel bathroom. The base of the toilet oozed what I hoped was only soft black tar, and the shower nozzle mounted on the wall between the sink and the toilet spattered less than a stream of coldish water. But my ultimate challenge was the battalion of sturdy black cockroaches scurrying out of the hair dryer when I switched it on. That night, I fell exhausted into bed, on perpetual guard against my roach roommates. My throat burned as I breathed in the rancid mix of chemicals and biological waste.

Welcome to Tashkent.

In each city we held open meetings in the Jewish cultural centers, where we introduced UCSJ, our role, goals, and policies. Then we consulted privately with Jewish families who had specific problems, leaving our Moscow bureau staff to collect data and answer technical questions on emigration.

In Tashkent, I set out to the meeting with the organizer of the day's event. The glaring sun was unforgiving as the two of us walked to the school the Jewish cultural center had arranged for us to use for our meeting. I decided to feel her out and asked what specific issues the community wanted us to address. She warned, "Talk about emigration, but do not say anything about anti-Semitism." As we approached the large groups of Jews converging on the school's playground, my companion vanished abruptly, leaving me with the impression she didn't want to be seen with me. Inside the school were several hundred Jews and at least one identified KGB agent who was particularly aggressive. We managed to keep him at bay.

Our introduction focused on UCSJ's non-paternalistic partnership orientation; then Micah and I sat in the corner of the gymnasium to meet privately with families. I was intent on hearing from the victims to verify or disprove reports of anti-Semitic violence. It was the reason we were here. Leonid brought a middle-aged man to us. His face was carved with deep lines of a father's worry. He told us that his son, Yaakov Shtelman, had been arrested on false charges, beaten to unconsciousness during the investigation, and sentenced based on the verbatim, fabricated accusation. He was desperate for us to publicize his son's case and gain his release. Another tragic father was Boris Kats. His son had been murdered by the military, and he was receiving anonymous phone calls threatening him to stop his investigation. These weren't rumors.

Lyudmila Alexeyeva, the legendary Russian human rights leader and a founding member of the Moscow Helsinki Group, had put Leonid in touch with a journalist from Intersoyuz. She briefed us, explaining that the democratic movement in Uzbekistan had died young, leaving in its wake various ethnic groups vying for domination. A cauldron of clans and castes of Uzbeks, Turks, Tajiks, Crimean Tatars, and Turkish Meskhetians found a shared goal under the rabid Birlik movement: "Foreigners Out." Foreigners meant Russians and Russian-language speakers, a great many of whom were Jews.

During the Fergana Valley pogrom, the inflamed crowd originally targeted Meskhetian Turks, but it was Russian homes that were burned down, while the military stood by without action. Pogroms broke out in Kokand, Tashkent, and Dushanbe. The government-sanctioned violence left everyone vulnerable, especially the remaining Jews in Uzbekistan.

Then, in May 1990, there was a pogrom in Andizhan. The official story was that it started with young drunks who, disappointed by a football game, started attacking wealthy people, but a Jewish Bukharan leader whose family was among those murdered told us otherwise. Yakov Bangiev explained that a day or two before the pogrom, government authorities confiscated every weapon that could be used for self-defense. They knew what was coming or had planned it themselves. At the game, Uzbek trade groups' placards read: "We'll kill Jews and Armenians and then the Russians will run out themselves." When the violence erupted, the government cut off the electricity, assisting the pogromists, who were under orders to stop just short of killing. When it was over, fifteen houses had been burned to the ground and a Jewish woman raped.

We had heard rumors of Andizhan for a year. When the pogrom was denied by both Israel and the US State Department, we had sent Chernobilsky from our human rights bureau, who had confirmed government complicity. Now we were here to verify and analyze conditions for emigration against this backdrop of violence. But where was the Israeli government?

We weren't alone in asking the question. Aryeh Levin, who would become Israel's ambassador to Russia, thought his government wasn't doing enough. He wrote: "This abhorrent incident was not publicized and the Ministries of the Interior and Foreign Affairs, which I contacted, feigned total ignorance."[2]

The political turbulence and ethnic strife in Central Asia and Russia, the poisonous anti-Semitism dramatically illustrated by the serialization of *Mein Kampf* in the Soviet Ministry of Defense's magazine, and the deteriorating socioeconomic conditions all combined to threaten Jews everywhere in the dissolving Soviet Union. By delaying their emigration, Israel and the United States only increased their risk. A quarter of a million Jews in the five Central Asian republics were looking for an escape hatch.

UCSJ's Expedited Emigration Proposal

For UCSJ, emigration wasn't the problem; it was the solution. Family reunification to the United States and Jewish repatriation to Israel was our two-track strategy. The warnings from our Moscow meeting hadn't fallen on deaf ears. The problem was that the American government was moving too slowly. At the embassy in Moscow, American immigration officials were interviewing 132 people a day to determine refugee status, and there was a backlog of 100,000 Jews waiting for their slot in line. The situation called for a massive rescue. For evacuation.

About six weeks before our trip to Central Asia, the Israelis had reacted venomously to our proposal that the United States waive the annual quota of fifty thousand for Soviet Jewish émigrés. UCSJ urged that the more than 100,000 Soviet Jews who had already applied for refugee status be immediately evacuated to be reunited with their close families in the States.

Our evacuation proposal brought antipathy from Israel, which feared our plan would divert Jews from Israel to the United States. By the time we arrived in Central Asia, the controversy had spread through the Jewish organizational bureaucracy. Micah and I tried dampening it down with letters to editors, reiterating the obvious: UCSJ's plan was strictly limited to Jews with close family in the States and who had already applied to

---

2. Aryeh Levin, *Envoy to Moscow: Memoirs of an Israeli Ambassador, 1988–92* (London: Frank Cass, 1996).

emigrate. It didn't alter *who* was coming to the States; it only altered *how quickly* they would arrive.

Leading former refuseniks, including Leonid, of course, as well as Boris Kelman, Yuri Cherniak, and Mark Kotlyar, had endorsed our plan as a one-time emergency action to evacuate Jews separated from their families. Our plan was widely appreciated in Central Asia. Tashkent activists had read about the UCSJ initiative to evacuate Jews from Central Asia and endorsed it. Their view was reiterated throughout our meetings. But for the Jewish Agency, Lishka, and Foreign Ministry, the threat of expediting the US emigration process was tantamount to putting a blow torch to a parched forest.

Late one afternoon in Tashkent, having agreed to accommodate one family's request to meet them at their home, Micah, Leonid and I set off, address in hand. We walked down an alley flanked by corrugated metal barriers. It looked as if we were in a run-down industrial zone. I was sure we had the wrong address. But, confident as always, Leonid urged us on. Eventually we came to a heavy, corrugated gate. Hesitantly, Micah pushed it open. Before us lay a breathtaking garden of Eden. A blooming lemon tree dominated a flowering courtyard. A dark-skinned couple, clearly Sephardic, graciously welcomed us. Their home, sprawling across a single floor, was a courtly residence adorned with sparkling silver Judaica. Persian carpets hung on the walls, and colorful tiles lined the floors. On the domed ceiling was an ornate painted mural.

Their home testified to the long and rich history of Central Asia's Jews, who had lived there for over a thousand years. They had built synagogues, mikvahs, and schools, and they had thrived, accumulating wealth. Now forced to flee and leave everything behind, they faced the prospect of starting again from the very beginning. This was the story of my people.

In Central Asia nothing was as it seemed. Corrugated metal hid opulence. Alleged profession of peace and security masked seething anti-Semitism. Jewish cultural society activists denied the presence of anti-Semitism. Slowly, we were scratching the surface, trying to find what lay beneath.

Bukhara

A short morning flight west took us to Bukhara. The medieval city on the Silk Road hadn't changed much over the centuries. It was among the most isolated and oldest Jewish communities in the world – some say from the era of King David. Now this chapter of Jewish history was coming to an end.

Shura and Ifraim Borokhov were waiting for us at the airport, pre-dictably with another group of young people from the Jewish cultural center. The Borokhovs were refuseniks with a long, troubled history of harassment. While Ifraim drove us to our community meeting at the syn-agogue on Tsentralnaya Street, Leonid reviewed our schedule, explaining what we needed to learn during our short stay. Squeezed in the back seat with Micah and me, Shura warned us not to talk about anti-Semitism. One of the organizers of the community meeting, she was afraid KGB would identify her as the source of unfavorable information passed to "Western agents."

Privately, Jews described the bureaucratic obstacles that were making emigration a nightmare. While there were no limitations or hurdles for emigrating Germans and Greeks, Jews had to travel to distant cities for customs, where they encountered officials who didn't want to accept their baggage. With so many restrictions on what they could take out, they were forced to come to Israel as beggars.

Our schedule was short, rigorous, and demanding. Even if I could get a phone connection to America from the hotel, there was no time. But I knew if I needed to reach Lenny, I could rely on Leonid's local resources.

Samarkand

From Bukhara, we flew to Samarkand. The image I had of the storied city of Genghis Khan and Tamerlane, the majestic Rome of the East, shattered with our first visit, to the Shamalov family. Hanging in the living room was a striking painting of a young, handsome man with piercing eyes, his dark hair slicked back. Beneath the portrait, Mariya, his sister, barely man-aging her grief, told us the story that had ripped apart their lives. Ifraim was a twenty-one-year-old foreman when his coworkers, two Arabs and an Iranian, bludgeoned him with a hammer, hitting him hard enough to break the hammer's shank. Covering him with plastic, they threw him into their car trunk. They grabbed a young girl who had witnessed the attack and pulled her into the car. Then they drove off into the mountains. Later, the girl later testified she could hear Ifraim screaming, "Mama." They took him out, doused him with gasoline and burned him alive, while they danced and chanted, "Look how this Jew burns like a Negro."

They threatened the girl, assuring her that they would do the same to her if she reported them, and let her go. But she reported the murder. Two out of the three assailants were arrested. Inside the courtroom, the proceedings exposed the antagonism between Uzbeks and Jews; outside, an Uzbek shouted, "Your turn is next. We should kill all of you." Mariya told us the murderers threatened to avenge themselves on the Shamalov family, and they were all terrified the murderers would be given an early release. The Shamalovs had been given refugee status, but how long would they have to wait for their place in the immigrant line? Would it be in time? We extended every assurance that we would remove obstacles to their entry to the United States.

It was dusk when we left our meeting at the Bukharin synagogue and walked to the apartment of the Chabad rabbi, Imoniel Shimonov. Night had invaded the perimeter of the small room, but a nearby floor lamp bathed his handsome face in a golden light. He was young, with dark, curly hair and intense eyes. He was passionate and charismatic. Micah, Leonid, and I huddled together with him, catching some of the glow around him. It was a scene Rembrandt might have painted: these three people with a young bearded rabbi, drawn into a light that seemed more spiritual than physical.

He told us there were between twelve and fifteen thousand Jews in Samarkand, and most wanted to leave. He operated an afterschool cheder three times a week for four hundred children to learn about Judaism and the Torah. He taught an ulpan for four hundred adults to learn Hebrew, employed fifteen teachers, and published *Shofar,* a weekly paper that commented on the Torah portion and provided information that Jews in Samarkand lacked.

Rabbi Shimonov burned away the dark horror of Ifraim Shamalov's murder and left me awestruck. In this remote corner of the world, a young man was paving a path to the tomorrows in Jewish history. He was educating, leading, guiding. I wasn't exactly sure what it was, but I knew he had something, understood something, that I didn't, and in all that golden light, I felt the shadow of an empty melancholy.

I assured Shimonov our tourists would bring the books, tefillin, and siddurim he wanted to our Moscow bureau for him to pick up. He couldn't have known he was one of those remarkable Jews who etched their lives onto my own. Looking back, I anxiously wonder whether I did enough to help this man who unknowingly touched my yet-unidentified nostalgia for what I was missing: a relationship with Torah Judaism.

Dushanbe

The next morning, we flew south to Dushanbe, Tajikistan, just a few hundred miles from the Afghanistan border, in a valley surrounded by snow-capped mountains.

Yuna Dotkharev, a leader of the omnipresent Jewish cultural society, introduced the UCSJ and our activities to a surprisingly large gathering at the local synagogue. Speaking to the crowd, I was preoccupied with one of the main reasons I had come to Dushanbe – to find Sueleimon Masterov. Free from the podium, I went to search him out, only to learn that he had left.

Left? He was there and left? Why hadn't I found him before the meeting or made arrangements to meet him? I was sure he was as anxious to meet us as we were to meet him. His wife had been murdered, her throat cut. The murderer scalped her before he escaped. Authorities didn't investigate. The file was closed. Half a world away, in my office in Chicago, I had heard about her, and I had come all this way only to learn that her husband had been there with us but had fled. Why didn't he stay? Had they threatened him? Was he afraid of being associated with a Western or Jewish organization?

His wife's death was far from the only atrocity. There was the carpet dealer who was stabbed nine times before dying, and the dentist Tamara Yakubov's two sons, who were stabbed at home. Grigory Buryagev's son was attacked, his hands tied behind his back, their apartment confiscated and their packed suitcases stolen. It was known that they were all leaving for Israel.

Mira Bacheveva was our briefer in Dushanbe. Her son had been followed by KGB for a year and then severely beaten by the children of local officials. She was one of the few Jews in Central Asia who spoke openly and honestly. Mira and her family had permission to leave, but they were planning, like others, to protect themselves by going into hiding during the departure process, to avoid the anti-Semitic attacks that preceded the twin processes of expulsion and expropriation.

After Mira's briefing, the Jewish cultural society's leaders rounded us up and herded us to Meir Chaim Gavreilov's home, where conversation alternated between culinary praise for the fragrant pilaf heaped beneath clay domes and exaggerated claims of gains under Gorbachev. Mira, who had briefed us so openly, wasn't included. Leaders of the cultural societies in all these republics worked hard to isolate us from anyone who might give us a view of reality. They were firmly under the thumb of the authorities.

When the two of them were alone, Micah confronted Dotkharev: we knew he was suppressing information. Away from other leaders of the cultural society, he acknowledged "the situation is dangerous. We Jews are caught in the middle of conflicting political forces. We are all awaiting an 'Andizhan Pogrom.'"[3]

What would happen to these Jews? Would they be able to leave? What trajectory would their lives take? Their individual stories, the stories of their fathers, and their fathers' fathers, going so far back in time: their hopes and successes, struggles, losses, agonies would eventually be absorbed in the historical process, and I would never hear from them again.

I do know, however, that everyone who wanted to leave ultimately left.

Alma Ata

The next flight carried us north to Alma Ata (now Almaty) in Kazakhstan. Somewhere in the mix of exhaustion, the emotional vortex of horror stories that were too real, the itinerary of meetings and speeches and presentations, I had lost a sense of who I was. I was exclusively operating on behalf of the movement, the Union, focused only on the needs of Jews who needed to leave, frantically writing notes and memos, lists of actions to be taken, ideas to discuss. During travel time, Micah, Leonid, and I chewed everything over and strategized for the next session. The work was so all-consuming, it was even consuming me.

Five or six young Jewish men, really just teenagers, from Alma Ata's Jewish cultural society were on the tarmac waiting for us. We were making introductions and gathering suitcases when I noticed a man in a raincoat, lagging behind us with a large camera case slung over his shoulder. We were the only group still on the tarmac, and it seemed he was tracking us, but I was distracted by these affable teenagers who were leading us to their small bus. It wasn't until the end of the trip, when we returned to the airport and I saw him following us, that I confirmed that the man with the camera had been sent for us.

On the bus, we mingled among each other, chatting amiably with our charming English-speaking guides as they peppered us with questions.

---

3.   Yuna Dotkharev, in conversation with Micah Naftalin, April 1991.

One of the boys was an especially sweet, innocent-looking, tall, skinny kid wearing a Chicago Bulls cap. Hearing I was a Chicagoan, Vadim Gytis excitedly started talking about his hero, Michael Jordan. Already marked by Jewish history, Vadim confided in me that his grandparents were among the nearly thirty-five thousand Jews the Germans and Ukrainians had murdered in Kiev in the ravine at Babi Yar. One of his friends took me aside and told me that Vadim had been among the first sent to clean up after the nuclear catastrophe in Chernobyl, Ukraine – sent without gloves or mask, without any protection. The nineteen-year-old Jewish Chicago Bulls fan was dying of lymphoma. One more tragic Jewish victim of Russia.

Micah, Leonid, and I were anxious to get started on our packed schedule, but the boys from the Jewish cultural society had another agenda. Unknown to us, they were being handled by KGB, which had insinuated itself into the Jewish cultural societies, and they were in turn handling us. Oblivious to the bus driver's route, we didn't realize at first that we were being kidnapped. On the pretense of taking us on a sightseeing tour of a newly constructed dam, they were driving deeper into the heavily forested mountains, away from our schedule. Meanwhile they continued to ask us questions and videotape our responses with what I later realized was the camera brought by the suspicious-looking man at the airport. We demanded the driver turn back, but only when Micah tried to grab the steering wheel did the boys relent.

Finally released from their grip, we rushed to the courthouse for the trial of the Bodner brothers. Dominating the courtroom at front left was a lion's cage with a padlocked door, surrounded by a dozen armed militiamen. In the cage were the two Bodner brothers, who looked to be in their twenties. The procurator – the prosecutor – sat silently at a long table facing the cage. From inside the cage, Felix Bodner, a slim man in T-shirt and jeans, was conducting their defense, his hands gesticulating between the bars. The judge permitted him to be taken from the cage to address the supposed expert witness on the stand. The heavy padlock was opened. He approached the witness and destroyed her testimony. The Bodners had been imprisoned for two and a half years, and their trial had the potential to go on for many more years. The court planned to call 830 witnesses to testify against the brothers for a financial crime they didn't commit. It was a show trial.

Reports about the Bodners' arrest, incarceration, and the investigation had been reaching us for months. Our Moscow bureau had uncovered evidence to prove their innocence. We also had plenty of proof of the illegal machinations of the procurator and the court, which was still operating under the former Russian code. After all, that's what we did. That's how we were able to conduct the campaigns that proved the innocence of Sharansky and Mendelevich and Edelstein and Kholmiansky and Lein and dozens of other Jews who had been framed over the past twenty years. We brought out the state's fabricated accusations and so-called evidence and conducted the accused's legal defense in the American media, with the US government, and even with Soviet authorities.

From his seat, Leonid signaled to their defense attorney to meet him outside the courtroom. Leonid had made contact with him, and he was expecting us. The lawyer wanted us to meet the head of Kazakhstan's Supreme Court, Sergei Duvanov, to express the concern of the American public and the government about the case, especially in light of the upcoming Moscow Conference on the Human Dimension.

The surprisingly well-dressed, sophisticated Duvanov met us upstairs in his small, wood-paneled office. Surprisingly, he greeted us graciously, proffering chairs in front of his desk and offering tea. Leonid made the introductions in Russian and translated back and forth throughout the meeting.

To protect the Bodners from anti-Semitic reaction to our intervention, we associated ourselves with our Moscow Human Rights Bureau, not the Union of Councils for Soviet Jews. Step by step, Leonid argued the brothers' innocence and showed that the evidence being used to prosecute them was fabricated.

After Leonid's exacting legal defense, Duvanov, a sociologist, gave us a panoramic political and sociological analysis of Kazakhstan, sometimes contradicting himself, but affirming that the old Communist system was fully operational.

He had listened carefully to Leonid, and we left him hoping he would intercede. Ultimately the Bodner brothers were freed. Many years later, on a Shabbos morning at Rabbi Eliezer Dimarsky's Russian Heritage Synagogue in West Rogers Park, a man excitedly introduced himself to me. He was the nephew of one of the brothers. He told me the Bodners knew they had been released because of our intervention. That alone was worth our trip to Central Asia.

The questions raised publicly at our meeting with the Jewish cultural society in Alma Ata were more provocative and suspicious than in any of the other cities. Reflecting the Kremlin's dangerous assertion of the insidious, anti-Soviet nature of Zionism, someone from the floor pointedly asked whether we were a "Zionist organization." I could feel everyone in the room prickle, wondering how their ties to us "anti-Soviet Zionists" would later rebound on them and their families. The luncheon the Jewish cultural society was hosting in our honor was held at the hotel of the Communist Party. Their ties to the party were obvious.

We insisted that our handlers take us to the grave of Rabbi Levi Yitzchak Schneerson, the father of the famed Lubavitch rabbi Menachem Mendel. Stalin had arrested him for teaching Torah and distributing matzah. For more than a year, he had been imprisoned, interrogated, and tortured. Finally he was sentenced to exile in Khazakhstan, where he died and was buried, in this far-flung edge of the world where someday, there would be no Jews. Stalin. Hitler. Those who resisted. Jews who tried to scale the steep precipice of history, hanging on with bloody fingers, leaving their mark, their path for others to follow, for their children. For me.

Meanwhile, the boys continued to videotape us throughout the public meetings, but we wouldn't allow them to record any private conversations. It turned out that the suspicious man I had seen on arrival at the airport, Boris Poliyak, was a Jew. Throughout our stay in Alma Ata, he mysteriously appeared, disappeared, and reappeared. Asked if he planned to leave, he told us that he couldn't: "They have their hands on me." He worked in a military border control unit under KGB. I had a sickening feeling in my gut when I saw Boris on our flight back to Moscow. He didn't look at us. He didn't speak to anyone. We were certain he was taking the videotape back to Moscow to give to KGB.

And we were right. Months later, a Soviet news channel aired the footage of anti-Soviet Zionist provocateurs, identifying Leonid, Micah, and me, including footage taken by our charming guys who tried to keep us away from the Bodner trial.

I was more than ready to get out of Central Asia. I would have dreaded having to return, so it's a good thing we don't know the future.

It had been a long but productive trip. Micah, Leonid, and I came away exhausted, physically and emotionally, but with a solid grasp of the key Jewish issues. The Central Asian Jewish cultural centers weren't the only centers of current KGB activity. KGB was creating organizations and penetrating existing ones to produce disinformation before and during the Moscow human rights conference that would obscure their support of Pamyat and their continued abuse of human rights. We were able to put the pieces together and report our findings to the State Department, the administration, and Congress with emphasis on the issues that needed to be addressed at the upcoming Moscow conference.

The plane couldn't fly home fast enough. I was more than ready for our family vacation in Switzerland. Josh was coming home from the University of Kansas; Scott was arriving from Boston, where he had taken root after Brandeis; and Brooke was taking time off from her job in Chicago. We rented a car in Zurich and drove around the lake to Lucerne, on to the Bernese Oberland, to Zermatt and Kandersteg. Lenny and I shared our favorite hikes with the kids, up the steep grade to Oeschinensee, through the rock-pitted pine forest to Blausee, and on the forested path on the ridge to Furi, skirting the Matterhorn. Lenny and I drank in the laughter and camaraderie of our adult children, and I was back in my personal world, my safe harbor, without which I could never have left port. The trip swallowed our days, and too quickly the kids headed home, leaving Lenny and me to drive on to Italy, trying not to feel guilty for such indulgent pleasure.

CHAPTER 25

From Geneva to Moscow to Vilnius, 1991

The CSCE Meeting of Experts on National Minorities in Geneva

In June 1991, Boris Yeltsin became the first popularly elected president in Russia's history. Yeltsin had expressed support for greater autonomy for the Soviet republics and a market-driven economy, and his election was seen as a mandate for change.

That summer, I was asked to be a public delegate to the CSCE Meeting of Experts on National Minorities in Geneva. I couldn't refuse the official acknowledgement of UCSJ's work, though I wanted desperately to stay home. Micah was laid up after surgery. I'd be at a loss without him, but at least Leonid would be there representing UCSJ.

I checked into the Drake-Longchamps Hotel in Geneva and recovered from jet lag on a Lake Geneva ferry boat with Leonid. In spite of the picturesque waterscape, my attention was on Leonid, who was recollecting his family's life under Stalin. With astounding recall, he related strings of stories about the people he knew who had been informed on by neighbors and arrested, of the persecuted writers, his father's arrest, his mother's resistance. Under the burning sun, I listened, mesmerized by his account, regretting I didn't have a tape recorder.

In Geneva, as part of the US delegation, I could raise UCSJ's issues among our own delegation as well as with the European delegates. Given the forthcoming CSCE Moscow Conference on the Human Dimension, human rights should have been front and center in Geneva. But in the midst of the Soviet dissolution, the focus had moved to conflict resolution. I was the sole human rights advocate among a slew of mediation professionals in the delegation. I was expert at advocating UCSJ's positions and didn't have experience in the mediation field. I knew my time would be better spent meeting with other delegations on behalf of our issue. Frustrated, I made a couple of distressed and teary calls to Lenny. It didn't help that my old nemesis, Morris Abram, was there in his capacity as the permanent representative to the United Nations in Geneva. Morris did host a splendid reception for the European delegations on the lawn of the stately US residence on the lake. Leonid and I circulated among the delegates, urging them to raise our issues at the Moscow Conference on the Human Dimension in September, but they were preoccupied with what Bush had called a new world order.

The fifteen Soviet republics were struggling toward independence. Indigenous Jewish activists were already allied with leaders of the secessionist democratic movements, and UCSJ followed suit. The largest grassroots Soviet Jewry organization, we believed, could not spurn aspirations for democratic reform and independence without compromising the remaining Jews still living in those very republics. We were encouraged at the time by some of the Western-minded, reformist leaders' assurances of guarantees for the rights of their Jewish minorities, whether they wanted to emigrate or not.

The Jewish Establishment reacted with accusations that we were moving the goalposts and manufacturing new priorities to "stay in business." Their unofficial whisper campaign argued that the long-term refuseniks were leaving or had already left. What did the Union want now, a free Lithuania, the willing partners in the Holocaust? A free Ukraine, home of horrific pogroms?

The truth is, in hindsight, history's circuitous path has validated some of their concerns. As I write this, Lithuania, Ukraine, and Poland are still soaked in anti-Semitism. The brightest hopes for the Lithuania of President Landsbergis and the Poland of Lech Walesa died a long time ago. Then again, so did the flash of hope for human rights enshrined in Russia.

But with history, context and perspective is everything.

The Failed Coup

The USSR was a shambles in 1991. The scarcity of food and medicine had increased the already long lines of people hoping to buy a pair of children's shoes, a loaf of bread, a chicken. Inflation was over 300 percent. Factories couldn't pay salaries. Fuel supplies wouldn't meet the winter's needs.

Economic desiccation exacerbated the political instability, and a vast underground reservoir of hate seeped out from beneath the Russian soil. Gaining strength, Pamyat launched its own newspaper and radio station, accusing the "Zionist conspiracy" of every evil and problem in the country. The Writers' Union complained of "kike masons." The Russian rightist ultranationalists were calling for a military dictatorship, fearing that more of the union republics would secede. The head of KGB called for a state of emergency.

A few weeks before our Vilnius alternative human rights conference, Micah called our house and, with uncharacteristic urgency, ordered me to turn on the news.

It took a while for me to process the images of armored units and paratroopers rolling into Moscow. On Monday, August 19, desperate to preserve the central power of the Soviet Union, communist hardliners had staged a coup against the Gorbachev government. Masses of Russians, protesting the coup, had erected protective barricades around the White House, Russia's parliament building. Boris Yeltsin joined the protesters and, surrounded by reformers, unarmed democrats, and parliamentarians, went out to meet the tanks in front of the White House. He crawled atop one of them and addressed the crowd. He urged the troops not to attack and declared a general strike until the Gorbachev government was reinstalled. The hardliners responded with a call for a state of emergency and cut off the only independent radio station. In the resulting skirmishes, three demonstrators were killed.

We were desperate for information, but it was impossible to get a phone call through.

The revolt collapsed a few days later, propelling Boris Yeltsin and his reformists to the forefront. In the immediate aftermath, mobs tore down the statue of the founder of Stalin's secret police, the notorious Felix Dzerzhinsky, the symbol of KGB and the reign of Soviet terror. Gorbachev remained in power, but the end was in sight.

In the middle of the furor, Brooke became engaged to David, the young man who had monopolized her conversations and attention during our Switzerland trip. I shifted gears and centered attention on a January wedding. Within a week, all the arrangements had been decided, and my mother had located a beautiful gown for her granddaughter. We congratulated ourselves on our efficient decision-making and that we kept our eyes on the upcoming marriage and not the distracting small details. With some angst, though, I associate that week of wedding preparation with Brooke's bat mitzvah party. We had held that celebration in a tent in our yard, and the next morning, before dawn, before she opened her gifts and we could relive the moment together, I allowed a limousine to carry me off to the airport for a flight to DC for our annual meeting.

Maybe that's when I began asking the Almighty to take care of my children as I was trying to take care of His.

Our Vilnius conference was only weeks away. With the political unpredictability and Lithuania still under the influence of the Soviets, I sent a memo to our executive committee, suggesting we reconsider, but my intrepid colleagues wanted to move ahead.

When I arrived in Moscow a couple of weeks later, black smoke still stained the White House.

Moscow, Vilnius, and Shavel

Maybe it was the same hopeful euphoria that brought down Dzerzhinsky's statue, but this time when we landed in Moscow, the bright September sunlight dispelled the city's perpetual gray. The changes were palpable. Thin scents of freedom were wafting through Russia. On the Arbat, English-speaking Russians hawked relics of a crumbling empire: metal miniatures of Lenin and Dzerzhinsky, red banners imprinted with the Cyrillic letters of the now-defunct CCCP, even newly made wallets with the letters of KGB. The Arbat's free market attracted tourists and merchants, artists and artisans. The White House, symbol of the Yeltsin democrats, was washed in light. But the dry dirt of Moscow rose from the city's ravaged streets, and the cost in rubles for the Arbat's little pretties exceeded what was in anybody's wallet.

On the streets of Moscow, I was infected by the presence of hope, ephemeral as it might have been. Leonid's friend, Ilya Zaslavsky, who was on Yeltsin's team, opened the doors of the Parliament for Micah, Leonid, and me. Walking through the halls of the White House, we were greeted by young Americans, Eastern Seaboard Ivy League types, working as parliamentarian aides. They buzzed around the halls, infused with optimism and purpose like that seen in the congressional buildings in DC. Their optimism was contagious, if fleeting. For that brief moment, there was vibrant hope for a new Russia, for its incipient democracy, for privatization, even capitalism. When I returned a few months later, that hope had already died.

Some of UCSJ's heavyweights had flown in for the conference: David Waksberg; June and Ron Daniels; Stephen Cohen, UCSJ Lawyers Committee chairman; and Donna Arzt, head of UCSJ's Legal Advocacy Center. Vladimir Matlin, from Voice of America radio, also joined us. We all met up in Moscow for briefings with our bureau, refuseniks, and former prisoners, then we took the overnight train to Vilnius, which had settled down in the aftermath of the attempted coup. The Vilnius Alternative Conference was cosponsored by UCSJ and the International Helsinki Federation and included the president of Lithuania, Vytautas Landsbergis. Emmanuel Zingeris, a former Jewish activist who had been named chairman of Lithuania's International Committee of the Parliament, presided over the meetings.

Representatives of our consortium of human rights organizations reported on continuing Soviet violations in respect to the official Moscow CSCE human rights conference that we were boycotting. Among the many issues addressed was that of prisoners – their continuing abuse, and the Soviets' failure to meet their obligation to change the penitentiary system. Political prisoners Yuri Massover, Samuel Rombe, Dmitri Berman, and the Bodners were still being held. Authorities refused us permission to visit them in the camps.

At our conference, we met an elderly Lithuanian Jew who had been collecting evidence of Nazi atrocities in Lithuania, facts long denied by the Soviets. Holocaust denial and the denial of collaboration was a hallmark of Soviet dogma. Consequently, Jewish refuseniks had focused on the Holocaust, identifying mass killing sites and commemorating the victims. My own family had lived and died in Lithuania. Some were among those murdered. Micah's grandparents also came from Lithuania. This elderly Jew took Micah, Leonid, and me to view a self-styled gallery of his collected photographs of Lithuania during the Holocaust, displayed on an apartment wall. A passionate docent, he recounted the barbarism of Lithuanians who were complicit with the Nazis. He reminded us that when the Soviets liberated Vilnius in 1940, they paved the streets with Jewish tombstones.

The photos threw me back to a time when Vilnius was Vilna, the great city of Jewish scholarship, the center for Jewish publishing and the home of the Gra, the famed Vilna Gaon, as well as the Vilna Shul. I wanted this man to take me to the city of Siauliai, Shavel in Yiddish, where my grandfather and great-grandparents had lived. He had recently discovered the Shavel cemetery and told us we could drive there and back in a day.

After visiting the site of the Vilna Shul, Micah and I wedged into the back seat of the man's small car and headed to Shavel. Leonid, in the front, translated. I felt like we were driving back in time. We passed no villages, gas stations, or rest stops. Occasionally we went by a dilapidated wooden shack that may or may not have had electricity or running water.

Finally, the man pulled the car up to the edge of a field bordered by a low stone wall and a solitary cottage. The field had gone wild. Tall grass blew in the wind. This was the Shavel cemetery, in use from the seventeenth century until the Soviets destroyed it. Somewhere in this field, my great-grandparents, the Bermans, were buried. I was standing on the ground where my family had said kaddish for Reb Dovid, Grandpa Charlie's father, and for his mother. Yet there were no headstones. There was nothing to indicate that this was a cemetery at all and not just another wild field. The Nazis had tried to erase our existence, chopping us off at our roots, exterminating generations of Jews. The Soviets tried to erase even the memory of our existence. In hundreds of shtetls like Shavel, Jewish lives, past and present, had been snuffed out. Micah, Leonid, and I headed in different directions, and I stumbled across the wild grass. Here and there I found a crumbled, thrown-over tombstone. In this field, my dream of finding my great-grandparents' graves vanished. There was no way I would ever find them. All I could take away were some pebbles from the site.

We drove on to Tels, where Micah's grandparents had lived, and where I think my grandfather must have learned at the great yeshiva. We parked in front of a nondescript, red-brick building, which our driver assured us was the site of the yeshiva. At the back, a door opened to a shoe factory. There was no indication that this had been one of the great, holy sites of Torah scholarship in Europe. Try though I might, I could not sense the holiness that must have been left behind.

In Shavel, I was searching for the imprint of our past that would stamp our future. I have come to understand that our history – the lives, hopes, values, and beliefs of those who came before us – is, in fact, a small but sturdy seed in each of us. When watered, that seed roots and springs to life. Our beloved children and grandchildren are evidence that both the Nazis and the Communists failed. Now I can only pray that each of them

will continue to strengthen their spiritual DNA so that they will be able
pass down what our grandparents and great-grandparents lived for but
also died for.

From Lithuania, Leonid, Micah, and I went back to Moscow to
hold press conferences based on the findings of the Vilnius Alternative
Conference. I reported, "The system is still collecting hostages. In the past,
the Soviets usually made concessions in advance of CSCE meetings, such
as releasing some long-term refuseniks. This time there was nothing."[1] We
urged the CSCE to call upon the Kremlin and each of the republics to
immediately allow all refuseniks to leave. We also brought our findings to
the NATO delegations. In spite of political changes, we had reams of documentary evidence of the continuing violations of the Helsinki accords and
the follow-up documents.

Leonid, Micah, and I met one afternoon with the head of the US delegation to the official Moscow human rights conference, Max Kampelman,
at an outdoor cafe. Max was a distinguished-looking, grey-haired diplomat with a familiarly Jewish face, a long State Department service record,
and a fine reputation that I considered marred by the fact that he had been
a conscientious objector during the war that nearly annihilated his people.
We were talking informally about human rights. Max said we couldn't set a
universal human rights standard for the Soviet Union. He was saying that
what is right for the United States is right for the United States, and what
is right for Russia is right for Russia. I nearly choked on my coffee. The US
delegation's role was to weigh Soviet compliance with the universal human
rights principles adopted by the Helsinki Final Act, an accord signed by
the Soviets. Our delegation head had just suggested that such a standard
could not be universally applied. It was moral relativism, and the outra-
geousness of it bounced in my head for weeks afterward. We expected the
United States to raise the issue of refuseniks with the Kremlin. Now we
wondered whether they would.

Several dozen refuseniks had the same worries. A group of them were
holding their own parallel meeting in a Moscow apartment. Svetlana
Sorkin, whose husband Roman was denied permission on the pretext of
having access to state secrets, bitterly noted that the State Department
declined to commit to their issues. "[Secretary of State James] Baker used

1.   Pamela Braun Cohen, press conference, Moscow, September 1991.

to meet with us when he came here, now we can't get his attention. What has changed?"[2] What had changed was that the world was ebullient with the hope of change, and the Jewish world was focused on the number of those leaving rather than the number of those refused.

Unintended Policy Consequences in Israel, and the End of the Soviet Union

From Moscow, I headed to Israel to meet Lenny, Brooke, Scott, and Josh for my niece's wedding, where I got my first glimpse of the effects of a policy gone wrong. A few former refuseniks, also wedding guests, greeted me warmly but with raw cynicism: *What was I doing in Moscow? Now, everyone can leave, and besides, this wave of emigration is flooding Israel with non-Jewish Ukrainians and Russians whose right of return is based on one Jewish grandparent.* Burning with frustration, I tried to make myself heard, but the music was too loud for them to hear and they weren't listening anyway. They were complaining about the consequence of the hard-fought battle that UCSJ had lost. In spite of our strongest objections, America had closed its gates except for family reunification cases. It was the Lishka, Israel's foreign ministry, the National Conference on Soviet Jewry, and their supporting Jewish bureaucracy that had closed the freedom of choice option. In doing so, they had set the stage for an influx of non-Jewish immigrants who would have chosen America but, with no other option, had come to Israel. I was enraged and silent.

Besides, there *were* still Jews in Russia, like the Sorkins, who were being refused. The much-touted official Moscow human rights conference hadn't helped them, and it hadn't helped alleviate the tragedy of people like Dmitri Berman, a Jew from Ukraine. Three years before, in August 1988, Dmitri had been waiting for permission when he was accused of knifing a Moldavian Soviet navy ensign at a cafe in the Bug River port of Nikolayev, Berman's hometown.

The twenty-eight-year-old factory worker was in prison for the sailor's murder. In nine courtroom appearances, Dmitri claimed innocence, but the investigator relentlessly demanded he confess. When he refused, they confined him in three psychiatric hospitals, forcibly gave him hallucinogenic drugs, and finally convicted him without evidence. David Leopold,

---

2.   Alexander Lesser, "The Forgotten Refuseniks," *Jerusalem Report*, October 3, 1991.

a Cleveland attorney on UCSJ's board who worked at our Moscow bureau, said, "This was never a murder case. This is a human rights case. Dimitri was framed from the beginning."[3]

Then suddenly, in an unlikely twist, the Ukrainian prosecutor dropped the case. Finally free, Dmitri proceeded with his emigration plans. Just days before he was to fly to Israel, he was informed that, on orders from Moscow, his case was to be reopened. Fleeing Ukraine, Dmitri went to Moscow and sought help from our bureau. Under Leonid and Micah's direction, the staff arranged for him to seek refuge at the Canadian embassy, where he was sheltered for more than a year while we mobilized our grassroots activists to urge Gorbachev to relent and let him go. Ultimately he left the embassy on his own, managed to disappear, and went to Israel.

At that time, Gorbachev's days were numbered. Four months after the attempted coup against him, on December 25, 1991, he resigned. The Union of Soviet Socialist Republics was no more. Russia was independent. Ukraine was independent. The captive Baltic nations, independent. But whether Russia and the other republics would move toward democracy or implode into chaos was still unknown.

---

3.   "Changes in USSR Mean Little Yet for Soviet Jew Accused of Murder," Jewish Telegraphic Agency (JTA), September 3, 1991.

PART FIVE

Endings and Beginnings

CHAPTER 26

Canaries of History: Moscow, Kiev, and Leningrad, Spring 1992

Russian-American Cooperation on Human Rights and Democracy

In spring 1992, just a few months after the dissolution of the Soviet Union, Micah, Leonid, and I traveled to Moscow for a UCSJ symposium, the Russian-American Cooperation on Human Rights and Democracy, convened with former dissidents, now democrats.

Given Russia's history, recent and distant, the promise of its transformation into a democracy that would provide a safe future for its Jews seemed uncertain. The ongoing exodus might eventually empty the country of most of its Jews, leaving the Russians to sort out their future for themselves. But at this point, not all Jews were leaving, especially the vast number of those who had never before admitted their Jewish identity on line five of their internal passports. For them, freedom of religion, freedom of speech, the right to demonstrate, and freedom of movement were the promises that they might live Jewish lives without persecution.

Although we remained focused on emigration and the persistent question of whether doors would remain open, under Leonid's direction, we brought together a consortium of human rights and Jewish activists to work together to push new governments to adopt guarantees for the full individual human rights agenda.

In the post-Soviet era, UCSJ was grappling again with the relationship between the Jewish emigration movement and the broader human rights and democratic movements. UCSJ's involvement with human rights groups had always been controversial in the eyes of Israel and the Jewish Establishment, which wanted an explicitly Jewish and Zionist agenda. The Kremlin's interests were also served by keeping these groups separate.

KGB was at its most ferocious when persecuting Jewish activists who participated in the human rights movement, like Sharansky.

Now UCSJ was trying to work to build safeguards for human rights in the developing republics, supporting our long-held position that individual human rights guarantees protect all minorities. At our conference in Moscow's Foreign Literature Library, addressing the most prominent Jewish and Russian activists, including Yelena Bonner, Larisa Bogoraz, and Father Gleb Yakunin, I restated UCSJ's position: "The struggle for human rights is the guiding principle behind UCSJ. It is essential for Jewish organizations to cooperate with human rights organizations since anti-Semitism is one of the first and earliest signs of fascism. The struggle against anti-Semitism is the struggle for the rights of all individuals. Once a totalitarian regime suppresses its Jews, it persecutes any manifestation of independent thought and dissent. Resistance to anti-Semitism has to begin at its first sign."[1]

The conference also looked at another issue gaining traction. Some, including local Jewish activists in the former Soviet republics, wanted special rights for national minorities. Alexander Podrabinek, a former political prisoner, a dissident, and also a Jew, made the point that exceptionalism spawns hostility. If the Jewish movement's mission – the right to leave a country and return – was structured in isolation from the broader human rights agenda, both the Jewish beneficiaries and their organizations would be isolated and spurned by the very movements driving reform. UCSJ held that identity need not be compromised in broader coalitions.

The conference gave UCSJ the privilege of honoring Yelena Bonner. The widow of Andrei Sakharov, Bonner was a giant in her own right. A commanding figure in her sixties, her salt-and-pepper hair pulled back severely in a bun, Bonner was the international icon of the human rights struggle. Under Stalin, her father had been arrested and shot, her mother sentenced to ten years of prison camp. A founding member of the Moscow Helsinki Group, her apartment had become the epicenter of the satellite of human rights groups and Western correspondents. She built a life of resistance. She and Sakharov had vigilantly defended emigration activists, attending many of their trials and sending information about the proceedings to the West.

---

1.   Pamela Braun Cohen, speech given at UCSJ conference, 1992, archives of Pamela Braun Cohen, American Jewish Historical Society, New York.

After an international campaign, the Kremlin let Bonner leave for medical treatment abroad. When the Kremlin barred Sakharov from accepting the Nobel Peace Prize in 1975, Bonner, already out of the country, went to Oslo to accept the award for him. Even after her husband's exile in 1980, the Kremlin continued to harass and denounce Bonner until they arrested her in 1984 for anti-Soviet agitation and propaganda. They sentenced her to five years of exile in Gorky. But by 1987, Gorbachev was showing a human face to the West and brought both of them back to Moscow. Two years later, Sakharov was dead.

Our symposium was an assembly of activists who were determined to use the moment to enact real change. Bonner pointed to the importance of international law in the process but warned that violence and discrimination against Jews still was rampant in the fifteen republics.

The conference was an important shift in the mindset of leaders of the Jewish, human rights, national, and ethnic movements. They acknowledged the primacy of human rights to the reorganization of a developing multinational society, and Podrabinek and others lauded UCSJ's contribution to that effort.[2]

UCSJ's Kiev Bureau and a Turning Point

Ukraine's human rights groups had been urging UCSJ to host a conference and open a Ukrainian-American Human Rights Bureau in Kiev along the lines of our bureau in Russia. After months of logistical wrangling, Leonid, Micah, and I headed to Kiev to mark the bureau's opening. In the fourteen years since Lenny and I had been there, a lot had changed, crucially Ukraine's independence. But one pernicious symbol remained: the statue of the viciously anti-Semitic Cossack, Bogdan Chmielnicki, triumphantly mounted on his stallion in Kiev's central Sophia Square. He led pogroms that slaughtered some three hundred thousand Jews between 1648 and 1653, murdering a staggering 30 percent of the Jewish population. That his statue was still standing should have served as a signal to the Jews of Ukraine to get out.

At the opening of the bureau, I said, "Activists want us to hold up a mirror to Ukrainian society, they want us to tell the truth: that there are no human rights here." With Chmielnicki in mind, I raised concern for

---

2. Alexander Podrabinek, "A Move in the Right Direction," *Express Chronicle* 17, April 21–28, 1992.

the rising anti-Semitism. "Jews have been likened to canaries in the coal mines. Miners used to take caged canaries into the mineshafts ahead of them because of their susceptibility to dangerous levels of humanly undetectable coal gas. If canaries died, the miners knew they had to clear out. In the history of civilization, Jews have been in the role of the canaries. How a nation treats its Jews forecasts what is to come."[3] The new sovereign nation of Ukraine should take heed of its canaries. We were calling on the republics to denounce Jew-hatred and protect their Jewish minority.

Two days of intensive briefings made it only too clear that the remaining problems of "poor relatives," secrecy refuseniks, and anti-Semitism in a framework without the rule of law demonstrated how removed the new republic was from securing legal protection for human rights. The deputy chairman of the parliament said what we all thought: "It will take many years to get across the idea that the individual is not less important than the big collective, and even more time for the idea to sink in that individual rights should be greater than collective rights, even national rights."[4]

Later in the week, I met the well-known Ukrainian Jewish poet Abram Katsnelson, who had written a poem and dedicated it to me, using the metaphor of canaries to express the tragic irony of Jewish history. Jews are the canaries of history. Maybe the first victims, never the last. The artist Adolf Goldman honored me also, with the gift of a painting. Written in Cyrillic, King Solomon's words of Ecclesiastes, or Kohelet, are descending from heaven and rooting in the soil. The gifts of these Jewish artists revealed the depth of their connection to our shared purpose.

Leonid had asked Dr. Semyon Gluzman to head our new Ukrainian-American Human Rights Bureau. A psychiatrist, Semyon had spent seven years in labor camps and three in Siberia for exposing the horrifically abusive psychiatric practice used to suppress political dissent.

It was a long few days. Leonid, Micah, and I were sitting with Semyon, who was always austerely pensive, in the living room of the apartment that housed our new Ukrainian bureau. As we sat around reviewing the meeting, a broad-framed, heavy-footed, middle-aged woman came into the apartment. She spoke to Semyon in Ukrainian, and then he turned to me and translated. She wanted to thank us for supporting her son. Her son

---

3.   Pamela Braun Cohen, speech given in Kiev, spring 1992.
4.   "Rights Groups Targeting Ukraine," *Forward*, May 15, 1992.

was Anatoly Marchenko, one of the best-known dissidents, who had spent more than twenty years of his life in prisons, labor camps, and internal exile, and who was the husband of Larisa Bogoraz. Marchenko had died in Chistopol Prison in 1986, while serving a ten-year term for anti-Soviet agitation and propaganda.

We were accompanying her to the door when she suddenly turned to me. She took a step toward me, lifted her gnarled fingers, and made the sign of the cross across my body. By the time I recovered from the shock, the door had closed behind her.

That night, when I finally closed the bedroom door behind me and got ready for bed, the woman's gesticulation followed me. I closed my eyes but couldn't sleep; her gesture, while intended as a blessing, was shattering. I felt I had been slapped hard across the face. Humiliation, embarrassment, were rising red. Who was I? What was I doing in Ukraine? Suddenly I heard the voice of my beloved deceased grandmother, my Nanny: "What are you doing in this land of pogroms – and just after Pesach? After Easter, when Jewish blood ran in the streets? Go home."

Spasms of unbidden thoughts broke into my consciousness. When could I leave? It was Friday night. Shabbat. I should have lit candles. Why didn't I? The great Jewish refuseniks, exemplars of Jewish leadership who had led the struggle for Jewish identity, whom I had helped and supported, had all left. They had left a vacuum. Now in Kiev there was no one left to light Friday night candles. And in their absence, I didn't. What kind of a Jewish leader was I? I, who questioned the qualities of authentic Jewish leadership? Who was I? I felt contaminated by my own sense of loss. I knew nothing about mikvah, but I wanted to purge myself.

It was as if this struggle for democratic, human rights principles in the new Russia, Ukraine, and Lithuania had revealed a gaping interior void. Struggling against anti-Semitism was legitimate, but the void created by the emigration of refuseniks whose identity had shaped my own left me off-balance. Much of my adult years had been spent working night and day for my people, helping them to emigrate and to live Jewish lives. But what made me a Jewish leader? At this point, how was I different from the Russian and Ukrainian dissidents and democrats – idealistic, good people who were born Jewish, but who were fighting for causes that couldn't be guaranteed to benefit their own people. What didn't I understand? It was like there was something just outside my line of vision that I knew was there but couldn't quite see.

I had defined identity in terms of the continuum of history, people-hood, survival, Israel. But beyond that, what was the substance? What was the foundation that it all was built on? Who was I? The old questions of my teenage years bubbled up to the surface. That night in Kiev, something snapped. Up until now, the sum total of my Jewish identity had been expressed through my support for those fighting to go to Israel and live Jewish lives. Now, with them gone, I didn't know who I was or what I was doing there.

I felt an abyss open inside me.

The Leningrad Duma

Our Kiev bureau established, Micah, Leonid and I took the train to Leningrad, where refuseniks were impatiently waiting on the platform. They offloaded our suitcases, grabbed a porter to stack them on his cart, and briskly shepherded us through the Leningradsky station to the street. We were late for the plenary session of the Leningrad Soviet (or Lensoviet, also known as the Duma), which, after a recent election, had a democratic majority.

It's a good thing I wasn't forewarned: on the way there, they told me I was expected to address the Duma. I don't know how many Jewish women in Russia's long history have ever addressed a legislative body – let alone a Jewish woman who also happened to be American. Scurrying so quickly, pushing into taxis, there was no time to register anxiety.

Except for factual briefings, I avoided extemporaneous speeches, so I was surprised by the scaling trills of anticipation I felt as the taxi maneuvered through Leningrad's streets. Here I would have the opportunity to be heard by some of the Russians who wanted to make changes.

The fact that the Duma had a human rights committee showed a remarkable change in the atmosphere. Its chairman, Yuri Ribakov, was a former dissident who had been arrested by KGB in 1976. I knew we shared common ground.

The taxi dropped us off at St. Isaac's Square, just across from the Blue Bridge. In front of us was the imposing Mariinsky Palace, now home to the Duma.

The deputies were already seated in descending rows by the time Leonid, Micah, and I arrived, rather breathlessly, in the chamber. No time for more than a cursory welcome, Ribakov led me to a raised podium. After a few words of introduction to the Duma members in Russian, Ribakov switched to English and presented me with a miniature copper sailing vessel on a small wooden block. It was a symbol of Leningrad, he said. Today, it sits on my kitchen desk together with the treasured medal Leonid presented me at our annual meeting in Moscow.

And so I spoke. I spoke as a Jew for all those Jews I was representing. I spoke in English, pausing while Leonid translated, but I spoke in the language these reformers understood, the language of human rights, the right to leave a country and return – not as an exception, but as a right guaranteed by law.

Perhaps it was Leonid's translation, which gave me time to craft my thoughts. I suspect it was a combination of Leonid's consummate diplomatic and oration skills and my passion that transmitted the core of our commitment. Whatever the case, the speech was greeted with enthusiastic applause.

CHAPTER 27

Yad l'Yad and Dinner at the White House, 1992

Pivoting to Meet New Needs

By the time the Soviet hammer-and-sickle flag was lowered at the Kremlin for the last time in December 1991, it was clear that Gorbachev's market reforms had been too little, too late. The desiccated economy, massive inflation, and bloated bureaucracy finally gave way to the national secessionist movements of the republics that had been clamoring at the USSR's gates. All fifteen Soviet republics were now independent. Along with the Soviet Union's political system, its social and economic infrastructure had also collapsed, and there was nothing to replace it. It was a tectonic shift that exposed vast, incalculable Jewish need.

Once illegal underground Jewish organizations had become officially registered. UCSJ's councils were tracking Jewish groups sprouting up out of the social rubble all over the former USSR, struggling to meet every imaginable need. At CASJ, Marillyn, Hetty, and Natasha were overwhelmed by the magnitude of requests in the aftermath of the vacated social systems. Activists in small towns in Russia and Ukraine told us heartbreaking stories of the crashing infrastructure that left elderly Jews, some Holocaust survivors, to decide between buying food or medicine, paying for heat or a burial plot. Many were alone, too elderly to emigrate. Simultaneously, an emerging interest in Judaism demanded massive infusions to fill the need from the ground up. And it all had to be exported, jump-started from the outside. Like our sister councils in the Bay Area, South Florida, Boston, and elsewhere, CASJ scrambled to find resources to assist.

UCSJ's mandate and specialization was Jewish emigration, freedom of movement. Over the years, council leaders had developed partnerships with Soviet Jewish activists, who were now taking the first steps to fill the vacuum in the wake of the Soviet collapse. By extension, their new challenges became ours. During the Soviet era we had provided religious and cultural assistance to refuseniks who were trapped against their will; now UCSJ's extensive grassroots network could be marshaled to support soup kitchens, meals on wheels, and aid to the elderly, and to assist activists in developing Jewish educational programs and social services. The challenge was colossal.

Piece by piece, the way forward became clear. The grassroots could be mobilized using the framework of our refusenik and prisoner adoption programs. By harnessing local Jewish institutional and communal resources, I was confident we could create a network of shared responsibility. Just as these groups had previously adopted refusenik cases, they could now adopt fledgling projects in the former Soviet Union. And so, at CASJ we gave birth to Yad l'Yad (hand to hand), a strategic innovation to mobilize the expertise and material resources of American synagogues and organizations to assist Jewish religious, social, communal, and cultural groups crawling out from under the rocks of the centralized communist state. Natasha Stonov's presence in Chicago was providential. As a Russian-speaking activist, she established and perpetuated connections between our American adopters and small cities where there were no English-speakers and where the need was hidden but enormous.

The Stonovs rolled up their sleeves and went to work. Marillyn and I brought together CASJ's social action and Soviet Jewry chairmen from local synagogues and organizations who were already emigration activists. At this Yad l'Yad seminar, we introduced an innovative concept to marshal their intervention. We asked that they reach out once again to establish a personal connection, a partnership, with contacts we assigned in various cities. The goal was to deliver material and medical assistance, educational materials and resources, to their adopted groups, depending on their needs. Soup kitchens were urgently needed. Medicines had to be collected and delivered, packages sent, and Jewish educators and rabbis dispatched.

At our follow-up Yad l'Yad meeting, CASJ's door opened to a woman whose dark, chin-length hair didn't conceal a pair of small earrings, one a Magen David, the other a Torah scroll. I pointed her out to Marillyn: "Someday this woman will be our successor." I wasn't wrong. Eventually, Susie Futterman, a local synagogue's Soviet Jewry chair, worked with Natasha and Marillyn to assume oversight and responsibility for the scores and scores of our Yad l'Yad projects. Eventually she succeeded Marillyn as the chair of CASJ.

Councils were overloaded with requests to meet an ever-growing need. At CASJ, Marillyn, Susie, and Natasha were consumed with finding synagogues to carry the burden of increasing requests from places like Mogilev, Chernivtsi, Minsk. CASJ was beginning to look like a cross between a pharmacy and a post office, filled with medicines, cartons, and packaging.

State Dinner for Boris Yeltsin

Desperately needing an escape, Lenny and I scheduled a trip to Prague, Budapest, and Vienna, and two luxurious weeks driving through northern Italy. It was our time to be alone together.

When the White House called, I presumed I was being invited to a human rights forum. But no, it was the White House social secretary. President Bush and his wife were extending an invitation to a state dinner at the White House for President Boris Yeltsin during their first summit. Realizing the dinner conflicted with our trip, I gingerly inquired whether UCSJ's national director could represent us. No, this is a personal invitation and invitations are not transferable.

For the next several days, Lenny and I relentlessly dissected the invitation. Surely invitations were being widely extended to donors and organizations. With hundreds if not thousands of guests, we'd be relegated to a secondary area with proceedings projected on screens. For that, we'd give up this opportunity to be together in Europe? It was too great a sacrifice. On second thought, it *was* a state dinner, and the first between the new Russia and the United States. It was a once-in-a-lifetime experience. So we decided to fly to Washington in the middle of the trip. I sent my new formal ball gown to Washington, and off we went to Eastern Europe.

The shops on Prague's busy Wenceslas Square were filled with tourists, locals, and pickpockets. I didn't notice immediately that my purse was lighter, but when I did, I discovered our airplane tickets, traveler's checks, and passports were gone. It was Friday afternoon. We were flying to Washington on Sunday. The state dinner was on Tuesday. Without passports, we were going nowhere.

Back at the hotel, Lenny frantically started making calls. We had two hours to get to the US embassy before it closed for the weekend. If we didn't make it, we'd have to wait until Monday for new passports and would miss the dinner. We needed passport pictures. Minutes were ticking away, and the once-in-a-lifetime experience we had once considered rejecting but now desperately wanted was slipping from our grasp. Rushing back to the square, our hearts stopped when we found the photographer's kiosk and he wasn't there. Minutes later, he showed up, and with pictures in hand, we taxied to the embassy. Thirty minutes before closing, they issued our new passports.

Next was navigating through the maze of purchasing agents, trying to make connections to Washington in time for the dinner. I was ready to throw in the towel, but Lenny stubbornly persisted. With outsize effort resulting in several sets of tickets, he got us our connection to Washington.

At the Willard Hotel, Tuesday dawned bright and hot, and we dressed, downed a coffee, and walked the few blocks to the White House for the official welcoming ceremony before the evening's events. Having been cleared for security in advance, we were led through the East Wing, past the First Lady's garden, onto the back lawn, where guests were milling. We were ushered to the designated area for the dinner guests, a small roped-off area about forty feet from the speaker's podium. Near us was the area reserved for members of the cabinet. One by one, they arrived: Secretary of State James Baker, chairman of the Joint Chiefs of Staff Colin Powell, and the others, along with the Secret Service. We were talking to the former chairman of PepsiCo, Donald Kendall, and the actress Betty White, when Condi Rice came over to greet us.

There was a buzz of excited expectation. A military parade, the contingent in full dress uniform, marched across the green, and the band signaled President and Mrs. Bush's approach with "Hail to the Chief."

Then a long, black limo pulled up, and the Russian president and his wife stepped out, greeted by an outburst of applause. The Bushes and Yeltsins approached the podium, waiting respectfully as the military band played the American and Russian national anthems, followed by a twenty-one-gun salute. Both presidents made their remarks, and the Old Guard Fife and Drum Corps marched past in revolutionary uniforms. It was thrilling.

That evening, in tuxedo and formal ball gown, Lenny and I walked to the White House. Lingering tourists might have wondered who we were, but in truth, the two of us were the only guests without celebrity status.

While we gathered with the other guests, waiting to be announced, NBC sportscaster and former NFL player Ahmad Rashad turned to me and apologetically said, "Excuse me, but I think you're standing on my wife's gown." Indeed I was.

We wandered into the library of American authors, then the room where presidents delivered radio addresses to the nation. Guests were arriving, Russian and American government officials, American commercial and banking executives, people who interfaced or wanted to interface with the new Moscow. There was excitement and expectation, heightened by the unpredictability of the moment, and we were wide-eyed from the glitter and glamour, the clothing and jewelry. I was jittery, nervous, trying desperately not to show it. Lenny and I periodically caught each other's eyes, signaling silently to each other. Was this really happening? Even Betty White confided to us that she was nervous. Condi Rice, always calm and regally elegant, took us over to the display cases lined with porcelain dinnerware sets used by the various presidents, and I wondered whether the antique Staffordshire Marillyn had donated was among them.

Then guests filed up the white marble staircase, picked up table assignments, and pooled expectantly. Soon it was our turn. Awaiting us was a young naval attaché, brilliant in formal whites, brass buttons gleaming, a sheathed saber clinging to his side. He proffered his arm and, with Lenny immediately in our wake, led me down the long, white-carpeted hallway past the orchestra. Again there was a pause as he asked how we wanted to be introduced. My heart was beating louder than the Mozart sonata. "Mr. and Mrs. Leonard Cohen," the loudspeaker boomed into a room of about fifty people. Every twenty seconds the loudspeaker broadcast the names of other guests: the secretary of state; Supreme Court justices; Sam Nunn, who was the chairman of the powerful Senate Committee on Armed Services; the presidents of Motorola and other companies; Arnold Scaasi, who created Mrs. Bush's purple, floor-length lace gown; representatives and senators. I looked around to see whether there were any other NGOs in the room. I didn't see any.

The president and Barbara Bush were in the reception line with Boris Yeltsin and his wife Naina, who looked stereotypically Soviet in brown. One by one, we were introduced. The First Lady, obviously well briefed, caught me off guard when she commented on my work for Soviet Jews. A military honor guard ushered Lenny and me down the red-carpeted corridor, past a musical ensemble, to the East Room, where my worst fear was realized: our table cards showed we were seated separately. In what I considered a well-earned reward for years of emotional and financial support for a wife who worked full time as an unsalaried volunteer, Lenny had been seated at the most prestigious table. He was seated with Russian Prime Minister Igor Gaidar, Vice President Dan Quayle, Colin Powell, and Dwayne Andreas of Archer-Daniels-Midland, with whom I had testified at the hearings on grain sales.

Mine was a working dinner. I was seated with Sergey Kovalev, chairman of the Russian Supreme Soviet Committee on Human Rights, whom I knew from Moscow. Also at my table were several corporate heads looking to expand into Russia, and I drew their attention to the fact that their commercial interests depended exclusively on Russia's advancement of the rule of law in all areas, especially the guarantees of human rights. I was also seated next to Dennis Ross, whom I knew from his role as Bush's director of policy planning at the State Department. Our conversation was interrupted by violinists serenading tableside, the formal table service, and finally by Yeltsin himself, who defiantly broke protocol and titillated the crowd by sweeping the wife of RJR Nabisco's chairman into his arms for an impromptu whirl between the tables. Yeltsin dominated the evening. Tanned, charismatic, and probably more than a bit tipsy, he broke through decades of Cold War relations, having announced he was cutting Russia's nuclear arsenals by one-third. He had charmed the Bushes, the press, and the nation. I wondered what he would do with his own country. After dessert, Lenny found me and admonished me to hurry – his new friend, Vice President Quayle, wanted to meet me.

We returned to our hotel close to midnight. Lenny recaptured his astonishment at being seated next to the vice president of the United States and the world's most powerful military figure, Colin Powell. He reminded Powell that it was because of his intervention that Micah and I were able to get our visas to travel to Russia in 1988. He also struck up conversations with Sam Skinner, the White House chief of staff. It was a glorious evening, and in the morning, we packed away our memories along with our formal clothing and flew off to Italy to make some more.

CHAPTER 28

Back to Central Asia, December 1992

Kyrgyzstan in the Dead of Winter

The reset that had broken the Soviet Union into pieces was playing itself out in Central Asia in a way that spelled the end of a thousand years of Jewish life.

In the former Soviet Muslim republics, an estimated quarter of a million Jews were particularly vulnerable and isolated, precariously feeling their way through the political and economic turmoil, interethnic violence, and anti-Semitism. Most were trying to put it all behind them, scaling mountains of obstacles to leave. The heads of the new republics were untested, unknown, and, in Central Asia, most were communist relics, suppressing the media and all opposition to establish control. Islam Karimov, president of Uzbekistan, was one of the worst, supporting the use of torture even in the judiciary.

Since our 1991 trip, reports about vigilante attacks on Jews in Uzbekistan had continued. Three men broke into the home of a Jewish family in Chilanzar, not far from Tashkent, beat several family members, and, with threats of more violence and anti-Semitic slurs, forced them to hand over fifty thousand rubles. A fifteen-year-old Jewish boy in Dushanbe, Tajikistan, was arrested, beaten in prison, threatened with rape and death.

Activists from Central Asia had been coming to our bureau staff in Moscow to explore ways to attract America's attention to the problems in their republics, especially those facing the Jews. So persistent were the requests that Leonid himself flew to Central Asia to consult with local Jewish activists. They urged UCSJ to convene a public human rights conference and establish a human rights bureau in Central Asia. Assuring us that Jews would benefit from the dialogue, they also believed the international press attention and conference reports would yield a more realistic policy from the US State Department. Most important, the resulting attention would light a fire under our drive to front-load all the remaining separated families into the States and to push the Israelis to add more flights to airlift Jews out of danger.

Neither the American nor Israeli government seemed adequately responsive to the plight of Jews in Central Asia. Besides its interest in opening new diplomatic relations with the former Soviet republics, Israel's housing shortages were challenging its ability to accommodate the influx of new immigrants. On the American side, the Jewish organizational infrastructure was already stretched to meet the absorption costs of new immigrants in both Israel and the United States. Rabbi Yechiel Eckstein, the head of the International Fellowship of Christians and Jews, launched a televised fundraising campaign appealing to Christians to help fund a historic return of beleaguered Jews from the troubled Central Asian republics to Israel. We understood that these appeals were needed because Israel and American Jewry were not doing enough to evacuate Central Asian Jews.

With the bureau in Moscow and Jewish activists in Central Asia, Leonid was putting the pieces together. By November, we were ready to set in motion our plan for a Central Asian conference on human rights.

I dreaded going back to Central Asia, and Kyrgyzstan in the dead of winter wasn't exactly on my bucket list. I packed whatever could insulate me from the cold: long underwear, thick wool socks, and a heavy pair of Dr. Martens black oxfords. So much for fashion. I also took my mandatory wire immersion burner for instant coffee and a box of granola to eat dry in the mornings. I couldn't count on much else.

Micah and I made it through the obstacle course at Sheremetyevo without incident on a frigid dark night and checked into the Hotel Moskva, where Leonid was already waiting with our briefing instructions. With us was Bay Area activist Ron Naymark, Leonid's determined, protective gray shadow. Ron's father was Sherman Naymark, the naval captain who had developed the engine for the USS *Nautilus*, the first nuclear-powered submarine.

Our plane sat on the tarmac on the first day of December in arctic cold. Naymark, an aeronautics expert with degrees in aerospace, mechanical, and nuclear engineering, was glued to his window surveilling the wings of our plane in quiet alarm. Noticeably pale, he turned to me across the aisle. The wings had iced over. There was no de-icing equipment on the tarmac. It would be impossible to take off with so much ice on the wings. He was panicked, and his panic was contagious. This flight was going down. As the plane rattled down the runway, I was in high terror, begging God: *Please, we are on this flight to help Your children. God, please save us, please hold this plane steady in the air, carry us to do our job.*

Several hours later, our white-knuckle flight passed over staggering panoramas of snow-covered peaks as we approached Kyrgyzstan's Ala-Too and Tien Shan mountain ranges. When we landed, it was already dark, and we were taken to Bishkek's Ala-Too Hotel. The stripped-down reception area should have given us a hint. The receptionist who checked us in made no pretense of even the most basic guest services. It was the second clue I missed. By the time I figured it out, it was too late: I was already in my room and wasn't leaving it. The guest rooms were used as much for servicing tourists as for male clients, who throughout a very long night banged drunkenly on the doors on my floor, calling for their turn in a Kyrgyz that even I understood.

Grateful to have survived both the flight and the night, in the morning I met Micah and Leonid in a surprisingly cheerful cafe with President Askar Akayev's aide. Tursembek Akhunov looked like an academic. He was a small, tanned man speaking Oxford-accented English, wearing outsize square glasses, a snappy tweed sports jacket, and an open-collared white shirt. He was casually friendly, chatting amiably over coffee about the changes in Kyrgyzstan. I managed to keep my composure when he disclosed that his grandfather had killed his granddaughter with his own hands for a prohibited romantic relationship. He assured us that changes in the country's norms precluded such behavior today. Before we separated, he gave me a charming ceramic figurine dressed in traditional Kyrgyz costume as a symbol of welcome to Kyrgyzstan.

For a sliver of time, Kyrgyzstan offered some fitful hope for Central Asian Jewish and human rights activists. After the fall of the Soviet empire, it elected as president a physicist, the head of the republic's Academy of Sciences. At first a democrat, Askar Akayev's early reforms were attracting millions in foreign aid and US State Department advisors. When UCSJ, our Moscow bureau, and a local human rights consortium had approached him about our conference, Human Rights and the Fate of Nations, he offered to host the conference in Bishkek. Bishkek had interesting demographics, with an astounding 10 percent Jewish population. The rest was Russian or Ukrainian.

The night after our arrival, President Akayev held a reception for us in the presidential residence. About fifteen or twenty of us were led to a starkly undecorated, cavernous ballroom that looked as if it had been resurrected from decades of disuse to welcome us. We were all seated at a long table that seemed diminished by the massive size of the room. In the center sat the round-faced, bald president, who warmly welcomed our delegation and the local human rights activists. At the far end was an *alte Yid*, an old Jewish man with a long white beard, wearing the traditional black velvet yarmulke, white shirt, and black jacket. He seemed paradoxically out of place in the mix of Western Jewish activists and indigenous Central Asian human rights representatives. He was introduced as Akayev's advisor. I wondered, was he the "court Jew," the *shtadlan*? Was he a showpiece for us? But he disappeared before I could talk to him. He was an enigma, like so much in Central Asia.

House Arrests, an Abduction, and Our Escape over the Mountains

In the auditorium the next morning, as delegates were taking their seats, I noticed that Leonid was visibly disturbed. He had learned that Jews from nearby republics of Uzbekistan and Kazakhstan who were on their way to Bishkek for our conference had been physically removed from trains. Some Jews, apprehended at the Kyrgyzstan border, had been detained and then placed under house arrest.

In spite of our anxiety, we had to launch the proceedings. Participants were equipped with headphones for instantaneous translation. Akayev led off the line-up of speakers, welcoming over 250 participants from at least eight nations, including the United States, and was followed by other Kyrgyz officials. Leonid spoke, announcing the first reports of the Jews who had been detained and placed under arrest. Then I spoke, addressing an audience of mostly Muslim men, as almost all of the Jews had been prevented from entering the country. From the podium, I asked them what I thought they must be thinking: What was a woman – a Jewish woman – doing at a conference filled with mostly Muslim men, speaking about the absolute need to secure under law and in practice the fundamental rights of all men and women: freedom of speech, religion, press, the right to assemble, and the right to leave one's country and return?

I spoke about the celebration of diversity and about the issues we had in common – mutual respect and the guarantees of human rights grounded in law. I was unprepared for what came next. Leaving the auditorium after the program, scores of these men were clapping their hands rhythmically. They burst into a spontaneous dance, accompanying me out of the hall. A few took my hands for me to join them. I was honestly afraid they might put me on their shoulders and carry me out. There were unrestrained smiles of appreciation. Never before or since have I had such a euphoric reaction to a talk. Decades later, when someone accused me of Islamophobia because of my defense of Israel and concerns about terrorism and violent anti-Semitism in America, I fantasized an instant replay video of that moment, when Muslim men came together with a Jewish woman to celebrate diversity and protect fundamental rights.

In stark contrast to the jubilation of that moment, the day wore on with sporadic reports of more house arrests – all Jews prevented from coming into Kyrgyzstan. We had to get the reports out to the West, so Leonid called a press conference with reporters from Radio Free Europe and *Moscow News*, Russia's only independent paper. And we knew our embassy in Kyrgyzstan was reporting back to the State Department. These flagrant, provocative detentions were bold illustrations of how far Uzbekistan and Kazakhstan would go to suppress Jewish involvement in our conference. Meanwhile, speakers at the conference continually recited the names of those who had been detained and prevented from participating in this significant first: a human rights conference in Central Asia.

It was the end of the final day of the conference that had addressed a long menu of human rights concerns in Kyrgyzstan and neighboring republics, especially the issue of scores of Jews who had been denied the right to travel to the conference and were subsequently arrested. Leonid was deftly putting off reporters waiting for a press conference. It wasn't going to start without Abdumanov Pulatov, who, we planned to announce, was to head UCSJ's new Central Asian human rights bureau. A young human rights activist and democrat from Uzbekistan, Pulatov had helped Leonid put together the conference and bring in the top governmental and nongovernmental participants. He was bronzed, slight in stature, with enviably chiseled cheekbones and a wide, open smile. His equanimity belied an inner intensity. I liked him from the first. He was Muslim, married with small children, and had a long history of human rights activity. And he was late for our press conference.

With the press corps increasingly impatient, anxious to return to Moscow, Leonid sent scouts to find Pulatov. His absence was out of character, as he was exactingly punctual. Leonid, Micah, and I waited, trying to mask our rising concern. Then I saw Leonid huddling with a couple of men, whispering in Russian. Reading their faces, my heart sank. Reports had come in that Pulatov had been spotted in the parking lot where we were holding our press conference. He had been dragged into a waiting white van, which then sped off. There were no license plates.

I tried assembling the pieces, but they were scrambled, nothing fit. The Kyrgyz president himself hosted the very conference Pulatov had organized. Would an oppositional movement try to discredit the president by assaulting his event's coordinator in broad daylight? Weren't they constrained by the fear they would be observed? Every theoretical conjecture was met by an opposing one. Was this a provocation, a setup? But by whom? Communists? Like everything unpredictable, it took a while to sink in. We were in denial, thinking, any minute he'll walk in with a credible explanation, and we'll laugh at ourselves and our nervous conjectures. But meanwhile, Pulatov wasn't showing up.

Leonid was trying to make sense of it all. He talked to government officials and activists, but there were too many missing pieces. How was it possible that government security didn't know what had happened? Assuming the worst, Leonid called the minister of internal affairs, who gave him his absolute assurance that the van carrying Pulatov would be stopped by the border guards and would not be permitted out of Kyrgyzstan. We just had to wait.

Somehow, Leonid pulled himself together for the press conference. Then, drenched in miserable silence, Leonid, Micah, and I went back to the hotel. As we arrived, a big black ZIL pulled up to the curb behind us. Tursembek, the smartly dressed aide who had welcomed us so warmly on that first morning, left his driver and got out of the car. It was freezing, a December afternoon, already growing dark. The three of us stood together on the sidewalk watching him approach us. His entire persona was transformed: the formerly open and friendly diplomat now spoke exclusively to Leonid, in Russian. Micah and I, coats flapping in the furious wind, unsuccessfully tried to extract the meaning behind the rapid staccato of Tursembek's words and his terse intonation. Message delivered to Leonid, Tursembek turned back in the wind to his car, without even a nod of good-bye to Micah or me.

In the lobby, Leonid filled us in. Abdumanov had been kidnapped. The Kyrgyz didn't stop the van at the border as Leonid had been promised. Tursembek had also said that Bishkek wasn't safe for us either. We had to leave Kyrgyzstan immediately. President Akayev was sending a car and driver to take us out.

Ron Naymark, Micah, Leonid, and I threw our suitcases into the trunk of the president's car just as night fell on Bishkek. Micah got into the front, next to the driver, who spoke no English, and I squeezed between Leonid and Ron in the backseat with a view of the mute driver's uniformed arm guiding the steering wheel, and too clear a view of the car's front window.

The long hood of the black ZIL started its ascent into the mountains just as gigantic flakes of snow began to cascade out of a pitch-black sky. Soon, the narrow road was covered. Micah had given in to a threatening cold and was asleep, his heavy regular breathing the only sound other than the motor. On my left, Leonid finally gave in to exhaustion. Only Ron and I kept watch. Our eyes never left the front windshield. Through the snow-storm, we watched the mountains grow steeper, huge inclines guarding each side of the road. There were no gas stations, no signs of civilization. There were no lights, no guardrails, and if there were lane markings, the snow had long covered them. Not that it mattered: there was no oncoming traffic. In fact, there were no other cars, no other headlights to perme-ate the night. It felt like we were the last people in the world, on a night so black it seemed the sun might never penetrate it. The snow piled ever higher. And Ron and I watched.

Not bothering to conceal his anxiety, Ron nudged me and whispered to ask me to wake Leonid to tell the driver in Russian to slow down. But I didn't want to wake him. Mustering a confidence I didn't feel, I did my best to reassure Ron we'd be all right.

Ron and I continued our watch. A while later, Ron again whispered, begging me to ask Leonid to speak to the driver. I attempted again to assure Ron. The driver continued at an inadvisable speed, negotiating steep and icy passes, with the only light coming from our headlights. Voicing a rising panic that mirrored my own, Ron again poked me to wake Leonid. Leonid, breathing in peaceful tranquility, couldn't be awakened. Micah snored quietly, oblivious.

And so Ron and I were on high alert, eyes on the snow-cloaked road, muscles tight, prepared for the tailspin that would catapult us a thousand feet into nothingness, where we would be lost forever.

Four endless hours later, the driver pulled into Alma Ata, Kazakhstan.

The hotel lobby was warm and brightly lit, with a real reception desk, a welcome change from the unsavory character of the Ala-Too Hotel. I called Lenny immediately from the phone booth in the lobby, to let him know where I was and assure him that we were safe, in case he heard any news broadcasts. But the instant I told him we were in Kazakhstan, the line was cut. Desperately, I tried again, but the line was dead. All the phone lines in the hotel had been cut. Something bigger than we had imagined was happening.

It started to dawn on us that Pulatov's abductors might have made border crossings that would have required the consent of multiple republics. Micah went out to find a public phone booth to call William Courtney, the American ambassador, who told us to come to the embassy first thing in the morning.

I was exhausted and worried, desperate for this day to end, when a group of Central Asian men burst into the lobby. Speaking rapid-fire Russian, clearly frightened, they told Leonid that they were afraid of being arrested in Bishkek. They had fled, and more people were coming. How did they know where we were staying? None of us knew who was moving the chess pieces, nor could any of us predict the next move. Would one of us be targeted next?

Concerned for my safety in the midst of this chaos, Micah spent the night in a chair outside my room. It was a good decision. Not long after, more escapees arrived, pounding on my door, frightened and looking for help.

In the morning, Ambassador Courtney opened the embassy to our needs, turning over desks, fax machines, and secure phone lines for calls to our families and then to the congressional Helsinki Commission and other members of Congress. Leonid, Micah, and I debriefed the State Department in DC about the detention of Jews from Kazakhstan and Uzbekistan and reported the abduction of Pulatov. We spent the day writing reports, faxing, making calls.

As new information trickled in, the puzzle pieces assembled to make an orderly picture. Karimov, the president of Uzbekistan, had issued a warrant for Pulatov's arrest. The Kyrgyz minister of internal affairs, who had assured Leonid that the van would be stopped at the border, later revised his statement, saying that the van had already crossed the border before he could stop it. In fact, at the time of their initial assurance, the van could only have been twenty or thirty miles from Bishkek. Karimov must have asked Akayev for his consent to let the van pass across the Kyrgyz border. Akayev apparently acquiesced, the border guards let the van through, and it traveled two hundred miles to bring its human cargo, Pulatov and two other human rights monitors, to a prison in Tashkent, Uzbekistan.

The host of our human rights conference was a conspirator in the illegal arrest of the organizer of that conference. Kyrgyzstan's Ministry of Internal Affairs later said it permitted Pulatov's abduction under an agreement between the two countries that allowed the extraterritorial arrest of criminals. By cutting the phone lines at our hotel, the Kazakh government revealed its hand in the conspiracy. After widespread criticism from UCSJ and the press, the Kyrgyz ministry later tried to whitewash its behavior, claiming it might have acted differently had it known there was a human rights dimension to Pulatov's arrest.

Even before we arrived back in the States, UCSJ began working on Pulatov's release. In January, he was freed from prison. He flew to Chicago, where a local attorney working with CASJ arranged for his refugee status. UCSJ hired him to work in our Washington office to operate our human rights division.

At Odds with the Establishment

In spite of the chaos at the end of our conference, we knew we had left in place an infrastructure for ongoing human rights advocacy. Not long after, Leonid appointed Evgeny Zhovtis, a lawyer who had spent many years in human rights activity, to head UCSJ's Kazakhstan-American Bureau on Human Rights and Rule of Law. Leonid, UCSJ's foreign minister par excellence, continued to oversee all the bureaus. By 1993, UCSJ was operating human rights bureaus in Russia, Ukraine, Kyrgyzstan, and Kazakhstan, while Micah and I continually tried to raise funds for an increasingly wider operation.

While UCSJ was working in one direction, the Jewish Establishment took a step in another. In the summer of 1993, the Conference of Presidents announced a reception, cosponsored by the Israeli mission at the United Nations and the National Conference on Soviet Jewry, honoring the presidents of several Central Asian republics in recognition of their new diplomatic relations with Israel. It included Uzbekistan and Tajikistan, among the worst human rights abusers. Though a member of the Conference of Presidents, UCSJ was not consulted. Their failure to consult with the largest grassroots movement working with and on behalf of Jews in the former Soviet Union elicited strong reactions from our board. But that was far from the only problem.

Israel was pursuing its national interests in furthering these diplomatic relations with the newly independent republics. But pulling in American Jewish umbrella organizations, especially one that ostensibly carried a Soviet Jewry brief, was objectionable. It was unacceptable for Jewish organizations claiming to advocate for Central Asian Jews to simultaneously honor dictators who failed to protect them. Though National Conference claimed the reception wasn't an endorsement of the republics' policies, we maintained that these human rights–abusing governments "should not be seen as having 'friendly relations' with the American Jewish community."[1] In a statement to the press, David Waksberg pointed out, "They [Conference of Presidents] offered to raise human rights issues at the reception, which we thought was a constructive response, [but] they didn't."[2] As a result, at a press conference UCSJ announced our resignation in protest from the Conference of Presidents.

---

1. "Group Quits Conference of Presidents in Protest over a Diplomatic Reception," Jewish Telegraphic Agency (JTA), July 13, 1993.

2. *Jewish Bulletin of Northern California*, July 16, 1993.

CHAPTER 29

Transitions, 1993

Unraveling Mysteries

It was a beautiful summer afternoon. I was at home, working on an article on human rights for a Central Asian Jewish newspaper, and I was curious about what the Torah might say about the subject. Apparently, the troubling episode in Kiev was still working on my subconscious, pulling me to evaluate my activity in terms of classical Jewish thought, whatever that meant. I knew the Jewish maxim that to save one life was to save an entire world, but I wondered what the Torah says about human rights or the struggle to achieve them. I went to our Jewish book collection and began a hunt through the indexes, picking up one volume after another, when I came upon a book I didn't recognize. I opened the cover and found two inscriptions on the flyleaf. One was dated 1981 and signed by Rabbi Zechariah Fendel, the book's author. He had added "with best wishes" in English. I was intrigued. There were more words in Hebrew, but I couldn't read them.

I didn't know Rabbi Fendel. In truth, I didn't even recognize his name. I couldn't piece it together. An insatiable collector of Russian and Jewish books, I know every volume in my library and where I found them. But not this one. I wracked my memory.

The second inscription deepened the mystery. On the facing page, in a strong, determined, European script, was a note dated June 30, 1984: "To Josh: One of the reasons our people survived is because they were helping each other in need, and your parents are the best example of this tradition. GO ON." It was signed: "With love, Mike."

Mike? Who was Mike? It certainly wasn't the handwriting of my brother-in-law Michael. I didn't know other Mikes.

"To Josh?" Was he referring to our son, Josh? Some other Josh? It's a common Jewish name.

Unable to resolve the puzzle about the mysterious book, I set it aside and resumed my non-productive hunt through the indexes, with rising frustration that was exacerbated by the intrusion of the telephone.

The person on the phone identified himself as Rabbi Ezra Belsky. Linda Opper's daughter had recommended that he call me, and he asked if I wanted to learn with him. I wasn't about to turn down one-on-one learning with an expert. Seizing the opportunity, I asked if he knew what the Torah had to say about human rights. He assured me we could discuss it when we met. I asked Marillyn to join us. Her razor-sharp intellect and open, questioning mind would be drawn to whatever new concepts he might offer.

Meticulous in a pressed white shirt and black suit, wearing a smart Borsalino hat, Rabbi Belsky sat with the two of us in CASJ's conference room and asked why we wanted to learn.

I inhaled deeply. Where to begin? The world was upside down. In his speech during his historic visit to Denver, Pope John Paul II didn't raise the hideous crimes of Serbia's Slobodan Milosevic during the recent Yugoslavian war. Though grisly images of Bosnian Muslims in concentration camps were broadcast nightly, there was no protest, not even from Christian leaders. It distressed me that, again, the world was silent. Again, apathy. Where were the world's leaders who had echoed the Jewish call "never again?" Did history count for nothing?

Rabbi Belsky's question once again brought to mind the lonely echo of that night when I felt like a lost Jew in Kiev – what did it mean to be a Jew? The question couldn't be silenced. It only added to those I had struggled with for years.

"God created the world," I answered, "but He made a terrible mistake when He created humanity. A humanity without leaders to guide us? Where are our authentic, moral, religious Jewish leaders?"

The old question. We volunteers had struggled with all our might to ensure the survival of our people, through emigration and in securing the right to live as Jews without persecution. In that effort, we had found few religious leaders in America ready to speak out. The greatest leaders I encountered – in fact, the greatest Jews of my generation – were those hidden heroes forged by refusal.

He answered instantly. "If you believe God created the world, don't you think He had a plan? Why not reserve judgment until you read the plan?"

And so Rabbi Belsky introduced Marillyn and me to "the plan": the plan was Torah, which instructs us how to live. Once I had struggled to read an edition of the Five Books of Moses, but without commentary, it read like Aesop's fables. Rabbi Belsky recommended the Chumash with Rabbi Samson Raphael Hirsch's commentaries, and I began spending long Shabbos afternoons grappling with Rabbi Hirsch. I needed a Hebrew dictionary, but first I needed to learn the Hebrew alphabet. From a *machberet* I found in Josh's room, I taught myself the aleph-bet and looked up my first pivotal Hebrew words in Rabbi Hirsch's commentary. Step by step, the misty film cleared from the lens. I began to see with unexpected clarity that the world revealed a breathtaking symmetry. A hidden reality emerged. I began to understand that life is not haphazard. Nothing is accidental, nothing random, nothing driven by chance. Everything and everyone, every act and every thought, is fraught with meaning and purpose and drives consequence. And, as the saying goes, God is in the details. Rabbi Belsky had appeared at exactly the right time, to provide answers to questions I had asked for most of my life.

I was reminded of a remarkable story Rabbi Yaakov Bleich, the chief rabbi of Ukraine, had once told me. He recounted a trip to post–Soviet Union Ukraine with Rabbi Kook, the chief rabbi of Rehovot. They went to Uman, where Rabbi Nachman of Breslov was buried. Though in later years, tens of thousands of Jews would pour into Uman every Rosh Hashanah, back then, the site was nearly forgotten except for the few Breslov Chasidim who came to pray at his grave.

Rabbi Bleich hoped to find an indication that some Jews might still live in Uman. A Ukrainian they stopped to question directed them to a small house, not far away. An old man opened the door, his eyes widening in astonishment at the sight of two bearded, black-frocked men with black hats, clearly from a time gone by. Tentatively, he let them in, but in his face was the question, what do you want with me? The awkward moment dissolved in Bleich's enveloping warmth.

After a few moments, Rabbi Bleich asked if the man had any *seforim*, any Jewish books. The old man went to his shelf and returned with a prayer book, the pages frayed and yellowed. His gnarled fingers turned the pages, and he looked up, helplessly. "It was my father's. I can't read it." Rabbi Bleich turned to Shema Yisrael, pointed to the enlarged print, and gently asked the old man to repeat the words after him, one by one. When

Rabbi Bleich looked up, tears were running down the old man's face as he said, over and over, "I remember. I remember."

I was like that old man. My grandfather's prayer books were on my bookshelves, too, and I also couldn't read them. In the beginning of my studies, as the week was ending and he was preparing for Shabbos, I once told Rabbi Belsky that Fridays brought me a wave of nostalgia. "Nostalgia?" he questioned. "How can you feel nostalgia for something you never had?" But I felt it. Buried in the recesses of my subconscious was a rich Jewish treasure chest that I longed to pry open.

Although I couldn't identify it at first, my learning had begun to reorient my views and to fill the void that had become so apparent in Kiev. Lenny and I began questioning whether our lives conformed to the truths we were confronting. We had long been schooled in the power to change by men and women who risked everything for what they believed, and we began making choices that included Sabbath observance. We began to be aware of a certain instant late on Fridays when light seemed to alter, when time itself altered, creating a distinct separation from the rest of the week. It was time, drenched in holiness. Somewhere in my DNA, there was a residual spark of what my great-grandfathers and great-grandmothers had experienced but could not pass down. It was what I realized I had been searching for at the cemetery in Shavel and why I had been so devastated when I couldn't find it. Now Lenny and I were reclaiming it. It was ours. We were living it, breathing it, and praying it wasn't too late to pass down what we were given at Sinai to our children and grandchildren.

Misha Edelman

Several months later, making room on my overcrowded bookshelves, I pulled out that mysterious volume written by Rabbi Fendel and took a closer look at it: *Legacy of Sinai: A History of Torah Transmission, with World Backgrounds; From Creation to the Close of the Geonic Era.* Remarkable. Skimming through, I was astounded to see the transmission of Torah documented in a written record, from generation to generation, all the way back to Sinai, passing from teacher to disciple, to our present generation.

What a fascinating little book, sitting on my shelves all these years, apparently just waiting for the right moment to leap down into my hands.

Even as I was pulled into its pages and into history, the mystery of the inscription from "Mike" continued to be unsettling. Soon the book and the mystery were once again shelved, until one day when I was searching through photographs taken years earlier in Jerusalem, at Josh's bar mitzvah, summer of 1984. Suddenly Misha Edelman's picture leaped out at me: Misha, at Josh's bar mitzvah party, dancing.

Misha had come into our life in 1980, when he came from Israel to our annual meeting in Washington. Misha was a big, Kojak-skulled hulk of a man who chanted Kiddush with a haunting sweetness that hung over the room. He briefed us on the realities facing former Soviet Jews trying to live and work in Israel and regaled us with jokes deriding the Soviets and communism:

> It's October 1980 and the phone rings in a Moscow apartment.
>
> "Alexander Yefimovitch? I'm calling to inform you that the automobile you ordered last week will be delivered to you on October 15, 1991, in the morning."
>
> "October 15, 1991? I'm sorry, that's impossible. It will have to be delivered in the afternoon: I've got the plumber coming in the morning!"

Misha was born and grew up in Riga when it was blooming with Jewish schools, shuls, and Yiddishkeit. When the Nazis invaded Latvia, he was working on a merchant ship heading toward Europe. The Nazis boarded his ship and arrested the crew. Misha, managing to hide his Jewish identity, was held as a prisoner of war for four years. When the war was over and he returned to Riga, it was to another world. Everything was gone, even his wife and children. Misha began again. He married Feiga, raised a family, and then began the struggle to leave for Israel, finding himself and his family for many years in the Kafkaesque world of refusal before finally receiving permission in 1978.

Misha was the essence of contradiction. He wasn't tall, but his massive, craggy appearance occupied substantial space, belying a sweet and gentle nature. During one of several visits to our home, he wanted to prepare for us the gefilte fish that his mother and grandmother had made in Riga for Shabbat. At the grocery, this man who looked like a tough dockworker artfully presided over the ordering and filleting of the fish. In our kitchen, wearing my one-piece apron, he used his huge hands with the dexterity of a violinist to chop, mix, and finally stuff the fish into its moist, delicate skin, lovingly laying the pieces into the fish soup that he colored with beets. It tasted of pre-war Riga.

In the several times Marillyn and I brought Misha to Chicago to speak, he captivated his listeners as he did me. On the way to speaking engagements, he lovingly sketched the scenes of his youth in a lost Riga, the center of Jewish learning that gave rise to Torah scholars, so rich in Yiddishkeit. Somehow I sensed that it was my loss, too. After he left, he would send letters filled with jokes and puzzles for our children.

There was a grievous sense of loss when we learned that he had died. Misha gave us so much when he was alive.

Finally, with that photograph of Misha dancing at Josh's bar mitzvah, I understood. The mysterious book on my shelf was a gift to Josh from a wondrous man, filled with goodness, a man born Moishe in Riga, who became Misha under the Soviets after the Holocaust, and who had become Mike in his message to Josh.

This precious book, inscribed by the author, ended up in the hands of Misha Edelman, who signed it over to Josh for his bar mitzvah and delivered it to me just when I was looking for it. Misha continued to give, even after he was gone.

Some people call that a coincidence.

Warsaw and Kiev

In October 1993, Micah and I traveled to Poland for the Warsaw CSCE meeting. After I gave a talk at one of the working sessions on the role of NGOs, we met with various NGOs and delegations, but the atmosphere for human rights discussion, just as it had been in Geneva in 1991, was clouded by a focus on international dispute settlement, mediation, and conciliation.

At the end of the conference, Micah and I stepped into a past that hung over our generation like a heavy pall. Within the walls of what had been the Warsaw ghetto, we walked on the fallen leaves among teetering headstones at the Jewish cemetery. Each lost in our own dark thoughts, we went to the *umschlagplatz* on Stawki Street, where the Nazis herded more than 300,000 Jews onto the cattle cars that carried them to the gas chambers, decimating the largest Jewish community in Europe.

After a briefing at the synagogue, we went to the famed site of Mila 18, a command bunker during the Warsaw Ghetto uprising. How often had I invoked those resistance fighters in my talks, reminding listeners that in 1943, Mordechai Anielewicz and the others were unknown to us. But today, in our struggle, we know the names of Yosef Mendelevich and Sylva Zalmanson and the other Leningrad trial defendants. It was a kind of mantra.

It was a short flight to Kiev for consultations at our Kiev bureau with two Jewish Ukrainian former prisoners, our bureau chief Semyon Gluzman and Josef Zissels. Both were remaining in Ukraine to take on leadership roles – Gluzman to advance the rule of law, and Zissels to develop communal institutions for Jews who weren't planning to emigrate.

Both knew UCSJ's record. They had firsthand knowledge of how our council leaders had turned their reports of human rights violations into weapons of protest and public advocacy. They understood that our crack team of volunteers had turned hairline cracks in the Iron Curtain into fissures, until the whole structure collapsed on itself.

Disintegration had created a new agenda for Jewish survival, and our Yad l'Yad initiative was a natural progression from the model of case-by-case refusenik advocacy to community-to-community social advocacy. Gluzman and Zissels laid out the broad spectrum of Jewish need throughout all of Ukraine. Micah, Leonid, and I reported how Yad l'Yad was confronting that need by marshaling American synagogues to support projects in both Ukraine and Russia. We described Yad l'Yad as the machinery to build the new infrastructure to prevent Jews from falling through the cracks.

Jews who were staying hadn't experienced the crucible of refusal, where so many refuseniks had forged their Jewish identity. Many, if not most, were Jewishly illiterate. New indigenous Jewish activists were seeking an infusion of Yiddishkeit, teachers, rabbis, caring role models, schools, Torah. Yad l'Yad was addressing the physical side of Jewish survival, but how could we foster the spiritual side – the mentoring, the education, the guidance? More and more, I was seeing myself among the Jewishly illiterate and consequently unable to personally supply them with what I myself didn't have.

Weeks before the trip to Kiev, Rabbi Belsky had recommended I contact Rabbi Yaakov Shteierman, who was involved in building a spiritual renaissance in Kiev. It was one of those many connections in my life that appeared to have been prepared for me all along. In another extraordinary circumstance, Rabbi Shteierman planned to be in Kiev for a meeting of the Union of Religious Organizations at the same time as my trip. So, as planned, on Thursday morning I taxied to Kiev's Great Choral Synagogue to meet Rabbi Shteierman, a slightly built man with a commanding presence. The Brooklyn-based powerhouse was instrumental in running Yad Yisrael, which had sent Rabbi Yaakov Bleich to Kiev to establish an entire Jewish communal structure. Out of the ashes of communism, they were building day schools, camps, an orphanage, and social services.

Rabbi Shteierman became an indispensable consultant. When he came to Chicago to give a talk for CASJ, he made an instantaneous and long-lasting connection with Marillyn. I also asked him to come to the UCSJ Annual Meeting to address the new unfortunate phenomenon of the Christian missionaries who were invading Ukraine and preying on vulnerable Jews, who, without money for heat or burial plots or food, were desperate enough to take payment for conversion.

Just as he had forged the introduction to Rabbi Shteierman, Rabbi Belsky later encouraged me to meet with the Novominsker Rebbe. Rabbi Yaakov Perlow, the head of the Novominsker Chasidic dynasty and also the president of the prestigious Agudath Israel of America, had just returned from Baku and Kuba, Azerbaijan, and had come to Chicago to raise desperately needed funds for the Jews there. He was clearly invested with the emotional intensity characteristic of UCSJ activists.

As Rabbi Belsky had arranged, Marillyn and I went to meet with the Novominsker the following day. We were more than a little nervous at the thought of meeting the leader of a community with which we had no previous contact. But we found a warm, soft-spoken, intelligent man with refined features and a commanding but welcoming presence. He listened thoughtfully as I outlined the role and activities of UCSJ. It was clear the commitments he made during his trip left him overwhelmed, and Marillyn and I offered CASJ's help to deliver on the assurances he had given.

As a result, Hetty, at her efficient, masterful best, arranged for a shipping container to be installed in the parking lot behind CASJ's suburban office. It took about a month for the community-wide kosher food drive to fill the container we then shipped to Baku.

I too felt buried by the sheer immensity of the need. Over the coming months, the onslaught of requests for help poured in to CASJ from throughout the former Soviet republics. Multiple times every day, Natasha was on the phone to Jews with long lists of needs in Chernivtsi or Simferopol or any of a number of far-flung places. To meet their needs, Susie and Marillyn were continually creating new Yad l'Yad partnerships, and Frances Peshkin was bringing in more and more medical supplies and medications. Unable to meet all the requests, we were compelled to make choices about priorities. But how to decide which community had the greatest, most urgent need? The Novominsker had given me his home phone number, and I began to call him for consultation. What should come first and where and to whom? When I phoned his home, his wife always greeted me pleasantly. "You're the woman from Chicago?" He didn't get calls from women. But there was never even one time that he didn't take mine.

We sent the next food lift to Lvov, now Lviv, in Ukraine, at the request of our extraordinary partner Meylakh Sheykhet, whom I had first met at our annual meeting in Moscow in 1989. Always a supporter of UCSJ and Chicago Action, Meylakh had tirelessly and selflessly built from scratch the very first infrastructure for Jewish survival in Lviv after the fall of the Soviet empire. CASJ helped support his meals-on-wheels program to deliver food to the elderly and infirm, but when it became clear this was insufficient, we sent the shipping container of foodstuffs to Lviv.

UCSJ made Meylakh our official representative to advocate with the new Ukrainian government, and in that capacity, he fought Ukraine's plans to build shopping centers and highways on Jewish cemeteries, attempted to regain Jewish property, and confronted anti-Semitism. He had also begun his search for unmarked graves, the kevarim, of our holy rabbis, and when my brother Chip became ill, Meylakh went to those graves to pray for him. As UCSJ was assisting him in Lviv, we were also helping Jews in Orel, Kremenchuk, and other former Soviet communities reclaim Jewish property that had been destroyed by anti-Semitic hate crimes or confiscated by the government.

I had found the characteristics of Jewish leadership in the refuseniks and other Jewish activists who had led the movement during the Soviet era and after its dissolution. They were guided by a vision, by a passionate, selfless commitment to the twin principles of Jewish survival and the survival of Jews. That survival would depend on continuity and security, identity and freedom, built on the shoulders of the giants of past generations. Along with former Soviet Jews like Meylakh, I was now encountering American Jewish leaders – like Rabbi Shteierman and the

Novominsker – who mirrored UCSJ's values while also infusing communities with much-needed Yiddishkeit. They consulted with Jews on the ground, working with them to assess their needs and objectives. They, like our UCSJ activists, tried to fill that need by taking personal responsibility, one Jew at a time, one community at a time, providing material help and advocacy. Instead of paternalism, they demonstrated empathy; instead of promoting personal interest, their consultations promoted their constituents' needs; instead of conveying patronizing authority, they conferred dignity and respect upon every Jew, simply because they were family, one people. They believed they could change the world with small acts of kindness. They were the new conscience of Jewish survival.

Our lives were changing. Marillyn's broken hip began a downward spiral that kept her from the office, leaving CASJ's Yad l'Yad in Susie and Natasha's capable hands. Micah and Leonid were pursuing grants from USAID to build human rights consortia to combat the mushrooming anti-Semitism in the former Soviet Union. For years, Micah, Leonid, and I had worked together with synchronized steps that moved UCSJ in one direction, and it was nearly inconceivable that one of us would willingly separate us.

But it was time for others with different resources to step up. In 1996, after ten years, I turned the UCSJ presidency over to a young, budding Jewish leader, Yossi Abramovich, and gave up my desk at Chicago Action. As excruciating as it was to break up the triumvirate with Micah and Leonid, whose lives, along with Marillyn's, had been so tightly entwined with mine, it was time to change. It was time to focus on my family, to make cookies for my grandchildren, to bake challah, to open my home for classes and for Shabbat dinners, to learn Torah.

"If I Forget Thee, O Jerusalem"

I had progressively come to see myself as the mirror image of Soviet Jews. Though for different reasons, we had both been cut off from our cultural and religious roots, and consequently, I did what many refuseniks had done: I turned to Jewish education, for myself and others in the North Shore. Lenny and I raised the initial funds to launch the Komimiyus North Shore Torah Center. From our Deerfield home, Rabbi Belsky began teaching classical Jewish texts and basic, pre-denominational Judaism, with each course providing the building blocks for the next. Lenny and I began hosting Friday-night dinners, and gradually, I felt like I was coming home, taking back what had been lost. To anchor our growing Torah university, Komimiyus bought a home in Deerfield for David and Ali Begoun, a young rabbi and his wife, whose classes and Shabbos dinners helped augment the Jewish education movement that had become a vital part of our lives.

The more we learned, the more we yearned to be a part of the main current of the Jewish people, not only its past history, but its mission. After thousands of years, the Jewish people had a country, and we were privileged to be in a generation to see the miracle of return. In 1997, Lenny and I bought an apartment on a cobbled street lined with orange trees near the bustling, noisy, colorful Machane Yehuda market and began living lives in two countries. Several years later, we began to feel that the pristine sterility of the Chicago suburbs was too stark a contrast to the rich intensity of Jerusalem, where Hebrew mixed with Russian, English, and French, and where there were classes, lectures, and the shuk that brought together Jews from throughout the world, each with a story. We left Deerfield for West Rogers Park, the heart of Chicago's Jewish community. Soon after, we moved from our original Jerusalem apartment in bustling Nachlaot to quiet Rehavia, to a small apartment with a large garden bursting with bougainvillea.

Our Chicago friends certainly thought we had lost our minds, but Lenny and I were like salmon, fighting against the current to swim upstream. Never a renegade, I wasn't entirely a conformist, either. And besides, as our Rabbi Zev Cohen says, to live is to change.

During the dark years of Soviet repression, I was traveling on the road Yosef Mendelevich built – except I didn't have to pave it myself, by burying the unearthed bones of Jews the Nazis shot at the edges of pits or by paying an incalculable cost for the struggle to cover my head in prison. I didn't have to use my fingernails to scratch out the image of Shabbos candles on a prison wall and encircle them three times with my arms before saying the blessing to welcome the Sabbath. I didn't have to trade nine years of my life in a prison camp for the privilege of going to Israel. I was traveling the road paved by every refusenik I ever met – and the thousands I never met. They struggled for the right to live in Israel, where Lenny and I had an apartment we didn't have to pay for with years of indignity, suffering, and persecution. I was traveling the road paved by Sharansky, but I didn't have to endure the torture of a hunger strike and forced feeding for the right to have my Tehillim. What made these psalms so valuable that it was worth submitting one's body to torture to retain them? What did Sharansky know? What did Mendelevich know? What did earlier generations of my family know? In my studies, I had begun to find the answers to these questions and had opened the golden treasure chest of my people.

Traveling on this road in my direction came a rabbi, with a black hat and a key to open doors I didn't even know were locked.

Afterword

Lenny and I are back from the Kotel, down the russet-colored steps under an army of bushes reaching over us, and the door opens to Friday's smells: challahs right out of the oven, Lenny's grilled vegetables, marinating chickens. With my flowers arranged, I'm looking around our apartment, our home, marveling at the complicated chain of events that brought us here. Our table is extended fully for friends of more than thirty-five years. We've been soldered together by a shared vision. They've seen me at my best and at my worst. Like me, they were full-time unpaid volunteers who gave fully of their personal resources. All of us were on a path that began in the Soviet Union but led us home, to Israel.

In a few minutes it will be late enough to phone our kids in America, Brooke and David, Scott and Kathy, Josh and Lizzy. Our grandchildren will be trying to call and text us before Shabbos. They come often to visit, to tour, to study, on summer programs, some to learn in yeshiva. Our happiest times are when they are seated around our Shabbos table in Jerusalem. In the meantime, we go back to Chicago for a few months each year.

Here in Jerusalem, we are in the center of the universe, where it is said Heaven and Earth kiss. Certainly it's the center of the Jewish biblical and historical narrative. The refuseniks and former prisoners have already been here for many decades and now have Israeli grandchildren. Most have served in the army or in national service. Recently we ran into Ari Volvovsky at the shuk. We see Dina Beilina, Evgeny Lein, Lev Utevsky, Misha Elbert, the Sharanskys, and Yosef Mendelevich. Some, like the Slepaks and Kosharovsky, have died. These national Jewish heroes, hidden heroes, unknown to younger generations, are slipping out of visibility. But they made their mark both on history and on us.

Jerusalem is the magnet that has drawn so many UCSJ activists who stepped out of the convention of their former lives because, once again, they believed they could make a difference, this time in Israel. Each of us was brought separately on a current that ran through the Soviet Union and then back to Judaism and Jerusalem. And here, we are close enough to walk to each other to share Shabbat.

The founder of Seattle Action for Soviet Jewry, Judy Lash Balint, and her husband Zev made aliyah. Judy spearheaded UCSJ's campaign opposing the Soviet infiltration of the US-Soviet sister city programs by Soviet-backed parallel organizations that mimicked and undermined authentic human rights groups. Rae Sharfman, founder of the Detroit Action Committee for Soviet Jewry and a UCSJ board member who campaigned for the Poltinnikovs, came in her eighties to live out her dream. June and Ron Daniels from the Des Moines Action Committee for Soviet Jews are here. It was June and Ron who flew from Moscow to Israel to deliver Natan Sharansky's message of encouragement to Avital before his arrest. Because of them, their Iowa senator, Chuck Grassley, became a steadfast supporter of Soviet Jews and UCSJ.

Enid Wurtman and her husband Stuart, a UCSJ president, made aliyah in the 1970s, simply because Yuli Kosharovsky and so many others could not. They came to Jerusalem, where she continued her activism, advocating for newly arrived immigrants overburdened with financial need and documenting the movement in a substantial archival collection.

Ruthie Newman, active on the Washington Committee for Soviet Jewry and on UCSJ's board, now lives in Beit Shemesh. Ruthie was responsible for UCSJ's protests against Soviet non-delivery of mail, testifying before several congressional hearings. Jackie and Michael Abels, who worked with Hinda Cantor and Joel and Adele Sandberg at the South Florida Conference on Soviet Jewry, commute between Jerusalem and Florida.

Then there's Lessa, Lenny's sister, who, with her late husband Michael, went to the USSR from Tacoma, Washington, and then made aliyah with their three children. She became an activist with Enid Wurtman and Yuri Shtern at the Soviet Jewry Education and Information Center. Glenn Richter, Avi Weiss, and Irwin Cotler are regularly in Israel.

Their journeys, like ours, brought them to Jerusalem.

And then there's Luba. Unlike the rest of us, who had easy paths, Luba's road was rock-strewn, unique to her and yet representative of so many Zionist refuseniks.

My friend Luba has spiky, short grey hair. Her most striking feature is her hands, which she uses like an orchestra conductor to accompany her stories. I've seen those hands, with surgical precision, carve delicate papercuts into an intricate tapestry and apply the thinnest gold filaments on parchment. You see, Luba is an artist.

Luba grew up in Sverdlovsk, formerly Ekaterinburg, where the last Russian czar and his family were shot during the final days of the Soviet revolution. While Luba was preparing for university entrance exams, her tutor, an underground Zionist activist, introduced her to the Jewish world, to the concept of the Jewish national home, and to Jews struggling to go to Israel. In the summer of 1969 – two years after the Six-Day War and a year before a group of desperate Soviet Jews tried to hijack a plane out of the USSR – the dark-haired nineteen-year-old girl found herself at a Zionist camp, swimming, learning about Israel, singing Hebrew and Jewish songs, and forging a Jewish identity.

Soon after starting university, the youngest of the underground Zionist group, Luba arranged to receive a *vysov*. When it came, she hid it under her mattress, away from her parents' sight.

At a Chanukah party with refuseniks, Luba signed an appeal to the Kremlin to commute the death sentences for two Leningrad trial defendants. Five days later, everyone who had signed the appeal was arrested and interrogated. Refuseniks had instructed Luba how to respond to KGB in the event of an interrogation. She was to repeat that she was not anti-Soviet; she wanted to go to Israel to marry. She couldn't find a Jewish husband in Sverdlovsk. That was her line, and she stuck to it.

With warnings not to engage in subversive activity, she was released, and soon after, she applied to emigrate. In April 1971, just as the movement was getting underway, this precocious girl received her exit visa. By Pesach, Luba had left her family behind and was on her way to Israel, by way of Vienna. At a Seder in Vienna arranged for emigrants, Luba made her way to the long tables and found a seat. Sitting next to her was an Israeli, the first she had ever met, a handsome man studying medicine in Vienna.

Simcha was there in Vienna, waiting for her at the Seder. There are no coincidences in this world. Luba and Simcha Bar Menachem were later married in Israel. Now they live around the corner from us.

Luba's parents wanted to follow their daughter, but the Soviets denied them permission. Recalling the tragedy of the Poltinnikov family, both of Luba's parents died in the USSR, prevented from seeing their daughter and grandchild.

Looking back, I often wonder about my past self, that young girl with her unanswered questions, her love of Jewish books, and a reluctance to speak publicly. I do remember the young mother, happy to be home with three small children, cooking something wonderfully fragrant, reading stories aloud, content with her world and with her lot, not looking for change. But that contentment and complacency were buried in the rubble left by an unstoppable drive to help her people. The questioning girl, the young mother, the volunteer activist, now mitzvah observant. To me, it seems like a miracle.

Without guarantees that our choices would flower, I only had the free will to choose where to put down one foot, then another. After a few steps, I could still see the beginning but had no idea where I would end up. Now, I am where I wanted to be all along, though I hadn't known it. During the journey, I was absorbed in each moment, struggling with challenges, moving from one emergency to the next. Appearing with exquisite precision exactly when I needed them, as if they were waiting for me, were inspiring refuseniks and prisoners of conscience, role models, partners, colleagues, activists, teachers, rabbis. They changed Lenny and me, and we altered our lives to accommodate those changes. I so wanted to carry on what my great-grandparents left behind in that graveyard in Shavel, Lithuania. We wanted to be part of the continuum that started at Sinai, to carry and transmit that meaning into the future.

Only in retrospect, after the Soviet Union collapsed, did I comprehend the enormity of the challenge we, our voluntary strike force, had faced: the urgency of arrests and threats, house searches and trials, that demanded our first-response chain of action; the inconceivable scope of our day-to-day activity, including messenger phone calls, tourist briefings, direct aid, demonstrations, data collection, documentation, and information distribution; and the ever-expanding grassroots advocacy, confronting Soviets in international venues and conducting press conferences and government briefings. We had been witnesses to nothing less than the miracle of redemption for over two million Jews.

We were not only witnesses. All of us, volunteers in the independent grassroots movement, had tied our lives to the lives of our people in a far-off country and had participated in what may be the only mass rescue movement of Jews in Eastern and Central Europe in our long history.

Our rabbis tell us the Beis Hamikdash, the Temple in Jerusalem, was destroyed and our nation dispersed into a long and dark exile because of baseless hatred, undermining jealousy, and *lashon hara* – literally, evil tongue. I've come to believe that the exodus of Jews from the enormous post-Soviet landmass was a cosmic reaction to the antithesis of baseless hatred – the unifying factor of baseless love. Love between Jewish activists in the West and refuseniks – the shared worry, the shared pain, the shared burden, the shared responsibility, the shared joy – might have been a power so great as to trigger a miraculous force that not only brought out millions of Jews but ripped apart the very structure that imprisoned them. This is the story of hidden heroes, both inside and outside the former Soviet Union.

These hidden heroes leave a priceless legacy: life gives us freedom, freedom to choose and freedom to change. Some of us have the courage to change ourselves. Some of us can change ourselves and, in the process, inspire others. Some of us can change ourselves, inspire others, and in the end, change the world.

Union of Councils and Affiliate Members

Alabama Council to Save Soviet Jews
Alamo Council for Soviet Jewry
Arizona Council on Soviet Jewry
Baltimore Council for Soviet Jewry
Bay Area Council for Soviet Jews
Boston Action for Soviet Jewry
Burlington Action Committee for Soviet Jews
Chicago Action for Soviet Jewry
Cincinnati Council for Soviet Jewry
Cleveland Council on Soviet Anti-Semitism
Colorado Committee of Concern for Soviet Jewry
Connecticut Committee for Soviet Jews
Des Moines Action Committee for Soviet Jewry
Detroit Soviet Jewry Committee of the Jewish Community Council
Greensboro Action for Soviet Jewry
Soviet Jewry Action Council of Harrisburg
Houston Action for Soviet Jewry
Kansas City Council for Soviet Jewry
Knoxville-Oak Ridge Council for Soviet Jews
Long Island Committee for Soviet Jewry
Los Alamos Committee on Soviet Anti-Semitism
Minnesota-Dakotas Action Committee for Soviet Jewry
Newport News Soviet Jewry Committee
Soviet Jewry Committee of the Jewish Federation of the North Shore
Oceanfront Council for Soviet Jewry
Oklahoma Commission for Soviet Jews
Omaha Committee for Soviet Jews
Soviet Jewry Council of the JCRC, Philadelphia

Pittsfield Council for Soviet Jewry
Sarasota Conference on Soviet Jewry
Seattle Action for Soviet Jewry
Soviet Jewry Committee, Jewish Federation of South Bend
Jewish Federation of South Broward
South Florida Conference on Soviet Jewry
Southern California Council for Soviet Jews
Vancouver Soviet Jewry Action Committee
Waco Council of Concern on Soviet Jewry
Washington Committee for Soviet Jewry
West Palm Beach-Jewish Federation of Palm Beach County

Affiliates

Comité des Quinze
London 35s Women's Campaign
Canadian 35s
Student Struggle for Soviet Jewry
Center for Russian and East European Jewry
Medical Mobilization for Soviet Jewry
Legal Advocacy Center
Soviet Jewry Action Center

Index